D1129984

*Confederate Ireland, 1642–1649*

# Confederate Ireland
# 1642–1649

*A Constitutional and Political Analysis*

Micheál Ó Siochrú

FOUR COURTS PRESS

Set in 10.5 on 12 point Adobe Garamond for
FOUR COURTS PRESS
Fumbally Lane, Dublin 8, Ireland
e-mail: info@four-courts-press.ie
*and in North America*
FOUR COURTS PRESS
c/o ISBS, 5804 N.E. Hassalo Street, Portland, OR 97213.

A catalogue record for this title
is available from the British Library.

ISBN 1–85182–400–6

Printed in Great Britain
by the MPG Books Ltd, Bodmin, Cornwall.

To my parents, Dorren and Oisín

In memory of Dónal Cregan

# Contents

# Illustrations

# Preface

This project began back in October 1991 in less than auspicious circumstances. I am greatly indebted to Professor Aidan Clarke of Trinity College, for showing faith in me then, and for supporting my endeavours ever since. His vast knowledge of early seventeenth-century Irish history (as well as particular insights into my own topic) has been of inestimable value to me. I hit a major crisis around late 1994, at which time I had the good fortune to meet Dr Jane Ohlmeyer, whose infectious energy and enthusiasm sustained me through this difficult period and beyond. Éamonn Ó Ciardha also provided plenty of encouragement in the latter stages, as well as sharing many of my ideals and aspirations. Staying in the history field, I would like to thank Dr Tadhg Ó hAnnracháin for his help with the *Commentarius* (and all the stimulating chats), Dr Matthew Stout for preparing the maps, Dr Bríd McGrath for the biographical information on the members of the 1640-1 Irish parliament and Dr Pádraig Lenihan for illuminating a whole variety of military issues in his doctoral thesis.

Having spent most of the last six years in libraries, both here and in England, I am grateful to all the staff who helped me during this time, especially Ann Walsh and Mary Higgins, in the Berkeley Library, Trinity College. Family and friends have been tremendously supportive as they watched me stumble along, while the editorial comments of my father proved invaluable in preparing the final drafts. Thanks in particular are due to my parents for giving me the opportunity to live in Baile na nGall while writing the book, to Joyce for the translation of French documents, and to Karan for helping me shift through the interminable lists of confederate names. She more than anybody else will always be associated with this period of my life, having shared many of the experiences of the last six years. I am also extremely grateful to Michael Adams of Four Courts Press for making the publishing process as painless as possible.

Finally, I would like to acknowledge my debt to the late Dr Dónal Cregan, as this book is very much a continuation of research he began over fifty years ago. He may not have agreed with a number of my conclusions, but he was always delighted to argue the point. Despite all the wonderful assistance I have received with this project, I am aware that much work remains to be done on Confederate Ireland, and any mistakes in the text are wholly my own responsibility. As for the dates, I have in all instances adhered to the convention of dating according to the Old Style (Julian) calendar for the day and month, and the New Style (Gregorian) calendar for the year.

# Abbreviations

| | |
|---|---|
| Add. Mss | Additional Manuscripts |
| BL | British Library, London |
| Bodl. | Bodleian Library, Oxford |
| HMC | Historical Manuscripts Commission |
| IHS | Irish Historical Studies |
| IMC | Irish Manuscript Commission |
| NA | National Archives, Dublin |
| NHI | Moody, T.W., Martin, F.X. and Byrne, F.J.(eds) *A new history of Ireland*, vol. 3, *Early modern Ireland, 1534-1691* (Oxford 1991) |
| NLI | National Library of Ireland, Dublin |
| PRO | Public Records Office, London |
| RIA | Royal Irish Academy, Dublin |
| SP Ire. | State Papers relating to Ireland |
| TCD | Trinity College, Dublin |
| TCP | Transcript of the Carte Papers, National Archives, Dublin |
| UCD | University College Dublin |

# The storm breaks

ↂ

## OCTOBER–DECEMBER 1641

> In the year 1641, on the 22 of October, the conspiracy was discovered
> which occasioned the war in Ireland, a war of many parts, carried on
> under the notion of so many interests, perplexed with such diversity of
> rents and divisions, among those seemed to be of a side, as will transmit
> to posterity observations perhaps as useful, although not so memorable
> and full, as a war managed with more noise, greater power and between
> princes, whose very names may bespeak attention for their actions.
>
> Richard Bellings, *History of the late war in Ireland* (1670s)[1]

On 22 October 1641 the native Irish of Ulster, led by Sir Phelim O'Neill, captured a number of key towns and fortifications in that province. Within weeks
they had forged an alliance with the old English of the Pale, and controlled a
large swathe of territory as the revolt spread throughout the country. After an
initial period of confusion and chaos, the insurgents began to organise themselves, united by an oath pledging loyalty to God, king and country. This was
the beginning of confederate Ireland, a period from 1642 to 1649 when the Irish
governed a unitary state, covering most of the island, and engaged in a bitter
conflict with royalists, parliamentarians, and Scots covenanters. Despite the
pressures of war, the confederates developed a highly sophisticated system of representative government, from which emerged the genesis of modern Irish
nationalism.

The study of confederate Ireland, however, has suffered from a relative
neglect by historians on both sides of the Irish Sea. Sandwiched between the
1641-2 Ulster massacres (of both catholics and protestants) and the apocalyptic
Cromwellian invasion in 1649, the 1640s appear at first to be characterised by
nothing more than bloodletting, treachery and internecine factionalism. Even
the war seems like an unfruitful area for research, remarkable only for its lack of

---

1 Gilbert, J.T., *History of the Irish confederation and the war in Ireland* (Dublin 1882-91), i, p. 1.
Manuscript versions of Bellings' memoirs survive in Trinity College, Dublin and the British Library (TCD Mss 747; BL Add Mss 4763), but references in the text are to the published version.

major engagements, and totally overshadowed by endless dreary negotiations. This negative perception was partly created by the destruction of confederate records in two fires. The first blaze in 1711 destroyed all political, administrative and judicial material, while the surviving records (mainly financial) perished in the second during the civil war in 1922.[2]

All was not lost, however, due mainly to the efforts of a number of individuals, particularly James Butler, the first duke of Ormond, who dominated the Irish political landscape in the seventeenth century. During the 1640s, as the king's representative in Ireland, he took part in protracted peace negotiations with the confederates. Fortunately, Ormond preserved most of his correspondence, as well as making copies of official documents. His biographer, Thomas Carte, brought together the vast bulk of this material, which is now preserved in the Bodleian Library in Oxford. The 272 volumes of the Carte collection (each containing hundreds of original manuscripts) are unquestionably the major source for any seventeenth-century Irish historian.[3]

Carte published a fraction of these letters and documents in his biography of Ormond. At the end of the last century, the antiquarian J.T. Gilbert produced an invaluable seven-volume history of the confederates, consisting of material from his own private collection, as well as a significant cross section from the Carte manuscripts.[4] These volumes also contain the most important contemporary account of the period, written by Richard Bellings in the 1670s. Bellings, as secretary of the confederate supreme council from 1642 until 1646, played a vital role in the politics of that decade. Returning from exile after the restoration of Charles II, he dedicated his history (which is staunchly royalist in tone) to the duke of Ormond.[5]

Gilbert had already published a three-volume history of Irish affairs during the 1640s, the principal part of which consisted of the anonymous (and highly entertaining) memoirs entitled *Aphorismical discovery of treasonable faction*.[6] The

---

2 The court of claims in the 1660s had access to these records, before they were eventually placed in storage in Lower Essex Street. On 5 April 1711, a great fire destroyed most of the documents, except for the books of public accounts. These survived until the destruction of the Four Courts building in June 1922, during the assault by Free State forces. See 20th report of the deputy keeper, appendix 4, *Public records in Ireland* (Dublin 1888) pp 24-7. I have heard accounts of how in 1922 anti-treaty soldiers used bundles of documents to block windows! 3 Bodl. Carte Mss 1-272. 4 Carte, Thomas, *History of the life of James the first duke of Ormond* 6 vols (Oxford 1851 edition); Gilbert, J.T., *Irish confederation*, 7 vols (Dublin 1882-91). 5 Bellings' memoirs are scattered throughout the seven volumes of Gilbert, *Irish confederation* (1882-91). 6 Gilbert, J.T., *A contemporary history of affairs in Ireland from 1641-1652*, 3 vols (Dublin 1879). These memoirs are bitterly critical of the duke of Ormond, and supportive of the Ulster Irish general Owen Roe O'Neill. A number of other leading confederates produced memoirs which have been published at various times, including the earl of Castlehaven and Nicholas French, the bishop of Ferns. Tuchet, James, *The earl of Castlehaven's review or his memoirs* (London 1684); Bindon, S.H. (ed.), *The historical works of the right reverend Nicholas*

letters (and observations) of Ulick Bourke, marquis of Clanricarde, who although not a confederate, remained close to the leadership in Kilkenny, are another important source. Originally contained in four letter-books, they cover the years 1641-52, and provide a unique insight into catholic royalist Ireland. The first and fourth letter-books were published in the eighteenth-century, the second in 1983 by the Irish Manuscripts Commission.[7] Unfortunately, the third letter-book, covering late 1647 until 1650, a vital period in confederate history, is missing. A number of histories hostile to the confederates also appeared during the course of the seventeenth-century. These contain copies of important documents from the 1640s, and provide invaluable information on the attitudes in Dublin and London to the events unfolding in Ireland.[8]

The historian J.P. Prendergast, a contemporary of Gilbert, spent many years working on the confederate records stored in Dublin's Four Courts. He made extensive notes on their contents, prior to their destruction in 1922, which can be consulted in the King's Inn library.[9] The other major surviving source is the published work entitled *Commentarius Rinuccinianus* based on a contemporary account by two Irish clerics of the mission to Ireland of the papal diplomat, Giovanni Battista Rinuccini, archbishop of Fermo. The work contains Latin translations of scores of original documents relating to confederate politics. The six volumes, published between 1932 and 1949 (once again by the Irish Manuscripts Commission), are the best surviving copy of the original work, destroyed during the Second World War.[10]

The historian of confederate Ireland can also consult significant collections of original manuscripts in the Bodleian Library (Clarendon and Tanner papers), Public Records Office, London (State Papers relating to Ireland), British Library (various collections), and the National Library, Dublin (Ormond papers).[11] In addition, a considerable number of institutions in Ireland have retained papers directly relating to the confederate period.[12] The destruction of the confederates'

*French D.D*, 2 vols (Dublin 1846). **7** Bourke, Ulick, *Clanricarde memoirs* (London 1747); Lowe, John (ed.), *Clanricarde letter-book 1643-1647* (Dublin 1983). **8** The most famous of these is Temple, John, *The Irish rebellion or an history* (London 1646) which was reprinted on a number of occasions over the next 200 years. See also Borlase, Edmund, *The history of the execrable Irish rebellion traced from many preceding acts to the grand eruption the 23 October 1641, and thence pursued to the act of settlement, 1662* (Dublin 1680), and Nalson, John, *An impartial collection of the great affairs of state*, 2 vols (London 1682-3). **9** King's Inns, Prendergast Papers vols 1-14. **10** O'Ferrall, Richard and O'Connell, Robert, *Commentarius Rinuccinianus, de sedis apostolicae legatione ad foederatis Hiberniae catholicos per annos 1645-9*, ed. Stanislaus Kavanagh 6 vols (Dublin 1932-49). Rinuccini's letters and reports to Rome were published in Italian by G. Aiazza, and translated into English by Annie Hutton. See Aiazza, G., *The embassy in Ireland of Monsignor G.B. Rinuccini, archbishop of Fermo in the years 1645-49*, translated by Annie Hutton (Dublin 1873). **11** Bodl. Clarendon Mss 20-36; Tanner Mss 57-60; PRO SP Ire. 260-6; BL Add Mss 4,763 and numerous others (see bibliography); NLI Ormond Papers Mss 2307-15. **12** For example, the Dublin City Library, Franciscan Archives, Marsh's Library, Jesuit

records means that a detailed study of their general assembly and supreme council, along the lines of those on the Scottish and English parliaments, is not possible.[13] Nonetheless, a surprising amount of information can be retrieved, allowing
the historian to reconstruct much that was thought to be lost forever.

As for secondary material, only a few general histories were written prior to
this century, the most readable being C.P. Meehan's book published in 1882.[14] A
minor renaissance began, however, in the 1930s with the appearance of two
works on confederate Ireland. Michael Hynes published a biography of
Rinuccini, while Hugh Hazlett's PhD thesis provided an overview of the military
conflict in the 1640s. Unfortunately, neither historian produced any further significant studies on the confederates.[15] Dónal Cregan's PhD thesis in 1947, written almost exactly three hundred years after the dissolution of the confederate
association, was the first detailed study of its structure and personnel.[16]

Cregan never completed his pioneering research, and only segments were
ever published, but it remains required reading for any student of confederate
Ireland.[17] Patrick Corish wrote a number of excellent articles on religious issues
during the 1640s, and his two chapters in the third volume of the *New History of
Ireland* provide the most comprehensive chronological narrative of Ireland during this period.[18] J.C Beckett raised the profile of confederate Ireland with a
review article which appeared in the *Historical studies* series in 1959, and shortly
afterwards an English student, John Lowe, constructed a detailed account of the
complex negotiations between Charles I and the confederates.[19] Compared to

Provincial Archives, Royal Irish Academy, Trinity College Dublin. **13** Keeler, M.F., *The long
parliament, 1640-1641: A biographical study of its members* (Philadelphia 1954) is a comprehensive study of the situation in England, while Young, J.R., *The Scottish parliament 1639-1661: A
political and constitutional analysis* (Edinburgh 1996) attempts something similar for the
Scottish parliament. **14** Meehan, C.P., *The confederation of Kilkenny* (Dublin 1882). **15** Hynes,
Michael, *The mission of Rinuccini, nuncio extraordinary to Ireland 1645-1649* (Louvain 1932);
Hazlett, Hugh, "A history of the military forces operating in Ireland 1641-1649", 2 vols (PhD
thesis, Queen's University Belfast 1938). **16** Cregan, Dónal, "The confederation of Kilkenny:
Its organisation, personnel and history" (PhD thesis, UCD 1947). **17** See bibliography. The
last article to appear was Cregan, Dónal, "The confederate catholics of Ireland: The personnel
of the confederation, 1642-9" *IHS* vol. 29, no. 116 (Nov. 1995) pp 490-512. **18** Corish, P. J.,
"Bishop Nicholas French and the second Ormond peace 1648-9" *IHS*, vol. 6, no. 22 (Sept.
1948) pp 83-100; "The crisis in Ireland in 1648: The nuncio and the supreme council:
Conclusions" *Irish theological quarterly*, vol. 22 (Jan. 1955) pp 231-57; Moody, T.W., Martin,
F.X. and Byrne F.J. (eds) *A new history of Ireland*, vol. 3, *Early modern Ireland 1534-1691*
(Oxford 1991) chaps.11-12 (hereafter referred to as NHI, iii). **19** Beckett, J.C., "The confeder-
ation of Kilkenny reviewed", *Historical studies*, vol. 2, (London 1959) pp 29-41; Lowe, John,
"The negotiations between Charles I and the confederation of Kilkenny 1642-9" (PhD thesis,
University of London 1960) is a long and detailed work, but contains comparatively little
analysis of internal confederate politics. The article Lowe, John, "The Glamorgan mission to
Ireland 1645-6", *Studia Hibernica*, no. 4 (1964) pp 155-96, includes the most significant information from the thesis. Another book from around this time, is a confused account of the

the historical writings on the 1790s however, or the early decades of this century, the study of confederate Ireland was largely neglected.

More recently, in 1981 a Scottish scholar, David Stevenson, examined the links between Ireland and Scotland during the 1640s, and in the last few years, Irish scholars have produced three major theses on the confederates.[20] First out of the blocks was Jane Ohlmeyer's fascinating biography of Randal MacDonnell, earl of Antrim. Unfortunately for the purpose of this book, Antrim, while undoubtedly a colourful character, was a peripheral figure in confederate politics for much of the 1640s. Ohlmeyer went on to edit a collection of essays on Ireland covering the period between 1641 and 1660, but only one chapter (her own on diplomacy) deals directly with the confederates.[21]

Tadhg Ó hAnnracháin's reappraisal of Rinuccini was long overdue, providing a more balanced and sophisticated view of this much maligned cleric. His thesis, however, does not attempt to unravel the inner workings of confederate government, which so preoccupied the papal diplomat. The third PhD, by Pádraig Lenihan, examines in detail the confederate military machine, concentrating principally on the army of Leinster. On the negative side, the impressive minutiae at times tend to overshadow broader considerations, particularly the question of who determined confederate military strategy.[22]

While these superb new studies have provided fresh impetus for a re-examination of the period, they do not seriously challenge the traditional assumptions about confederate politics. The standard interpretation outlines how the old English and native Irish, forced together by a unique set of circumstances, forged an uneasy alliance which began to unravel over the crucial issue of religious concessions. The catalyst for this collapse, according to this scenario, proved to be the arrival of the papal nuncio, Rinuccini, with his unrealistic demands for full recognition of the Roman Catholic Church. The nuncio's hard-line thus alienat-

1640s from a traditional Irish catholic nationalist perspective: Coonan, T.L., *The Irish catholic confederacy and the puritan revolution* (Dublin 1954). **20** Stevenson, David, *Scottish covenanters and Irish confederates: Scottish- Irish relations in the mid-seventeenth century* (Belfast 1981). **21** Ohlmeyer, Jane, "A seventeenth-century survivor: The political career of Randal MacDonnell, first marquis and second earl of Antrim, 1609-83" (PhD thesis, TCD 1990), later published as *Civil war and restoration in the three Stuart kingdoms: the career of Randal MacDonnell, marquis of Antrim 1609-1683* (Cambridge 1993). See also Ohlmeyer, J. (ed.), *Ireland from independence to occupation 1641-1660* (Cambridge 1996). **22** Ó hAnnracháin, Tadhg, "'Far from terra firma': The mission of Gian Battista Rinuccini to Ireland 1645-1649", 2 vols (PhD thesis, European Univ. Inst. 1995). Most of Rinuccini's contemporaries were sharply divided over his intervention in Irish affairs, while Hynes' biography was largely based on an uncritical reading of the *Commentarius.* Hynes, *Mission of Rinuccini* (1932). Lenihan, Pádraig, "The catholic confederacy 1642-49: An Irish state at war", 2 vols (PhD thesis, UCG 1995). Two other recently completed theses, although not directly concerned with confederate Ireland, provide an abundance of information on the period. Armstrong, Robert, "Protestant Ireland and the English parliament, 1641-7" (PhD thesis, TCD 1995); McGrath, Bríd, "A biographical dictionary of the membership of the House of Commons, 1640-1" (PhD thesis, TCD 1998).

ed the old English, for whom reconciliation with the king remained the primary goal. The native Irish, however, resentful from the beginning of their old English allies, readily embraced the clerical position, thus precipitating the outbreak of civil war in May 1648.

The collapse of the confederate association, therefore, is blamed almost exclusively on internal pressures, with Rinuccini and the native Irish portrayed as the principal culprits. The old English are charged with a misguided rather than malevolent influence, caught between the unreasonable demands of their confederate allies and the extreme policies of their English parliamentary enemies.[23] This analysis, while attractive in its simplicity, is fundamentally flawed on two levels. In the first instance, the unduly negative approach of historians, concentrating on confederate weaknesses, obscures the many achievements of the association between 1642 and 1649. Secondly, a political model based on ethnicity does not appear to stand up to serious scrutiny.

The ultimate destruction of Irish catholic political and military during the 1650s undoubtedly influenced subsequent interpretations of confederate Ireland. Nonetheless, the outcome of the war was by no means inevitable, and the fact that confederate government functioned effectively for over six years constituted a major achievement, particularly as its enemies (except for one brief period in 1647) enjoyed a significant military advantage in numbers at least.[24] The confederates established their association in 1642 to provide effective civil government on a national level, to counter the immediate military threat posed by the royalists and the Scots in Ulster, and to negotiate a settlement with the king. Insufficient credit is given to the fact that by the time of Cromwell's arrival in Ireland in August 1649, the association had already obtained these primary goals and voluntarily disbanded.

While confederate infighting did delay a peace settlement with the king, other factors were possibly more significant. Despite the anxiety of the confederate leadership for peace with the royalists, a final agreement eluded them for over three years. This delay allowed the leadership's opponents in Kilkenny sufficient time to organise effective resistance to the treaty published in July 1646. The role of Ormond in particular during this period needs to be seriously re-examined. Entrusted with the responsibility of negotiating a deal with the confederates, the lord lieutenant proved unwilling to grant even the most basic of concessions on the issue of religion, despite receiving sufficient authority from the king.[25] This reluctance placed Ormond's allies in Kilkenny in an impossible position, and

23 This analysis first appeared in the Restoration period, as a number of leading old English confederates tried to justify their participation in the rebellion. Principal among these was Richard Bellings, whose memoirs had an enormous impact on subsequent historical writings. 24 Lenihan, "Catholic confederacy" p. 170 illustrates the relative strengths of the various standing armies in Ireland during the 1640s. 25 The negotiations on the religious issues are discussed in detail in chapter 2.

contributed greatly to the difficulties experienced by the confederates from 1645 onwards.

Developing on the theme of factionalism, the traditional interpretation of confederate Ireland also stresses the alleged ethnic basis for political divisions between old English and native Irish.[26] During the early part of the seventeenth century, however, ethnic boundaries between catholics in Ireland became increasingly blurred, especially among the upper classes, through intermarriage and a common interest in land and political power.[27] By the 1640s, ethnicity appears to have been less important than social status in determining an individual's political outlook. The old English aristocracy, for example, displayed no hostility towards their native Irish counterparts, working in close co-operation with them throughout the period.

Animosity towards the native Irish in confederate ranks was directed almost exclusively at the lower social orders, principally those from the province of Ulster. The demands of landless peasants in Ulster, supported by dispossessed exiles, for overturning the plantation process posed a serious threat to the existing order. The catholic landed elite, across the ethnic boundaries, vehemently opposed any such moves, while the physical destruction caused by the Ulster army and its camp followers aroused much resentment within the Pale.[28] By 1648, Owen Roe O'Neill, the great hero of Gaelic Ulster, was abandoned by most of the native Irish land holders in the province, with class and self-interest taking precedence over ethnicity, sentiment or tradition.[29]

Even a cursory examination of confederate divisions appears to confirm this interpretation. Large numbers of the native Irish land owning class – Donough MacCarthy, Viscount Muskerry, Barnaby Fitzpatrick, the lord of Upper Ossory, Dermot O'Shaughnessy, and Donough O'Callaghan among others – sided with the so-called "old English" party. Opponents of this group, apart from the Ulster Irish, included at times leading old English figures, such as Piers Butler, Viscount Ikerrin; Maurice, Viscount Roche; Hugh Rochford; and Roebuck Lynch. Religious devotion and local political rivalries account for some of this, but clearly the ethnic model is not entirely satisfactory in explaining political affiliation.

---

**26** Even the most recent accounts persist with such an interpretation. Corish, *NHI*, iii, p. 331; Ohlmeyer, *Civil war and restoration* pp 164-5 etc. **27** As Clarke has written, all men of sufficient property and station were within the pale of the gentry. Clarke, Aidan, "Ireland and the general crisis", *Past and present*, no. 48 (Aug. 1970) p. 90. See also Jackson, Donald, *Intermarriage in Ireland 1550-1650* (Montreal 1970) for a discussion on the extent of intermarriage between the various ethnic groups in Ireland. **28** Hostility towards the Ulster army was expressed in numerous letters of that period. For example, 18 April 1647, Robert Preston to Thomas Preston (PRO SP Ire. 263/105 f.176), 20 April 1647, Patrick Darcy to Thomas Preston (PRO SP 263/108 f.180), 26 April 1647 – to Thomas Preston (PRO SP 263/119 f.200) etc. **29** Phelim O'Neill, Myles O'Reilly, Alexander MacDonnell and others who already held estates in

The simple two-party model (old English and native Irish) comes under particular strain from 1646 onwards. Moves in August and September of that year to reject the peace settlement with the marquis of Ormond received support across ethnic boundaries. The following general assembly, in January 1647, supposedly dominated by the clerics and their native Irish allies, confirmed the rejection of the peace treaty, but exonerated its authors from any blame.[30] The papal nuncio described the penultimate assembly in November 1647 as wholly dominated by his opponents, and yet once again its actions were characterised by compromise.[31]

Finally, by the time the last assembly met in September 1648 civil war had erupted within the confederate association. With Rinuccini and Owen Roe O'Neill in close alliance, none of their supporters attended this meeting. Despite this, the assembly did not rush into an agreement with the marquis of Ormond. For almost four months the confederates insisted on all the religious concessions sought by the nuncio. Only news of the king's impending trial in England prevented a complete breakdown of negotiations, and the assembly in a dramatic gesture of loyalty agreed to a compromise settlement.[32] It is impossible to explain these developments using the traditional two-party model.

A re-examination of the sources reveals that instead of two factions (old English and native Irish) there were in fact three – a peace party, a clerical party and a loose grouping of non-aligned moderates. Furthermore, social standing, rather than ethnicity, proved the determining factor in the formation of the these factions. The peace party consisted of existing catholic land owners, both old English and native Irish, whose primary interest revolved around preserving the existing social and economic order, and obtaining political influence commensurate with their wealth and standing. In the interests of self-preservation, as much as anything else, they proved anxious for an early reconciliation with the king. The clerical party consisted of catholic bishops, returned exiles and those gentry and nobility excluded from power in Kilkenny by the dominant clique. This group also wished to come to terms with the king but only after obtaining major concessions on religious issues, and a significant redistribution of land. The leading figures in both the peace and clerical parties can be easily identified.[33]

---

Ulster, supported the attempts to negotiate a second peace treaty with Ormond, despite the violent opposition of Owen Roe O'Neill. "Journal of Colonel Henry McTully O'Neill" in [Lodge, John (ed.)], *Desiderata Curiosa Hibernica* (London 1772), vol. 2 p. 511. **30** The new government formed by the clerical faction in September 1646 contained names such as O'Neill, Plunkett, O'Sullivan Beare, Roche, O'Shaughnessy, Butler. Gilbert (ed.), *Irish confederation*, vi, pp 144-6. The assembly's declaration against the peace in February 1647 is in Bodl. Carte Mss 65 f.364. **31** Rinuccini to Cardinal Panzirolo, 24 Dec. 1647 (Aiazza [ed.], *Embassy* pp 343-6). **32** Richard Blake [chairman of the general assembly] to Ormond, 28 Dec. 1648 (Bodl. Carte Mss 23 f.123). These negotiations are examined in chapter 6. **33** The principal leaders of the peace faction were Viscount Muskerry, Richard Bellings, Viscount Mountgarret, Gerald

Evidence of a third grouping of non-aligned moderates only begins to emerge from 1644 onwards. These moderates sought a compromise peace settlement, with significantly better terms than those offered by Ormond, but not necessarily all the concessions favoured by the clergy. They used the legislative general assembly as a forum to articulate and promote their views. The split in confederate ranks over the 1646 peace treaty presented the moderates with an opportunity to exploit the balance of power, while at the same time preserving confederate unity. Although numerically insignificant, they gained crucial support across the political spectrum, and dictated confederate policy until the end of 1647. A series of military defeats followed by the outbreak of civil war temporarily undermined their influence, but the resurgent peace faction was subsequently forced to adopt the political middle ground created by the moderates in order to reach an agreement with Ormond acceptable to a majority of confederates.

Identifying these moderate leaders is not an easy task. As in England, political "parties" in seventeenth century Ireland bear little resemblance to their modern day equivalents. They consisted of loose groups of individuals, dominated by one or two personalities, sharing a common goal. The vast majority of active confederates in the general assembly were for the most part uncommitted politically, ready to be swayed by the arguments of the day, and generally more concerned with local rather than national issues.[34] The moderates exercised their influence by exploiting the balance of power, first siding with one group, then switching to the other. Nicholas Plunkett of Meath, the most influential and popular of all confederates, was undoubtedly the most effective proponent of this strategy.

Born in 1602, Plunkett was the third son of Christopher Plunkett, Lord Killeen (an old English nobleman from the Pale) and Jane Dillon, sister of the earl of Roscommon. After graduating from Gray's Inn in London, he sat as a representative for County Meath in the parliament of 1634-5, and again in 1640-1. Plunkett's family, legal and parliamentary background provided him with an extensive network of contacts which he exploited with consummate skill.[35] From 1634 until the 1670s Plunkett participated in many of the major political events in Ireland. A reluctant rebel at first, he quickly assumed a central role in Kilkenny, where his tactics were invariably those of compromise and moderation.[36] Plunkett's political strategy, as it evolved during the 1640s, consisted of

Fennell and Geoffrey Browne. Rinuccini and the bishops led the clerical faction, but other figures such as Dermot O'Brien and Oliver Plunkett, Lord Louth, also played an important role. **34** For a discussion on the nature of political parties in England at this time see Underdown, David, *Pride's purge* (London 1985) p. 46, Hexter, J.H., *The reign of King Pym* (Cambridge 1941) pp 63-7, and Pearl, Valerie, "Oliver St John and the "middle group" in the long parliament: August 1643-May 1644", *English historical review*, vol. 80 (1966) pp 492-6. **35** In 1622 Plunkett was sent to Gray's Inn. Cregan, D.F., "Irish catholic admissions to the English inns of court 1558-1625", *Irish jurist*, vol. 5 (summer 1970) p. 109. **36** Plunkett was elected as chairman of the

formulating a settlement with the king which would satisfy the aspirations of moderate catholic land-owners and churchmen. It is principally through his manoeuvrings that a political middle ground began to emerge within the confederate association.

Plunkett's pivotal role in events underlines the strong element of continuity, both of personnel and political demands, before and after the 1641 uprising. The majority of confederate leaders were active in the Irish parliaments of 1634 and 1640-1, while the terms of the Ormond peace treaties in 1646 and 1649 (except for the crucial religious and constitutional clauses) are closely linked to the Graces of 1628.[37] This continuity, however, should not obscure the radical nature of confederate policies, particularly concerning the operation of central government. From 1644 onwards, the general assembly passed a number of reform initiatives to ensure the greater efficiency and effectiveness of confederate governmental institutions. These reforms tackled the fundamental issues of collective responsibility, the accountability of the executive supreme council and the primacy of the legislative general assembly.[38] The battle between the executive and legislature is of particular interest, not only from a constitutional point of view, but also because the radicalisation of the assembly coincided with the emergence of the moderates, led by Nicholas Plunkett, chairman of that assembly.

An understanding of the inner workings of confederate government, and the political alliances formed during this period, has been facilitated by the discovery of vital new material. The identification of two further attendance rolls for the general assembly (giving a total of four out of nine) and the completion of the supreme council lists (a task begun by Dónal Cregan over fifty years ago), enables a more detailed analysis of the political process to be carried out.[39] While the main events of the 1640s have been well chronicled by a number of historians, they do little more than provide a basic narrative structure. This study, by exploiting new data, and moving away from the concept of negative, ethnically based, politics, will help provide a better understanding of a fascinating, albeit extremely complex, period.

As the main thrust of this work concerns the confederate government, it is not necessary to dwell for long on the period leading up to the uprising itself. It

first and all subsequent general assemblies, except the final one in 1648, and sat on every supreme council and most of the negotiating committees. **37** Statistical continuity is examined in appendix 1. The Graces, concessions promised to Irish catholics by Charles I, are published in Clarke, Aidan, *The old English in Ireland 1625-1642* (London 1966) pp 238-54. **38** Three confederate reform documents still survive. 1644 (Marsh's Library Mss z 3.1.3); 1646 (Bodl. Carte Mss 16 ff 470-80); 1647 (Gilbert (ed.) *Irish confederation*, vi, pp 208-23). **39** The assembly lists for July 1644 and March 1647 are already published. The two new lists are for 1642/3 and 1645. The lists are discussed in detail in appendix 1. A full membership list for the supreme council appears in appendix 2 (table 13), while committee membership is outlined in chapter 7. See also Cregan, D.F. "Confederate catholics of Ireland" *IHS* pp 510-12.

would be inadvisable, however, to launch into a discussion of confederate Ireland without providing at least a basic synopsis of the early decades of the seventeenth century. The 1641 rising has been the subject of controversy over the years, and many confederates, along with their protestant opponents, wrote at length about the causes of the rebellion. Despite the obvious agenda underpinning these memoirs they nonetheless provide a fascinating contemporary insight into events.[40] More recently, Perceval-Maxwell's epic book is close to being the definitive work on the period 1640-1, while Clarke and Kearney have also produced invaluable studies on the preceding decades.[41]

The plantation policies of the Stuarts in Ulster provide the obvious starting point for the following review. These policies, combined with sporadic religious persecution, created widespread insecurity and resentment among catholics of all classes in Ireland. The native Irish, with few exceptions, had been almost completely disenfranchised politically, their lands confiscated, their last great stronghold in Ulster overrun with Scottish and English settlers, and their principal leaders in exile. Although most adapted as best they could, many hankered for a return of the old order and were encouraged in such aspirations by those who had fled to Flanders, Spain and Rome. The rapidity with which the uprising spread throughout the country in late 1641, suggests not only an element of planning and organisation, but also that the vast majority of native Irish remained unreconciled to the new regime.[42]

The old English, although still the main landholders in the kingdom, also suffered under the Stuarts. Famously described as "half-subjects" by James I, they were politically loyal but religiously suspect.[43] The policy of exclusion from government office, begun under Elizabeth I, was retained by her Stuart successors. Recusancy fines proved a sporadic irritant and the process of plantation left many feeling insecure about their estates. Whereas the native Irish tended to look abroad for leadership, the old English placed their hopes on the Irish parliament, in which they retained a powerful, if no longer dominant, influence. Through parliament they sought to safeguard their estates, mitigate the worst excesses of religious discrimination and regain some political influence. This policy achieved what appeared to be a major success with the granting of the Graces by the king in 1628, including a crucial statute of limitations on royal claims to

40 On the confederate side, the most important published accounts were by Richard Bellings, James Tuchet, the earl of Castlehaven and Nicholas French, bishop of Ferns. On the protestant side, the two most famous books are by John Temple and Edmund Borlase. See notes 5-8. 41 Perceval-Maxwell, M., *The outbreak of the Irish rebellion of 1641* (Dublin 1994). Clarke, *Old English* (1966) and numerous articles (see bibliography). Kearney, Hugh, *Strafford in Ireland 1633-41: A study in absolutism* (Cambridge 1989). 42 Two maps in Perceval-Maxwell, *Irish rebellion* pp 215, 253, illustrate the speed with which the disturbances spread throughout the kingdom. 43 Clarke, *NHI*, iii, p. 217.

lands in Ireland. The subsequent failure to implement these concessions caused intense resentment and bitterness.[44]

The 1630s proved a traumatic time for the catholic elite in Ireland. The increasing use of arbitrary power by the lord deputy, Thomas Wentworth, negated any residual influence they still enjoyed in parliament, while his plantation policies threatened their estates, principally in Connacht. Denied the protection of the Graces, and with the king whole-heartedly supporting his deputy, their future looked bleak. The outbreak of conflict in Scotland in 1637, however, transformed the situation, as Charles, anxious to mobilise support in Ireland, could no longer afford to ignore catholic grievances.[45] As opposition to the king escalated in Scotland, and Wentworth prepared to use Irish catholic troops against his enemies, the political situation in Ireland became increasingly unstable.

At this time, a number of catholic landholders in Ulster, deep in debt and worried by the violently anti-catholic rhetoric of the Scottish covenanters and English parliament, initiated contacts with influential Irish exiles. The old English leaders, similarly concerned with developments in the other Stuart kingdoms, successfully colluded with their protestant colleagues in the Irish parliament (and Westminster) to bring about the execution of the hated Thomas Wentworth. One consequence of this co-operation, however, was the renewed interest of the English parliament in legislating for the kingdom of Ireland. With Charles seemingly unwilling or incapable of granting serious concessions, the catholics of the Pale reluctantly considered a resort to arms. The catholic troops recruited by Strafford remained in the country, a potential source of support for any uprising.[46]

These various conspiracies (royalists, Ulster Irish, Pale catholics) became briefly entangled during the course of 1641, although no consensus exists among historians as to what exactly took place.[47] One by one, however, most potential conspirators fell away, as a settlement between Charles and the Scottish covenanters temporarily defused the political crisis. The catholics of the Pale, encouraged by the king's agreement to an act of limitation to royal claims to land in Ireland, and by the attitude of the new lord lieutenant, the earl of Leicester, reverted to

44 Clarke, Aidan, *The Graces 1625-41*, Irish history series no. 8 (Dundalk 1968). 45 The earl of Castlehaven, a leading confederate, described in his memoirs how fear of the Scots, as well as admiration for their achievements, motivated the Irish rebels. Tuchet, *Castlehaven memoirs* p. 21. 46 Many of these troops were later to become the backbone of the confederate armies. Lenihan, "Catholic confederacy" p. 36; Hazlett, "Military forces" p. 53. On 24 October 1641, Viscount Montgomery wrote to the king that the uprising was "chiefly supported by those, who under the colour of going to serve the king of Spain, had commissions to levy forces" (PRO SP Ire. 260/23 f.121). 47 Witness the recent controversy in the *Historical Journal* vol. 35, no. 4 (1992) pp 905-19 and vol. 37, no. 2 (1994) pp 421-37 between Jane Ohlmeyer and Michael Perceval-Maxwell over the possible involvement of the earl of Antrim in a royalist plot.

parliamentary politics.[48] The Ulster leaders, however, pushed ahead regardless with their pre-emptive strike, hoping to negotiate with Charles I from a position of strength. Instead their limited actions unleashed a nation-wide uprising which, lacking a strong central leadership, quickly threatened to escalate out of control.

The immediate events surrounding the outbreak of the rebellion on 22 October 1641 are familiar to all students of Irish history. In Armagh, Sir Phelim O'Neill took advantage of a dinner invitation to capture the strategic fortress at Charlemont, while in Dublin, Owen O'Connolly slipped away from a group of drunken conspirators and betrayed their plans to the authorities. These stories, richly embellished over the centuries, are an engaging mix of tragedy and farce. At the time they simply confirmed for many the racial stereotypes of Irish catholics, as a deceitful and untrustworthy people, with a propensity for drink. The lurid and often wildly exaggerated accounts of the massacre of Ulster protestants, taken in the form of depositions from those who fled to Dublin, were subsequently used to justify the wholesale expropriation of catholics and their demotion to the status of second-class citizens.[49]

It is necessary, however, to make a clear distinction between the people who initiated the uprising and the forces they mobilised in the process. The conspirators, for the most part, belonged to the landed elite, the so-called "deserving Irish", and played an active role in political affairs, on a local and national level, albeit in permanent opposition to the administration in Dublin. A number of them, like Phelim O'Neill and Philip O'Reilly, sat in the Irish parliament, while others served as sheriffs or justices of the peace in the shires. Their actions were motivated by a mixture of fear, grievance and financial worries.

The anti-catholic policies of the Westminster parliament, and its attempts to claim jurisdiction over Ireland, gave credence to rumours of a second conquest, led by an army of Scots covenanters.[50] Moreover, the Ulster conspirators bitterly resented their exclusion from royal service and restrictions on the practice of their religion. Although they had received lands in the plantation process, adapting to the new regime proved difficult, and many found themselves deep in debt. Frustrated by the failure of previous attempts at redress, they claimed to have taken up arms in self-defence, with the tacit (and in some cases explicit) support of the king. They vowed to continue in their actions until, "we be at better leisure to make our great grievances known unto his Majesty, and he have

---

**48** Leicester's role in diverting the Old English from the path of rebellion is described in Perceval-Maxwell, *Irish rebellion* pp 201-4.   **49** Thirty-three volumes of the depositions (including an index and various related documents) form part of the Trinity College Dublin manuscript collection. TCD Mss 809-841. **50** Early petitions of the rebels in 1641-2 refer to this threat from Westminster and Scotland. For example, "General declaration of the catholics of Ireland, Dec.1641" (Franciscan Mss D IV f.29); "Remonstrance of the Irish of Ulster, 1641" (Gilbert [ed.], *Contemporary history*, i, pp 450-60).

more power to relieve us".[51] The violent reaction of the administration in Dublin to developments, and the gradual collapse in social order, undermined these modest goals.

The administration in Dublin, the Ulster conspirators' principal target, could hardly have been expected to welcome the actions of Phelim O'Neill and his colleagues, but the ferocity and indiscriminate nature of its response exacerbated an already explosive situation. The lords justices issued a proclamation on 23 October accusing "evil affected Irish papists" of disloyalty, and displayed a marked reluctance to arm the Pale gentry, or indeed any catholics in the face of encroachments from the Ulster rebels.[52] They also failed to restrain the murderous activities of Charles Coote and William St Leger, in Leinster and Munster respectively, both of whom seemed intent on provoking a national uprising. By forcing catholic landowners to take up arms, the administration effectively created a pretext for confiscating their lucrative estates.

Meanwhile, the initial success of the rebels ensured that a growing number of people flocked to their banner, drawn "by the common habit of joining the winning side".[53] Local leaders, having assumed authority in their areas, found it increasingly difficult to control their supporters, who began to unburden themselves of generations of bitterness and resentment. Initially, such actions were confined to theft and destruction of property but after suffering a number of defeats at the hands of government forces, the insurgents became more inclined to murderous extremes.[54] Catholic landowners now faced the grim prospect of being squeezed on the one side by an increasingly hostile and aggressive administration, and on the other by a populist rising careering out of control.

---

**51** "Remonstrance of the catholics of Ireland, Dec.1641" (Gilbert [ed.], *Contemporary history*, i, pp 360-1. Canny, Nicholas, "In defence of the constitution? The nature of Irish revolt in the seventeenth century", *Culture et pratiques politiques en France et en Irlande 16ème-18ème siècles*, eds Louis Cullen et Louis Bergeron (Paris 1990) pp 23-40. The rebels loudly proclaimed their loyalty to Charles I, and in early November Phelim O'Neill issued a proclamation, allegedly sent by the king, authorising them to take arms in his defence. Although undoubtedly a forgery, the proclamation may well have appeared convincing to many at the time. Clarke, *Old English* pp 165-8; Corish, *NHI*, iii, pp 292-3. **52** Nalson, *Impartial collection*, vol. 2, p. 522. The grudging retraction six days later did little to assuage catholic fears. *A declaration by the lords justices and council …*, Dublin 1641 (BL Thomason Tracts 669 f.3). The catholic earl of Clanricarde, governor of the city and county of Galway, complained bitterly about the actions of the Dublin administration during this period. Bourke, *Clanricarde memoirs* pp 22, 25, 33 etc. Leading confederates blamed the lords justices for provoking the revolt. Tuchet, *Castlehaven memoirs* p. 35; "Roman catholics reply to the answers of the protestant commissioners, 12 March 1662" (BL Add Mss 4781 f.276-300) etc. **53** The papal nuncio made this comment, in a different context, after his return to Rome in 1649. "Report on the affairs of Ireland" (Aiazza [ed.], *Embassy* p. 499). **54** This development has been examined in some detail in the case of Armagh. See Simms, Hilary, "Violence in County Armagh, 1641" *Ulster 1641: Aspects of the rising*, edited by Brian MacCuarta (Belfast 1993) pp 122-38.

On 17 November, the Irish parliament formed a delegation to approach the Ulster insurgents and discover the causes for their actions. The principal figures behind this initiative – the earl of Antrim, Viscount Gormanston, Nicholas Plunkett, Roebuck Lynch and Richard Bellings among others – subsequently became leaders of the confederate association. The decision of the lords justices, however, to prorogue the parliament that same day fatally undermined any efforts at reconciliation, leaving the catholics of the Pale isolated and vulnerable. In the circumstances, they had little alternative but to seek some form of accommodation with the rebels.[55] The success of the Ulster forces on 29 November at Julianstown, against government troops sent to relieve the town of Drogheda, finally drove the Pale leaders to initiate contact with them.

A few days later, in a carefully choreographed meeting on the Hill of Crofty in Meath, the old English leaders of the Pale, and their Ulster Irish counterparts, formed a loose alliance. Loyalty to Charles I, and a determination to defend the ancient liberties of the Irish kingdom were the underlying principles of this arrangement.[56] A second meeting a week later, on the symbolic Hill of Tara, cemented the union, which Bellings later represented as a dramatic coming together of traditional enemies, who forty years earlier had been bitter foes.[57] On the contrary, however, these developments merely formalised a process which had been taking place over a number of years.

The leaders on both sides were closely related through marriage, worked together in parliament, and shared the common concerns of all landholders.[58] The indiscriminate policies of the lords justices, along with the fear of a popular uprising, helped bring them together politically. This was not a merging of old English and native Irish interests in a historic new departure, but rather the coming together of a conservative landed interest in the face of pressure from two extremes. Their principal concern was not to redress historic wrongs or to create a new egalitarian society, but rather to preserve (and expand) their role within the existing system. The insurgents, as in England, distinguished between

55 Richard Bellings (and others) stressed the importance of the decision to prorogue parliament, thus denying catholics a legitimate forum in which to express their grievances. Bellings' History in Gilbert (ed.), *Irish confederation*, i, pp 18-22. 56 This meeting, and the subsequent one at Tara, are described by Edward Dowdall in a statement to the authorities, given on 13 March 1642. He also includes a list of the names of those who attended, including Nicholas Plunkett "the lawyer" at Tara, but not apparently at Crofty (TCD Mss 816 f.44). On 22 March 1642 Garrett Aylmer similarly identified Plunkett among those present at Tara (TCD MSS 840 f.13). 57 Bellings was always keen to stress the differences between the old English and native Irish, particularly in later years when it came to apportioning blame for the uprising and the subsequent killings. Bellings' History in Gilbert (ed.), *Irish confederation*, i, p. 38. See also Corish, *NHI*, iii, p. 293. 58 The leading rebel Rory O'More for example was married to a daughter of Patrick Barnewall of Kilbrew, while Conor, Lord Maguire had married into the Flemings of Slane. Corish, *NHI*, iii, p. 290. Jackson, *Intermarriage in Ireland* (1970) provides a wealth of information on the various marriage alliances.

the institutions of government, which they supported, and the present occu-
pants, in this case the lords justices in Dublin, whom they bitterly opposed.
They fought against bad governors, not against a bad system of government.[59]

For the next four months rebel energies would be concentrated on the siege
of Drogheda and the creation of effective military units. Battlefield engagements
with royalist forces proved few and far between, as instead men like Viscount
Mountgarret and Malachy O'Queely, the archbishop of Tuam, sought to curb
the worst excesses of the populist uprising.[60] Apart from restoring order, it was
also imperative that the rebels organise themselves politically before they could
begin to negotiate a peace settlement with the king. The political and religious
elite took the first tentative steps in this direction early in 1642.

**59** Both John Morrill and David Smith make similar points about the opposition to Charles I
in England. Morrill, John, *The nature of the English revolution* (London 1993) p. 14; Smith,
David L., *Constitutional royalism and the search for a settlement, 1640-49* (Cambridge 1994) p.
328. **60** Bellings claimed that Mountgarret personally intervened to prevent pillaging in
Kilkenny city. See Bellings' History in Gilbert (ed.), *Irish confederation*, i, p. 57. O'Queely
actually raised his own private force to maintain order in his diocese. Gillespie, R., "Mayo and
the rising of 1641", *Cathair na Mart*, vol. 5 (1985) p. 41.

# CHAPTER 1

# Government formation

ℰᎧ

## JANUARY 1642–NOVEMBER 1642

Our constitution is what the dissensions of our time will permit: not such as were desired, but such as the persistent strife of wicked citizens will suffer it to be.

John Milton, *Defence of the people of England* (1651)[1]

The initial months of the insurrection were characterised by increasing disorder as, after the failure to capture Dublin, the uprising spread across the island in a series of uncoordinated local attacks. Royalist forces, isolated and undermanned, could do little more than launch punitive raids, while the northern insurgents, with the help of Pale catholics, concentrated their efforts on capturing the town of Drogheda.[2] That long (and ultimately unsuccessful) siege reflected not only the bankruptcy of ideas among the rebels, but also the limits of their military capabilities. By February 1642, the rebellion had affected most parts of the kingdom, forcing the catholic gentry and nobility to become more actively involved. Before long, the necessity of some sort of political organisation began to be felt; apart from concerns over the collapse of authority, the rebel leadership gradually realised that any peace settlement would require extensive negotiations with the king.[3]

The opening moves in this direction occurred during the first few weeks of the uprising. The lords justices reported that the insurgents had framed an oath, modelled very closely on the Scottish covenant, pledging their loyalty to the crown, country and religion, with "copies scattered abroad for all mens' view".[4] This oath was distributed haphazardly throughout the country, mainly through

---

1 Ashton, Robert, *The English civil war: Conservatism and revolution 1603-1649* (London 1978) p. 317. 2 The gradual spread of the rebellion throughout the kingdom has been outlined in some detail in Perceval-Maxwell, *Irish rebellion* pp 213-60. 3 Viscount Muskerry's letter to the earl of Barrymore on 17 March 1642 vividly describes the dilemma facing catholic nobility at this time (BL Add Mss 25,277 f.58). See also Corish, *NHI*, iii, pp 295-7. 4 Lords justices and council to the lord lieutenant, 25 Nov. 1641 (PRO SP Ire 260/37 f.154a). Oaths were produced in both English and Irish. Acts of the general assembly, 1642 (Gilbert [ed.], *Irish confederation*, ii, p. 85).

the network of parish clergy. To what extent an element of coercion existed in this process is unclear, although the earl of Clanricarde bitterly criticised priests for forcing people to take the oath. The significant number of gentry in the Pale and Galway who remained neutral suggests that compulsion by no means always succeeded.[5]

Whatever the case, by the end of 1641, evidence begins to emerge of crude attempts to forge the disparate groups then in arms into some form of alliance. In December the Pale lords urged the nobility and gentry of Galway to join their "association", while Clanricarde reported to the king that the entire kingdom was "in a strange combination and confederacy by vows and covenants".[6] These early developments concentrated primarily on military affairs, rather than on political matters. The rebel leaders may well have believed that an early settlement with the king was inevitable, whereas the threat from the Dublin administration, coupled with widespread social disorder, demanded immediate military action.

On 26 February, however, a royal proclamation reached Dublin calling on those in arms in Ireland to surrender to the authorities. This came as a major blow to the insurgents, who had proclaimed their loyalty to the king from the beginning.[7] News of the king's intervention had a profound impact on the Pale gentry, and a number of prominent individuals, including Lord Dunsany and Patrick Barnewall of Kilbrew, surrendered voluntarily to the Dublin administration. The vindictive actions of the lords justices, imprisoning and torturing these people, shocked Irish catholic opinion and almost certainly precluded the possibility of large-scale surrenders.[8] Indeed, the entire rebellion could well have collapsed at this time if the authorities in Dublin had reacted in a more conciliatory fashion.

---

5 As late as June 1642, a significant number of leading Pale gentry (including Nicholas Plunkett and James Bathe) were pledging their continued loyalty to Clanricarde, and the same is true in Galway, where the earl listed Patrick Darcy, Roebuck Lynch, Richard Blake and Richard Martin among his supporters in the city. Clanricarde to lords justices, 18 May 1642; Clanricarde to lords justices, 27 June 1642 (Bourke, *Clanricarde memoirs* pp 19, 75, 81, 141, 177). It is undoubtedly significant that Bishop Dease of Meath opposed the rebellion, while in Galway, the collegiate church resisted the authority of Archbishop O'Queely who supported the rebels. (thanks to Tadhg Ó hAnnracháin for this point). 6 Pale lords to the nobility and gentry of Galway, 29 Dec. 1641; Clanricarde to duke of Richmond, 23 Jan. 1642 (Bourke, *Clanricarde memoirs* pp 62, 67). 7 Corish, *NHI*, iii, p. 295. All the early declarations, petitions and letters from the rebels stressed their loyalty to Charles. "Copies of the proclamation of Phelim O'Neill and others, 24 Oct. 1641" (PRO SP Ire 260/27 f.135); "The general declaration of the catholics of Ireland, 28 Dec. 1641" (Franciscan Archives Mss D IV f.29); Phelim Molloy to William Parsons, 17 March 1642 in *HMC* 2nd Report, Appendix (London 1874) p. 218 etc. 8 According to Nicholas Plunkett the actions of the lords justices forced the rebels to "assume a government to preserve themselves". "Roman catholics reply, 12 March 1662" (BL Add Mss 4,781 ff 276-300).

This hard-line policy mirrored developments at Westminster, where on 19 March the English parliament implicitly assumed control of Irish affairs by forcing the king to sign the adventurers act. The act used Irish land as security to raise loans to send forces to Ireland, and more importantly prohibited the king from granting pardons to the rebels without the consent of parliament, which alone could declare an end to the rebellion. These developments confirmed the worst suspicions of catholics about the intentions of the English parliament towards Ireland, and with the king seemingly unable to defend his own prerogatives, there seemed little alternative to the present strategy of armed opposition to the Dublin administration.[9]

On the military front, the arrival of Colonel Monck in Dublin with 1,500 foot to help suppress the uprising in the Pale, forced the rebels to abandon the siege of Drogheda in early March. The following month, the vanguard of the Scottish army landed in Antrim, and the rebels suffered two significant military reverses at Kilrush, County Kildare (April 15), and Lisburn, County Antrim (April 29). It became increasingly clear that the insurgents could not gain a quick victory in the war, while the possibility of a negotiated settlement appeared remote.[10] In order to prevent a slide into anarchy, the catholic leaders needed to organise some form of government to administer the areas under their control.

The impetus for this new strategy came from Ulick Bourke, fifth earl of Clanricarde, a leading catholic lord, and the major landholder in County Galway. Clanricarde had been born and raised in England, and spent most of the 1630s at the court of Charles I. Although new to Ireland in September 1641, the earl was by no means a novice in the political affairs of the kingdom. He had been closely involved with the Irish parliamentary delegation in London, including such figures as Viscount Gormanston and Nicholas Plunkett, during the course of the summer. His arrival in Ireland shortly before the outbreak of the rebellion certainly proved very opportune for the king's fortunes there. As a catholic royalist and office holder (governor of the town and county of Galway), with extensive estates and contacts in both Ireland and England, the earl proved uniquely placed to provide a channel of communication between the rebels and their monarch.[11]

---

9 Irish catholics frequently referred to the threat posed by English parliament, and the adventurers act in particular. "General declaration of the catholics of Ireland, 28 Dec. 1641" (Franciscan Mss D IV f.29); "Petition of catholics to Ormond, 31 July 1642" (Bodl. Rawlinson Mss B. 507 f.43); Confederate treaty commissioners to Ormond, 28 Sept. 1644 (Gilbert [ed.], *Irish confederation*, iii, p. 311) etc. 10 Bellings stressed this point in his memoirs. Bellings' History in Gilbert (ed.), *Irish confederation*, i, p. 81. In an appendix to his thesis, Robert Armstrong lists all the troops sent to Ireland at this time. "Protestant Ireland", pp 304-7. 11 The earl also held an English title (earl of St Albans), with lands in Kent and Hertfordshire, and the future parliamentarian general, the earl of Essex, was his half-brother. Lowe (ed.), *Clanricarde letterbook* p. xvii; Little, Patrick, "'Blood and Friendship': The earl of Essex's efforts to protect the earl of Clanricarde's interests, 1641-6" *EHR*, vol. 112, no. 448 (Sept. 1997), pp 927-41.

The initial outbreak of the uprising, however, left Clanricarde vulnerable and isolated, as a number of his relatives and associates joined the uprising. The earl bitterly criticised the provocative actions of the lords justices in Dublin, particularly when they failed to provide him with sufficient arms to counter rebel incursions into Galway.[12] The insurgents, for the most part, left him alone, in the hope that he would eventually join their cause. Although Clanricarde understood the pressures which had forced many catholic leaders to take up arms, and sympathised with many of their demands, he nonetheless felt unable to condone their actions.[13]

From the beginning of the insurrection, the earl made a clear distinction between the leaders and their followers. On first hearing of the uprising he described those risen in arms as "loose people", and expressed his relief that none of the gentry or lords "either of English descent or ancient Irish" had become involved. As the revolt spread he specifically directed his criticism at the northerners whom he believed were "generally of more haughty and ambitious spirits than those in other parts of the kingdom".[14] He began to moderate his views, however, taking a generally sympathetic view of rebel actions, in response to the violent reaction of the lord justices. He argued that the policies of the Dublin administration were counter-productive and placed the Pale nobility in an impossible position.[15]

The earl decided, therefore, to contact the rebel leadership to explore the possibility of a speedy settlement to the conflict. He received vital assistance in this task from the citizens of Galway, particularly the lawyers Patrick Darcy and Richard Martin. Both Darcy and Martin belonged to leading Galway families, were closely related through their respective marriages, and had attended the Middle Temple in London.[16] During the 1630s, despite the difficulties faced by catholic lawyers, they emerged at the forefront of the legal profession in Ireland, representing the catholic and protestant nobility. In 1636 the two men clashed with the lord deputy, Thomas Wentworth, while acting on behalf of catholic landowners in Connacht (including Clanricarde), in opposing the plantation of that province. Wentworth, clearly impressed by their legal talents, described Darcy as "a lawyer. . in as great practise as any other of his profession".[17]

---

**12** Clanricarde to Charles I, 22 Jan. 1642 (Bourke, *Clanricarde memoirs* p. 61). **13** Ibid. p. 15. Although loyalty to the king was an important motivation in Clanricarde's stance, he may also have been concerned at losing the income from his English estates. He continued to receive rents until at least late 1646. Little, "Blood and Friendship" pp 935-8. **14** Clanricarde to earl of Bristol, 14 Nov. 1641; Clanricarde to earl of Essex, 15 Nov. 1641; Clanricarde to Charles I, 22 Jan. 1642 (Bourke, *Clanricarde memoirs* pp 14, 15, 61). **15** Clanricarde to duke of Richmond, 23 Jan, 1642 (Bourke, *Clanricarde memoirs* p. 63). **16** The Darcy and Martin families belonged to the "tribes of Galway", and Margaret, sister of Patrick Darcy's wife, Mary French, had married Richard Martin. O'Malley, William, "Patrick Darcy, lawyer and politician, 1598-1668" (MA thesis, UCG 1973) p. 35. Darcy was admitted to Middle Temple in 1617, Martin five years later in 1622. Cregan, "Catholic admissions" pp 112-13. **17** Kearney,

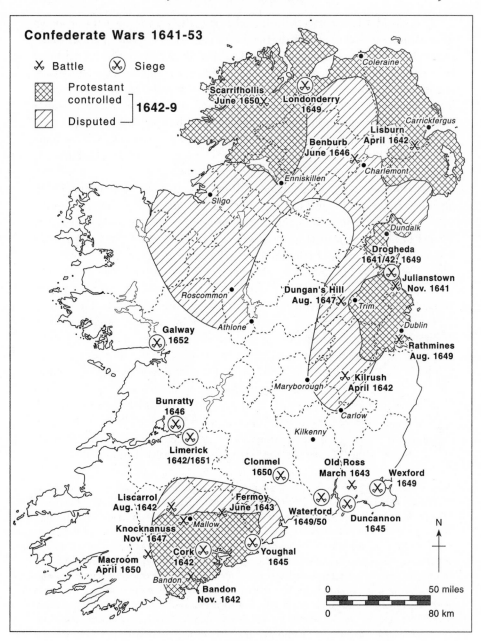

*Map 1: The confederate wars, 1641-1653* This map marks the major engagements (sieges and battles) in a war dominated by skirmishes and raiding, which affected most parts of the country.

Darcy and Martin later helped orchestrate the campaign to bring down Wentworth and were returned to the parliament in by-elections held in 1641.[18] After the outbreak of the rebellion in October, the Galway men joined other leading catholic parliamentarians in Dublin for an emergency two-day session. Perceval-Maxwell contends that Darcy allied himself with the protestants at this time, but probably more in an attempt to forestall intervention from England or Scotland, than from any particular hostility towards the rebels. Claims in the *Aphorismical discovery* that Darcy moved the motion to prorogue parliament are contradicted by the lawyer's presence on a committee (with Nicholas Plunkett) calling for a continuation of the session.[19]

After the proroguing of parliament on 17 November the movements of both men become more difficult to track. They maintained regular contact with the earl of Clanricarde, informing him of happenings in Dublin, and of their continued loyalty. On 12 December, however, the earl received yet another letter from Darcy confirming the spread of the rebellion throughout the country, and "by the manner of his expressions I did then conjecture that his own inclinations were wavering and leaning that way".[20] Controversy surrounds the exact timing of Darcy's (and Martin's) return to Galway and their role in subsequent events.

A number of statements in the 1641 depositions outlined developments in Galway city during the early months of the rebellion. Despite some differences in detail, they all ascribed a central role to both men as members of the new ruling body, the "council of eight". Later as a prisoner of the Cromwellian regime, Darcy denied having taken part in any assembly or council in Galway until the first confederate general assembly in October 1642, by which time the English civil war had already broken out. The weight of surviving evidence, however, suggests that Darcy's own recollections could not be relied upon, as he desperately sought to clear himself of any charge of disloyalty towards the king.[21]

*Strafford in Ireland* pp 92-4. Darcy's legal clients included the earls of Antrim, Clanricarde, Cork and Ormond. O'Malley, "Patrick Darcy" p. 28; Ohlmeyer, *Civil war and restoration* p. 36.  **18** Both Darcy and Martin were returned to the parliament in by-elections in 1641. Kearney, *Strafford in Ireland* p. 193; Clarke, *Old English* p. 259. See Perceval-Maxwell, *Irish rebellion* (1994) for the role played by the Galway lawyers in the parliament during 1640-1. It was during this parliament that Darcy wrote his famous "argument", dealing with the relationship between the executive, parliament and the king. Darcy, Patrick, *An argument delivered by Patrick Darcy esquire by the express order of the commons in the parliament of Ireland, 9 June 1641* (Waterford 1643; reprinted 1764).  **19** Perceval-Maxwell, *Irish rebellion* pp 243-5. The author of *Aphorismical discovery* loathed Darcy (who he described as "a perfidious member to his nation") and blamed him for a variety of vile deeds. Gilbert (ed.), *Contemporary history*, i, p. 12; *Journal of the House of Commons of the Kingdom of Ireland*, vol. 1 (Dublin 1796) p. 293.  **20** Narrative in Bourke, *Clanricarde memoirs* p. 38.  **21** In a statement given on 14 Aug. 1643, William Hamond described Darcy and Martin as "the men that first moved the town of Galway to rebellion" (TCD Mss 830 f.134b). In May 1643 Joseph Hampton similarly accuses them of leading the rebellion (TCD Mss 830 f.138b). According to the testimony of

Whatever the truth, it is clear that both Darcy and Martin had arrived in Galway city by early 1642. Reluctant rebels, they proved anxious to maintain contact with the earl of Clanricarde.

The province of Connacht, due mainly to the earl's influence, remained relatively quiet during the initial months of the uprising. This distance enabled Clanricarde to realise, perhaps earlier than most, the full extent of the dilemma facing the rebel leadership. By failing to capture the administrative centre at Dublin, they found themselves isolated from the king and opposed by a government intent on destroying them by force. A series of uncoordinated local attacks simply contributed to the general breakdown in authority, and created a power vacuum in the provinces. Clanricarde and his Galway allies now attempted to provide some direction and purpose to events.

Early in 1642, Valentine Browne, a Franciscan friar, returned to Galway with a letter from Viscount Gormanston addressed to Clanricarde. Gormanston complained at length about the actions of the lords justices and the threat from Westminster, while at the same time reassuring the earl that the Irish had not "revived the old quarrel" against the English.[22] Not long afterwards, Clanricarde received another communication from a more local source in Connacht. The catholic gentry of Roscommon, assembled at Tulske in a "union of faith", declared their loyalty to the king and the existing laws, except where they discriminated against catholics, and urged the earl to take command of their forces.[23] Although Clanricarde declined this offer, these assurances of rebel loyalty to the crown spurred him into action. On 4 February 1642 he replied to the gentry of Roscommon, informing them of his intention to travel to Galway to confer "with persons of ability there". Unfortunately, he fails to identify these people, but subsequent events suggest the involvement of the leading lawyers in the city, including Darcy and Martin.[24]

Margaret Rolwick on 12 March 1643 "the rest of the English were not interrupted in their estates until such time as Mr Patrick Darcy and Mr Richard Martin did come to the said town" (TCD Mss 830 f.166). On the same day, Oliver Smith swore that Darcy and Martin arrived in Galway in January 1642 and sat on the "council of eight" which controlled the city (TCD Mss 830 f.158). In 1653, however, Darcy stated that he arrived in February, and "was not present in any assembly or council in Galway" (TCD Mss 830 f.263). **22** Gormanston to Clanricarde, 21 Jan. 1642 (Carte, *Ormond*, v, pp 285-6). Another statement on 13 March 1642 by Edward Dowdall, a prisoner in Dublin castle, suggests Browne may have been sent specifically from Galway to contact the rebel leadership. Gilbert (ed.), *Irish confederation*, i, pp 268-78. The "old quarrel" in this context referred to efforts to expel the English out of Ireland. **23** *A true copy of the laws and rules of government, agreed upon and established by the nobles of several counties of Ireland* ..., London 1641/2 (BL Thomason tracts E138 f.5); Gentlemen of Roscommon to Clanricarde, 23 Jan. 1642 (Bourke, *Clanricarde memoirs* pp 67-9). **24** Clanricarde to the gentlemen of Roscommon, 4 Feb. 1642 (Bourke, *Clanricarde memoirs* pp 68-9).

On 21 February 1642, a few weeks after this meeting, Clanricarde wrote to the earl of Westmeath, an intimate of the Pale lords, suggesting that "noblemen and persons of quality" should prepare a remonstrance of their grievances to present to the king.[25] Clanricarde followed up this suggestion by initiating direct contact with the Pale leaders. In a letter to Viscount Gormanston, Clanricarde argued that the rebellion would only "divert the disposing of places of trust on deserving natives which is justly to be desired and expected". His personal chaplain, the Dominican friar Oliver Bourke, acted as an intermediary underlining the important role played by the clergy in political affairs. Apart from this letter, Bourke also brought with him a number of papers which Clanricarde claimed had been offered for his consideration "by some gentlemen of this province [Connacht]".[26]

The first paper described the present condition in Connacht, stressing the abuses committed by the English garrisons there. The authors bemoaned the lack of communication between the various counties in the kingdom, and warned of the danger of massive intervention from both England and Scotland. They recommended (as Clanricarde had suggested to the earl of Westmeath just a few days previously) that the insurgents send a remonstrance to the king, presented "with such moderation as may not justly endanger a denial". Others of "quality" who had not yet joined the revolt might be encouraged to sign the petition, which Clanricarde would present at court. The document concluded with a plea to the rebel leadership to seek a truce from the king "until his pleasure be declared".[27]

Aware that his actions might be construed as treasonous, Clanricarde claimed in his memoirs to have undertaken these contacts simply to buy time until sufficient help arrived from England. Nonetheless, the earl clearly sympathised with some of the insurgents' demands and shared their anxiety that the wilder elements within their ranks be controlled. There was nothing inconsistent between this initial approach and his subsequent policy of attempting to facilitate a compromise settlement, using his numerous contacts in both Dublin and Kilkenny.[28]

His memoirs fail to mention two further crucial papers which Oliver Bourke carried with him. According to Edward Dowdall, who witnessed Bourke presenting the documents to the Pale leadership, one of these contained "a model for a form of government [to be] observed throughout the kingdom during the

25 Clanricarde to earl of Westmeath, 21 Feb. 1642 (Bourke, *Clanricarde memoirs* p. 76). 26 Clanricarde to Gormanston, 23 Feb. 1642 (Bourke, *Clanricarde memoirs* pp 78-80). The clergy often acted as personal agents for the nobility. For example, Patrick Crelly, the Cistercian abbot of Newry, played the same role for the earl of Antrim. Ohlmeyer, *Civil war and restoration* pp 191-2 27 Propositions brought by Oliver Bourke, Feb. 1642 (Bourke, *Clanricarde memoirs* pp 78-80). 28 Narrative in Bourke, *Clanricarde memoirs* p. 81. For later attempts at moderating confederate demands see in particular Clanricarde's approach to the confederate supreme council during the assault on Dublin in November 1646. Clanricarde to supreme council, 14 Nov. 1646 (Lowe [ed.], *Clanricarde letter-book* pp 309-15); Supreme council to Clanricarde, 15 Nov. 1646 (Bodl. Carte Mss 19 ff 369-70); Supreme council to Thomas Preston, 24 Nov. 1646 (PRO SP Ire. 262/31 ff 193-4).

said troubles".[29] This is the first specific reference to the creation of an alternative government, while the title and form of the document echoes plans implemented by the confederates shortly afterwards. The Connacht proposals involved the establishment of a national supreme council, with subordinate provincial and county councils. Unfortunately, Dowdall's statement provides no further details. Another contemporaneous document contains what appears to be a summary of these proposals, including the creation of a judicature to enforce law and order, and the framing of an oath of association.[30]

The final paper consisted of certain demands to be presented to the king, which Dowdall described as "exorbitant".[31] Once again he failed to elaborate on this point, but the composite document outlined a number of propositions, quite similar to the confederate position during the subsequent peace negotiations with the royalists. The list included full religious freedoms, the restoration of church livings to catholic priests, a free parliament without interference from Westminster, which would adjudicate on the restoration of plantation lands, and finally that all military installations in the kingdom be garrisoned by troops of the nation.[32]

Oliver Bourke intimated that Clanricarde would bring the terms to "the king's immediate view".[33] Needless to say, the earl could hardly publicly admit to any role in facilitating confederate efforts to establish an alternative government, but it seems highly unlikely that he was unaware of the contents of the documents conveyed by his personal chaplain. The general tone and content of the propositions, calling for an oath "to settle a perfect union", and implementing measures for "setting the baser sort to look to their business", appear consistent with the general thrust of the earl's strategy of using the catholic gentry to control and moderate the uprising.[34]

Edward Dowdall, who saw all three original documents, reckoned they had been written by somebody "learned in the laws", and the evidence already presented strongly suggests the involvement of Patrick Darcy and Richard Martin. The lawyers, close allies of the earl of Clanricarde, the main sponsor of the initiative, had recently arrived in Galway from where the document emerged. Moreover, both men were subsequently involved in drawing up the confederate

---

**29** Examination of Edward Dowdall, 13 March 1642 (TCD Mss 816 f.44). Dowdall's deposition was also published in Gilbert (ed.), *Irish confederation*, i, pp 268-78. **30** This document, entitled "Plan for a national convention in Ireland, 1641-2" is in Gilbert (ed.), *Irish confederation*, i, pp 289-90. **31** Dowdall's condemnation of the proposals is hardly surprising given he was a prisoner of the Dublin administration at this time. Examination of Edward Dowdall, 13 March 1642 (TCD Mss 816 f.44). **32** Gilbert (ed.), *Irish confederation*, i, pp 289-90. The list of demands concludes with the statement they were nothing more than Scotland already had, illustrating again the influence of events elsewhere in the Stuart kingdoms. **33** Examination of Edward Dowdall, 13 March 1642 (TCD Mss 816 f.44). **34** Gilbert (ed.), *Irish confederation*, i, pp 289-90.

model of government along very similar lines.[35] Darcy played a leading role in Kilkenny politics as *de facto* lord chancellor, while Martin served on the first confederate judicature, established in August 1644.[36] From the beginning of the uprising, therefore, and throughout the confederate period, they helped shape political developments in Ireland.

Instead of going directly to Viscount Gormanston and the other Pale lords, Bourke first visited a number of catholic gentry in Meath who remained as yet uncommitted. This group assembled in the house of Lawrence Dowdall, former MP for Navan, and those present included his renowned parliamentary colleague Nicholas Plunkett.[37] During the 1630s he established close relations with such leading figures as Gormanston, whom he accompanied to England in 1641 to negotiate with the king on the issue of implementing the Graces. Although primarily a Pale politician, Plunkett's link with Connacht stretched back to 1636, when he represented Galway landowners in their dispute with Thomas Wentworth.[38]

At the outbreak of the rebellion, Plunkett supported the initiative by the Irish parliament to contact the rebels, but as soon as the lords justices prorogued the session he returned to Meath. Plunkett attended the second meeting between representatives of the Pale and the Ulster insurgents at the Hill of Tara, and was appointed legal adviser to the new council of war along with Garrett Aylmer and Richard Berford.[39] Nonetheless, despite this close association with the rebel leadership, Plunkett's assessment of developments in the kingdom closely resembled that of Clanricarde and his Galway associates.

Plunkett argued that the initial uprising in 1641 was "only the act of a few persons of broken and desperate fortunes", supported by "a rude multitude". For this reason, he concluded, these developments could not be described as the work of "the whole nation". Developing this theme, he drew a clear distinction between those "of English extraction, though born in Ireland", who would have opposed the uprising if possible, and the men of Ulster.[40] He qualified this eth-

---

**35** On 1 November 1642, the confederate general assembly established a committee to "lay down a model of civil government", headed by Patrick Darcy and including Richard Martin among others. Gilbert (ed.), *Irish confederation*, ii, pp 73–90. **36** Martin reporting on the first general assembly to the earl of Clanricarde, described how Darcy sat bareheaded on a stool, like those who sat on the woolsack in parliament. Richard Martin to Clanricarde, 2 Dec. 1642 (Bourke, *Clanricarde memoirs* pp 296-8). The general assembly established the judicature at the end of the 1644 session. Gilbert (ed.), *Irish confederation*, iii, pp 266-7. **37** Once again Edward Dowdall is the source of this information. Examination of Edward Dowdall, 13 March 1642 (TCD Mss 816 f.44). **38** See Clarke, *Old English* (1966), Kearney, *Strafford in Ireland* (1989) and Perceval-Maxwell, *Irish rebellion* (1994) for information on Plunkett's career pre-1641. **39** According to Garret Aylmer, Plunkett attended the meeting, having received a summons from the sheriff of Meath (Nicholas Dowdall) at the direction of Viscount Gormanston. Examination of Garret Aylmer of Balgriffin, 14 March 1642 (TCD Mss 840 f.13). Nicholas Dowdall confirmed this in a statement given in Dublin on 17 March 1642 (Gilbert [ed.], *Irish confederation*, i, p. 281). **40** Plunkett out-

nic division by explaining how the actions of the lords justices forced the "English Pale" *and* the rest of the native Irish into taking up arms. The problem, therefore, centred not on all native Irish people, but only the Ulster Irish, and their "barbarous" behaviour.[41]

This prejudice against the Ulster Irish existed in confederate politics throughout the 1640s, and even Plunkett, the great conciliator, proved suscepti-ble to such arguments. Nonetheless, while conceding that the murders of 1641 were inexcusable, Plunkett insisted that the principal blame lay with the lords justices, who harboured a "grand plot of extirpation" against all Irish catholics. Indeed, he continued, "the said Ulstermen did not engage in blood 'till the provocation of that kind was first given by executing the said Lords Justices orders". Recent research on the depositions has proven this statement to be largely accurate, and his assessment of events became the standard defence of the catholic position over the next three hundred years.[42]

The day after the encounter in Dowdall's house, all those who had attended met with Viscount Gormanston, Viscount Netterville and James Bath of Ath-carne for further discussions. Rory O'More also became involved, while Plun-kett travelled to Naas for a meeting with Richard Berford, another prominent lawyer.[43] Eventually, in early March, the Pale leadership responded to the Conn-acht initiative, accepting the model of government and Clanricarde's role as mediator. Viscount Gormanston requested that the earl arrange a truce to enable the rebel leaders in the various provinces to discuss his idea of a remonstrance. A number of catholic noblemen, including Viscount Mountgarret, Viscount Clanmorris and Lord Mayo, received letters at this time to inform them of developments.[44]

For his part, Clanricarde sent his cousin, Terence Coghlan, to Dublin with "dispatches to the state for a cessation of arms, until the king's pleasure were declared upon some humble addresses prepared for his view". In a letter to Sir Charles Coote, the earl advocated a cease-fire, explaining how many rebels "were compelled by the threats and strength of their neighbours, to run to those cours-es contrary to their own inclination".[45] Coote, a notorious anti-catholic bigot,

lined his opinions in a series of papers presented to Charles II in 1661-2 (BL Add Mss 4,781 ff 155-61, ff 276-300). **41** BL Add Mss 4,781 ff 276-300. **42** BL Add Mss 4,781 ff 276-300. Simms, "Violence in Armagh", *Ulster 1641* (1993), is a detailed study of the area in which a number of atrocities took place. A much earlier work based on the depositions also illustrates that government forces in Munster initiated much of the bloodshed in that particular province. Fitzpatrick, Thomas, *Waterford during the civil war* (Waterford 1912). **43** Examin-ation of Edward Dowdall, 13 March 1642 (TCD Mss 816 f.44). Berford, like Plunkett, attend-ed Gray's Inn and after the establishment of the confederate association was appointed to the judicature along with Richard Martin in 1644. Cregan, "Catholic admissions" p. 108; Gilbert (ed.), *Irish confederation*, iii, pp 266-7. **44** Gormanston to Clanricarde, 5 March 1642 (Bourke, *Clanricarde memoirs* pp 104-5); Dowdall Examination, 1642 (TCD Mss 816 f.44). **45** Clanricarde believed that his efforts at mediation were seriously undermined by the seizing of

remained unmoved by such pleading and time was fast running out for the possibility of a compromise settlement.

Increasingly desperate, Gormanston and his allies in the Pale contacted another leading catholic nobleman, the earl of Castlehaven, seeking his mediation with the government in Dublin and access to the king. Castlehaven passed the letter on to the lords justices, who reproved him for not arresting the original bearer of the message, and ordered him to hold no further correspondence with the insurgents. To his horror, the earl subsequently discovered that he "stood indicted of high treason". Shortly afterwards he travelled to Dublin, only to be arrested and thrown into jail.[46] The treatment of Castlehaven, along with the arrest of another intermediary, Colonel John Reade, convinced the rebel leadership of the futility of sending a remonstrance to the king until they could defend themselves from government aggression.[47]

On 14 April Clanricarde received a letter from Viscount Gormanston declaring an unwillingness to proceed with the original plan, "without the advice of the select of the county". Gormanston also confided his suspicions of those neutrals, like Nicholas Plunkett, who appeared to be "more cautious of their own than careful of the common safety".[48] In this the viscount reflected not only a hardening of the insurgents' attitude towards a settlement, but also the hostility felt by many catholics towards those co-religionists who refused to associate with their cause. The cleric Hugh Bourke described them as "the pest of a sound commonwealth and as it were its woodlouse", and in the years to come confederate authorities instigated a number of measures against catholics who refused to join the association.[49]

In his memoirs, the earl wrote that as a result of Gormanston's intervention he decided not to continue with his efforts, but in fact a more pressing crisis had emerged to direct his attentions closer to home. In late April an internal power struggle forced Patrick Darcy and other moderates to flee the city of Galway, although they returned shortly afterwards at Clanricarde's insistence.[50] The

an English ship in Galway harbour in March. Clanricarde to Sir Charles Coote, 17 March 1642 (Bourke, *Clanricarde memoirs* p. 95, 104-6). **46** Correspondence of the earl of Castlehaven, 1641-2 (TCD Mss 840 f.41, 45); "A remonstrance of the right honourable James, earl of Castlehaven, and Lord Audley" in [Lodge, John (ed.)], *Desiderata curiosa Hibernica*, vol. 2 (London 1772) pp 124-7. **47** According to Bellings, the torture of Reade "did complete mens' aversion of the state". Bellings' History in Gilbert (ed.), *Irish confederation*, i, p. 82. Plunkett also argued that the treatment of Castlehaven clearly demonstrated that the lords justices would not allow any access to the king. "Roman catholics' reply, 12 March 1662" (BL Add Mss 4781 ff 276-300). **48** Gormanston to Clanricarde, 14 April, 1642 (Bourke, *Clanricarde memoirs* p. 123). **49** Hugh Bourke to Luke Wadding, 10 July 1642 (*Report on Franciscan manuscripts* [Dublin 1906] p. 160); The new supreme council, on 11 June 1642, ordered that neutrals refusing to take the oath of association "be dealt with as enemies" (PRO SP Ire. 260/67 ff 234-53). **50** Clanricarde sent directions to Patrick Darcy, Richard Blake, Richard Martin, Roebuck Lynch and others "to reside there till former bad humours be clearly spent and quieted by

mayor, Walter Lynch, informed Clanricarde of a new oath "for our just and nat-ural defence". This in effect signalled Galway's intention to join the rebellion, and shortly afterwards local forces besieged the fort. On 11 May Clanricarde managed to establish an uneasy truce, much to the chagrin of the lords justices, who ordered the earl to receive no further submissions from the rebels, but instead "persecute them with fire and sword".[51]

Nonetheless, Clanricarde persisted with his efforts to secure a nation-wide truce, writing to the king in June expressing his doubts about the policies of the lords justices and requesting that "some other course of moderation or distinc-tion may be directed".[52] The other ideas proposed by Darcy and Martin, and sponsored by Clanricarde (principally that of the catholic elite organising them-selves to assume control of the uprising), did not disappear entirely. Instead they were eagerly embraced by the only national institution supportive of the insur-gents, the Catholic Church, and for the next three months the political initiative passed to the clergy.

The 1641 depositions graphically illustrate the extent of clerical involvement from the early days of the insurrection. In most accounts, they acted as a moder-ating influence on the rebels, counselling restraint and preventing the massacre of protestant settlers on a number of occasions. In Connacht, the archbishop of Tuam, Malachy O'Queely, went as far as to raise a body of troops to maintain some semblance of order.[53] The uprising presented the catholic hierarchy with something of a dilemma. On the one hand, many bishops belonged to substan-tial landowning families, and feared for their property and possessions; while on the other, the Catholic Church as an institution stood to profit substantially should the rebellion prove successful.[54] The hierarchy, therefore, supported the uprising but abhorred the breakdown in social order which accompanied it. For this reason, the clerics favoured imposing an oath of association, which provided some form of social cohesion as the old order crumbled away.

their means and good endeavours". The earl sought the suppression of private councils, with the town once again ruled "by the ancient form of government'. Clanricarde to lords justices, 18 May 1642 (Bourke, *Clanricarde memoirs* pp 138-42). **51** O'Sullivan, M.D., *Old Galway* (Cambridge 1942) pp 240-4; Walter Lynch to Clanricarde, 21 March 1642; Lords justices to Clanricarde, 13 June 1642 (Bourke, *Clanricarde memoirs* pp 101, 139-40, 167). As Sir Maurice Eustace later commented in a letter to Ormond, "the greatest cowards are observed to be the most merciless men". Eustace to Ormond, 8 Oct. 1647 (Gilbert [ed.], *Irish confederation*, vi, pp 206-8). **52** Clanricarde to Charles I, 28 June 1642 (Bourke, *Clanricarde memoirs* p. 181). **53** Nicholas Canny has done excellent research on the depositions, described in numerous arti-cles. See for example Canny, Nicholas, "In defence of the constitution? The nature of Irish revolt in the seventeenth century", *Culture et pratiques* ... op. cit. pp 23-40; Gillespie, R., "Mayo and the rising of 1641", *Cathair na Mart*, vol. 5 (1985) pp 38-44. **54** The approximate holdings of these episcopal families are listed in Cregan, Dónal, "The social and cultural back-ground of a counter-reformation episcopate, 1618-60", *Studies in Irish History presented to R. Dudley Edwards*, (eds) Art Cosgrove and Dónal MacCartney (Dublin 1979) pp 85-117.

The clergy's first major contribution to the development of a civil government occurred as the initiative sponsored by the earl of Clanricarde began to flounder. On 22 March 1642 a synod assembled in the town of Kells, presided over by Hugh O'Reilly, archbishop of Armagh.[55] The clergy, although supportive of the rebels, had become increasingly concerned as the situation in the country at large tended "towards anarchy". The synod issued a declaration, urging the creation of a council of lay people and ecclesiastics to enforce law and order, and passed a sentence of excommunication on those guilty of murder, plundering or trespass.[56] Clerical support for the establishment of a new civil government echoed the Connacht initiative. The motivation of the clergy was essentially reactionary in nature, in direct contrast to their desire for radical religious reforms. This conservatism appealed to the catholic gentry, and proved a major factor in the alliance which subsequently developed.

As Scottish and English forces inflicted further defeats on the insurgents, the need for some form of central authority to help co-ordinate the war effort became increasingly urgent. A national ecclesiastical congregation, convened in Kilkenny from 10 to 13 May 1642, provided a forum to discuss the various options. This meeting reaffirmed many of the decisions taken at Kells regarding the maintenance of public order and the organisation of the rebel forces. The bishops declared that any conflict fought to defend catholic religion, the royal prerogative and the liberties of the kingdom, was "lawful and just". They pleaded for co-operation between all the provinces, and ordered the clergy to fund the war with the proceeds of church livings.[57] Apart from legitimising catholic participation in the war, the assembled clerics focused primarily on the establishment of a provisional government.

They outlined the need to frame an oath of union for all catholics "which they shall devoutly and Christianly take and faithfully observe". To preserve this union, and defuse potential ethnic tensions, they recommended that no distinction should be made between the old English and "ancient Irish". A general council, consisting of clergy, nobility and lay people (three from every province), would rule the kingdom, with the assistance of subordinate provincial councils, until a national assembly had an opportunity to meet.[58] With these proposals, which bear a remarkable similarity to those sponsored by the earl of Clanricarde, the essential framework of confederate government finally began to emerge.

After their deliberations, the bishops invited the nobility and gentry to join them in Kilkenny to discuss developments.[59] According to Geoffrey Barron, the

55 Apart from Armagh, the only other bishops present were Eugene MacSweeney of Kilmore and Heber MacMahon of Down/Conor. Moran, P.F. (ed.) *Spicilegium Ossoriense, being a collection of original letters and papers illustrative of the history of the Irish church from the reformation to the year 1800* 3 vols (Dublin 1874-84), ii, p. 8.  56 Gilbert (ed.), *Irish confederation*, i, pp 290-2.  57 Acts of the ecclesiastical congregation, 10-13 May 1642 (BL Stowe Mss 82 ff 271-4).  58 Idem.  59 This gathering was "casually met", according to Richard Bellings, who personal-

"temporal estates" were represented by the lords in person and "by two out of each county, city and corporate town", but how exactly this was organised remains unclear.[60] The assembly took a number of steps to organise the financial and military affairs of the insurgents, while attempting to enforce as much of existing law as possible in the circumstances. The members, representing the catholic gentry, were concerned that rents continued to be paid, and that existing tenants did not abandon the land.[61]

The assembly also ordered that a "general oath of association" be administered by the clergy to all catholics. As the only catholic body with an existing national structure, the Catholic Church proved ideally placed to perform this task, while the high regard for the clergy among the lower social orders ensured a high degree of compliance. As a consequence of this decision, however, the Catholic Church became the *de facto* arbiter of the oath, a fact the bishops were to exploit with devastating effect in the dispute over the Ormond peace treaty.[62] Finally, the assembly established a supreme council, consisting of "one general, one bishop, one temporal lord, eight gentlemen whereof one to be professor of the law, out of each province". Future councils would be "chosen or confirmed by the general provinces", and to ensure a degree of unanimity in decisions, at least seven members had to be present before any "laws" could be passed.[63]

ly attended the sessions. Cregan, D.F., "Confederation of Kilkenny" (PhD thesis) p. 44. Events suggest, however, that the meeting was more formally organised. Unfortunately, complete records for the June assembly no longer exist, but a document in the Public Records Office in London provides some information. Entitled "Acts, orders and constitutions made and established by the lords and gentry of the confederate catholics within the kingdom, assembled together at the city of Kilkenny, 7 June 1642" (PRO SP Ire. 260/67 ff 234-53), it is unclear how the document ended up in London. **60** Geoffrey Barron to Luke Wadding, 8 August 1642 (*Report on Franciscan manuscripts* [Dublin 1906] p. 171). Barron was a nephew of the influential Irish cleric Luke Wadding, and had been sent to France by Viscount Gormanston to recruit the veteran soldier Thomas Preston to the rebel cause. In a letter written to the earl of Clanricarde, shortly after the meeting in Kilkenny, the new supreme council informed the earl that only three provinces sent agents to "this assembly", as the representatives from Connacht were absent. By tacitly recognising Clanricarde's authority in Connacht, the council hoped he would be tempted to join them in opposing "the puritan anarchical faction". The confederates repeated this strategy later in the year, when the post of general in the western province was left vacant by the general assembly in anticipation of the earl taking the confederate oath. Mountgarret etc. to Clanricarde, 11 June 1642; Richard Martin to Clanricarde, 2 Dec. 1642 (Bourke, *Clanricarde memoirs* pp 171-2, 296-8). **61** On the military front, the assembly sought to create a national army to complement the efforts of the various provincial forces. This new army, commanded by Colonel Hugh O'Byrne, would (in theory at least) consist of 4,000 foot and 500 horse, supplied equally by the four provinces. "Acts ... 7 June 1642" (PRO SP Ire. 260/67 ff 234-53). **62** "Acts ... 7 June 1642" (PRO SP Ire. 260/67 ff 234-53). Early in the year, Clanricarde noticed the active role of the clergy in forcing people to subscribe to an oath of association. Narrative in Bourke, *Clanricarde memoirs* p. 81. **63** The wording of the order establishing the council is ambiguous and confusing, but Bellings wrote

In terms of sovereignty, it is interesting to note that even at this early stage the council issued laws rather than orders, conferring a veneer of legitimacy on the new regime. Geoffrey Barron explained this in a letter written to his uncle, the influential cleric Luke Wadding. Barron outlined the role of the new council "by whose wisdom and providence the whole affairs of the kingdom shall in the nature of a free state be governed, till the present tumults be accorded".[64] With the Dublin administration controlled by "the malignant party", and all access to the king denied, the insurgents had little option but to assume governmental authority.

The new council sat from 11 June until 13 July, organising the war effort. The council appointed receivers in each barony to collect the rent from the royal estates in Ireland, an important source of income for the insurgents. Tenants abandoning their farms had to pay a fine and surrender their leases, and strict measures were introduced against anybody entering lands without permission. Neutrals refusing to take the oath of association were "to be dealt with as enemies", while the raising of private forces became a capital offence. The council also established a system of courts to enforce order on a local level, with varying degrees of success.[65]

The nature of these orders underlines the conservative outlook of Irish catholic leaders, both lay and clerical. Forced by political circumstances to assume an executive role, they sought (above all else) to restore some semblance of law and order, protect private property, and control the populist uprising. The collapse of the old regime terrified the land-owning elite, who longed for the security of monarchical government, albeit with certain modifications. The rebel leadership tried as best they could to preserve the existing social system until a settlement could be reached with the king. For the moment, however, the authority of the supreme council was "as absolute as the full consent of the persons who met could make it".[66]

In the course of the summer of 1642 the royalist and Scottish offensives in Ireland ground to a halt, due mainly to disease and a chronic lack of supplies.[67]

---

that only two were nominated out of each province, which along with the bishop, general, lord, and Viscount Gormanston as president, gives a total of twelve people on the first council (unfortunately no list survives). Bellings also claims that Mountgarret acted as president, whereas the document clearly states that Gormanston was elected to the post. The latter was unquestionably the most dynamic and influential catholic leader, while the former fulfilled the role of senior statesman. At the first general assembly in October of that year both men were appointed onto the supreme council, but with Mountgarret as president. "Acts, orders and constitutions ..., 7 June 1642" (PRO SP Ire. 260/67 ff 234-53). Bellings' History in Gilbert (ed.), *Irish confederation*, i, p. 87. **64** Barron to Wadding, 8 Aug. 1642 (*Report on Franciscan manuscripts* [Dublin 1906] p. 171). **65** "Acts, orders and constitutions ..., 7 June 1642" (PRO SP Ire. 260/67 ff 234-53). **66** Bellings' History in Gilbert (ed.), *Irish confederation*, i, pp 87-8. **67** Lenihan, "Catholic confederacy" p. 127. According to Armstrong, the royalist army in Leinster lacked ammunition, while only half the troops were fit for service.

As the prospect of negotiated settlement re-emerged, the supreme council presented a petition of grievances at the end of July to the royalist military commander, James Butler, earl of Ormond, seeking above all else access to the king. The outbreak of the English civil war shortly afterwards appears to have strengthened the position of the moderates in the Dublin administration, and the petition reached Charles by the end of October.[68] The king's response to this document eventually led to a truce the following year and the beginning of protracted peace negotiations.

In the meantime, however, Irish catholics continued to consolidate their authority throughout the kingdom, with the supreme council embarking on a regal-style tour of various towns and cities, the purpose of which was "to settle in the minds of the people a veneration for the new magistracy, without venturing to let them feel the affects of their power".[69] In Clonmel, for example, the civil administration remained undisturbed, but the citizens had to make an individual contribution to the war effort according to their means.[70] Clearly the provisional government required a broader mandate to underpin its legitimacy, and this could only be provided by a full assembly of the kingdom.

Although it has long been accepted that the first general assembly met on 24 October 1642, the meeting in June of that year also involved catholic clergy and laity. Furthermore, the earl of Clanricarde claimed to have seen writs of summons issued to all counties on 31 July for a meeting at the end of August. On 3 September, the earl received news of an important gathering at Kilkenny from his cousin Terence Coghlan, who informed him that "they intended to sit a fortnight longer". No information survives of what took place at this time, and according to Clanricarde the participants had dispersed by mid-September "without concluding much more than to lay a ground-work for their future intendments, having appointed to meet again the 18th of the next month".[71]

There is no reason, despite the slight inaccuracy in the dating, to question the earl's account. Why then do all other records clearly show 24 October as the opening day of the first general assembly? The lack of progress, mentioned by Clanricarde, perhaps explains why earlier meetings appear to have been overlooked by historians. The absence of Connacht representatives is another possible reason the June or August/September assemblies could not be termed nation-

Armstrong, "Protestant Ireland" p. 60. Undoubtedly, the escalating crisis in England affected supplies to troops in Ireland. **68** The lords justices had rejected any possibility of a truce in June, confirming the hard-line position of the English parliament. Apart from Clanricarde, the earl of Ormond and Lord Ranelagh also opposed this policy of confrontation. Lords justices to Clanricarde, 13 June 1642; Ormond to Clanricarde, 13 June 1642; Lord Ranelagh to Clanricarde, 22 June 1642 (Bourke, *Clanricarde memoirs* pp 168-70). The original petition was sent to the king in letters to Secretary Nicholas, dated 12 October 1642 (TCD Mss 840 f.59). **69** Bellings' History in Gilbert (ed.), *Irish confederation*, i, pp 87-8. **70** Burke, W.P., *History of Clonmel* (Waterford 1907) pp 62-4. **71** Narrative in Bourke, *Clanricarde memoirs* pp 240, 266.

al.[72] Moreover, the outbreak of the civil war in England gave a certain credibility to confederate claims to be fighting for the king against his parliamentary enemies. Writs of summons issued in May or July would not fit such an interpretation and it may have been considered opportune at a later stage to claim an October starting point.

In any case, the session which began on 24 October 1642, and finished four weeks later on 21 November, was without question the most important meeting of that dramatic year, formally establishing the confederate association. For the first time since the rebellion began, representatives from all four provinces, including Connacht, attended a national assembly. After the upheavals of April-May, the moderates had regained the initiative in Galway city, culminating in the election of Richard Martin as mayor at the beginning of August. Apart from internal tensions, an uneasy truce also existed between the city government and Captain Anthony Willoughby, English commander of the fort. The summoning of an assembly in Kilkenny, therefore, proved an attractive proposition to Martin and Patrick Darcy, both of whom travelled south with a strong Connacht delegation.[73]

Clanricarde noted Darcy's departure on 20 October with the "intention to declare for the other side", indicating that until then he had not publicly joined the insurgents. Once in Kilkenny, Darcy provided legal advice to the assembly, acting as *de facto* lord chancellor, while Martin refused to take the oath of association, so as not to upset the delicate power balance in Galway.[74] The representatives of catholic Ireland, probably on Darcy's advice, adopted a unicameral structure for the new assembly, with bishops, lords and commons sharing the same chamber.[75] Anxious not to challenge the principle of royal authority in Ireland, the confederates (as they could now be termed) insisted that they did not intend "this assembly to be a parliament, or to have the power of it".[76] As Bellings later explained,

> for though they endeavoured their assemblies after the model of the most orderly meetings, yet they avoided, so far as was possible for them, all cir-

72 During September, the Connacht provincial assembly was meeting in Ballinrobe, County Mayo. Assembly at Ballinrobe to Clanricarde, 15 Sept. 1642 (Bourke, *Clanricarde memoirs* p. 258). 73 Martin's election as mayor is recorded (Galway corporation records book A f.179). Walter Bourke named the entire Connacht delegation, bar the city of Galway, in a sworn statement to the Dublin administration on 12 December 1642 (TCD Mss 831 f.170). 74 Richard Martin to Clanricarde, 2 Dec. 1642 (Bourke, *Clanricarde memoirs* pp 296-8). Darcy sat on every confederate supreme council from 1642 onwards, except between September 1646 and March 1647, when he headed the judicature. See appendix 2 (table 13) for the full list of council membership. 75 Only the bishops were entitled to sit in the assemblies. The other clergy sat in the convocation which met at the same time in Kilkenny, but was not a constituent part of the assembly. It functioned in a similar role to the Westminster assembly of laymen and ministers which advised the English parliament on matters of religion. Cregan, "Confederation of Kilkenny" (PhD thesis) p. 68; Morrill, John, *The nature of the English revolution* (London 1993) p. 18. The structure of the assembly is discussed in greater detail in chapter 7. 76 Petition of the Confederates to the King and Queen, Dec. 1642 (Bourke, *Clanricarde memoirs* p. 299).

cumstances that might make it be thought they had usurped a power of convening a Parliament, the calling and dissolving whereof the supreme council, by their petition sent to the king, after adjournment of this assembly, avowed to be a pre-eminence inseparable from his Imperial Crown.[77]

This subtle distinction made little impact on contemporary commentators, including Giovanni Giustinian, the Venetian ambassador to London, who in his reports on Ireland to the Doge referred to the assembly as a parliament. Similarly, Clanricarde discussed with his kinsman Roger Shaughnessy the implications of "the proceedings of the great parliament in Kilkenny".[78] The general assembly may have been a parliament in all but name, but the confederates were careful never to assume the title, remaining steadfast in their declared loyalty to the Stuart monarchy.[79] Nonetheless, it is clear that the assembly (whatever title the confederates chose to give it) acted in a sovereign manner over the next six years, passing laws, raising taxes, issuing coinage and dispatching envoys abroad.

Returning to the first session, the assembly appointed Nicholas Plunkett as chairman, a position he retained at every subsequent assembly.[80] This selection is of particular interest, given Plunkett's reluctance to commit himself to the rebel cause earlier in the year. Viscount Gormanston, for example, criticised his stubborn neutrality, which had helped undermine the Connacht peace initiative the previous April. Nonetheless, Plunkett clearly enjoyed tremendous support on the assembly floor throughout the 1640s.[81] His record of defending Connacht landowners during the 1636 plantation controversy, and of opposing the lord deputy, Thomas Wentworth, must have endeared him to many Irish catholics. Plunkett's extensive family contacts also proved invaluable in attracting support, particularly in the Pale area.[82]

**77** Bellings' History in Gilbert (ed.), *Irish confederation*, i, pp 111-12. Richard Martin described the assembly as "a general meeting, to consult of an order for their own affairs until his majesty's wisdom had settled the present troubles". Martin to Clanricarde, 2 Dec. 1642 (Bourke, *Clanricarde memoirs*, pp 296-8). **78** *Calendar of state papers, Venetian*, vol. 26, pp 168, 238 etc.; Clanricarde to Roger Shaughnessy, 30 Oct. 1642 (Bourke, *Clanricarde memoirs* p. 287). **79** The loyalty of the catholic Irish is discussed in O'Buachalla, Breandán, "James our true king: The ideology of Irish royalism in the seventeenth century", *Political thought in Ireland since the seventeenth century*, eds D. George Boyce, R. Eccleshall, V. Geoghan (London 1993) pp 7-35. The constitutional issue is discussed in Clarke, Aidan, "Colonial constitutional attitudes in Ireland 1640-1660", *PRIA*, vol. 90, section c, no. 11 (1990) pp 357-75. **80** Richard Martin to Clanricarde, 2 Dec. 1642 (Bourke, *Clanricarde memoirs* p. 298). During Plunkett's absence in Rome during 1648, another Galway lawyer and former parliamentarian, Richard Blake, assumed the position of chairman of the assembly. Blake used the title in all his official correspondence in late 1648 (Bodl. Carte Mss 22 f.325, 389, 453 etc.). **81** The extent of Plunkett's support can be gauged from the fact that in the elections to the supreme council in February 1646, he received 92 votes from the Leinster delegates, out of a total of 106. Rinuccini to Cardinal Pamphili, 7 March 1646 (Aiazza [ed.], *Embassy* p. 131). **82** Plunkett's

After the collapse of the Connacht peace initiative in April 1642, Plunkett kept a low profile, refusing to commit himself to any side. During the summer, along with a number of prominent Pale gentry, he pledged his loyalty to the earl of Clanricarde, whose continuing neutrality afforded them some protection.[83] As the conflict escalated, however, Plunkett came under increasing suspicion from a sceptical administration in Dublin. Viscount Valentia informed Maurice Eustace that the lawyer was "a most dangerous man, and suspected to be one of the first contrivers of the rebellion". Shortly afterwards the burning of his house and crops by government troops convinced Plunkett to throw in his lot with the insurgents.[84]

In an account written twenty years later, Plunkett blamed the lords justices for provoking the general crises in the kingdom, and claimed that as the old order crumbled away, the establishment of some form of government proved necessary "to avoid confusions and disorders". He saw the confederate association as a reactive rather than a revolutionary organisation, concerned primarily with maintaining law and order. The confederates were not rebels, but had been forced to "assume a government to preserve themselves".[85] This interpretation of events, helps explain Plunkett's initial hesitation in joining the uprising, and the reason he eventually changed his mind.

On 1 November, with Nicholas Plunkett and Patrick Darcy now occupying the two pivotal positions within the association, the assembly established a committee to "lay down a model of civil government". The body, chaired by Darcy, consisted of members from each of the four provinces, including Richard Martin of Connacht, Richard Bellings of Leinster, Gerald Fennell of Munster, and Phelim O'Neill of Ulster. All the lawyers in the assembly were ordered to assist the committee in its work, emphasising the importance of lawyers in confederate politics.[86] Despite the large number of people associated with the project, the leading role assigned to Darcy (and Martin's involvement) suggests a direct link between the confederate "model of government" and the earlier initiative from Connacht.

---

nephew, Christopher Plunkett, was the earl of Fingal. A sister Joan, married Richard Nugent, earl of Westmeath, while another (Eilís) married William Fleming, Lord Slane. There were other family connections with the Dillons of Roscommon and Prestons of Meath. McGrath, Bríd, "Biographical dictionary" pp 244-6. See also Cokayne, G.E., *The complete peerage*, 12 vols revised edition (London 1910-59). **83** Apart from Plunkett, the list included William Hill and James Bathe of Athcarne who had also been prominent in the Connacht peace initiative. Clanricarde to lords justices, 27 June 1642 (Bourke, *Clanricarde memoirs* p. 177). **84** Valentia to Maurice Eustace, 20 July 1642 (Carte, *Ormond*, v, pp 338-40); Extract from Carte papers in *HMC*, appendix to 2nd report (London 1874) pp 227-31. **85** Plunkett's papers presented to Charles II in 1661-2 (BL Add Mss 4,781 ff 155-61, 276-300). **86** Acts of the general assembly of the Irish confederation, 1 Nov. 1642 (Gilbert [ed.], *Irish confederation*, ii, pp 73-90). See appendix 1 (table 9) for the list of those members of the assembly with legal training.

The earl of Castlehaven claimed the model had been prepared in advance of the assembly, and indeed it closely resembled the plans originally proposed in March and developed during the meetings that summer. The model of government survives in the form of 33 points, establishing the principles and methods by which the confederates governed themselves over the next six years.[87] It began with a preamble, praising the glory of the Roman Catholic religion and proclaiming the confederates' determination to defend the royal prerogatives as well as "our liberty and our lives". This combination of loyalty and self preservation pervaded all confederate declarations and appeals, and was echoed in their motto *"Hiberni unanimes pro Deo, rege et patria"*.[88]

The first item of the model called for the restoration of the privileges and immunities enjoyed by the Catholic Church from the reign of Henry III until the Reformation in the 1530s.[89] This demand, effectively seeking to overturn over a century of anti-catholic measures, remained the primary objective of the clergy who had done so much to bring about the confederate association in the first place. Simple toleration no longer sufficed, as Irish catholics sought full legal recognition of their religion. Although Charles I, a protestant monarch, had neither the personal inclination nor the political ability to grant such a concession, religious issues dominated the subsequent peace negotiations. Moreover, for Kilkenny to obtain aid from the catholic courts of Europe, the confederates felt it necessary to portray their actions as a religious crusade, rather than a revolt against a legitimate authority.[90]

The second item ordered that all persons "bear true allegiance to king Charles", a call consistent with the confederates repeated assertions of loyalty to the Stuart monarchy. The declaration that English common law continue to be observed, except of course where directed against the catholic religion, underlined confederate determination to preserve the existing social order. They recognised that the pressures of war would necessitate a deviation from certain

---

**87** "Orders of the general assembly met at Kilkenny 24 Oct. 1642" (BL Add Mss 4,781 ff 4-11) is one of the many copies of this document which survives. Castlehaven's comment appears in his memoirs, and the preparatory stage possibly refers to the previous assembly meeting in September. Tuchet, *Castlehaven's review* p. 55. **88** This multi-layered allegiance is graphically illustrated on confederate banners, which contained not only ecclesiastical symbols, but also the cross of Ireland and the imperial crown, with the refrain "long live King Charles". Moran (ed.), *Spicilegium Ossoriense*, ii, pp 17-18. The confederate motto is strikingly similar to the Scottish covenanters' pledge of loyalty "to God, to our King and country", reflecting once again the influence of Scottish affairs in Ireland. This issue is examined in detail in Stevenson, David, *Scottish covenanters and Irish confederates: Scottish- Irish relations in the mid-seventeenth century* (Belfast 1981). See also Gardiner, S.R., *The constitutional documents of the puritan revolution, 1625-1660* (Oxford 1962) pp 124-34. **89** Orders of the general assembly ... 24 Oct. 1642 (BL Add Mss 4,781 ff 4-11). **90** The supreme council practically admitted as much in a letter on 12 Dec. 1644 to Hugh Bourke, a confederate agent travelling to Spain (Gilbert [ed.], *Irish confederation*, iv, pp 90-5).

laws and statutes but they hoped nonetheless to retain "the substance and essence thereof".[91] The confederates saw themselves as the true guardians of the legal heritage of the Irish kingdom, which they believed had been subverted by a corrupt administration in Dublin.[92]

To ensure a unity of purpose, confederates subscribed to an oath of association, stating unequivocally their loyalty to God, king and country. Oaths of this nature had been in existence since the beginning of the insurrection, to try to enforce some discipline on the disparate rebel groups. The previous assembly in June established one such oath, but this latest attempt proved to be the most systematic and comprehensive application of the pledge to date. The bishops distributed copies in both English and Irish to priests, who administered it at public meetings (after confession and sacraments) in parish churches throughout the kingdom, "to all and every of their parishioners". All catholics, without exception, had to join the confederate association, which morally at least would be policed by the clergy.[93]

According to the model of government, the primary function of this oath was "to prevent the springing up of all national distinctions", and all catholics who resided in the kingdom, whatever their national origin, were invited to join the association. Furthermore, the confederates would not tolerate any distinction to be made between old Irish and old and new English, "upon pain of highest punishment". The assembly ordered that "every person or persons whatsoever talking or discoursing, in writing or otherwise of the enemies, shall not call them by the name or names of English or protestants, but shall call them by the names of puritanical or malignant party" . Such moves emphasised the importance to confederates of avoiding ethnic conflict, which always had the potential of undermining their fledgling association.[94]

The most radical provisions of the model of government concerned the creation of new power structures. Apart from the legislative assembly, the confeder-

---

**91** Orders of the general assembly ... 24 Oct. 1642 (BL Add Mss 4,781 ff 4-11). The retention of English common law also ensured the continued importance of the lawyers who had all received their training in England. **92** James Cusack's appointment by the assembly "to be his Majesty's attorney-general in this realm" confirms this view. Gilbert (ed.), *Irish confederation*, ii, p. 89. **93** For examples of the various oaths in circulation during 1641-2 see TCD Mss 812 f.243; PRO SP Ire. 260/92 ff 310-11; BL Stowe Mss 82 f.66. As administrators and arbiters of the oath, the clergy wielded enormous authority, which the supreme council may later have attempted to curtail by appointing lay officials to perform the task. Sometime after 1642 James Bryan, for example, was appointed a commissioner for the oath in the diocese of Ossory. Talon, Geraldine (ed.) *Act of settlement 1662: Court of claims* (IMC forthcoming) pp 215-6. **94** Orders of the general assembly ... 24 Oct. 1642 (BL Add Mss 4,781 ff 4-11); Gilbert (ed.), *Irish confederation*, ii, p. 85. At the very beginning of the rebellion the lords justices in Dublin had tried to divide Irish catholics, issuing a proclamation condemning the "old meer Irish in the province of Ulster", and not the "old English of the Pale, nor of any other part of the kingdom". *A declaration by the lords justices and council* ..., Dublin 1641 (BL Thomason tracts 669 f.3).

ates established an executive supreme council, consisting of 24 individuals chosen from provincial lists, "being equally extracted out of the four provinces", 12
of whom at least sat as resident or permanent members. Nicholas Plunkett and
Patrick Darcy and Viscount Gormanston, each of whom had been involved in
the attempt to establish some form of government at the beginning of the year,
served on this council.[95] A president, "named of the assembly", had to be
appointed from among the residents, as well as a secretary who retained possession of the confederate seal. Viscount Mountgarret acted as president, and
Richard Bellings as secretary of every council until the rejection of the first
Ormond treaty in August 1646.[96]

The supreme council combined the administrative, executive and judicial
functions of government, while ultimately answering to the legislative assembly.
The model of government clearly delineated the council's powers, outlining how
"the said council shall have power to order and determine all such matters as by
this assembly shall be left undetermined, and shall be recommended unto
them". The orders of the council remained "of force until the next assembly and
after, until the same be revoked". The council, in its judicial role, had the right
to hear all military, capital, criminal and civil cases, except the right or title of
land.[97] By creating a powerful executive, accountable to the legislature, the confederates displayed an innovative mindset which foreshadowed developments in
England. In February 1644, Westminster established the committee of both
kingdoms, comprised of members of parliament and the Scottish commissioners
in London. Like the supreme council, it controlled all aspects of the war except
the declaration of peace or war, which was to remain the sole responsibility of
the parliament.[98] Before long, conflict emerged in both countries between the
legislative and executive arms of government.

The confederate "model of government" also established a hierarchy of councils at provincial and county level. Provincial councils consisted of two members

**95** Gilbert (ed.), *Irish confederation*, ii, p. 85. The composition of confederate councils is discussed in detail in chapter 7. **96** Orders of the general assembly … 24 Oct. 1642 (BL Add Mss
4,781 ff 4-11). The positions of president and secretary are also discussed in chapter 7. **97**
Orders of the general assembly … 24 Oct. 1642 (BL Add Mss 4,781 ff 4-11). This exemption
clause underlines the sensitivity of the land issue, which was to arouse controversy during this
first assembly meeting and indeed throughout the 1640s. Richard Martin informed the earl of
Clanricarde that, despite the opposition of the clergy, the assembly insisted that the return of
lands to the Catholic Church could only be done by act of parliament. Richard Martin to
Clanricarde, 2 Dec. 1642 (Bourke, *Clanricarde memoirs* pp 296-8). **98** Surprisingly little work
has been done on the role and powers of the various parliamentary committees during the
1640s. Roberts, Clayton, *The growth of responsible government in Stuart England* (Cambridge
1966) tackles some of the wider issues raised in the struggle between the executive and legislative arms of government. Morrill, John, *The revolt of the provinces: Conservatives and radicals
in the English civil war 1630-50* (London 1976) is the best detailed study of the various layers of
government at national and local levels.

from each county, and in theory at least sat four times annually, fulfilling functions as the "Judges of Oyer and Terminer and Gaol Delivery were wont to do". The provincial councils had the authority to review the judgements of the county councils. The latter, consisting of two members from each barony, enjoyed the powers previously assigned to justices of the peace. The confederates planned to appoint the entire range of government officers (sheriffs, coroners, constables etc.) in every county. Cities and corporate towns also retained their former rights, reflecting the strong element of continuity at the heart of these proposals.[99]

This power structure, a fascinating mixture of conservatism and innovation, was in many ways born of necessity. Unlike the covenanters in Scotland, the confederates never gained control of the administrative centre of the Irish kingdom, thus denying their actions a certain legitimacy and forcing a degree of improvisation. Nonetheless, they claimed the sole right to establish temporal government in the kingdom, as long as Dublin remained in the hands of a "malignant party", hostile to the royal interest. Their proceedings, therefore, were "as near and consonant to the laws of the kingdom as the state and condition of the times did or can permit".[100]

The remaining provisions of the model of government dealt with military, educational, financial and property matters. To consolidate authority on a local level, the confederates prohibited private forces, and insisted that fugitive soldiers, a constant source of worry, be returned to their commanders.[101] Efforts to control the behaviour of soldiers, however, proved largely ineffective and complaints of abuses abounded throughout the 1640s, mainly associated with the Ulster army. Successive assemblies attempted various remedies but the excesses of the confederate troops (no worse than their European counterparts it must be said) resulted in a growing reluctance to contribute towards the upkeep of the provincial armies.[102]

A meeting of officers in Kilkenny agreed to "lay down a model or course for the martial government to be established in this kingdom".[103] The assembly appointed continental veterans as generals in three provinces – Owen Roe O'Neill for Ulster, Thomas Preston for Leinster, and Garrett Barry for Munster.

**99** Orders of the general assembly … 24 Oct. 1642 (BL Add Mss 4,781 ff 4-11). **100** Beckett, J.C., "The confederation of Kilkenny reviewed", *Historical studies*, 2 (London 1959) p. 35. The outbreak of the civil war in England gave added credibility to confederate claims that they were loyal subjects fighting against a corrupt faction in the Dublin administration. **101** Orders of the general assembly … 24 Oct. 1642 (BL Add Mss 4,781 ff 4-11). **102** Numerous complaints about the Ulster forces survive in the sources. Colonel Edmund Butler to Thomas Preston, 24 April 1647 (PRO SP Ire. 263/117 f.196), Nicholas Plunkett to Thomas Preston, 27 April 1647 (PRO SP 263/124 f.209) etc. ; The 1644 general assembly for example introduced a number of measures to contain the violent behaviour of their own soldiers (Marsh's Library Mss z 3. 1. 3); In late 1646, Rinuccini, an enthusiastic advocate of an aggressive military strategy, noted the existence of a general war weariness throughout the kingdom. Considerations on the general assembly, 30 Dec. 1646 (Aiazza [ed.], *Embassy* p. 238). **103** Gilbert (ed.), *Irish confederation*, ii, p. 88.

In Connacht, John Bourke received the title of lieutenant-general, in the hope "one day to confer the generalship upon a person more in their eyes and wishes" (meaning the earl of Clanricarde).[104] Plans for a national army, led by Hugh O'Byrne, were confirmed, but this force eventually amalgamated with the Leinster army. As Lenihan outlines in his thesis, this combined Leinster force effectively operated as a national army, at least until 1646.[105]

On the question of a supreme commander, the intense rivalry between Owen Roe O'Neill and Thomas Preston, based primarily on professional jealousy, although ethnic considerations may also have played a part, flourished on their return to Ireland. Their mutual hatred proved a constant factor in confederate politics over the next six years. On one occasion during the assembly, only the intercession of the clergy helped resolve a potentially violent dispute between the supporters of the two men.[106] Earlier in the year, the confederate envoy, Matthew O'Hartegan, wrote to Mountgarret recommending that, as a means of avoiding problems over precedence, "the state itself, if it be well settled, should keep all the authority".[107]

The assembly favoured this option and indeed at no stage during the 1640s did the confederates appoint a supreme military commander.[108] Moreover, on a provincial level they similarly restricted the power of the generals, with Preston for example not permitted to arrange truces for longer than 14 days before obtaining the supreme council's approval. Council members also demanded that Preston keep them informed "of all your enterprises and designs of consequence, and your grounds and reasons for them".[109] Despite their best efforts, the civilian administrators did not always succeed in controlling the generals.

Lenihan argues that the failure to create a "running army" restricted confederate military operations to defensive and localised campaigns. On the contrary, the provincial arrangements made perfect sense from a military and administra-

---

**104** Richard Martin to Clanricarde, 2 Dec. 1642 (Bourke, *Clanricarde memoirs* pp 296-8). **105** Lenihan, "Catholic confederacy" p. 27. After the cessation with Ormond in September 1643 there was no fighting in Leinster until the rejection of the peace treaty in August 1646. This enabled the Leinster forces to take part in offensives in Ulster (1644), Munster (1645) and Connacht (1646); According to Hazlett, the failure of the supreme council to provide proper supplies to O'Byrne forced him to become Preston's subordinate in the Leinster army. Hazlett, "Military forces" p. 244. **106** Richard Martin to Clanricarde, 2 Dec. 1642 (Bourke, *Clanricarde memoirs* pp 296-8). **107** On 22 Aug. 1642, O'Hartegan wrote to Luke Wadding, informing him of his recommendations to Mountgarret (*Report on Franciscan manuscripts* [Dublin 1906] p. 180). **108** The appointment of a supreme commander would also have caused problems politically as apart from O'Neill and Preston, the earls of Antrim and Castlehaven coveted the post. The assembly appointed Antrim to the post of lieutenant-general of the confederate forces in late 1643, but the position had no real power attached to it, and fell into abeyance the following year. Ohlmeyer, *Civil war and restoration* pp 128-49. **109** Appointment of Thomas Preston by the supreme council, 14 Dec. 1642 (Gilbert [ed.], *Irish confederation*, ii, pp 92-6).

tive standpoint.[110] The local population proved less hostile towards troops from their own area, making it easier to raise supplies and provide winter quarters.[111] Moreover, the military threat facing the confederates remained disparate in nature throughout the 1640s, divided between the Scots in north-east Ulster, Ormond in Dublin, Inchiquin in Cork and a host of smaller outposts. Whenever necessary, however, the provincial forces could be used outside of their own areas for specific campaigns, as happened on a number of occasions.[112] The division of confederate forces into four separate armies, therefore, was designed to maximise their potential.

Regarding financial matters, the model of government ordered the use of royal rents and those of enemies to finance the war, with collectors and receivers being appointed by the county councils. Protestant ecclesiastical livings were to become catholic ones, but crucially church lands and tithes in catholic ownership before the troubles would be left to those who joined the confederate cause. To preserve the existing system of land ownership, anybody taking land since the outbreak of the troubles had to return it, unless the original owner had been declared an enemy. In that case, the supreme or provincial councils would redistribute the estate in a manner they considered appropriate.[113]

The collapse of royalist government, therefore, across most of the kingdom did not result in a large-scale redistribution of land, except in cases authorised by the confederate government. The application by the provincial of the Augustinians to the assembly for the return of the order's property aroused much hostility, as a number of leading confederates, including the new president and secretary of the supreme council, held monastic lands.[114] Assembly members informed the clergy that any transfer of land could only be done by act of parliament, and that lay ownership of ecclesiastical property had been legitimised by Cardinal Pole. They also declared their determination to observe the act dissolving the abbeys.[115] This policy appears to contradict earlier assertions that laws inimical to the Catholic Church would no longer be obeyed, but self-interest proved the decisive factor in this case.

110 Lenihan, "Catholic confederacy" p. 139. Such a division of forces was not unique to confederate Ireland. It must be remembered, that until the emergence of the New Model Army in 1645, forces in England were similarly localised, with the various association forces operating in effect as provincial armies. 111 Attacks by the local population in Connacht and Leinster on soldiers from Ulster, and the difficulties they experienced in finding winter quarters outside of their native province, clearly illustrate the extent of these problems. 112 In 1646, for example, Leinster troops participated in the siege of Bunratty castle in Munster, while the bulk of the army (under Thomas Preston) captured Roscommon in Connacht. 113 Orders of the general assembly ... 24 Oct. 1642 (BL Add Mss 4,781 ff 4-11). 114 The list of confederates holding monastic lands include Richard Bellings, Viscount Mountgarret, Geoffrey Browne, Richard Blake and the earl of Westmeath. Ó hAnnracháin, "Far from terra firma" pp 203-5. 115 One report stated that the provincial of the Augustinians was hissed out of the house. Croker, T.C., *The tour of the French traveller Monsieur de Boullaye le Gouz in Ireland AD 1644* (London 1837) pp 86-9. Richard Martin

The same held true for the equally contentious issue of plantations. Although anxious to halt the plantation of Connacht, where many of them held extensive estates, assembly members appeared less concerned about overturning the policy in Ulster. Many of the confederate leadership from the Pale area, as well as Ulster (the "deserving Irish"), had profitted from the plantation process. Satisfying the claims of the dispossessed in that province would call into question many existing land titles. The confederates limited their demands, therefore, to the issue of compensation which could be raised in a future parliament – a parliament controlled by those already in possession of the land.[116] This conservative policy meant that the hopes of the religious orders and dispossessed native Irish for the recovery of their estates would for the most part remain frustrated.

One of the assembly's final acts involved the appointment of agents to reside in the catholic courts of Europe. Churchmen proved ideal for this role, as they possessed the necessary educational qualifications (including Latin) and could rely on extensive European contacts for introductions at court.[117] Their use as envoys also reinforced the image abroad of the war in Ireland as a religious conflict, which the government in Kilkenny hoped would lead to more generous contributions from catholic monarchs. The confederates also appointed lay figures, however, for specific missions, such as Bellings' visit to the continent in 1645 to raise supplies for the confederate war effort, and Nicholas Plunkett's trip to Rome in 1648 to seek papal support for a renewed peace deal with the royalists.[118]

Before dispersing, the confederates concluded business by dealing with the issue closest to their hearts after their estates, namely official salaries. The severe lack of coinage in the country resulted in the establishment of a mint in Waterford, although many confederates thought this "an unnecessary invasion upon the prerogative royal".[119] Despite this shortage, the assembly delegates voted themselves an allowance of five shillings a day for burgesses, 10 shillings for knights, for each days attendance at the assembly and for ten days before and

described this debate in his report to Clanricarde on 2 Dec. 1642. Bourke, *Clanricarde memoirs* pp 296-8. **116** An article to this effect was included in the second peace treaty on 17 January 1649 (Gilbert [ed.], *Irish confederation*, vii, pp 184-211). **117** Clerics functioning as resident confederate agents abroad included Luke Wadding in Rome, Matthew O'Hartegan in Paris and Hugh Bourke in Brussels and then Madrid. See Ohlmeyer, J., "Ireland independent: Confederate foreign policy and international relations during the mid-seventeenth century", *Independence to occupation* pp 89-111. **118** In one case Captain Oliver French was accredited as confederate agent to the United Provinces in 1648, because a catholic clergyman would not have been acceptable in this protestant state. Speech delivered by Captain Oliver French, agent of the supreme council to the states general of the United Provinces, 5 May 1648 (Bodl. Carte Mss 22 ff 91-2). Geoffrey Barron, nephew of Luke Wadding, also acted as confederate ambassador to Paris, between 1645 and 1647, to replace the erratic O'Hartegan. Supreme council accreditation to Geoffrey Barron, 28 April 1645 (Bodl. Carte Mss 14 f.441). **119** Richard Martin noted that despite opposition to the creation of a mint the motion was carried in the assembly. Martin to Clanricarde, 2 Dec. 1642 (Bourke, *Clanricarde memoirs* pp 296-8).

after. At a conservative estimate, discounting what the lords and bishops may have received, the wages bill for the first assembly alone would have exceeded £3,500, although this may well not have been paid in cash.[120]

Considering that papal sources only provided £20,000 in cash to Ireland during the 1640s (the largest single contribution from abroad), the association clearly could not afford such exorbitant wages.[121] The appointment of a multiplicity of officials at local and national levels exacerbated the problem, so it is hardly surprising that before long some confederates began to voice criticisms of a ravenous bureaucracy which devoured a major proportion of available resources. The author of the *Aphorismical discovery* complained bitterly that "the most part or rather all was spent in daily wages of the supreme council, judges, clerks and other mechanical men, and little or nothing went to the military".[122]

The general assembly finally dispersed on 21 November, and arranged the next meeting for 20 May 1643, although "if urgent occasion be, the supreme council may convoke this assembly sooner". In the meantime, all authority resided in the supreme council "and what the council shall do therein, we do and own, approve and allow as the acts or acts of this assembly".[123]

Events during the course of 1642 clearly demonstrate that the motivation to establish an alternative form of government was essentially reactionary rather than revolutionary in character. Fears about social order, combined with the realisation after April 1642 that the conflict in Ireland would not be of short duration, forced the catholic elite into a radical position, although they tried to disguise their actions under a cloak of legitimacy. Excluded from office for decades because of religious discrimination, the confederate leaders suddenly faced the daunting responsibility of civil, military and judicial authority. This inevitably created great difficulties and tension, but to their credit, they adapted quickly to the realities of power.

The other main point of interest in 1642 concerns the emergence of the earl of Clanricarde and Nicholas Plunkett as key players in confederate politics. Although Clanricarde did not formally join the association, his close ties with the Galway representatives enabled him to influence developments in Kilkenny. His attempts at mediation continued throughout the 1640s with varying degrees of success. Plunkett, after his initial flirtation with neutrality, became an ardent and active confederate, but he remained committed to the principal of compromise, seeking to preserve unity by extracting significant concessions from the king. Indeed, for the next six years, the terms of a peace settlement would dominate confederate politics.

**120** Acts of the general assembly, 21 Nov. 1642 (Gilbert [ed.], *Irish confederation*, ii, p. 89). Given the consistent shortage of coin in confederate areas throughout the 1640s, assembly members, officials and others may have received land or property in lieu of payment. **121** Ohlmeyer, "Ireland Independent", *Independence to Occupation* p. 108. **122** Gilbert (ed.), *Contemporary history*, i, p. 78. **123** Gilbert (ed.), *Irish confederation*, ii, p. 87.

CHAPTER 2

# Peace talks

## NOVEMBER 1642–MAY 1645

The sin of their [confederates] extirpation will be equally shared between the Parliament that covets their land and thirsts for their blood and themselves that will accept of no conditions but such as for no earthly consideration his Majesty can grant nor any honest protestant of his can be an instrument to convey unto them.

Minute by the marquis of Ormond
on the state of peace negotiations, 1645.[1]

The crucial developments during the period from January to October 1642 were the formation of a coalition of the disaffected catholics of Ireland into the confederate association, and the assumption by that association of civil power throughout most of the country. There then followed a period of two and a half years, which witnessed several inconclusive military campaigns and two essentially political processes. The first and most prominent of these consisted of lengthy negotiations with the marquis of Ormond (representing the king), while the second involved the evolution of the political system within the confederate association. The latter resulted in the emergence of demands for reforms to establish the supreme authority of the general assembly, as envisaged in the original confederate "model of government". The reformers envisaged that all other institutions (including the executive supreme council) would derive their mandate from the legislative assembly.

Between 1642 and 1646, the confederates engaged in almost continuous negotiations with the royalists. Initially concerned with securing a cessation of arms (achieved in September 1643), the talks subsequently tackled the issue of a final peace settlement. From 1643 until 1646, with military engagements a mere side-show, arguments raged in Dublin and Kilkenny over the terms of this settlement. The intricate nature of the negotiations have discouraged many historians, but the talks (and attendant truces) dominated events in Ireland during the 1640s. Indeed, according to Rinuccini they were "the ruin of the whole affair"[2].

1 Bodl. Carte Mss 16 f.573. 2 Rinuccini to Monsignor Nuncio of Spain, 26 April 1647 (Aiazza

It is crucial, therefore, to examine the principal issues at stake before proceeding with an account of the negotiations themselves.

Confederate negotiators faced the formidable task of reaching an agreement with the king which would safeguard their estates and political position on the one hand, while not totally alienating the clergy, political exiles and their supporters on the other. The talks encompassed all aspects of life in Ireland, including political, religious, administrative, financial, military and educational matters. Petty arguments over particular wording often stalled negotiations for weeks, but the bulk of concessions sought by the confederates, while important, proved not to be contentious.[3] The real difficulties in any prospective deal with the king lay in the extent of religious concessions demanded by the confederates, and the constitutional nature of guarantees to ensure that the peace treaty would be properly ratified and honoured.

Regarding the first issue, all shades of confederate opinion agreed on the unsatisfactory nature of the existing religious settlement in Ireland. Penal laws, directed against the catholic population, had been on the statute books for roughly 80 years prior to the outbreak of the revolt in October 1641. These laws affected all areas of life, religious, political and professional. Catholic clergy remained officially outlawed, and recusancy fines were sporadically imposed on those who failed to attend services of the established church. Moreover, the protestant clergy received tithes from all sections of the community, regardless of religious affiliation. On a political level, appointees to government positions had to take the oath of supremacy, a stipulation which in effect barred catholics from public office.[4]

The accession of James VI of Scotland to the English throne had been warmly welcomed by Irish catholics, who believed the new king to be less hostile towards catholicism than his predecessor.[5] To their dismay, however, the penal legislation remained on the statute books, implemented at the discretion of the exclusively protestant administration in Dublin. During the 1630s, Charles I and his lord deputy, Thomas Wentworth, adopted a pragmatic approach to religious issues. They showed a willingness to make concessions, including lifting restrictions on practising in the courts, in return for political and financial support. As a result, by the end of the decade catholic clergy operated openly throughout the country, while catholic lawyers increasingly dominated the legal profession.[6]

[ed.], *Embassy* p. 275). The exception here is John Lowe whose PhD thesis was based on the negotiations between the confederates and royalists. See Lowe, John, "Negotiations between Charles I and the confederation of Kilkenny" (PhD thesis 1960). **3** An example of the word games being played by both sides is Ormond's suspicion at the supreme council's switch from signing themselves "your lordships humble servants" to "your lordships loving friends". Ormond to Clanricarde, 16 January 1645 (Carte, *Ormond*, vi, pp 231-3). **4** For a discussion of the period prior to 1641 see Clarke, *Old English in Ireland* (1966) and Kearney, *Strafford in Ireland* (1989). **5** Ó Buachalla, Breandán "James our true king" p. 11. **6** Lawyers like Nicholas

Nonetheless, catholics merely obtained a degree of tolerance, rather than any official recognition, from the state. As long as repressive legislation remained in place, a hostile administration in Dublin could continue to make life very uncomfortable for Irish catholics. The Pale gentry, who had traditionally served in the top administrative positions, bitterly resented their exclusion from public office, while the clergy were forbidden from exercising their ecclesiastical jurisdiction or enjoying any church livings. The success of the Scottish covenanters in their religious dispute with Charles I, combined with the aggressive tones of the puritans at Westminster, increased the sense of insecurity among Irish catholics. At the same, however, these developments clearly demonstrated what might be achieved through a policy of political and military confrontation.[7]

In the early days of the insurrection catholics united in opposition to the perceived puritan threat, but once organised politically, two distinct strategies began to emerge. Catholic landowners appeared content with limited concessions, enabling them to partake fully in political and professional life and at the same time to worship in private without fear of punishment.[8] The Catholic Church, however, sought a full restoration of its rights and property. This fundamental difference could be glossed over while contact with the king took the form of remonstrances and petitions, but once full negotiations began the rift in confederate thinking became increasingly difficult to ignore.[9]

The second main issue to engage confederate negotiators proved no less important, dealing as it did with the question of trust. Having experienced at first hand the failure of Charles I, and successive administrations in Dublin, to implement the Graces of 1628, the confederates realised the dangers of accepting

Plunkett, Patrick Darcy, Richard Martin and James Cusack represented clients from all sides of the political spectrum and were particularly prominent in the Irish parliament. For the role of lawyers in Stuart Ireland see Cregan, D.F., "Irish catholic admission to the English inns of court", *Irish jurist*, vol. 5 (summer 1970) pp 95-114 and "Irish recusant lawyers in politics in the reign of James I" *Irish jurist*, vol. 5 (winter 1970) pp 306-20. The list of catholic "leaders" in the House of Commons includes seven lawyers. Perceval-Maxwell, *Irish rebellion* pp 136-7. **7** This point was made by the earl of Castlehaven, among others. Tuchet, *Castlehaven memoirs* pp 5-21. **8** This opinion was most famously expressed by Robert Talbot, who according to the author of the *Aphorismical discovery* swore "that he would neither contest with his prince or lose himself a foot of his estate for all the martyrs in Ireland; that it was indifferent to him to have mass with solemnity in Christ or St. Patrick's church, as privately at his bedside". Gilbert (ed.), *Contemporary history*, i, p. 66. Admittedly, this writer was extremely hostile to any compromise on the issue of religion, but the terms of the first Ormond peace treaty in 1646 confirm that the confederate leadership at that time were content with the minimum of religious concessions by the king (Gilbert [ed.], *Irish confederation*, v, pp 286-310). **9** As early as 1644, members of the confederate negotiating team were making it clear in a statement to the king that they would be happy with simple freedom of religion. Gilbert (ed.), *Irish confederation*, iv, pp 104-7. For the position adopted by the clergy see Ó hAnnracháin, Tadhg, "Rebels and confederates: The stance of the Irish clergy in the 1640s", *Celtic dimensions of the British civil wars*, ed. J.R Young (Edinburgh 1997) pp 96-115.

a royal pledge at face value.[10] They faced a difficult problem (along with the parliamentary party in England) of how to guarantee the implementation of any treaty terms. Their political instinct, and experience, led them to seek the consolidation of royal concessions by parliamentary enactment.[11] The constitutional status, therefore, of the kingdom of Ireland, or more precisely, the Irish parliament's relationship with the king and Westminster, was of central concern to them.[12]

The main areas of contention revolved around the operation of Poynings' law and claims of jurisdiction by the English parliament over its Irish counterpart. Lord-Deputy Edward Poynings introduced his famous statute in 1494, primarily as a check on Geraldine power in Ireland. Under the provisions of this new law, the lord deputy and the Irish council certified to the king and his council, under the seal of Ireland, the reasons for holding a parliament and drafts of the intended legislation. In return, they received a licence under the great seal of England to hold the parliament, introducing those bills approved by the king and council.[13] In this manner, Henry VII hoped to keep the earl of Kildare, reappointed as lord-deputy in 1496, under closer supervision.

Unforeseen changes in the Irish political landscape during the sixteenth century meant that the effect and conception of Poynings' law altered with each generation.[14] As long as the earls of Kildare retained royal favour the application of the law proved extremely flexible and uncontroversial. The political climate changed drastically, however, with the collapse of Geraldine power in 1534–5, followed by the 1541 kingship act. The latter transformed Anglo-Irish relations as the monarch and the English court became more actively engaged in Irish politics. The Irish parliament began to exploit the provisions of Poynings' law in order to obstruct the legislative initiative of the new generation of English governors in Ireland, appointed to replace the earls of Kildare. Parliament would refuse to consider bills that had not received prior certification in England, and

---

10 Although Charles consented to the Graces in 1628, a number of crucial clauses had still not been implemented by the time the rebellion broke out in October 1641. 11 Clarke, "Colonial constitutional attitudes" p. 368. 12 This question had occupied a great deal of time in the 1640-1 parliament, and as most of the catholic members of that parliament became active confederates, it not surprisingly also figured prominently in negotiations during the 1640s. For a detailed account of the 1640-1 parliament see Perceval-Maxwell, *Irish rebellion* (1994). The list of active confederates who had parliamentary experience is in appendix 1 (table 8). According to Clarke, Irish legislative independence became a catholic cause in the 1640s. Clarke, "Colonial constitutional attitudes" p. 360. 13 The full text of the law is reprinted in Quinn, D.B., "The early interpretation of Poynings' law, 1494-1534", *IHS*, vol. 2, no. 7 (March 1941) pp 241-54. 14 Richardson. H.G. and G.O. Sayles, *The Irish parliament in the middle ages* (Philadelphia 1960) pp 273, 280; Quinn, "Early interpretation of Poynings" (1941); Edwards, R.D. and T.W. Moody, "The history of Poynings' law: Part 1, 1494-1615", *IHS*, vol. 2, no. 8 (Sept. 1941) pp 415-24; Clarke, A., "The history of Poynings' law, 1615-1641" *IHS*, vol. 18, no. 70 (Sept. 1972) pp 207-22.

then use their contacts in the English court to try and have the bills modified or rejected. The Dublin government, therefore, attempted on a number of occasions to have the law suspended or modified.[15]

The Poynings' issue re-surfaced at every parliament from 1536 onwards, but acquired a greater urgency as a result of Thomas Wentworth's aggressive tactics in the 1630s. Wentworth, as Aidan Clarke has outlined in some detail, used the act as a means of stifling domestic criticism, denying parliament any role in the drafting of the legislative programme for certification in England. Working in close co-operation with the king, the lord-deputy cynically manipulated the 1634-5 parliament, securing the passage of a generous subsidy bill in the first session, on the promise of concessions to the catholics in the second, which never materialised. As a result, proposed amendments to Poynings' law during the 1640-1 parliament received strong support from catholic MPs.[16]

An Irish parliamentary delegation travelled to England in 1640, to discuss a wide range of issues with the king.[17] They demanded the restoration of the convention whereby the lord deputy consulted the lords and gentlemen of Ireland (including catholics) on all bills prepared in advance of parliament, and that the Irish executive be denied the right to prevent the transmission of bills prepared by the parliament itself, once in session. The acceptance of the delegation's proposals would have led to a significant shift in the balance of power in Ireland, with the legislative initiative passing from the executive to the Irish parliament.[18]

The Irish parliament also sought to curtail administrative abuses perpetrated by Wentworth, a campaign which led indirectly to the issue of parliamentary

**15** The last time the government succeeded was in 1569, but only after agreeing to a compromise, whereby any future proposal for the repeal or suspension of the act required the consent of a majority in both houses. Quinn, "Early interpretation" p. 247; Edwards and Moody, "History of Poynings" pp 420-1. The lord chancellor, Richard Bolton, resurrected this act during negotiations in 1644, to frustrate confederate demands for the suspension or repeal of Poynings' law. Peace debates, Sept. 1644 (Gilbert [ed.], *Irish confederation*, iii, pp 280-1). **16** Clarke, "History of Poynings' law" pp 211-15. Wentworth's tactics during the 1634-5 parliament are also discussed in Kearney, *Strafford in Ireland* pp 42-68. **17** The delegation included Nicholas Plunkett, described by one source as "one of the great lawyers of this last age". "Account of the War and Rebellion in Ireland since the Year 1641" (NLI Mss 345 f.57). Patrick Darcy, only took his seat in parliament in May 1641 (after a by-election), and did not travel to England. However, he would unquestionably have influenced the delegation's strategy. **18** Clarke denies the radical intent of these amendments, claiming the delegation merely sought to restate the original provisions of Poynings' Law beyond any possible doubt. Clarke, "History of Poynings' law" p. 220. Perceval-Maxwell agrees with Clarke, describing the demands as conservative, an attempt "to return to the Irish parliament some of the initiative it had lost under Wentworth". Perceval-Maxwell, *Irish rebellion* p. 166. The right of the parliament to transmit bills once in session without executive interference was not part of the original bill, but included in a 1557 amendment. To what extent this consultation process ever operated is unclear, but the confederates clearly believed it was their right. Quinn, "Early interpretation of Poynings" p. 242; Edwards and Moody, "History of Poynings' law" pp 419-20.

independence. As Clarke explains, the primary purpose of Patrick Darcy's "Argument", presented to the Irish House of Lords in June 1641, involved addressing the illegality of various governmental practices. In the course of doing this, however, he claimed that Ireland was "annexed to the crown of England", and that the kingdom enjoyed legislative autonomy.[19] The Irish parliament agreed, declaring in July that

> The subjects of this his Majesty's kingdom of Ireland are a free people, and to be governed only according to the common-law of England, and statutes made and established by parliament in this kingdom of Ireland, and according to the lawful customs used in the same.[20]

The Irish parliamentary delegation in England failed to convince Charles and his council of the validity of their constitutional claims. Catholics in Ireland, increasingly concerned at developments in England and Scotland, bitterly resented the king's refusal to compromise on these issues.

The outbreak of the rebellion in Ireland destroyed the immediate prospects for political progress on constitutional matters, although the suspension or repeal of Poynings' law and an act declaring the independence of the Irish parliament resurfaced as key confederate demands during the 1640s. All early petitions from Irish catholics to the king demanded a redress of grievances through the Irish parliament, "without dependency of the parliament or state of England". In the oath of association, agreed upon in the summer of 1642, they swore to "defend, uphold and maintain ... the power and privileges of parliament of this realm".[21]

Constitutional issues assumed even greater significance shortly after the revolt began, when on 19 March 1642, Westminster passed the adventurers act, specifically designed to finance English military involvement in Ireland through the large-scale confiscations of catholic estates. In the face of Westminster's determination to legislate for Ireland, it became vital to proclaim the independence of the parliament in Dublin, and to clarify the exact nature of the constitutional link with England.

The confederates, comprised mainly of conservative land-owners and clergymen, never seriously contemplated severing links with the Stuart monarchy. Despite official discrimination against catholics, many retained a significant stake in the existing order, which they sought to enhance. Clerics and soldiers returning from the continent, although they had less to lose than their Irish-based counterparts, generally belonged to the same social class and abhorred the

19 Darcy, Patrick, *An argument* ... op. cit. According to Clarke, Darcy made the latter point "incidentally", after discovering no evidence of the legal authority of the English parliament within the kingdom of Ireland. Clarke, "Colonial constitutional attitudes" p. 359. 20 Clarke, "Colonial constitutional attitudes" p. 359. 21 The Stowe collection in the British Library contains numerous examples of confederate oaths. BL Stowe Mss 82 f.66, 92, 303 etc.

prospect of a collapse of authority. They also realised that any moves against the Stuarts would irrevocably split the confederate association, with disastrous consequences for all catholics.[22] On the basis of these self-imposed restrictions, the confederates struggled for six years to reach an accommodation with the royalists.

In early 1643, formal negotiations between the king and the confederates finally began when, in response to a petition from the supreme council, Charles authorised Ormond and Clanricarde to accept a remonstrance of grievances from those he termed "rebels". The confederates protested at this description, but eventually agreed to a meeting in the heart of the Pale, at Trim.[23] Along with the commission, Charles also sent a memorial to Ormond, outlining in some detail his position on the various concessions likely to be demanded by the confederates.[24] The royal council, after the experience of negotiations in London in 1641, was clearly familiar with Irish catholic grievances, and knew what to expect in any remonstrance.

This document proved one of the few occasions when Charles clearly stated his own policy, and it formed the basis for the royalist negotiating position over the next three years. On the crucial question of the repeal of penal laws, Charles believed that toleration of catholicism could not "be granted without apparent danger of ruin to the king's affairs"; he favoured instead the lenient application of existing legislation. Concerning a declaration of independence by the Irish parliament from Westminster, the king simply instructed Ormond to admit any concession only "by way of declaration of what is their right, not as granted *de novo*", thus preserving the status quo, as a declaration had no basis in law. On Poynings' law, Charles specifically prohibited the option of repeal, as "the whole frame of government of that kingdom would be shaken" by such an action.[25]

The document also dealt with the issue of land restoration, declaring that "no retrospect may be admitted farther than from the beginning of the king's reign". This proved a clever tactic, distinguishing between the more recent plantations undertaken by Wentworth, and the earlier, far more extensive, confiscations of church and native Irish property. Charles calculated (correctly as it tran-

22 There is little evidence of separatist sentiment among the confederates. For example, the book *Disputatio apologetica* by the Jesuit Conor O'Mahony, calling for the election of an Irish king, was unequivocally condemned by the confederate leadership, and publicly burned in Galway and Kilkenny (Galway corporation records, book A ff.191); Walsh, Peter, *The history and vindication of the loyal formulary or Irish remonstrance* (1674) pp 736-9. 23 The petition from the supreme council, dated the 31 July 1642 (TCD Mss 840 f.59), was received by the king sometime after 12 October 1642. The royal orders to meet the confederates were brought to Ireland by Thomas Bourke. Little, "Blood and Friendship" p. 11. The correspondence arranging the meeting is in Carte *Ormond*, v, pp 401-3 and Gilbert (ed.), *Irish confederation*, ii, pp 157-9, 163-4, 224-5. Charles had no love of representative assemblies, and described the gathering of royalist MPs in Oxford during the 1640s as the "mungril parliament". Smith, D.L., *Constitutional royalism and the search for a settlement, 1640-1649* (Cambridge 1994) p. 173. 24 Charles I to Ormond, 12 January 1643 (Carte, *Ormond*, v, pp 1-3). 25 Idem.

spired) that the majority of confederate leaders, whose families had benefited from the earlier confiscations, would be happy to accept this limited deal. Finally, the king insisted that royal appointees in Ireland could not be chosen exclusively from that kingdom, but he indicated a willingness to be flexible on the issue.[26]

On the evidence of this document, more or less restating his position during negotiations with the Irish parliamentary delegation in 1641, Charles appeared unwilling to make significant concessions to secure the active support of Irish catholics.[27] They could expect certain gains in return for providing vital military assistance, but no compromise on the religious or constitutional imperatives, at least for the moment. This conservative, cautious approach appealed greatly to Ormond, who as a leading protestant landowner in Ireland, and the king's representative in subsequent talks with the confederates, had to maintain a delicate balance between the interests of the crown and those of his co-religionists.[28]

On the confederate side, the remonstrance of grievances, delivered to the royalist delegation at Trim on the 17 March 1643, outlined their position. The document consisted of a list of 14 grievances and made a number of recommendations for their speedy redress. The preamble contained the familiar refrain that the confederates had been driven to arms in self-defence, but that they would continue to be "your Majesty's most faithful and loyal subjects".[29] This belief underpinned the confederate association, and they were anxious that Charles acknowledge the fact, particularly in light of his recent use of the term rebel.

Confederate grievances centred mainly on the legal disadvantages suffered by catholics in Ireland and the many abuses perpetrated by the administration in Dublin. The exclusion of catholics from public office, the denial of the Graces, the constant searching for defective titles, and the failure to recognise the many generous contributions they had made to the crown over the years, rankled most. According to the remonstrance, the blame, predictably enough, lay not with the king but with his corrupt officials, a line of argument used by most insurgents during the early modern period, including the English parliamentarians.[30]

---

**26** Idem. **27** The negotiations in 1641, which took place in London, are described in detail in Perceval-Maxwell, *Irish rebellion* (1994) pp 162-78. **28** In the face of a bewildering stream of confusing and often contradictory letters from the king, Ormond doggedly pursued the agenda set down by Charles in early 1643, unresponsive to subsequent developments. Whether Ormond's stubbornness was due to pressure from Irish protestants, lack of imagination or self-interest will be discussed later in the chapter. Its impact on the negotiating process, however, proved profoundly negative. **29** Remonstrance of grievances, 17 March 1643 (Gilbert [ed.], *Irish confederation*, ii, pp 226-42). **30** Roberts describes how the English parliament in 1640 did not take exception to the form of government but to the policies being pursued, and blamed the ministers because of the accepted maxim that the king could do no wrong. Roberts, *Responsible government* pp 70-5.

The document indicted the lords justices for a whole series of misde-meanours, which not only forced some catholics to take up arms in the first instance, but subsequently exacerbated the crisis. The royal prerogative alone protected catholics from such men, but this appeared to be under threat from those the confederates termed the "malignant party". The authors of the remon-strance reserved particular criticism for the adventurers act, disputing claims by the English parliament to be able to legislate for Ireland. The act, they argued, not only contravened the fundamental laws of the kingdom but also under-mined the rights and prerogatives of Charles as king of Ireland.[31]

The remonstrance outlined the major benefits to the king of a settlement in Ireland, including an increase in royal revenue and the prospect of 10,000 catholic troops to aid his cause in England. The main confederate demand involved the holding of fresh parliamentary elections, with no impediment on catholics either voting or sitting in parliament. This parliament, meeting in an unspecified neutral venue, would deal with confederate grievances, but only after the suspension of Poynings' law. The repeal of this law could then be con-sidered by the parliament in consultation with the king.[32]

These initial contacts between royalists and confederates took place against the backdrop of a power struggle within the Dublin administration. The divi-sions of the English civil war had not yet affected the protestant community in Ireland. United in their opposition to the confederates, supporters of the king formed an uneasy alliance with parliamentary sympathisers. Whereas Ormond controlled the army, the civil administration remained in the hands of individu-als extremely hostile towards catholic interests, none more so than the lord jus-tice, William Parsons. These administrators supported the English parliament's tough policy on the insurrection in Ireland, and constituted a major obstacle to the king's efforts at reaching a settlement with his Irish catholic subjects.

In October 1642, shortly after the outbreak of the English civil war, a delega-tion from Westminster had arrived in Dublin. Despite Ormond's opposition, they attended meetings of the Irish Council until their expulsion in February 1643, following an express order from the king.[33] At the same time, Charles

31 The confederates stated that the Irish parliament since the reign of Henry II had been "qualified with equal liberties, powers and privileges and immunities with the parliament of England and only dependent of the Crown of England and Ireland". Remonstrance of griev-ances, 17 March 1643 (Gilbert [ed.], *Irish confederation*, ii, pp 226-42). Charles, as king of England, had reluctantly assented to the adventurers act. By legislating directly for Ireland, Westminster by-passed the need for Charles' assent as king of Ireland. This point had assumed greater significance by March 1643 with the king and English parliament in open conflict. 32 Idem. The inadvisability of sending bills to England, particularly those granting concessions to catholics, no longer appeared in any doubt. 33 In September 1642, the English House of Commons appointed Robert Reynolds and Sir Henry Mildmay as commissioners to Ireland. Mildmay was then replaced by Robert Goodwyn. Corish, *NHI*, iii, p. 304; Armstrong, "Protestant Ireland" pp 67, 88.

authorised Clanricarde (a leading moderate) and Ormond, rather than the Dublin administration, to meet with the confederates at Trim. The latter remained with the army, however, rather than allow his rival, Lord Lisle, take command in his absence. On 18 March, the day after the presentation of the confederate remonstrance, the Leinster general, Thomas Preston, intercepted the royalist forces just north of New Ross in Wexford. Ormond inflicted the first of many defeats on the hapless Preston, though in strictly military terms the encounter proved insignificant.[34] More importantly, the victory strengthened Ormond's hand in his struggle with Parsons.

Shortly after these developments, Charles took another decisive step towards consolidating royal authority in Dublin. On 31 March, he issued an order dismissing Parsons as lord justice and replacing him with the more compliant Henry Tichborne. Three weeks later, following the collapse of peace talks in England, the king officially ordered Ormond to treat directly with the confederates for a cessation of military actions to allow negotiations to begin. With the royalists totally dominant in Dublin, Lord Lisle complained bitterly that they afflicted "by all possible means those that have been in earnest in this war".[35]

No doubt heartened by events in Dublin, the confederates responded enthusiastically to the royalist overtures for a cease-fire. Ormond dispatched Viscount Taaffe and Colonel John Barry to Kilkenny to lobby for peace, while the general assembly scheduled for 20 May provided the confederates with a speedy opportunity to appoint a negotiating team. This delegation consisted of eight members, two from each province, led by Viscount Gormanston.[36] He died shortly afterwards, and was replaced by two men, Nicholas Plunkett, chairman of the assembly, and Richard Barnewall, both from Leinster.[37]

These events marked a significant shift in the balance of power at Kilkenny. Viscount Gormanston appears to have been the dominant figure politically in

---

34 Lisle was later appointed as Westminster's lord lieutenant, and played an important role in Irish politics in 1646-7. See Adamson, J., "Strafford's ghost: The British context of Viscount Lisle's lieutenancy of Ireland", *Independence to occupation* pp 128-59. 35 Lord Lisle to countess of Leinster, 16 May 1643 in *HMC, Manuscripts of the Viscount de L'Isle*, vol. 6, 77th Report (London 1966) p. 431. The commission from Charles made no mention of rebels but instead described the confederates as "our subjects, who have taken up arms against us and our authority". Charles I to Ormond, 23 April 1643 (Gilbert [ed.], *Irish confederation*, ii, p. 267). 36 Order of the supreme council, 20 June 1643, based on order of the general assembly, 20 May 1643 to treat for a cessation (BL Stowe Mss 82 f.116). Cregan, D.F., "Confederation of Kilkenny" (PhD thesis) p. 127. 37 Will of Nicholas, Viscount Gormanston, 27 July 1643, *Analecta Hibernica*, no. 25 (Gormanston Papers) pp 157-8; Cregan, D.F., "Confederation of Kilkenny" (PhD thesis) p. 127; *A collection of all the papers which passed upon the late treaty touching the cessation of arms in Ireland ...*, Dublin 1643 (RIA vol. 38, box 34, tract 1). The full committee was as follows: Robert Talbot, Richard Barnewall, Nicholas Plunkett (Leinster); Viscount Muskerry, John Walsh (Munster); Lucas Dillon, Geoffrey Browne (Connacht); Turlough O'Neill, Ever Magennis (Ulster). Appointments to the various confederate committees are analysed in detail in chapter 7.

the confederate association, a fact underlined by his leadership of the delegation to Trim in March 1643. His death, however, eight months after that of another prominent nobleman, Lord Slane, resulted in the decline of Pale influence and the emergence of a new ruling clique led by Donough MacCarthy, Viscount Muskerry.[38] Muskerry, a brother-in-law of Ormond, sat in the Irish parliaments of 1634-5 and 1640-1 as MP for County Cork, and succeeded to the title in 1641 after the death of his father. A few months earlier, Muskerry had travelled to London as a member of the Irish parliamentary delegation sent to negotiate with the king.[39]

In March 1642, he joined the rebels in Munster for "maintaining the Catholic Roman Religion, his majesty's prerogative and royal attributes to the government and ancient privileges of the poor kingdom of Ireland established and allowed by the dominion law of England". Self-preservation provided the primary motivation, with the viscount fearing for his own safety having witnessed "burnings and killings of men women and children without regard of age or quality".[40] Muskerry attended the first general assembly in October 1642, and the following May assembly members elected him onto the delegation to negotiate a truce with the royalists.[41]

For the present, with the Pale nobility devastated by the loss of Gormanston and Slane, the new clique based on the Butler axis in south Leinster and Munster dominated confederate politics. As well as Muskerry, Viscount Mountgarret, president of the supreme council, was Ormond's great-uncle, and his son-in-law, Richard Bellings, acted as secretary to the council. Gerald Fennell, Ormond's physician and friend, also sat on the council board and corresponded regularly with Dublin.[42] Critics of this ruling group criticised these

---

**38** The death of Lord Slane is recorded by James Ware in November 1642 (TCD Mss 6404, Ware Manuscript, f.130). **39** Muskerry married Ormond's sister Eleanor Butler. Jackson, *Intermarriage in Ireland* p. 52. He succeeded his father on 20 February 1641. Cokayne, *Complete peerage* vol. 3 (1913) pp 214-5. Perceval-Maxwell identifies him as one of the catholic leaders in parliament. Perceval-Maxwell, *Irish rebellion* pp 136-7. **40** Muskerry explained his motivations in a letter to the earl of Barrymore on 17 March 1642 (BL Add Mss 25,277 f.58). On 6 March 1642, Captain Henry Stradling reported to Sir John Pennington that Muskerry was one of a number of people in Cork who had "taken an oath and entered into confederacy to extirpate the English" (PRO SP Ire. 260/58 f.214). ). **41** No list survives for the first general assembly, but John Purcell, examined on 15 November 1642 in Dublin after leaving Kilkenny, swore Muskerry attended the meeting. NLI Mss 2307 f.359. **42** Although they did not sit on the supreme council, Ormond could expect a sympathetic hearing from most of the Butler lords (Galmoy, Dunboyne, Cahir and Ikerrin). Other leading confederates close to Ormond, apart from Fennell, included Edward Comerford (estate manager) and Patrick Archer (business manager). These three men corresponded regularly with Ormond throughout the 1640s, keeping him informed of developments in Kilkenny. See NLI Ormonde Mss 2308 f.171, 357; Mss 2309 f.267; Bodl. Carte Mss 14 f.6; Gilbert (ed.), *Irish confederation*, iii, pp 116-17, and v, pp 329-30 etc.

close links with Ormond, and christened the leaders "Ormondists", a term still used by modern historians.[43]

Personal links, whether through marriage, land or patronage, played a central role in Irish (and indeed English) political life. The major nobility established their own personal network of relations and clients, which often cut across religious, national and even political boundaries.[44] The rebellion disrupted this system, without totally destroying it, and Ormond proved particularly adept at maintaining contacts within the confederate camp. Nonetheless, these links did not prevent people like Muskerry and Mountgarret from joining the rebellion in the first place, and holding out for the best terms available afterwards. Similarly, Ormond proved reluctant to make any concessions to the confederates, despite his close ties with the leadership in Kilkenny. Both sides simply sought to exploit such contacts to their own advantage. As Nicholas Plunkett explained,

> though some of them [members of the supreme council] have reason to wish well to Ormond or Clanricarde, yet when any good redounding to either of them shall come into competition with the public, all private respects are and must be laid aside, and in such case they are no more thought of then as enemies and men ill affected.[45]

Although Plunkett's statement reflected the official (somewhat idealised) position, the basic premise was correct. Muskerry and his associates represented those catholics who had most to lose from a prolonged rebellion, and most to gain from a speedy reconciliation with the king. In return for accepting minimum concessions from Charles, they hoped to consolidate their position politically and enhance their prospects for personal advancement. An advantageous peace settlement superseded any personal links, and they demonstrated a willingness to oppose Ormond when necessary.[46] For this reason, Muskerry and his

43 The author of the *Aphorismical discovery* talked of the "Ormond faction" as did Rinuccini, who described it as the root of all evil. Gilbert (ed.), *Contemporary history*, i, p. 40; Aiazza (ed.), *Embassy* p. 146. For use by modern historian, see for example Ohlmeyer, *Civil war and restoration* pp 164-5.   44 A good example of this is the extraordinary lengths to which the English protestant parliamentarian Earl of Essex went to protect the interests of the earl of Clanricarde, his Irish catholic royalist half-brother. Little, "Blood and Friendship", pp 927-41.   45 Plunkett's comments are contained in letter written on 9 January 1645 (on behalf of the supreme council) to Matthew O'Hartegan in Paris, after the latter's complaint about confederate factionalism (Gilbert [ed.], *Irish confederation*, iv, pp 119-21).   46 Gerald Fennell was probably the exception in this regard, and the author of the *Aphorismical discovery* claimed that he had deliberately stayed behind in Kilkenny to provide vital intelligence to Ormond. Gilbert (ed.), *Contemporary history*, i, p. 22. Indeed, even prior to the truce in September 1643, the two men had engaged in secret correspondence. After the cessation Ormond commented to his friend that "it is long since I durst write to you in this open way". Ormond to Fennell,

allies should more accurately be described as the peace faction. For the next three years, until August 1646, they dominated confederate politics.

Meanwhile, Ormond further consolidated his power in Dublin throughout the summer of 1643. In July he dismissed Parsons, Adam Loftus, Robert Meredith and John Temple from the council, and imprisoned them the following month on charges of supporting the English parliament against the king. Their detention removed the final obstacle on the royalist side to a truce, and negotiations with Kilkenny which had begun back in June continued apace.[47] In the confederate camp, the only sign of opposition came from the papal agent Scarampi, recently arrived from Rome. He argued, with some justification, that as the confederates had gradually gained the upper hand militarily, "not to go forward is to go backward". Moreover, he believed that a royalist victory in England would simply return catholics "to the miserable position in which we were before the war".[48]

Scarampi's concerns about the wisdom of an early settlement with the king represented the first tentative challenge to the dominance of the peace faction. For the present, the papal agent remained a lone voice, but once negotiations on peace terms began, dissent, particularly that led by the clergy, would not be so easily silenced. The earl of Clanricarde informed Ormond that certain confederates had expressed fears "of some tumultuous elections likely to be made of their own side". The earl suspected that these concerned individuals would prefer to gain concessions by agents "until it might be confirmed in a more settled time by act of parliament".[49] It appears that the peace faction, confident of controlling a negotiating committee, doubted their ability to manipulate a full parliament (or general assembly for that matter).

---

30 Sept. 1643 (Carte, *Ormond*, v, p. 468). **47** French, Nicholas, *Narrative of the earl of Clarendon's settlement and sale of Ireland* (Louvain 1668) pp 36-7. James Ware recorded the arrest of Parsons, Loftus, Temple and Meredith in his diaries (TCD Mss 6404 f.134). The confederate victory at Fermoy on 4 June 1643, their first in the field since Julianstown in November 1641, also increased the pressure on royalists to agree to a cessation. Armstrong, "Protestant Ireland" pp 104-5. **48** Scarampi's reply to Richard Bellings, Aug. 1643 (Gilbert [ed.], *Irish confederation*, ii, pp 319-27). On the military front, Galway fort had finally surrendered to the confederates in June 1643, and Owen Roe O'Neill, after an earlier set-back, defeated a royalist force near Trim. Moreover, the arrival of siege guns from the continent that summer greatly increased the confederate military capacity. Lenihan, "Catholic confederacy" p. 150. Shortly after the truce Clanricarde confided to Lord Cottington that the cessation was beneficial "considering the present strong power of the Irish, and the infinite wants of his majesty's forces". Clanricarde to Cottington, 25 Sept. 1643 (Lowe [ed.], *Clanricarde letter-book* pp 2-5). Although the advantage was by no means decisive, and Clanricarde was primarily concerned with mollifying sceptical royalists in England, the military initiative at this time unquestionably lay with the confederates. **49** These "well-affected" confederates almost certainly included Ormond's brother-in-law, Muskerry, who shortly afterwards led a delegation to Oxford. Clanricarde to Ormond, 3 Oct. 1643 (Carte, *Ormond*, v, pp 472-4). Clanricarde's letter is further evidence of the divisions in confederate ranks, long before the start of official peace negotiations and the arrival of Rinuccini in Ireland.

Ormond shared these fears of populist agitation and rejected demands for fresh elections during the truce negotiations in June 1643. He explained to Colonel John Barry that with the protestant community driven from most of the kingdom, "few but themselves [the confederates] are like to be of that parliament". For Ormond, this debate proved an unwelcome distraction from the task of securing a truce in Ireland and transferring troops over to England. The confederates at first angrily demanded an explanation for the refusal to summon a new parliament, but shortly afterwards accepted that present circumstances in the three kingdoms precluded such a development. Instead they would "in due time expect his Majesties pleasure therein".[50]

On 15 September 1643, after three months of talks, the two sides signed a cessation of arms (the first of many such arrangements), valid for one year, dividing the country into separate spheres of influence, royalist and confederate. The agreement made no mention, however, of the grievances which had caused the confederates to take up arms in the first place, but for the moment peace reigned between the king and his Irish catholic subjects.[51]

Although the truce relieved the pressure on royalist forces in Ireland, allowing troops to be transferred over to England, many Irish protestants and the king's supporters in England expressed unease at the situation. Edward Hyde (later earl of Clarendon) believed the cessation "had been the most unpopular act the king had ever done, and had wonderfully contributed to the reputation of the two houses of parliament". A number of leading English royalists defected to the parliament, citing the cessation as the principal cause, although other more credible reasons existed for the switch of allegiance.[52]

Less than two weeks after the truce, on 25 September, the Scots (whose forces in Ulster were not party to the agreement) signed the Solemn League and

---

50 Cessation debates, June-Aug. 1643 (Gilbert [ed.], *Irish confederation*, ii, pp 284-5, 308, 351, 353). Given that many leading figures had doubts about calling an election in the first place, this change of heart was hardly surprising. Although the king ultimately supported Ormond's position, the policy of continuing the present parliament clearly originated in Dublin. This assisted Irish protestant interests, rather than those of the king, a recurring theme in subsequent peace negotiations. Charles to Ormond, 2 July 1643 (Carte, *Ormond*, v, pp 455-6); Secretary Nicholas to Ormond, 17 Oct. 1643 (ibid. pp 475-6). 51 *A collection of all the papers which passed upon the late treaty touching the cessation of arms in Ireland …*, Dublin 1643 (RIA vol. 38, box 34, tract 1). In November, Charles appointed Ormond lord lieutenant of Ireland and made him a marquis, in recognition of his achievement in securing a truce. Cregan, D.F., "Confederation of Kilkenny" (PhD thesis) p. 139. Clanricarde also became a marquis a short time later. Lowe (ed.), *Clanricarde letter-book* p. xviii. 52 Lindley, K.J., "The impact of the 1641 rebellion upon England and Wales 1641-5", *IHS*, vol. 18, no. 70 (Sept. 1972) pp 169-73. Joyce Lee Malcolm estimates that Irish royalists conveyed over 22,000 troops (English and Irish) to England Wales and Scotland between October 1643 and June 1644, without which the king would have been unable to continue his war effort. Malcolm, J.L., "All the king's men: The impact of the crown's Irish soldiers on the English civil war", *IHS*, vol. 21, no. 83, (March 1979) p. 251.

Covenant with the English parliament. The covenant arrived in Ulster in December, and that same month the Scots general Robert Monroe was appointed commander-in-chief of the British forces in the province.[53] The following January, a large Scottish army invaded England, in a dramatic intervention which further increased the pressure on Charles I. Throughout 1644, therefore, the confederates directed their military efforts against the Scots in Ulster, while the earl of Antrim organised a small invasion force to the Western Isles, led by Alasdair MacColla. This troops, in alliance with the marquis of Montrose, achieved a number of spectacular victories during the course of 1644-5.[54]

Despite repeated pleas from the confederates to campaign jointly against the Scots in Ulster, Ormond proved reluctant to take the field against the covenanters.[55] Considering the negative reaction to the truce among protestants, a military alliance with Irish catholics, before the signing of any formal peace settlement, would have created serious problems politically for the royalists, and perhaps shifted the balance of power in Ireland dramatically in the confederates' favour. Nonetheless, in strictly military terms, Ormond squandered an excellent opportunity to root Scottish influence out of Ulster and relieve some of the pressure on Charles in England.[56]

Returning to the political arena, the confederate supreme council summoned a general assembly, the second that year, to meet in Waterford on 7 November.[57] Patrick Darcy kept Clanricarde informed of developments, and noted growing disturbances, not among the lower social orders, but "from turbulent people of the middle rank". Reports from the assemblies throughout the 1640s were infuriatingly vague, rarely identifying the individuals involved in particular events. Clanricarde's correspondence proved no different, although he did mention that

53 Armstrong, "Protestant Ireland" pp 118-24. 54 MacColla's dramatic campaign is analysed in Stevenson, David, *Alasdair MacColla and the Highland problem in the seventeenth century* (Edinburgh 1980). For Antrim's involvement in the Scottish enterprise see Ohlmeyer, *Civil war and restoration* pp 133-44. Lenihan argues that the confederates' concentration on Ulster and Scotland marked the subordination of a domestic military strategy to a pan-British one. Lenihan, "Catholic confederacy" p. 167. After the confederates signed the truce with Ormond in September 1643, however, the Scots were the only enemy remaining in the kingdom, until Lord Inchiquin and the Munster garrisons defected from the royalist camp in July 1644. For the 1644 campaigning season, therefore, the confederates had no alternative to an Ulster offensive. 55 Ormond even received authorisation from Charles for such a move. Charles I to Ormond, 27 Feb. 1645 (Bodl. Clarendon Mss 98 ff 63-4); The correspondence between the supreme council and Ormond on this issue is contained in Bodl. Carte Mss 14 f.164, 15 f.455, 526. Ormond helped raise the shipping for the expedition to Scotland, but refused to hand over a departure port to the confederates. Stevenson, *Scottish covenanters and Irish confederates* p. 172. 56 The importance of the Scottish campaign to the king's fortunes in England can be gauged from Digby's letter to Ormond on 4 January 1645. Digby wrote that he found "a greater effect from my lord Montrose's successes in Scotland toward peace here by means of the Scots Commissioners than by any other successes whatsoever" (Bodl. Carte Mss 13 f.256). 57 This was the only occasion that the assembly met outside the city of Kilkenny. See chapter 7 (table 1).

the bishops (and those aspiring to be bishops) constituted the principal trouble-makers.[58]

Clerical discontent suggests a connection with Scarampi's opposition to the truce. On this occasion, however, the bishops apparently could do nothing more than voice their general disquiet at recent events as the overwhelming majority of confederates fully supported the peace initiative.[59] The assembly voted sup-plies for the planned offensive in Ulster, and after a long discussion over treaty terms, appointed a new delegation of seven, led by Viscount Muskerry, to travel to Oxford and present a series of demands to the king.[60] Plunkett also travelled to England having emerged by this time as the Pale's most senior political spokesman. Plunkett's continued chairmanship of the assembly further enhanced his standing in the confederate association, and provided a possible counter-balance to Muskerry's increasing influence.

The cosy relationship between the confederate leadership and the Dublin administration was graphically illustrated when Muskerry sought advice from Ormond on how to approach the forthcoming conference in Oxford. Ormond replied that the viscount should behave respectfully at all times towards the king. He asked his brother-in-law to consider the merits of acquiring "the name of a loyal subject for that of a rebel", and to tailor confederate demands accordingly.[61] This advice contained nothing remarkable except that (technically at least) a state of war still existed between the confederates and royalists. Such intimate contacts between Dublin and Kilkenny invariably raised suspicions of secret deals, and encouraged the emergence of a vocal opposition in confederate ranks.

On 28 March 1644, the confederate delegation in Oxford presented their demands to the king's council, annexed to the Remonstrance of Grievances of March 1643. These propositions, along with 14 additional points added the fol-lowing September, formed the core of the negotiations over the next two years, and as such should be examined closely.[62] They began, predictably enough, with a call for the repeal of all acts against catholics and complete freedom of religion. The confederates also insisted that all acts, ordinances and attainders of the "pre-tended parliament" in Dublin be declared void, Wentworth's plantations

58 Clanricarde believed the opposition lacked any real influence in the confederate ranks. Clanricarde to Ormond, 13 Nov. 1643 (Lowe [ed.], *Clanricarde letter-book* p. 16). He was con-cerned, however, that the confederates had raised forces that went "beyond their skill to con-jure down or keep within the circle of obedience to their authority". Clanricarde to Ormond, 6 Dec. 1643 (Carte, *Ormond*, v, pp 532-5). 59 On 29 Oct. 1643, however, Inchiquin informed Ormond that intelligence he had received indicated that the clergy would insist on retaining churches, a point raised by Scarampi in his objections to the truce, and later to become a major sticking point in the peace negotiations (Carte, *Ormond*, v, pp 498-500). 60 The com-mission for the delegation to Oxford is printed in Gilbert (ed.), *Irish confederation*, iii, p. 65. 61 Ormond to Muskerry, 19 Dec. 1643 (Carte, *Ormond*, v, pp 540-1). 62 The initial demands of March 1644 are printed in Gilbert (ed.), *Irish confederation*, iii, pp 128-33. Additional points, ibid., pp 324-7.

reversed, the court of wards abolished, and land-holdings confirmed by a 60-year act of limitation.

They demanded that catholics be appointed to public office with equality and indifference, and enjoy the right to establish inns of court, universities and common schools. The confederates also favoured the introduction of residential and property qualifications for both the lords and commons in the Irish parliament, as well as stricter rules on the use of proxy votes.[63] In an effort to curtail administrative abuses, chief governors were to be restricted to a three-year term of office, limitations placed on the power and jurisdiction of the council board, and the standing army replaced by local county levies.

Crucially, an act of oblivion would be passed for offences committed since the outbreak of the conflict, while Poynings' laws and the adventurers act would be repealed. The confederates, mindful of the controversy surrounding the implementation of the Graces, declared their intention to retain a separate government until all concessions granted by the king had been passed in parliament.[64] Finally, in an effort to forestall any future attempts by Westminster at legislating for Ireland, the confederates requested "that an act shall be passed in the next parliament, declaratory that the parliament of Ireland is a free parliament of itself, independent of and not subordinate to the parliament of England, and that the subjects of Ireland are immediately subject to your Majesty as in right of your crown".[65]

This claim may well have appealed to Charles, embroiled in a bitter civil war with the English parliament, but his Irish advisers counselled caution. Members of the Dublin administration, summoned to Oxford by the king, vehemently opposed the confederate proposals, declaring that the granting of a new parliament and the suspension of Poynings' law would allow Irish catholics to "assume all power into their own hands". They explained to the king that few protestants remained in the country, and that the confederates controlled the machinery of local government through which election writs would be issued. As a result, "that which they call a free parliament must consist of papists for there can be very few or no protestants in it".[66]

---

**63** The reform of the court of wards, an act of limitation and confirmation of Connacht titles were all included in the Graces of 1628. Clarke, *Old English* pp 238-54. In 1640, the Scottish parliament, controlled by the covenanters, abolished proxy votes. Brown, Keith, *Kingdom or province? Scotland and the regal union 1603-1715* (London 1992) pp 119-20. **64** The confederates did not pursue this point in the negotiations, probably as there was no need to debate the issue with the king. The failure, however, to maintain confederate government until treaty terms had been ratified by the Irish parliament was one of the main charges levelled by the clerical faction against the supporters of peace in August 1646. "Declaration of the ecclesiastical congregation to the supreme council, 24 August 1646" (PRO SP Ire. 261/51 ff 207-10). **65** Confederate demands, 28 March 1644 (Gilbert [ed.], *Irish confederation*, iii, pp 128-33). **66** The delegates from the Irish council were William Stewart, Gerard Lowther, Philip Percivall and Justice Donelan. Answer to confederate propositions, April/May 1644 in *HMC, Egmont,*

A delegation sanctioned by the Dublin parliament proved even more strident in its opposition to confederate proposals, demanding "the establishment of the true protestant religion in Ireland", and the strict imposition of penal laws against catholics. They informed the king that Irish protestants expected the full restitution of all churches, and that future office holders be required to take the oath of supremacy. Finally, they wanted the confederates to pay reparations for the destruction of property since the beginning of the uprising, and an extension of the plantation policy throughout the kingdom. The king's Irish committee responded simply that "it would be impossible for the king to grant the protestant agent desires and grant a peace to the Irish".[67]

Nonetheless, the submission of the parliamentary delegation illustrated the depth of hostility felt by Irish protestants towards any peace agreement with the confederates. Faced with such opposition, and the increasingly hard-line counsels in Oxford itself, the king refused to commit himself to any major concessions.[68] On the question of religion, Charles offered nothing more than a guarantee not to persecute catholics once they returned to obedience. He agreed to the summoning of a new parliament, but only on condition that Poynings' law stayed in effect, and that the confederates agreed not to pass any bills which had not first been transmitted into England, or that would prejudice Irish protestants.[69]

As for the independence of the Irish parliament, the king's position as the constitutional head of both the English and Irish kingdoms presented him with an awkward dilemma. He tried, therefore, to steer a middle course, referring the question "to the free debate and expostulation of the two parliaments". Charles declared his neutrality on the issue "being so equally concerned in the privileges of either that he will take care to the utmost of his power that they shall contain themselves within their proper limits, his Majesty being the head and equally interested in the rights of both parliaments".[70] This sounded particularly hollow in view of the fact that the king had already signed the adventurers act into law, allowing the English parliament to redistribute over 10 million acres of Irish land.

On other, less important, issues there appeared to be more room for manoe-

vol. 1, part 1 (London 1905) pp 212-29. **67** The protestant delegation consisted of Francis Hamilton, William Ridgeway, Charles Coote, Captain Parsons and Mr Fenton. Rushworth, J., *Historical collections of private passages of state, weighty matters of law, remarkable proceedings in five parliaments* (London 1680-1701), vol. 5, pp 953-71. The petition "in the name of divers of his majesty's protestant subjects in this kingdom of Ireland" was read and approved by parliament on 17 February 1644. *Journal of the House of Commons of the kingdom of Ireland*, vol. 1 (Dublin 1796) p. 317. **68** Smith outlines how the hardliners in Oxford had been strengthened by the queen's arrival there in July 1643. The following January, an approach by peers and MPs at Oxford to the earl of Essex came to nothing, and further conflict in England seemed inevitable. Smith, *Constitutional royalism* pp 115-17. **69** The answer of Charles I to the confederate propositions appears in Gilbert (ed.), *Irish confederation*, iii, pp 175-8. These conditions would have effectively prevented Irish catholics from introducing any of their reform program. **70** Idem.

uvre. Charles claimed he did not have the power to declare void all acts of the Dublin parliament since 7 August 1641, as they had already received the royal assent. He believed, however, a full and general pardon would assuage the fears of catholics who had been indicted or attainted by that same body. He also declared a willingness to reverse the Stafford's plantation in Connacht, and to allow for the establishment of a university and free schools, but only if they agreed to be governed by statutes approved by the king.[71]

Charles announced simply that appointments to public office would be made according to merit, hardly encouraging for Irish catholics who had been ignored for generations. The court of wards would not be abolished and he refused to accept limits being placed on the term of office of the chief governor, but in both cases he promised action to prevent abuses. Finally, concerning the issue of lords and commons in the Irish parliament being estated in the kingdom, he referred the confederates to concessions agreed back in 1641, allowing them five years to purchase estates.[72]

Muskerry and his colleagues rejected these concessions, but rather than negotiate directly with the confederates, the king decided to pass the poisoned chalice of peace talks on to his lord lieutenant. The confederate delegation returned to Kilkenny empty handed, but on 24 June Charles instructed Ormond to proceed with the negotiations.[73] The supreme council summoned a new general assembly to discuss recent developments at Oxford, and the prospects for the forthcoming talks with the lord lieutenant. Surviving evidence at this time points to increasing divisions in the confederate camp over the direction and implementation of political and religious policy.

The concentration of power in the supreme council, and the arbitrary, cabalistic and secretive exercise of its authority, not surprisingly provoked resentment, aggravated in part by the lack of progress in the negotiations with the king. While the general assembly of July 1644 did eventually appoint the delegates to continue the talks with Ormond, it also debated demands for reform.[74] A detailed document, advocating a number of important changes in confederate governmental structures, signalled the emergence of a political middle ground, with a group of influential moderates acting as a balance between the clerical and peace factions. The main issues raised in the ensuing debate, and the substance of the document articulating the reform propositions are set out later in this chapter. At this point it is sufficient to state that they probably had only a minor impact on the actual conduct of the negotiations prior to May 1645, but assumed considerable importance thereafter.

71 Idem. 72 Idem. 73 The commission arrived in Ireland on 26 July 1644 (TCD Mss 6404, Ware Manuscript, f.140). The king wrote to Ormond on 17 July 1644 that he was "not ignorant how hard a part I put upon you in transferring to you the treaty and power to conclude a peace with the Irish" (Bodl. Clarendon Mss 98 f.36). 74 "Propositions touching the present government to the general assembly in June 1644" (Marsh's Library Mss z 3.1.3).

The main business of the assembly centred on the election of a delegation to negotiate a treaty with the marquis of Ormond. On 20 July 1644, in a move expressing complete confidence in their efforts to date, the assembly reappointed the entire delegation to Oxford to what became known as the committee of treaty. Another body, called the committee of instructions, comprised entirely of assembly members, was established to provide support and advice to the nego-tiators. Three weeks later on 10 August an additional six people joined the com-mittee of treaty.[75] Critics of the peace treaty later claimed the assembly had delib-erately increased the numbers because they remained suspicious of the Oxford delegation's close relationship with the royalists, but this seems unlikely.[76] The new members included Viscount Mountgarret, John Dillon and Richard Everard, all strong supporters of an accommodation with Ormond.

Despite the increasing dominance of the supreme council by a small clique, the assembly still maintained a degree of autonomy from factional control. A majority of members publicly rejected Ormond's policy of refusing to deal with catholic clergymen, causing great embarrassment to his confederate sup-porters. The lord lieutenant wrote personally to Muskerry on 9 August, plead-ing in vain that no cleric be appointed.[77] The assembly's firm stance on this occasion, however, proved largely symbolic as they chose Thomas Fleming, archbishop of Dublin, to represent the clergy. The archbishop, according to one account, was "exceedingly corpulent", and travelled with great difficulty. He does not appear to have been actively involved at any stage of the subse-quent proceedings.[78]

The commission granted by the assembly to the committee of treaty became a source of bitter controversy following the rejection of the first Ormond peace treaty. Unfortunately, no copy of this commission survives. Indeed, the cleric Walter Enos, examining the assembly record books in 1646, could find no trace of the document.[79] What does survive is the commission granted to the commit-

---

75 The original commission no longer exists, but Nicholas Plunkett informed Ormond of the additions to the committee of treaty on 11 August 1644. Gilbert (ed.), *Irish confederation*, iii, p. 252. Information on the committee of instructions is sparse and uninformative, although we do know that the leading Leinster confederate, Thomas Tyrrell, was the chairman. Confederate committees are discussed in chapter 7. **76** The Dublin cleric, Walter Enos, made this charge in his lengthy survey of the Ormond peace written at the end of 1646. Enos, Walter, "Survey of the articles of the late rejected peace" in Gilbert (ed.), *Irish confederation*, vi, pp 307-433. **77** Ormond to Muskerry, 9 August 1644 (Gilbert [ed.], *Irish confederation*, iii, pp 251-2). Bellings claimed that Ormond had objected to any clerical presence on the original delegation to Trim in 1643, and that the supreme council at the time decided not to insist upon it. Bellings History in Gilbert (ed.), *Irish confederation*, i, p. 123. **78** Rinuccini to Pamphili, 31 Dec. 1645 (Aiazza [ed.], *Embassy* pp 105-7). The signature of the archbishop of Dublin does not appear on any documents from the committee of treaty and his name is not mentioned during the negotiations. **79** Enos "Survey" in Gilbert (ed.), *Irish confederation*, vi, pp 362-3.

tee by the supreme council, after the dispersal of the assembly.[80]

Enos claimed that the council exceeded its powers in two crucial areas. In the first instance, the assembly instructed the council to give a commission to the committee of treaty to negotiate, but not to conclude a treaty. The only proof Enos offered to support this allegation centred on the repeated efforts by the committee to extend its powers at subsequent assemblies.[81] Lacking the vital evidence, all that can be said is that signing over all power to a committee to conclude a peace appears to be at odds with the assembly's demands to be kept closely informed of developments.[82]

The second change by the supreme council concerned the number of signatures necessary for an agreement to be valid. Enos claimed the council reduced the number from all thirteen members to just five. He admitted, however, that this reduction may have been justified by an act of the assembly on 23 August, which stated that commissions could be granted to as many committee members "to treat with the lord marquis of Ormond for establishing of a firm peace within this kingdom, or a further cessation, as the supreme council and the additional committee of instructions shall think fit".[83] This act may well have been passed to ensure the archbishop of Dublin's presence was not required in order to reach an agreement with Ormond. In any case, the possibility remains that the supreme council drastically altered the commission of the committee of treaty. Definite conclusions remain elusive but it is clear that the council, by stealth or legitimate means, obtained control of the negotiating process with serious consequences for the unity of confederate association.

In early September, after the disastrous failure of the confederates' summer offensive against the Scots in Ulster, negotiations with the royalists resumed.[84] The Oxford delegation travelled to Dublin, with the exception that Patrick Darcy and John Dillon replaced Alexander MacDonnell and Richard Martin. MacDonnell's omission, although he remained a member of the committee of treaty, meant that the remainder of the talks process took place without the direct involvement of an Ulster representative. With the archbishop of Dublin also absent, the interests of the dispossessed natives and the clergy, two vital components of the confederate association, were effectively side-tracked.[85]

**80** Commission for confederate delegates, 31 Aug. 1644 (Gilbert [ed.], *Irish confederation*, iii, pp 269-71). **81** Enos "Survey" in Gilbert (ed.), *Irish confederation*, vi, p. 367. **82** For example, the general assembly repeatedly pressed (unsuccessfully) for the full disclosure of the treaty terms in February 1646. Clanricarde to Muskerry, 14 Feb. 1646 (Lowe [ed.], *Clanricarde letterbook* pp 212-3). The same assembly also introduced reforms to make the supreme council, the executive branch of government, more accountable to the legislature. Orders of the general assembly, Jan. 1646 (Bodl. Carte Mss 16 ff 470-80). **83** Enos "Survey" in Gilbert (ed.), *Irish confederation*, vi, pp 368-9. **84** Unseasonably wet weather and a scarcity of supplies, effectively undermined an operation marked by suspicion and hostility between the two confederate commanders, Owen Roe O'Neill and the earl of Castlehaven. Wheeler, S., "Four armies in Ireland", *Independence to occupation* pp 51-2. **85** The earl of Antrim was also supposed to have

On the royalist side, the defeat of the king's forces at Marston Moor on 2 July 1644, followed shortly afterwards by the defection of Lord Inchiquin and the Munster royalists to the parliamentary camp, presented Ormond with a serious dilemma.[86] Although Charles urgently needed troops from Ireland (royalist or confederate), the necessary deal with the confederates would require concessions to be made to Irish catholics. Inchiquin's actions threatened to undermine the lord lieutenant's authority at this crucial juncture, while Westminster's policy of military intervention, precluding any compromise, proved increasingly attractive to the Irish protestant community.[87]

Despite these difficulties, Ormond's pre-eminence in Irish political circles and record of loyal service to Charles I made him the obvious candidate to undertake the delicate task of peace negotiations. The lord lieutenant proudly proclaimed his English protestant heritage on a regular basis, and presumably could be relied upon to safeguard the king's vital interests in Ireland.[88] Moreover, throughout the war he remained on close personal terms with a number of leading confederates, facilitating the prospect of a settlement with Kilkenny. Ormond, nevertheless, from the king's perspective at least, proved an unfortunate choice.

In many ways the lord lieutenant faced a daunting task. The conflicting submissions of the confederate and protestant delegations in Oxford, earlier in the year, provided little room for manoeuvre, and Ormond often struggled to win council approval for his policies.[89] Already disturbed by the cessation agreement, Irish protestants expressed a determined hostility to the idea of further concessions to catholics. According to Colonel Audley Mervin, an officer serving in Ulster,

> a peace with the Irish is generally a harsh sound to every ear and the reason of this is diverse. Some in conscience hold no toleration of their reli-

been involved in the talks, but left for England shortly after the assembly dispersed, disappointed over his failure to secure overall command of the confederate military forces. Ohlmeyer, *Civil war and restoration* p. 149. See chapter 7 for a discussion of committee appointments. **86** Inchiquin had travelled to Oxford at the beginning of the year, but was disappointed not to be appointed lord president of Munster. This failure, as much as his distaste for the truce with the confederates, probably prompted his switch in allegiance to the parliamentary side. *A letter from the right honourable lord Inchiquin and other commanders in Munster to his majesty …*, London 1644 (BL Thomason Tracts E8 f.37); *A manifestation directed to the honourable houses of parliament in England sent from the lord Inchiquin etc. …*, London 1644 (BL Thomason Tracts E6 f.10); Corish, *NHI*, iii, p. 309; Lindley, "Impact of 1641 Rebellion" pp 170-1. **87** Armstrong, "Protestant Ireland" p. 45. **88** In 1642 Ormond explained to Viscount Valentia that he was "not only by birth, extraction and alliance but likewise in my affections, wholly and entirely an Englishman and as true a lover of the religion and honour of that nation as any that has been born and educated there". Carte, *Ormond*, v, pp 356-7. **89** Armstrong, "Protestant Ireland" p. 266.

gion, some judge the blood of their friends yet unrevenged, some their personal lives not to be repaired, others that it is beyond the reach of state to provide for our security in the future, and not a few because the country is pleasant and held too good for them.[90]

Ormond's inability to reconcile his public duty as a servant of the king with his own personal interests as an Irish protestant land-owner undermined the prospect of a peace settlement with the confederates. In fact, despite his proud boast of Englishness and loyalty to the crown, Ormond's first, and consistent, priority seems to have been the best interests of Irish protestants. Charles recognised this fact long before the confederate leadership in Kilkenny.

The negotiations, however, which began again in September 1644 and continued for one month, witnessed rapid progress on a number of less contentious issues.[91] Ormond agreed to catholics regaining whatever property they held before the war, and to the removal of all records of indictments from the courts. The Connacht plantations initiated by Thomas Wentworth would be reversed, and provisions made for an act of limitation. The lord lieutenant promised to reform the court of wards, and to introduce restrictions on the jurisdiction of the council in Dublin. A number of other administrative abuses would be curtailed, including the farming of royal customs to officials and the purchase of land by chief governors.[92] Although these concessions fell far short of the confederates' core demands, at least some gains had been made.

The two sides remained divided on the more substantive issues, such as Poynings' law. The confederates argued for a suspension of the statute (at the very least), to speed up the process of ratifying the peace terms in the Irish parliament, and to protect against any alteration of the bills in England. The lord chancellor, Richard Bolton, explained how the agreement in the 1569 parliament meant in effect "that no bill be certified into England for the repeal or suspending of Poynings' Act before the same bill be first agreed on, in a session of parliament to be held in this realm ... and then to be transmitted to his Majesty according to Poynings' Act, for it does not rest in the king's power alone to do it". This procedure, the lord chancellor argued, would delay ratification of any treaty by up to four months.[93]

Moreover, Bolton dismissed fears of changes to the bills in England, as any alterations would constitute a breach of a legally binding treaty. The confederate

---

**90** Colonel Audley Mervyn to Ormond, 4 Feb. 1645 in *HMC, Manuscripts of the Marquess of Ormond*, vol. 1, 14th report, appendix part 7 (London 1895) pp 90-5. **91** Formal negotiations continued until the end of the month, and were then suspended while Ormond waited for further instructions from the king. Cregan, D.F., "Confederation of Kilkenny" (PhD thesis) pp 158, 164. **92** Ormond's answers to the confederate propositions are printed in Gilbert (ed.), *Irish confederation*, iii, pp 293-7, 313-19. **93** Peace debates, Sept. 1644 (Gilbert [ed.], *Irish confederation*, iii, pp 279-81).

delegation rejected the lord chancellor's interpretation of the 1569 amendment, and Patrick Darcy delivered a further report clarifying their position. He demanded an immediate suspension of the act in the first session of the new parliament, as otherwise "those bills to be now agreed upon could not pass in the new parliament without a new transmission". To allay royalist suspicions about confederate intentions, Darcy continued "that they desired it should only be suspended as unto the ratifying of the matters to be agreed on upon the treaty and to no other purpose".[94]

Darcy's "clarification" actually represented a major concession by the confederate leadership. In return for satisfactory treaty terms, ratified by the Irish parliament and accepted without alterations in England, they were prepared to drop demands for the repeal of Poynings' law. This move, prompted by confederate anxiety for a speedy settlement, proved a serious tactical blunder, as Bolton engaged the committee of treaty in a prolonged debate over the ratification of the treaty terms. The wider issue of who possessed the legislative initiative in Ireland (parliament or the administration), disappeared from the agenda.[95]

On the practicalities of holding a new parliament, the confederate delegation expressed concern that numerous catholic lords, gentry and freeholders remained outlawed, and therefore barred from voting or taking their seats. The committee of treaty wanted all records of outlawry removed from the files "and that in such cases formalities of law ought to be laid aside". In times of crisis, even the renowned constitutional lawyer Patrick Darcy preferred not to be constrained by the strict letter of the of law. In reply, Bolton cautiously suggested introducing a bill to the present parliament in Dublin. Darcy agreed with this approach but, conscious of the parliament's hostility towards catholics, hoped "that some more speedy way might be thought of for removing the attainders".[96]

94 Idem. The confederate and royalist legal teams would have known each other well, and Bolton appears to have been accepted by both sides (including Darcy) as *the* expert in constitutional law. The fact that he had access to parliamentary records undoubtedly helped in this regard. 95 By May 1645, when negotiations resumed after a gap of six months, Ormond confidently predicted no further trouble from the confederates on the issue of Poynings' law. The confederates, perhaps uncertain as to the best approach on the issue, appeared worn down by Ormond's persistent opposition to any changes. The lord lieutenant informed the king that "after much discourse upon it, they [the confederates] seem convinced that what your majesty intends them may be as speedily and securely conveyed to them, without the suspension as with it". Ormond to Charles I, 8 May 1645 (Carte, *Ormond*, vi, pp 278-83). 96 Peace debates, Sept. 1644 (Gilbert [ed.], *Irish confederation*, iii, pp 278-82). A large number of catholics were outlawed during the 1640s, although not all the records have survived. Five counties (Dublin, Cork, Meath, Kildare and Wicklow) are included in "Oireachtas library list of outlaws, 1641-1647", presented by R.C. Simington and John MacLellan, *Analecta Hibernica*, no. 22 (1966) pp 318-67. Between 1641-7, these counties constituted the core of royalist and parliamentarian influence in Ireland.

The following week, on 16 September, the debate shifted to the constitutional status of the Irish parliament. The confederate negotiators favoured a declaratory act of independence, while Bolton argued the case for a simple declaration
of both Houses. Although the lord chancellor explained (correctly) that the
English parliament was not bound by an Irish act, an act of parliament nonetheless carried more weight than a declaration, principally because it required the
king's consent.[97] After the formal submissions by both sides, the subsequent
negotiations progressed slowly, with neither the royalists or confederates willing
to make any meaningful concessions.

Ormond intervened at this stage of proceedings to restate the king's public
position, probably more to reassure his own supporters in Dublin than to make
any positive contribution to the talks process. The lord lieutenant accepted the
need for a new parliament, but only after the transmission of prospective bills to
England. He continued that Charles, "for diverse weighty considerations, will be
further advised before he do consent to the suspension of Poynings' Act".
Moreover, Ormond pledged to maintain a strict neutrality regarding the relationship between the two parliaments in Dublin and Westminster.[98] Undeterred,
the committee of treaty persisted with demands for an unconditional meeting of
parliament, and the suspension of Poynings' law.

The committee adopted an increasingly tough stance on the question of Irish
parliamentary independence. Darcy and his colleagues dismissed the notion of
the king's constitutional neutrality as he "was drawn to give the royal assent to
the acts of subscription [adventurers act]". The confederates repeated the
demand for a declaratory act, and stated that given the self-evident nature of
Ireland's independence from Westminster's jurisdiction, "to draw this into any
debate or question might prove of most dangerous consequence to this nation".[99]
Ormond faced the unenviable task of trying to agree acceptable terms with the
confederate catholics, while at the same time protecting protestant (and personal) interests in Ireland. He compounded these difficulties, however, by a stubborn refusal to grant any meaningful constitutional concessions to Kilkenny,
regardless of the changing political and military circumstances. This policy frustrated the hopes of the peace faction for an early settlement.

**97** Peace debates, Sept. 1644 (Gilbert [ed.], *Irish confederation*, iii, pp 286-7). As Clarke has
outlined, the administration adopted a pragmatic position, with officials stating that "it was
to be wished that there were such an act, but the time was not seasonable to desire it". Clarke,
"Colonial constitutional attitudes" p. 361. The confederates, however, clearly hoped to force
the king to take sides, and recognise the independence of the Irish parliament. **98** Answer of
Ormond to the confederates, Sept. 1644 (Gilbert [ed.], *Irish confederation*, iii, p. 294). With
the Irish protestant community continuing to fragment during the course of 1644 (between
royalist and parliamentarian supporters), Ormond came under increasing pressure not to concede ground to the confederates in the negotiations. **99** Peace debates, 1644 (Gilbert [ed.],
*Irish confederation*, iii, pp 307-11, 313-19).

Religion emerged as the other main area of contention during the negotiations. The confederates demanded a repeal of all anti-catholic acts and freedom of worship. In reply, Ormond stressed that while catholics could expect royal protection and leniency, he required further instructions from Charles before he could agree to repeal any acts. The confederates responded angrily that due to the nature of the threat from the English parliament and Scottish presbyterians, a reliance on the king's "grace and goodness" was wholly inadequate. They did modify their position, however, seeking instead a removal of penalties rather than a repeal of all penal laws.[100]

With the religious negotiations at a delicate stage, Ormond dramatically introduced a number of fresh proposals on behalf of the protestant clergy, including crucially the restoration of church property. This specific demand, the first time the issue had been raised by either side, almost resulted in the complete collapse of the talks.[101] Ormond's motivation in refocussing the agenda at this time remains unclear. Although anxious to mollify his supporters in Dublin, concerned at the prospect of a deal with Kilkenny, the lord lieutenant also abhorred, on religious grounds, the very idea of relinquishing churches to the catholics.[102]

Ormond's mistake was not in insisting on retaining churches (a policy fully supported by Charles until 1645) but in publicly raising the issue.[103] As the catholic hierarchy would never agree to returning property to the protestants, the confederate leadership in Kilkenny dealt with the problem by simply ignoring it. This strategy proved impossible following Ormond's intervention. To their supporters abroad the confederates presented a hard-line on religious matters. They claimed that Charles was prepared to remove the penal laws "though in a private and retired way, but for enjoying our churches or restoring the profession of our faith to its ancient splendour is a thing so odious to the king's party, and so ill-suiting with his Majesty's professions, that we must make it good by the same way we did obtain it".[104]

Two months letter the supreme council returned to the issue in their instructions to the cleric Hugh Bourke, travelling to Spain as a confederate agent.

---

100 Ibid. pp 289-311. 101 Ibid. p. 321. As already discussed Scarampi raised the issue in debating the merits of the cessation in August 1643, while Inchiquin informed Ormond in October of that year of the that the catholic clergy would insist on retaining churches. Scarampi's reply to Richard Bellings' statement (Gilbert [ed.], *Irish confederation*, ii, pp 319-27); Inchiquin to Ormond, 29 Oct. 1643 (Carte, *Ormond*, v, pp 498-500). The issue, however, had not been raised by the confederate negotiators. 102 Even during the crisis in late 1646, with Dublin under threat from confederate forces, Ormond would not agree to catholics retaining churches, but felt that freedom from penalties and the quiet exercise of their religion "ought to be given them". Ormond to George Digby, 25 Dec. 1646 (Carte, *Ormond*, vi, pp 485-6). 103 Until the summer of 1645, Charles was prepared to concede no more than a repeal of penal legislation. Charles I to Ormond, 27 February 1645 (Bodl. Clarendon Mss 98 ff 63-4). 104 The phrase "by the same way we did obtain it" presumably means holding onto the property by force. Supreme council to Luke Wadding, 26 October 1644 (Gilbert [ed.], *Irish confederation*, iv, pp 61-2).

Bourke could inform sceptics in the court of Philip IV that the moderate religious demands of the confederates were nothing more than a tactic to win time. The true goal remained "freedom in splendour" but only if they received substantial assistance from abroad.[105] This statement, whether true or not, would certainly have helped mollify the Irish clergy while, at the same time, increasing the prospect of financial and military aid from abroad.

A paper sent to the king, however, by three members of the committee of treaty, Viscount Muskerry, Geoffrey Browne and Nicholas Plunkett, contradicted the supreme council's reassurances. The committee members recognised religion as "the principal thing insisted upon" by the confederates, but also indicated a willingness to compromise. Charles responded positively to this approach, promising not to implement the penal laws in the event of peace, and that after the defeat of parliament he would "consent to the repeal of them by law". Browne replied that if the king's answers on the matters of plantations and an act of oblivion proved equally satisfactory "it will confirm them in that hope and belief and make the work less difficult as to all".[106]

This correspondence remained highly secret, with Browne and the others instructed by the king not to reveal the contents to anybody outside of the supreme council. Indeed, considering the make-up of that body (including five bishops) it is questionable if they even informed the entire council. This very secrecy, however, precluded the committee members from using the information to satisfy any sceptical confederates. Official negotiations, which had been suspended during the winter while Ormond awaited fresh instructions from the king, resumed in April 1645, but with little immediate progress.[107] Ormond wrote in frustration, on 8 May, that the talks had stalled as the committee of treaty, despite their apparent willingness to compromise, "would not venture to conclude anything without their [assembly members] approbation".[108]

Despite Ormond's frustration, however, it is clear from the preceding examination of the talks process that the primary responsibility for any delays lay with

105 Supreme council appointments, 12 Dec. 1644 (ibid. pp 90-5). 106 There is some confusion over the dating of the king's reply, but the original in the Clarendon collection suggests 15 December 1644, rather than 18 January 1645 as published by the catalogue of Clarendon's papers and Gilbert. (Bodl. Clarendon Mss 98 f.49, 107 and Gilbert [ed.], *Irish confederation*, iv, pp 104-7). 107 English parliamentarians had intercepted one group returning to Dublin with royal instructions, and Colonel John Barry did not arrive with a new set until 6 March 1645. Cregan, D.F., "Confederation of Kilkenny" (PhD thesis) pp 158, 164. These problems illustrate the difficult circumstances in which the negotiations took place. 108 Ormond to Charles I, 8 May 1645 (Gilbert [ed.], *Irish confederation*, iv, pp 249-54). This statement also suggests that perhaps Enos' suspicions, concerning the committee of treaty's commission, were in fact valid. If the committee had full power to conclude a treaty, why now were the members anxious to seek the assembly's consent? Was it that the power to conclude had only been granted by the supreme council and not the assembly, or simply that the terms on offer were so unsatisfactory that the committee was reluctant to proceed without further authorisation? Enos "Survey" in Gilbert (ed.), *Irish confederation*, vi, p. 367. A general assembly was scheduled to meet on 15 May 1645.

the lord lieutenant, rather than the confederates. This fact appears particularly damning in light of the king's express orders early in 1645, as a new campaigning season approached, to press ahead with a settlement. On 27 February, five days after the collapse of the Uxbridge negotiations in England, Charles instructed Ormond "to conclude a peace with the Irish whatever it costs", and he concluded that he would "not think it a hard bargain" to agree to a suspension of Poynings' law and a repeal of penal legislation in return for securing confederate support. The king wrote again on 13 May, pleading with Ormond to conclude a treaty with or without the Irish council's approbation.[109]

In Ormond's defence, it must be conceded that satisfying the demands of both Charles and Irish protestants was proving to be an almost impossible task. Moreover, the king's public and private instructions often contradicted one another. For example, on 22 January 1645 Charles issued a proclamation forbidding the repeal of the penal laws. Although he reversed this policy in his private letter to Ormond on 27 February, his position remained unchanged publicly until 13 May.[110] Writing the following year, Charles explained that his "intention was not to tie you [Ormond] to the literal but the true meaning of our letters".[111]

Nonetheless, despite the king's dissembling, the lord lieutenant's tactics (in particular the introduction of a specific demand for the return of churches) provided the greatest obstacle to a peace settlement. With the regime in Kilkenny anxious to agree terms, a deal appeared possible at minimum cost to Irish protestant interests. Instead the marquis refused to make even basic concessions and concentrated his efforts on fostering divisions among the confederates, thereby weakening the very people from whom the king needed assistance.[112] Ormond compounded the problem by allowing the negotiations to stall on the one issue (religion) guaranteed to arouse the greatest emotions in confederate ranks.

In October 1644, Clanricarde feared that "if the treaty be brought to this issue, to break upon that point will certainly be very prejudicial to his majesty's service, and of so great advantage to them [the confederates] both home and abroad, that it had been better not to have consented to any such treaty".[113]

**109** This final plea was made one month prior to the disastrous royal defeat at Naseby. The king's letters to Ormond survive in the Clarendon collection (Bodl. Clarendon Mss 98 ff 44-5, 55, 63-4, 77-8). The negotiations at Uxbridge had ended following the refusal of Charles to compromise on the issues of religion and the militia. Smith, *Constitutional royalism* p. 124. **110** Charles I to Ormond, 13 May 1645 (Bodl. Clarendon Mss 98 f.72). **111** Charles I to Ormond, 17 Feb. 1646 (Carte, *Ormond*, vi, p. 353). **112** On 13 January 1644, as the confederate delegation prepared to leave for Oxford, Ormond informed Digby that they could be divided "by gaining upon the ambition of the leading men". Ibid. pp 4-10. On 28 March 1645, Ormond suggested to Digby that "many considerable persons of the Irish" might abandon the confederates if offered a peerage. Ibid. pp 272-5. As the assembly gathered in May, Ormond confidently predicted that he could "ruin their supremacy by dividing their party". Cregan, D.F., "Confederation of Kilkenny" (PhD thesis) p. 170; Lowe, "Negotiations between Charles I and confederates" p. 282. **113** Remembrances for Viscount Taaffe, 12 Oct. 1644 (Lowe [ed.],

Ormond ignored these warnings, and presented the catholic clergy with an ideal opportunity to foment opposition among confederates frustrated by delays in concluding a settlement. Every passing week without a peace treaty increased the pressure on the peace faction in Kilkenny. The convocation of a general assembly in May 1645 provided critics (clerical and secular) of the supreme council's conduct of affairs with an ideal opportunity to demand changes in policies and procedures. This assembly, therefore, would be very different from the largely compliant institution dominated by the peace faction in the early years of the confederate association.

The rise of the clerical faction in 1645, however, was in fact preceded by a secular based opposition, whose reform proposals are outlined in a remarkable document already alluded to, entitled *Propositions touching the present government to the general assembly in June 1644*.[114] This detailed submission, by unknown authors, appeared just prior to the assembly meeting in July 1644, as the confederate delegates returned from Oxford. The proposals, clearly secularist in both tone and content, represented the opening shots of a wider struggle waged by elements in the general assembly to wrest control of confederate affairs from an increasingly authoritarian supreme council. This conflict emerged as a major factor in confederate politics over the next four years.[115]

The document itself contained sixty points, dealing with a variety of administrative, judicial, financial and military issues, but the most important proposals concerned the nature of confederate government itself. To encourage greater attendance and participation at meetings, the supreme council would be assigned a permanent location, as central and accessible as possible, with at least nine (rather than seven) signatures required to sign any order or public instrument.[116] On the issue of accountability, in future the council would be required to appear before a committee of the assembly, "who are to make report back to the assembly of all save only what shall be dangerous or mischievous to publish".[117] No evidence survives, however, to suggest that such a procedure was ever established.

The reformers also attempted to strengthen regional autonomy by prohibiting the levying of taxes on the provinces or counties without their consent.[118] In the confederate "model of government", established in 1642, the provincial councils answered directly to the supreme council.[119] The new proposals recommended instead that they "derive their power immediately from the assembly".

*Clanricarde letter-book* pp 111-4). **114** Marsh's Library Mss z 3.1.3 **115** There were at two other attempts to reform confederate government, initiated by the general assembly – 1646 (Bodl. Carte Mss 16 ff 470-80) and 1647 (Gilbert [ed.], *Irish confederation*, vi, pp 208-23). **116** During the 1640s the supreme council met in a number of different locations apart from Kilkenny, including Limerick, Waterford, Galway, Clonmel and Ross. **117** Marsh's Library Mss z 3.1.3. **118** Idem. **119** Orders of the general assembly met at Kilkenny, 24 Oct. 1642 (BL Add Mss 4,781 ff 4-11).

Throughout the 1640s, the *modus operandi* of confederate provincial government differed across the country. The Leinster council, based in Kilkenny, was entirely overshadowed by the supreme council, while little information survives on the Munster council (except that Viscount Muskerry acted at one time as its president).[120] The Ulster council functioned basically as Owen Roe O'Neill's war cabinet, convening wherever his army set up camp.[121] Only in Connacht did the provincial council meet on a regular basis, suggesting perhaps a Connacht influence in drawing up these reform proposals.[122]

That this reform document did not emanate from the clerics, hitherto identified as the main leaders of assembly opposition, is apparent from a number of proposals.[123] The document recommended for example that the clergy only have "cognisance of more spiritual things and of testamentary and matrimonial matters". Elsewhere, the clergy would become subject to temporal jurisdiction, especially those involved in the collection of tithes, or other financial impositions. The reformers also demanded that the clergy confine themselves to the limit of the law, and not "introduce into the land innovations of laws grounded upon foreign command", a clear reference to the threat to lay proprietors of church and monastic lands.[124]

As for the conduct of the war, the proposals envisaged the appointment of military men to sit on the supreme and provincial councils, "for the better management of military affairs". The provincial armies would receive "a certain and constant revenue" to pay costs and wages, and not be used outside of their own area "but by order of the general of the province". Soldiers would be kept in garrisons, rather than dispersed among the population, and receive training each week. The document recommended reducing the multiplicity of officers and commanders, and the employment of veteran soldiers "before others of less merit". Discipline, cost-efficiency and military effectiveness provided the guiding principles for these proposed reforms.[125]

The reformers revived the idea of a running or central army, to be paid from

---

120 During the crisis over the Inchiquin truce in 1648, the supreme council summoned representatives of Leinster and Munster to Kilkenny. It is unclear, however, if these were the provincial councils or assemblies. Gilbert (ed.), *Irish confederation*, vii, p. 68; O'Ferrall and O'Connell (eds), *Commentarius*, iii, pp 126-33; BL Add Mss 46,927 f.129 (Egmont papers) contains a petition from C.R. O'Callaghan complaining about illegal occupation of lands, addressed to Muskerry as "lord president of the council of Munster". 121 Most of the references to the Ulster council are in O'Ferrall and O'Connell (eds) *Commentarius*, i, pp 328-30, 573-5 etc., all referring to military matters. 122 The earl of Clanricarde was in regular correspondence with the Connacht provincial council during the 1640s. Bourke, *Clanricarde memoirs* p. 334, 442; Lowe (ed.), *Clanricarde letter-book* pp 84, 217, 243. 123 For the role of the clergy in the general assembly see Lowe (ed.), *Clanricarde letter-book* pp 173-7, 356-7; Ormond to [Walter Bagenal], 14 Jan. 1647 (Bodl. Carte Mss 20 f.135). Even the most recent study of confederate politics ascribes assembly discontent exclusively to the clergy. Ó hAnnracháin, "Rebels and confederates" *Celtic Dimensions* pp 109-10. 124 Marsh's Library Mss z 3.1.3. 125 Similarly

clerical livings, as decided in the previous assembly. Moreover, they recommended the establishment of a war council, created from supreme and provincial council members, "to determine all military causes and to give their opinion and advice for the management and conduct of the armies and war". The confederates clearly failed to implement this proposal, as Rinuccini complained shortly after his arrival in late 1645 that the confederates lacked such a council.[126] The reformers stressed the need to maintain law and order in the face of increasing chaos, by appointing sheriffs on a yearly basis, to ensure better accountability and efficiency, and four provost marshals in each county to punish thieves and vagabonds, "specially during the cessation wherein they increase more than at other times".[127]

The document concluded, however, with a remarkable political statement that the disposal of office by the supreme council was "not agreeable with the government of other commonwealths", where parliament performed this role. According to this new model the council was "but a committee of the general assembly and the assembly only ought to dispose of the places aforesaid, if they will not give all their power and dependency from them to their committee, which by the practise of parliaments are to conclude nothing but by the approbation of the parliament or both houses at least".[128] The reformers, therefore, not only saw the general assembly as a parliament (whatever they chose to call it), but also believed that the legislature should take precedence over the executive, echoing the arguments of the king's opponents in England.[129]

Corish denies the confederates ever actively enunciated a doctrine of executive responsibility, or that they protested at the extension of the supreme council's powers.[130] This document refutes both claims, even if on this occasion the reform efforts proved unsuccessful. Although the supreme council continued to dominate confederate politics, the assembly in 1644 at least began to voice its dissatisfaction. The reformers did register one spectacular success, however, achieving a separation of the executive and judicial functions, with the supreme council limited by instructions "to confine them wholly to matters of state and government".[131] The assembly established a new court of judicature, to try all civil and criminal cases, hitherto examined by the council, appointing five judges, including John Bourke, the bishop of Clonfert, who succeeded Patrick Darcy as lord chancellor. Apart

in England, both sides attempted to improve the efficiency of their war efforts. In February 1644, parliament and the Scottish covenaters delegated power to the new committee of both kingdoms, while in June the royalists, after a specially commissioned report, established committees in each county to check accounts for all money received and spent in the king's service. Roberts, *Responsible government* pp 145-6; Hutton, Ronald, *The royalist war effort 1642-1646* (London 1982) pp 93-4. **126** Report on the state of Ireland, 1 March 1646 (Aiazza [ed.], *Embassy* pp 139-40) **127** Marsh's Library Mss z 3.1.3. **128** Idem. **129** Roberts describes how Westminster's willingness to press for parliamentary nomination of ministers of state rose and fell with its military fortunes. Roberts, *Responsible government* pp 141-2. **130** Corish, *NHI*, iii, pp 300-1. **131** Marsh's Library Mss z 3.1.3.

from Clonfert, the strong legal team consisted of Richard Martin from Connacht, Richard Berford and John Dillon of Leinster and John Walsh of Munster.[132]

The reformers' primary concern, therefore centred on the efficient operation of central government. They stressed the subordination of the supreme council to the assembly, as envisaged in the original "model of government", created by Patrick Darcy, while the separation of judicial and executive functions tackled the monopoly of power established by a handful of individuals. They further hoped to curtail the excessive centralising of power through promoting provincial autonomy. Although the identity of these reformers remains unknown, an examination of the internal evidence in the document provides certain clues.

The proposed reforms were both secularist and populist in tone, with a strong legalistic flavour. The criticisms of the existing government suggests a group outside of the small ruling clique, while the limits placed on clerical power and the insistence that clergy be subject to temporal jurisdiction rules out the bishops. In fact, the court system, the provincial councils and the general assembly stood to gain most from the proposed changes. The two leading confederate lawyers, therefore, Nicholas Plunkett (chairman of the assembly), and Patrick Darcy (framer of the "model of government" and active Connacht politician) emerge as possible authors of the "Propositions" document.

Although they both sat on the supreme council, neither belonged to the inner sanctum of the peace faction. Their championing of the legislature in the face of executive misrule during the Irish parliament of 1640-1 found echoes in the 1644 document, while the support for provincial autonomy seems consistent with Darcy's active involvement on the Connacht council.[133] Plunkett had travelled to England in 1644, as part of the confederate delegation, and may well have been influenced by royalist and parliamentarian efforts at governmental reform. Moreover, the attempt in the document to reassert the original sense of the "model of government" strongly suggests the involvement of its author, Patrick Darcy.

From the beginning of the rebellion, catholic leaders in Galway, allied with Nicholas Plunkett, had been involved in efforts to create an alternative system of government. This document represented an attempt to swing the balance of power in their favour, away from the increasingly dominant peace faction. The strength of these reform proposals ultimately lay in their espousal of the primacy of the general assembly, but for the present, as the controversy centred on the religious question, the influence of Plunkett and his associates remained peripheral. Only when the confederates openly split into two hostile factions did the possibility arise for them to exploit the balance of power. Events over the next twelve months resulted in just such a rupture.

---

**132** Order by the commissioners of the general assembly, 30 Aug. 1644 (Gilbert (ed.), *Irish confederation*, iii, pp 266-7); Cregan, D.F., "Confederation of Kilkenny" (PhD thesis) p. 105. **133** For their parliamentary activities see Perceval-Maxwell, *Irish rebellion* (1994). Darcy's activities in Connacht are well chronicled by Clanricarde. See Lowe (ed.) *Clanricarde letter-book* pp 68, 74.

# CHAPTER 3

# Outside intervention

ℰℭ

## MAY 1645–SEPTEMBER 1646

> The catholics in any of his Majesty's dominions cannot prudently pro-
> pose to themselves any other advantage than by preserving the king's legal
> just power over the laws by which they may receive his grace and dispen-
> sation without avoiding and cancelling the laws themselves.
>
> Edward Hyde to Captain Brett, 6 January 1647[1]

The arrival of Edward Somerset, earl of Glamorgan, in late June 1645 dramatically transformed the Irish political scene. Whereas historians have concentrated on
the impact of the papal nuncio, Giovanni Battista Rinuccini, archbishop of
Fermo, who reached the kingdom four months later, Glamorgan's intervention
proved of greater consequence, at least until the collapse of the first peace treaty
in August 1646.[2] This statement is not intended to diminish the important role
played by Rinuccini in confederate politics, but rather to raise the profile of a
much maligned and misunderstood servant of the king.[3]

The main controversy associated with the earl of Glamorgan's mission centred on whether Charles I authorised his actions in Ireland. That the king commissioned the earl in late 1644 to agree a settlement with the confederates has
now been established beyond question.[4] Glamorgan, an ardent royalist and
devout catholic, seemed ideally suited for a mission to Ireland. In light of
Ormond's inability (or unwillingness) to conclude a peace settlement, Charles
clearly hoped Glamorgan would prove more flexible in his dealings with the

---

1 Bodl. Clarendon Mss 29 f.48. 2 A good example is Corish's two chapters on the 1640s in the
*New History of Ireland*. He takes the nuncio's arrival as the dividing point of the decade.
Corish, "The rising of 1641 and the catholic confederacy, 1641-5", *NHI*, iii, pp 289-316, and
Corish, "Ormond, Rinuccini and the confederates 1645-9", *NHI*, iii, pp 317-35. 3 Glamorgan
was arrested by Ormond in late 1645, publicly disowned by Charles I, and eventually abandoned by the confederates. Charles I to Ormond, 30 Jan. 1646 (Bodl. Clarendon Mss 98
f.112). 4 This issue is examined in some detail in Lowe, "Negotiations between Charles I and
the confederation" (PhD thesis). The main findings are published in Lowe, John, "The
Glamorgan mission to Ireland 1645-6" pp 155-96.

confederates.[5] More importantly, the leadership in Kilkenny unreservedly accepted Glamorgan's credentials as genuine.

The earl arrived in Ireland as the king's fortunes in England faced total collapse and peace negotiations between Ormond and the confederates reached crisis point. On 14 June, the New Model Army routed the royalist forces at Naseby, a battle which heralded an end to the civil war in that country. Although it took several months for the consequences of Naseby to be fully appreciated, in the short term Charles had no effective standing army at his disposal.[6] Glamorgan's departure to Dublin, shortly after this disaster, was directly linked to the king's desperate need for troops. From June 1645, therefore, the royalists' only hope centred on massive intervention from Ireland.[7]

A few weeks after the resumption of peace talks, the supreme council summoned an assembly for 15 May 1645 to discuss the terms of peace. The ferocity of clerical opposition to the religious concessions offered by Ormond caught the ruling peace faction hopelessly unprepared. The bishops enjoyed significant support among assembly members, frustrated by the lack of progress towards a settlement with the king and suspicious of the secretive manner in which the negotiations were being conducted.[8] The entire peace process appeared to be in jeopardy, with clerical resistance set to intensify, bolstered by news of the papal nuncio's imminent arrival in the kingdom.[9]

Despite the emergence of a vocal opposition in the confederate ranks, Ormond continued to insist on the restoration of church property to the protestant clergy. This demand placed the peace faction leadership in an impossible position, as the catholic clergy, supported by a significant section of the confederate rank and file, would never agree to such a transfer. Clanricarde, sent to

---

5 The secret nature of Glamorgan's mission also enabled Charles to denounce the earl once word of his deal with the confederates became public. Statement by Charles I, 24 Jan. 1646 (Gilbert [ed.], *Irish confederation*, v, pp 252-4). 6 Morrill, *Revolt of the provinces* pp 99-100. The remainder of the 1645 campaigning season proved equally calamitous for the royalists, with the defeat of Goring at Langport (July 10), the loss of Pembrokeshire after the battle of Colby Moor (August 1), and the surrender of Bristol in September. 7 On 21 June 1645, Lord Byron (royalist commander of Chester) informed Ormond that after the disaster at Naseby "Lord Glamorgan hath thought fit to hasten his journey into Ireland" (Bodl. Carte Mss 15 f.99). 8 The clergy denounced any treaty concluded "for temporal points", without insisting on significant religious concessions. Declaration by the clergy, 1 June 1645 (Bodl. Carte Mss 15 f.3); Unanimous resolution of the general assembly, 9 June 1645 (Bodl. Carte Mss 15 f.50); Clanricarde to Ormond, 26 May 1645 (Lowe [ed.], *Clanricarde letter-book* pp 155-7); Clanricarde to Ormond, 11 June 1645 (ibid., pp 167-8). 9 News of Rinuccini's appointment had reached Ireland as early as February 1645. Clanricarde informed Ormond of rumours of "a large relation of a rich Italian prelate styled bishop of Fermo, that is ready to come over to spend his revenue in this holy war". Clanricarde to Ormond, 27 Feb. 1645 (Lowe [ed.], *Clanricarde letter-book* p. 147).

Kilkenny by the lord lieutenant to act as an intermediary, reported that the religious terms on offer were "very sadly received" in the general assembly.[10]

The response to concessions on political matters proved more favourable, but Clanricarde insisted there could be no peace without a religious settlement. Assembly members, advised by their "spiritual guides", demanded that catholics not be disturbed in possession of church property until the confirmation of a peace treaty by an act of parliament.[11] From this moment onwards, months before the arrival of the papal nuncio, the catholic clergy grew increasingly vocal in their opposition to the religious settlement outlined by Ormond. Despite this development, the lord lieutenant refused to compromise, replying to Clanricarde that the king would not retract on the issue of church property.[12]

This may have reflected the king's attitude at one time, but as the royalist position in England deteriorated during the course of 1645, a peace treaty (resulting in significant confederate military assistance) took precedence over all other considerations. On 13 May 1645, Charles authorised Ormond to agree to a repeal of penal legislation.[13] Offered in conjunction with an understanding not to repossess church property before a meeting of parliament, such a deal would in all likelihood have been accepted by the general assembly. Ormond, however, conscious of the almost unanimous opposition in protestant Ireland to such a concession, did nothing.

Meanwhile, on the confederate side, a delegation of assembly members approached the clergy assembled in Kilkenny at this time, hoping to resolve the issue.[14] They questioned whether the oath of association obliged the confederates to insist on the retention of church property. On 1 June, the clergymen replied in the affirmative, declaring that the oath actually required a special article in the peace treaty to that effect.[15] For two years, clerical dissatisfaction with the direc-

10 Clanricarde to Ormond, 26 May 1645 (Lowe [ed.], *Clanricarde letter-book* pp 155-7). 11 Idem. 12 Ormond to Clanricarde, 29 May 1645 (Gilbert [ed.], *Irish confederation*, iv, pp 264-6). Publicly at least, Charles remained firm on the issue, assuring Prince Rupert that what he had "refused to the English I will not grant to the Irish rebels". Charles I to Prince Rupert, 3 Aug. 1645 (Carte, *Ormond*, vi, pp 311-2). 13 Bodl. Clarendon Mss 98 f.72. Charles had indicated back in February his willingness to repeal penal legislation, but Ormond did not pass the offer onto the confederate negotiators, for fear they would seek further concessions. Ormond to Charles I, 8 May 1645 (Gilbert [ed.], *Irish confederation*, iv, pp 249-54). 14 The congregation was assigned no official role in the confederate "model of government", but the practice of contemporaneous meetings dated back to May 1642, when the national synod of the Catholic Church in Kilkenny, invited secular leaders to join them in creating an alternative government structure (see chapter 1). In Scotland, the general assembly of the church played a similarly central role during the 1640s. Brown, *Kingdom or province* pp 119-20. 15 The clergy argued that the secular body had no jurisdiction over churches. They also insisted that catholic bishops sit in parliament and enjoy full power for the exercising of their jurisdiction. Cregan, D.F., "Confederation of Kilkenny" (PhD thesis) pp 174-5; O'Ferrall and O'Connell (eds), *Commentarius*, i, pp 524-36; Declaration by the clergy at the convocation

tion of negotiations had failed to impact on the policies of the peace faction. The oath of association, however, provided them with a powerful weapon to challenge their opponents in the confederate government.[16]

Clanricarde reported to Ormond that despite the clerical declaration the confederate leadership remained willing to compromise on the issue of church property. The peace faction argued that as long as neither side insisted on a definite article in the treaty for the retention of churches, the existing law of the land would ensure that, after the war, the protestant clergy regained their property. According to Clanricarde, Muskerry and his supporters followed the teachings of Saint Ambrose, who said "I may not deliver up my churches but if they be taken I ought not to resist".[17] The assembly, heavily influenced by the clergy, proved less conciliatory, resolving on 9 June that the commissioners of treaty refuse Ormond's request for the restoration of churches.[18]

Ormond retorted angrily that the problem over church property "was never 'till now discovered (it is very certain that it was never mentioned before by any of the confederates) to or by me".[19] The failure of confederate negotiators to inform him of the depth of hostility in their ranks to the reclamation of churches, or the extent of clerical influence in the assembly, rankled deeply. The lord lieutenant, however, could have had no doubts about the unwillingness of catholic clergy to hand over any property. It was his insistence on including a definite article, despite Clanricarde's misgivings, which had forced this confederate response, and provided the clergy with ammunition to oppose the peace treaty on religious grounds.[20] The whole episode proved a major tactical error by Ormond and almost brought about a collapse of the peace process.

---

house, 1 June 1645 (Bodl. Carte Mss 15 f.3); Ó hAnnracháin, "Far from terra firma" pp 216-7. **16** Numerous versions of the oath of association exist (see for example BL Stowe Mss 82 f.66, 92, 303), but the oath taken at the 1644 general assembly could be considered standard, at least until August 1646. Gilbert (ed.), *Irish confederation*, iii, pp 213-14. The oath played a crucial role in binding together the disparate group of individuals who comprised the confederate association. Confederates swore to defend royal prerogatives, the privileges of parliament and the fundamental laws of the kingdom. As regards religion, the oath simply calls for "the free exercise of the Roman Catholic faith and religion", with nothing specific about church property. The clergy acknowledged the limitations of the oath's religious clauses but insisted that churches, while not an absolute necessity, were a right. O'Ferrall and O'Connell (eds), *Commentarius*, i, pp 524-36. **17** Clanricarde to Ormond, 4 June 1645 (Lowe [ed.], *Clanricarde letter-book* pp 163-5). **18** Resolution of the general assembly, 9 June 1645 (Bodl. Carte Mss 15 f.50). **19** Ormond to Clanricarde, 9 June 1645 (Gilbert [ed.], *Irish confederation*, iv, p. 278). The lord lieutenant was clearly being disingenuous given the fact (already outlined) that Inchiquin informed him as early as October 1643 of confederate opposition to this demand. See note 101 p. 80 above. **20** In his thesis, Ó hAnnracháin claims that the whole issue of the retention of churches was first raised in the 1645 assembly by the catholic clergy. Ó hAnnracháin, "Far from terra firma" pp 210-11. As already outlined in chapter 2 (pp 80-83f), however, Ormond initiated the debate in late 1644. "Ormond's demands on behalf of the

As the crisis escalated, the convocation sent a delegation of clergy to the committees of instruction and treaty, consisting of Robert Barry, Walter Lynch, Thomas Rothe, Oliver Darcy and Nicholas French.[21] After a lengthy debate, in which Nicholas Plunkett and Patrick Darcy played a leading role, the two sides reached an agreement on 16 June, along those lines favoured by the confederate leadership.[22] The clergy accepted that the assembly would not be breaking the oath of association by not seeking a definite article on the retention of churches. They hoped some other method would be found to enable the Catholic Church to retain the property, which for the moment would remain in its hands.[23]

The reasons for this dramatic shift in clerical policy are unclear. Divisions among the prelates themselves may well have been responsible, as three bishops opposed the idea of a treaty clause insisting on the retention of churches. In a further twist, the authors of the *Commentarius* (hardly an unbiased source) claimed the committee members deceived the clerical delegation. Whereas the confederate leadership had already informed Ormond, through Clanricarde, that they would not oppose the reclaiming of churches by the protestant clergy, they then convinced the bishops that in practice this was unlikely to occur.[24]

Ormond's continued insistence on a definite article, supported by a letter from the king's secretary of state George Digby, undermined hopes of a compromise.[25] His stubbornness infuriated Clanricarde, who decided not to show Digby's letter to the confederates. By this time, according to Clanricarde, the assembly had split into two factions – those who favoured peace and a "violent

protestant clergy, Sept. 1644" (Gilbert [ed.], *Irish confederation*, iii, p. 321). The confederate leadership, recognising the sensitivity of the issue, simply ignored it. Once the catholic clergy in the assembly were informed of the religious terms on offer in May 1645, conflict proved inevitable.  **21** O'Ferrall and O'Connell (eds), *Commentarius*, i, p. 524. Rothe was dean of Ossory, while Barry, Lynch and Darcy were all consecrated as bishops after Rinuccini's arrival in Ireland – Barry (Cork), Lynch (Clonfert) and Darcy (Dromore). Nicholas French, bishop-elect of Ferns at this time, went on to play a leading role in confederate politics. Cregan, "Counter-reformation episcopate" p. 87.  **22** French, Plunkett and Darcy later became close political allies, advocating a moderate political course.  **23** Catholics were to retain churches on a *de facto*, rather than a *de lege*, basis. Cregan, D.F., "Confederation of Kilkenny" (PhD thesis) pp 174-5; O'Ferrall and O'Connell (eds), *Commentarius*, i, pp 524-36.  **24** Ó hAnnracháin believes that the members of the committee of treaty almost certainly lied to one or both sides at this point, with the clergy the main victims of the deceit. Ó hAnnracháin, "Stance of the Irish clergy", *Celtic dimensions* p. 110. The most likely source of clerical dissent was Dease of Meath, who had already been censured by a synod for his criticisms of the rebels, Rothe of Ossory and Tirry of Cork. O'Ferrall and O'Connell (eds), *Commentarius*, i, pp 524-36.  **25** Digby's claimed that the king would join with "the Scots or with any of the protestant profession, rather than do the least act that may hazard that religion which and for which he will live and die". Digby to Muskerry, 1 Aug. 1645 (Carte, *Ormond*, vi, pp 309-10). Digby also adopted a hard-line during the negotiations between royalists and parliamentarians in England. Smith, *Constitutional royalism* pp 124-5.

faction, though inferior in number and quality, are so active and industrious …
that the most considerable party dare not publicly avow their own concep-
tions".[26] The growing dissensions in the confederate ranks greatly increased the
pressure on the peace faction to extract some concessions from Ormond.

Clanricarde found that many confederates appeared reassuring in private
"but when they mix with their associates at their committees or Grand Assembly
they ever want judgement or courage to cope with the sages of law, who have
prevailing power to pervert the best ways". He also blamed the clergy for
fomenting trouble, but concluded that the only way to preserve the king at this
stage was by "the giving of power and encouragement to the catholics of both
kingdoms".[27] Although sent to Kilkenny by Ormond to moderate confederate
demands, Clanricarde now favoured a close alliance between the king and his
catholic subjects, and his recommendation (from Ormond's perspective at least)
verged on the treasonable.

The committee of treaty, anxious to deflect criticism from angry assembly
members, tried to recover some lost ground in the peace negotiations which
continued in Dublin throughout the summer. The confederate commissioners
(apart from the issue of churches) demanded a repeal of all penal laws and a suspension of Poynings' law. Ormond reluctantly agreed to an act of parliament
removing all penalties for the quiet exercise of religion, but refused to permit the
exercise of any papal jurisdiction in the kingdom, while the jurisdiction of the
protestant clergy would remain in place, although modified in certain respects.
The lord lieutenant also confirmed his opposition to any constitutional reforms
involving Poynings' law or the independence of the Irish parliament.[28]

Ormond's tough negotiating stance appeared to pay dividends, when on 21
June the confederate committee of treaty indicated a willingness to moderate
certain demands, offering some hope of breaking the stalemate. The commissioners requested "that the acts to be agreed upon in this treaty, if of necessity
they must be transmitted into England, may receive no alteration or diminution
there, and this to be expressed in the articles of the treaty", conceding in effect
the principle that the terms of any settlement had to receive approval in
England, as required by Poynings' law.[29]

On the other main issue, instead of a declaratory act, the confederate leadership agreed to settle for a declaration of "the independency of our parliament of
the parliament of England".[30] In his reply, six days later, Ormond, not surpris-

**26** Clanricarde to Ormond, 11 June 1645; Digby to the Irish agents, Aug. 1645 (Lowe [ed.],
*Clanricarde letter-book* pp 167-8, 181-2). Clanricarde had admitted to Ormond at the beginning of the assembly session that he sympathised with the confederate refusal to hand over
church property. Clanricarde to Ormond, 4 June 1645 (Carte, *Ormond*, vi, pp 297-8). **27**
Clanricarde to Ormond, 21 Aug. 1645 (Lowe [ed.], *Clanricarde letter-book* pp 173-6). **28** Treaty
negotiations, 1645 (Bodl. Carte Mss 15 f.86, 92, 102-5, 200, 211-12, 242, 251 etc.); See also
Gilbert (ed.), *Irish confederation*, iv, pp 289-351. **29** Ibid. p. 293. **30** Ibid. p. 294.

ingly, provided assurances that the articles of treaty would not be altered in England. Moreover, the lord lieutenant consented to any declaration made by both houses of Parliament "agreeable to the laws of the land ... and therewith the persons formerly attending us from your party [confederates] declared that they were satisfied".[31]

A rapid conclusion of the treaty with the royalists, at this time, might well have silenced the newly emerging opposition, and the peace faction desperately tried to remove any remaining obstacles to a settlement. The general assembly, however, proved unwilling to surrender the political initiative back to Viscount Muskerry and his allies. In early July 1645 the confederate leadership issued a denial (through the assembly) of rumours that the impending peace settlement would be contrary to the oath of association.[32] The publication by the parliamentarians of the king's letter of February 1645 (offering among other things to suspend Poynings' law), discovered in his baggage after the defeat at Naseby, further outraged opinion in Kilkenny. Assembly members accused the lord lieutenant of deception and duplicity, all of which provided encouragement to those described by Clanricarde as "not well affected persons".[33] As the atmosphere in Kilkenny continued to deteriorate, the prospects for peace diminished accordingly.

The limited concessions offered by Ormond proved insufficient to satisfy the confederates, prompting the dramatic intervention of the earl of Glamorgan. On 25 August, less than two weeks after Glamorgan's arrival in Kilkenny, both sides had signed a comprehensive religious settlement, in return for which the confederates agreed to send 10,000 men to the assistance of the king in England. The main points included free and public exercise of the catholic religion, exemption from the jurisdiction of the protestant clergy, and possession of all churches acquired by the confederates since 23 October 1641. On the vexed issue of clerical livings, they were to be secured by other means until an act of parliament could be passed.[34]

Crucially, the agreement was to remain secret until confederate troops arrived in England, which would only happen when the king performed his conditions and Ormond agreed to terms on civil matters. To safeguard his own position, Glamorgan drew up a defeasance, as he had no intention of binding

<hr/>

**31** Ibid. p. 317-8. **32** In future, anybody publishing such rumours would be considered guilty of high treason. Proclamation by the general assembly, 4 July 1645 (PRO SP Ire. 260/140 f.394). The launching of a joint military campaign that summer by confederates and royalists in Connacht further fuelled the suspicions of many at the assembly. **33** According to Clanricarde, the published letters arrived in Ireland from France. Clanricarde to Ormond, 21 Aug. 1645 (Bodl. Carte Mss 15 ff 478-9). The subsequent euphoria over Glamorgan's treaty spared Ormond the embarrassment of having to justify withholding the king's offer. **34** Articles agreed between Glamorgan and the confederates, 25 Aug. 1645 (BL Add Mss 25,277 f.62).

Charles to any concession "other than he himself shall please after he hath received these 10,000 men".[35] The religious treaty, although falling short of full official recognition of catholicism, represented a major advance on Ormond's offer. Nonetheless, Scarampi, the papal representative, distrusted Glamorgan, opposed the secrecy clause, and urged the confederates to wait for the arrival of the papal nuncio.[36]

The issue of secrecy dominated the subsequent dispute over the Glamorgan treaty. According to one account, the earl discussed religious terms with the confederate delegation in Dublin before accompanying them back to Kilkenny, where the assembly had reconvened after the July recess. In a statement made at the end of 1645, Glamorgan claimed he had negotiated exclusively with the committee of treaty, and refused to address the general assembly.[37] If the idea was to limit the number of people who knew about the agreement, the tactic proved spectacularly unsuccessful. Over half the members of the confederate negotiating team also sat on the supreme council, which by this time appears to have amalgamated with the committee of instruction.[38] As there is no dispute over the fact the bishops also received copies of the treaty, the question should really be (on the confederate side at least) who did not know the terms of the settlement with Glamorgan?[39]

Moreover, shortly afterwards, assembly members "unanimously" consented to a political treaty, and to send 10,000 troops to England. They also declared that the confederate association would remain intact until the Irish parliament ratified the articles of treaty, providing some reassurance for the sceptical.[40] This remark-

35 *The Irish cabinet or his majesties secret papers..taken in the carriages of the archbishop of Tuam* ..., London 1645/6 (RIA vol. 45, box 41, tract 4). The treaty and its implications are also discussed in Cregan, "Confederation of Kilkenny" (PhD thesis) pp 186, 328. 36 O'Ferrall and O'Connell (eds), *Commentarius*, i, pp 551-6. 37 Lowe, "Negotiations between Charles and the confederates" pp 332, 341-4. Glamorgan's answers to the interrogation after his arrest in December are contained in Bodl. Carte Mss 16 f.352, 63 ff 365-9. 38 Report on the state of Ireland, 1 March 1646 (Aiazza [ed.], *Embassy* p. 133). A full list of the members of the committee of treaty and supreme council in August 1645 can be found in chapter 7 (table 6) and appendix 2 (table 13). 39 According to Rinuccini, who arrived after the event, the supreme council ordered that every bishop receive a copy. Rinuccini to Pamphili, 1 Jan. 1646 (Aiazza [ed.], *Embassy* p. 108). This was confirmed by the discovery of a copy of the Glamorgan treaty in the papers of the Malachy O'Queely, archbishop of Tuam, after he was killed in a skirmish with parliamentarian troops near Sligo in October 1645. See *The Irish cabinet or his majesties secret papers..taken in the carriages of the archbishop of Tuam* ..., London 1645/6 (RIA vol. 45,box 41, tract 4). Lowe agrees that the bishops received copies of the treaty. Lowe, "The Glamorgan mission to Ireland" p. 166. 40 Glamorgan informed Ormond that the confederates were happy with the existing concessions on offer as long as they could petition the king for the rest, "and yet in the interim proceed to peace and supplies". Glamorgan to Ormond, 9 Sept. 1645 (Bodl. Carte Mss 15 ff 580-1); Declaration by the general assembly, 28 Aug. 1645 (Bodl. Carte Mss ff 558-9); Cregan, D.F., "Confederation of Kilkenny" (PhD thesis) p. 187.

able turn of events, considering the assembly's initial opposition to the terms on offer from Ormond, strongly suggests that even if assembly members had not seen copies of the Glamorgan treaty, they must have known of its contents.

On the royalist side, Lowe argues that Ormond believed Glamorgan's involvement consisted of convincing the confederates to accept a peace treaty and no more.[41] This interpretation is hard to credit considering the number of confederates who knew of the religious treaty. A quick glance through the list of the supreme council membership reveals at least one individual who remained in regular contact with the lord lieutenant throughout the 1640s. Moreover, on 29 August, Glamorgan sent Colonel Barry, a witness to the treaty and confidant of Ormond, to inform him of what took place, the details of which were "fitter for word of mouth", than a letter.[42]

The correspondence between Glamorgan and Ormond at this crucial stage becomes almost impenetrable (perhaps deliberately), with both men anxious not to commit any indiscretion to paper. Nonetheless, what was Ormond to make of Glamorgan's claim that a political treaty could now be completed within three days, and of the new confederate tactic of dividing negotiations into what could be agreed with the marquis, with the rest (principally religious terms) being sent in a petition to the king?[43] The surviving evidence strongly suggests, therefore, that Ormond must have been aware of the general thrust of Glamorgan's treaty, if not perhaps the full details.[44]

After Glamorgan's dramatic breakthrough negotiations between Ormond and the confederates resumed, presumably to resolve the outstanding political and military issues. The lord lieutenant insisted, however, that any compromise on his part should not be interpreted as giving consent to the practice of catholicism in churches. During the talks, the confederates opposed any article that could possibly contradict the terms agreed with Glamorgan, or preclude further concessions from the king.[45] Moreover, significant constitutional changes would also have greatly facilitated the implementation of any religious concessions.

---

41 Lowe, "Negotiations between Charles and the confederates" p. 419. Cregan appears unclear as to Ormond's involvement in the whole affair, arguing at first that the lord lieutenant remained completely ignorant of the treaty's existence, but adding later that it was inconceivable that he had no knowledge of developments. Cregan, D.F., "Confederation of Kilkenny" (PhD thesis) pp 186, 327. 42 Glamorgan to Ormond, 29 Aug. 1645 (Bodl. Carte Mss 15 f.534). Colonel Barry's name appears on the treaty itself. Glamorgan treaty (BL Add Mss 25,277 f.62). As already outlined, Gerald Fennell kept Ormond fully informed of developments in Kilkenny, and there may have been others who did likewise. 43 Ormond/Glamorgan correspondence in Bodl. Carte Mss 15 f.535, 580-1; 16 f.264, 319 etc. 44 On 31 January 1646, Glamorgan praised Ormond's "great prudence" in insisting on not seeing certain documents. This is the closest that either man comes to admitting that the lord lieutenant knew about, although he was probably not shown a copy of, Glamorgan's treaty (Bodl. Carte Mss 16 f.486). 45 Bodl. Carte Mss 65 ff 255-60 provides a summary of negotiations between September and November 1645.

The confederates, therefore, resurrected the demand for a suspension of Poynings' law, "until the articles of pacification be established and confirmed by parliament".[46] Ormond disapproved, but added that he would "cause whatsoever shall be further directed by his Majesty to be passed in parliament for and on behalf of his subjects, to be accordingly drawn into bills and transmitted according to the usual manner, to be afterward passed in parliament". In this way, concessions such as the Glamorgan treaty terms could in theory be passed by parliament, though the legislative initiative would remain with the king and his deputy. Ormond also refused the demand for a declaratory act, "that point being held unfit for any other determination than what his Majesty in his high wisdom hath declared in his answer to that proposition".[47]

Despite their differences, with the papal nuncio waiting to sail from France, both sides appeared anxious to conclude an agreement, before the arrival of "so unbidden a guest".[48] In early November (shortly after Rinuccini had landed in Munster), the confederate delegation suddenly announced that they would be content with an exemption from the oath of supremacy, the removal of penalties for the exercise of their religion, and the abolition of the court of high commission. Crucially, the treaty would contain no clause to prevent the granting of further concessions by the king, thus leaving the way open for the implementation of Glamorgan's terms. Ormond agreed, though stressing again that his consent should not be interpreted as allowing catholics to enjoy churches.[49] The confederate leadership, therefore, in effect presented the nuncio with a *fait accompli*, a fact he acknowledged in an early letter back to Rome.[50]

Rinuccini arrived in Ireland on 12 October 1645 with precise instructions from Rome on matters of policy, but very little practical guidance. Although expected to promote church reform, his primary objective was "to establish in Ireland an unalterable right to the public exercise of the catholic religion".[51] The papacy

---

**46** Enlargement of concessions desired by the confederates, 11 Sept. 1645 (Gilbert [ed.], *Irish confederation*, v, p. 88). **47** The confederates would have to be content with a simple declaration by the Irish parliament. With the peace faction back in control after the dissolution of the general assembly, Ormond was able to report in late 1645 that the suspension of Poynings' law "was denied upon such important reasons of law and state as hath given that satisfaction therein, as their agents insist no further upon it". Treaty negotiations, Oct.-Nov. 1645 (ibid., pp 115-6, 191). **48** This was Ormond's description of Giovanni Battista Rinuccini, archbishop of Fermo and papal nuncio to Ireland. Ormond to Glamorgan, 22 Nov. 1645 (Bodl. Carte Mss 16 ff 254-5). Considering Scarampi's opposition to the cessation in 1643, Glamorgan's treaty in 1645, and the general thrust of the peace negotiations, both royalists and the peace faction must have awaited the arrival of the papal nuncio with some trepidation. **49** Treaty negotiations in Gilbert (ed.), *Irish confederation*, v, pp 165-87. **50** Rinuccini to Pamphili, 23 Dec. 1645 (Aiazza [ed.], *Embassy*, pp 94-100). **51** Instructions to Rinuccini from Innocent X (Aiazza [ed.], *Embassy* pp xxvii-xlix); Rinuccini's interest in church reform is superbly analysed in Ó hAnnracháin, "Far from terra firma" pp 381-417, although claims that this was the nuncio's

opposed any truce, treaty or peace concluded without this concession, but adopted a more conciliatory line on political issues. Innocent X viewed the conflict in Ireland as a religious war, and hoped to use developments there to persuade Charles I to improve the position of catholics in England. For this reason he instructed Rinuccini to stress to the confederates that the practice of catholicism could be compatible with loyalty to the English crown.[52]

The arrival of Rinuccini in Ireland has been portrayed by historians as a major turning point for the confederates, and indeed his impact, as the highest ranking diplomat in Kilkenny, proved immediate and far reaching. However, far from creating discord and dissent, as some have argued, Rinuccini simply exploited existing tensions to pursue his own agenda.[53] The papal nuncio gave leadership and direction to those who, as the events during the assembly in 1645 clearly illustrated, already opposed the policies of the peace faction. From this time onwards, the clerical faction became closely identified with the personality and policies of Rinuccini.

Many of those favouring a speedy settlement did not have a problem with the appointment of a nuncio, but rather with the timing of his mission. As early as 1643, the supreme council had petitioned Rome for a nuncio, recommending the first papal agent Scarampi, but in late 1645 with a peace treaty imminent, Rinuccini represented a potentially ruinous obstacle.[54] Royalists expressed particular concern, and Queen Henrietta Maria sent her personal chaplain, George Leyburn, to Ireland in December 1645 to help counter the nuncio's influence. The lord lieutenant, not surprisingly, disapproved of Rinuccini's mission, while only the earl of Glamorgan appeared willing to try and win his support for peace.[55]

---

primary aim are difficult to credit. Rinuccini may have arrived in Ireland with reforming intentions but confederate politics soon consumed him.  **52** Instructions (Aiazza [ed.], *Embassy* pp xxvii-xlix). The link Rome made between Ireland and England is clearly illustrated in the terms of the treaty between the English royalists and Innocent X in November 1645 (ibid. pp 573-4).  **53** Ohlmeyer, for example, claims Rinuccini's "persistent meddling in Irish affairs ... wrought havoc within the Confederation and served to polarise the Catholic political factions and to undermine the confederate war effort". Ohlmeyer, "Independent Ireland", *Independence to occupation* p. 108.  **54** Supreme council to Urban VIII, 1 Oct. 1645 (Gilbert [ed.], *Irish confederation*, iii, pp 21-2). Another potential area of conflict was in the fact that a number of leading confederates held significant tracts of monastic lands, including Richard Bellings, Geoffrey Browne and Viscount Mountgarret. The council had already petitioned unsuccessfully for a papal bull confirming these titles, prior to Rinuccini's arrival. Supreme council to Luke Wadding, 28 June 1643 Gilbert [ed.], *Irish confederation*, ii, pp 278-9); Ó hAnnracháin, "Far from terra firma" pp 203-5. Innocent X hoped to regain church lands in private catholic possession, empowering the nuncio to treat with the existing owners for its return. Nonetheless, recognising the extreme sensitivity of the issue, the pope instructed Rinuccini to proceed with "great circumspection" and "by gentle means". Instructions (Aiazza [ed.], *Embassy* pp xxvii-xlix).  **55** Queen Henrietta Maria to Clanricarde, May 1645 (Lowe [ed.], *Clanricarde letter-book* p. 196). Ormond expressed his hostility to Rinuccini in a letter to

Among the confederates, Rinuccini detected a certain coolness in the welcome of Viscount Mountgarret, president of the supreme council, and divisions within the council itself. According to the nuncio, on the one side lay the peace party, wearied by conflict and driven by self interest, and on the other the clerical party, who had little confidence in their king and favoured expelling all enemies entirely from the kingdom.[56] He noted with concern the desire of the majority of the council to make peace on political grounds while remaining silent on ecclesiastical affairs, and remarked caustically in a letter to Rome "that the peace has long been fully determined on".[57]

The nuncio embarked on a pro-active strategy, insisting on further changes to the religious treaty. On 20 December Glamorgan agreed to certain additions, including the stipulation for a catholic lord lieutenant after Ormond, and permission for catholic bishops to sit in parliament. Furthermore, the terms of a settlement with Ormond were not to be published until the king had ratified the Glamorgan treaty, but in the meantime 3,000 troops could be sent for the relief of Chester.[58] The proposal for bishops in parliament went far beyond permitting full and free practice of the catholic religion. Rinuccini, however, already believed that any peace, regardless of the terms, would produce a rupture in confederate ranks. He simply wished to state his demands, while at the same time prepare the clerics and their allies for the inevitable clash with a council controlled by the lord lieutenant's "relations, friends, clients or dependants".[59]

The arrest of Glamorgan, in late December 1645, threw the entire peace process into confusion. Two months earlier, the archbishop of Tuam, Malachy O'Queely, had been killed in a skirmish near Sligo by forces loyal to the English parliament. They discovered among his papers a copy of Glamorgan's "secret"

---

Glamorgan. Ormond to Glamorgan, 22 Nov. 1645 (Bodl. Carte Mss 16 ff 254-5); Glamorgan replied on 28 November 1645 that he would obtain "a total assent from the nuncio" for the peace settlement (Bodl. Carte Mss 16 f.264). **56** On the supreme council at this time, the peace faction was represented principally by Viscount Mountgarret (president of the council), Richard Bellings (secretary), Viscount Muskerry, the earl of Castlehaven, Gerald Fennell and Geoffrey Browne. The four archbishops and the bishop of Clogher represented the clerics (though the archbishop of Tuam was killed just prior to Rinuccini's arrival). See appendix 2 (table 13) for the full list. **57** Rinuccini to Pamphili, 28 Nov. and 23 Dec. 1645 (Aiazza [ed.], *Embassy* pp 93-100). **58** O'Ferrall and O'Connell (eds), *Commentarius*, ii, pp 86-9. The issue of catholic bishops in parliament had been raised by the ecclesiastical congregation during the previous assembly. Ibid., i, pp 524-36. By late 1645 Chester was the last major English port in royalist hands. **59** Rinuccini wrote in his report to Rome on 23 December 1645 that "the sole aim of council is to the marquis" (Aiazza [ed.], *Embassy* pp 94-100). The nuncio convinced those bishops then present in Kilkenny (Dublin, Cashel, Ossory, Cork, Waterford, Clogher, Clonfert and Ferns) to sign a protest against the planned peace, which could be used at a later date. Hynes, *Mission of Rinuccini* pp 43-4.

treaty, which appeared in print shortly afterwards in London.[60] When news of this reached Dublin, Ormond, to forestall accusations of complicity in Glamorgan's actions, arrested the earl. As Thomas Nugent explained in a letter to George Lane, "I doubt not his Excellency had no hand in it other than of form".[61]

With the supreme council in recess for the Christmas holiday and the provincial armies scattered throughout their winter quarters, Rinuccini seized the initiative in Kilkenny. He convened a meeting of those council members still present in the city and urged an immediate assault on Dublin.[62] The arrival of Viscount Muskerry calmed the atmosphere, and he convinced the council to summon a general assembly instead, much to the nuncio's disgust. Rinuccini viewed the summons as nothing more than a delaying tactic by the peace faction, allowing them time to regroup. Muskerry substantiated the nuncio's suspicions, declaring, on hearing of Glamorgan's subsequent release, that he would have preferred to cancel the assembly.[63]

Despite the imminent meeting of the assembly, on 28 January the council ordered Patrick Darcy and Geoffrey Browne to proceed with the negotiations, "because no time should be omitted to bring the treaty of peace to a happy conclusion". Darcy does not appear to have travelled to Dublin on this occasion, and was replaced by John Walsh, another experienced lawyer. On 3 February, two days before the opening session of the assembly, Ormond wrote to Glamorgan in Kilkenny that, after meeting Browne and Walsh, there remained "no difference between my sense and theirs".[64]

Rinuccini's hopes of postponing the treaty appeared slim, particularly in view of accusations of electoral malpractice against the peace faction.[65] The arrival in Kilkenny of details of yet another peace treaty, however, concluded the previous November between Innocent X and Kenelm Digby, a representative of Queen Henrietta Maria, further confused the issue. The articles had been sent to Rinuccini by the pope (arriving at the beginning of February), along with autho-

---

**60** *The Irish cabinet or his majesties secret papers..taken in the carriages of the archbishop of Tuam ...*, London 1645/6 (RIA vol. 45, box 41, tract 4). The news of the treaty appears to have reached Dublin at the end of December. The warrant for Glamorgan's arrest was issued on 26 December (Bodl. Carte Mss 16 f.339). **61** Sir Thomas Nugent to George Lane, 13 January 1646 (Bodl. Carte Mss 16 f.413). Arthur Annesley, writing from Belfast on 6 Jan. 1646, speculated that Ormond was forced to arrest Glamorgan because "the people [Irish protestants] were so enraged to see religion betrayed". McNeill, Charles (ed.), *The Tanner letters* IMC, 30 (Dublin 1943) pp 201-2. **62** Rinuccini to Pamphili, 1 Jan. 1646 (Aiazza [ed.], *Embassy* pp 110-11). **63** Lowe (ed.) *Clanricarde letter-book* pp 201-2; Rinuccini to Pamphili, 1 Jan. 1646 (Aiazza [ed.], *Embassy* pp 110-11); Antrim and Clanricarde were among those who provided the bail for Glamorgan's release. Ohlmeyer, *Civil war and restoration* p. 165. **64** Supreme council to Ormond, 28 Jan. 1646 (Gilbert [ed.], *Irish confederation*, v, pp 255-6); Ormond to Glamorgan, 3 Feb. 1646 (ibid. p. 257). Supreme council orders, Jan. 1646 (Bodl. Carte Mss 16 f.461, 463). **65** The main complaint, however, that of appointing "ex officio"

risation to alter them according to the existing state of affairs in Ireland. Unfortunately for the nuncio he only received a coded copy, which could not otherwise be verified, but it proved a valuable instrument for delay nonetheless.[66]

In return for 100,000 crowns of Roman money, paid to Queen Henrietta Maria by Innocent X, catholics would enjoy the free and public exercise of their religion, a restoration of the ecclesiastical hierarchy, and possession of church property. The treaty terms also included the annulment of all penal laws since the reign of Henry VIII, and the enactment of all concessions in a free Irish parliament (independent of that of England). The principal offices and strongholds of the kingdom of Ireland would be in catholic hands, with royalist and confederate forces uniting against those of the Scots and English parliamentarians. In return, the royalists expected the confederates to send 12,000 troops over to England. All terms had to be fulfilled within a year or the pope would no longer be obliged to keep his side of the bargain.[67]

The general assembly session began on 5 February 1646, and two days later Rinuccini addressed the meeting. He argued that the Glamorgan treaty had been totally discredited by the earl's arrest, and urged assembly members to wait for the arrival of the original copy of the Roman treaty before committing themselves to any peace.[68] In the meantime, he supported sending troops to relieve Chester, the last major port in England still in royalist hands. Peace faction supporters replied that Ormond's authority to conclude a peace expired on 1 April, and might not be renewed. Moreover, the first article of the political treaty promised to make good religious matters in the future, whereas the Roman treaty would be strenuously opposed by protestants in Ireland and England.[69]

The nuncio insisted, however, that both treaties be published together, to ensure the implementation of all the terms. Crucially, Rinuccini had already obtained the earl of Glamorgan's agreement to withdraw his own treaty in favour of the one concluded in Rome. Even though Rinuccini's intervention threatened to undermine his plans, Glamorgan explained to Ormond that it would be impossible to carry the country "contrary to the nuncio's satisfaction".[70]

persons for enemy controlled corporations, made practical sense and was probably standard policy throughout the 1640s. Rinuccini to Pamphili, 13 Feb. 1646 (Aiazza [ed.], *Embassy* p. 116). **66** According to Rinuccini, the supreme council also received notification of the Digby treaty (ibid. p. 117). **67** Treaty between Sir Kenelm Digby and Innocent X (Aiazza [ed.], *Embassy* pp 573-4). **68** Two accounts of this assembly survive, one written by the nuncio at the time, the other by Richard Bellings almost thirty years later. Given their diametrically opposed views it is hardly surprising that the two versions differ considerably. Bellings' History in Gilbert (ed.) *Irish confederation*, v, pp 8-16; Rinuccini's account is contained in a series of letters to Cardinal Pamphili during February and March 1646 (Aiazza [ed.], *Embassy* pp 113-28). **69** Rinuccini to Pamphili, Feb./March 1646 (Aiazza [ed.], *Embassy* pp 113-28). **70** Glamorgan to Ormond, 8 Feb. 1646 (Bodl. Carte Mss 16 f.502). A shrewd observation as subsequent events demonstrated.

The supreme council, anxious not to jeopardise the peace settlement through a prolonged public debate, sought to defuse the crisis. Council members agreed to extend the truce with the royalists until 1 May, while sending troops to Chester without delay. If the Roman treaty had not arrived by that date, the responsibility for agreeing religious terms reverted to Glamorgan and the nuncio. Political negotiations could continue in the meantime, but until "a conclusion and publication of it [religious treaty], the other also may not be concluded or published".[71] Rinuccini celebrated the postponement of the Ormond treaty, remarking in a letter to Rome that the confederates had stepped back from the "precipice to which since last September they were tending".[72]

Bellings' memoirs, while confirming the basic details of the nuncio's account, differs in one crucial respect. He claimed that the full assembly read and approved *all* the articles of the Ormond treaty, and "looked on the performance of the condition for sending over the men [to England] as the sole obstacle which gave interruption to the conclusion of the peace". Furthermore, the assembly then ordered the new supreme council to meet with the old council, and the committee of treaty, on 1 May "to remove any obstruction which might occur in the way of a perfect conclusion of the peace".[73] According to Bellings, therefore, the assembly, having approved of the settlement terms, authorised the council to conclude a treaty. The clerical apologist, Walter Enos, agreed that on 2 March the assembly ordered the supreme council to prepare all matters concerning the peace treaty, but denied that the council possessed sufficient authority to order the committee of treaty to conclude a settlement.[74]

Unfortunately, the committee of treaty's original commission from the general assembly on 20 July 1644 no longer survives. However, following the dispersal of the assembly on 31 August 1644, the supreme council, on behalf of the assembly, granted the committee full power "to treat, agree *and conclude* with [Ormond] for a fine, lasting and settled peace within this kingdom".[75] The council (including a number of bishops) renewed this commission on at least two occasions prior to March 1646, and it seems hardly credible that any fundamental altering of the commission would have gone unnoticed in the assembly for so long.[76]

71 The agreement, signed on 19 February, also stated that there would be no change in confederate government until both treaties "maybe at once and together concluded and published by the approbation of the general assembly if it shall be seen necessary to the said lord nuncio and earl of Glamorgan to call it". Enos "Survey" in Gilbert (ed.), *Irish confederation*, vi, pp 419-20. 72 Rinuccini to Pamphili, 13 Feb. 1646 (Aiazza [ed.], *Embassy* p. 118). 73 Bellings' History in Gilbert (ed.), *Irish confederation*, v, pp 8-16. 74 According to Enos, the committee of treaty had petitioned frequently in assemblies for the power not only to treat and agree but also to conclude a treaty. He could not find any evidence of such a power ever being granted, unless "factionists" [i.e. peace faction] managed to slip "surreptitious orders" through a sparsely attended assembly meeting. Enos "Survey" in Gilbert (ed.), *Irish confederation*, vi, pp 365-6. 75 Ibid., iii, p. 269. The emphasis in the quotation is my own. 76 The commission was

If, as seems likely, the confederate commissioners possessed sufficient autho-risation to conclude a settlement with the lord lieutenant, why did their signing of the treaty cause such controversy? The issue of what exactly assembly mem-bers discussed during February 1646 now assumes crucial importance. Enos acknowledged that all members, including the bishops, consented to the Ormond treaty, but insisted that the actual terms (as published in August of that year) differed considerably, particularly on the question of religion. According to Enos, therefore, the terms changed between the assembly debate in February, and the end of March when the confederate commissioners signed the treaty with Ormond in Dublin.[77]

Although Enos specifically set out to discredit the treaty, letters in Clanricarde's collection reveal evidence of a dispute between the assembly and the supreme council about the peace talks. When the negotiations resumed in late January, Ormond (no doubt concerned at the prospect of a hostile protes-tant reception after the Glamorgan fiasco) insisted that a number of private con-cessions not be announced publicly in the assembly.[78] These probably refer to the king's earlier guarantee to abolish the penal laws, by act of parliament, once the war had been won.[79] The general assembly, however, proved reluctant to commit troops to Chester without receiving all the relevant information about the settle-ment. By way of a compromise, Clanricarde suggested that certain proposals be published and the rest verbally imparted to those "of quality and judgement".[80]

In a further letter to Viscount Muskerry, Clanricarde recommended an alter-native strategy, if the assembly continued to insist on full disclosure. He suggest-ed that the public terms be read first, and then the private presented "as proposi-tions of yours that had been debated here [Dublin] but not brought to a perfect conclusion". Muskerry should imply that obtaining them remained contingent on the rapid supply of troops for the king.[81] This tactic probably explains the

renewed on 5 April 1645 (signed by the bishop of Clogher among others) and again on 13 June 1645 (clerical signatories on this occasion included the archbishops of Armagh, Tuam and Cashel, as well as Clogher). April 1645 commission (Gilbert [ed.], *Irish confederation*, iv, p. 209); June 1645 commission (Bodl. Carte Mss 15 f.160). In March 1646, Rinuccini acknowl-edged that the existing committee of treaty retained the authority to conclude a peace, and was "obstinate to the last in not yielding up the absolute power vested in them by past com-mittees and therefore did not chose to refer or remit the whole question to the general meet-ing". Rinuccini to Pamphili, 5 March 1646 (Aiazza [ed.], *Embassy* p. 128). **77** Enos "Survey" in Gilbert (ed.), *Irish confederation*, vi, pp 425-30. **78** Clanricarde to Muskerry, 14 Feb. 1646 (Lowe [ed.], *Clanricarde letter-book* pp 212-13). **79** This secret correspondence between the king and the confederate commissioners (Browne, Plunkett and Muskerry) in late 1644, early 1645, is discussed in chapter 2. See [15 Dec.] 1644 Charles to Ormond (Gilbert [ed.], *Irish con-federation*, iv, pp 104-7). **80** Clanricarde to R.J., 13 Feb. 1646 (Lowe [ed.], *Clanricarde letter-book* pp 210-2). Clanricarde does not identify those "of quality and judgement", but presum-ably he meant those people who would be satisfied by such private assurances. **81** Clanricarde to Muskerry, 14 Feb. 1646 (ibid. pp 212-13). Rinuccini did not disagree in principle with the assembly members' (including the bishops) enthusiasm for sending an expeditionary force to Chester, and the resumption of peace talks in Dublin. Certainly, the assembly's final declaration before the meeting dispersed implied that an amicable settlement had been reached.[82] With both factions (clerical and peace) involved in a game of bluff and counter-bluff, trying to outmanoeuvre one another at every possible opportunity, the publication of any treaty was likely to cause disruption.

Although the assembly may have concluded on a harmonious note in respect of the negotiations, evidence exists of widespread discontent in assembly ranks at the general performance of confederate government, and a call for the implementation of further reform measures. The litany of complaints generating this demand (inefficiency, lack of accountability, and financial mismanagement) echoed those listed in June 1644, but the solutions on this occasion proved very different.[83]

To ensure greater efficiency in matters of government, the assembly reduced the supreme council in size, to "consist of nine and no more and those to be constantly resident". The ensuing elections saw the return of two existing members from each province, along with Richard Bellings as secretary. As five of the new council also sat on the committee of treaty, resulting in lengthy absences from Kilkenny, the assembly ordered that "five or more of the said council shall suffice to sit and sign". Once the negotiations had been completed, however, seven members would be necessary to hold a council meeting.[84]

As in 1644, the reformers emphasised the principle of accountability, and the subordination of the executive branch of government to the legislature. They introduced annual assemblies, rather than leaving the summons at the discretion of the supreme council. This directive, similar to the establishment of regular

council withholding information, arguing that "perhaps it is well not to reveal important deliberations to the whole of their number". On one occasion, he obtained concessions from his confederate opponents, who were afraid he might reveal all the facts concerning the treaty negotiations to the general assembly. Rinuccini to Pamphili, 13 Feb. 1646 (Aiazza [ed.], *Embassy* pp 118). **82** On 4 March 1646, the general assembly ordered "that anything contained in any order made during this assembly that may clash with or vary from the settlement made and ordered in, and by the Establishment made and concluded at this present general assembly shall not be binding but proceeding as in such matters to be made consonant and agreeing with the aforesaid Establishment, not withstanding any such orders" (Bodl. Carte Mss 16 ff 470-80). A statement like that must have been written by a lawyer! **83** The two reform documents are 1644 (Marsh's Library Mss z 3.1.3); 1646 (Bodl. Carte Mss 16 ff 470-80). **84** 1646 reforms (Bodl. Carte Mss 16 ff 470-80). The new council consisted of Viscount Mountgarret, Nicholas Plunkett (Leinster); Viscount Muskerry, Donough O'Callaghan (Munster); Lucas Dillon, Patrick Darcy (Connacht); Bishop MacMahon of Clogher and Alexander MacDonnell (Ulster); Richard Bellings (secretary). Mountgarret, Muskerry, Plunkett, Darcy and MacDonnell were also members of the committee of treaty. See appendix 2 (table 13) for a list of council members, while committee members are listed in chapter 7 (table 6).

parliamentary meetings by Scots covenanters in 1640, envisaged a more active role for the assembly in confederate politics.[85] Moreover, in future "an able clerk" would attend meetings of the council to keep a record of orders and dispatches, not only to ensure compliance with assembly directives but also as a means of monitoring performance.[86]

The reform proposals in 1646 differed most significantly from those in 1644 on the issue of provincial councils. In 1644 the reformers had favoured provincial autonomy as a means of curtailing the power of central government. The assembly in 1646 did not seek to restrict the role of the executive, but rather to increase its efficiency. This involved streamlining the confederate administration through the abolition of provincial and county councils, and by transferring responsibility to the clergy for the collection of tithes and rents on church lands. Clerical collectors did not have to be paid a salary, and would (in theory at least) be more honest in their dealings than the multitude of lay officials they replaced.[87]

This particular measure supports the notion that for the first time the clergy may well have backed reform measures directed against existing governmental practices.[88] This fact may also explain the successful implementation of the 1646 reforms, unlike many of the proposals in 1644. Evidence also exists of links between Nicholas Plunkett and the clerical faction, with one assembly member commenting to Clanricarde in February 1646 on the religious zeal which had transformed "our leading zealot [Plunkett]". He appears to have been greatly affected by the arrival of Rinuccini, and shortly after the assembly dispersed, joined the nuncio on a military sub-committee.[89] Their co-operation on reform

85 Brown, *Kingdom or province?* pp 119-20. 86 1646 reforms (Bodl. Carte Mss 16 ff 470-80). The assembly was clearly unhappy with the state of council records kept by the existing secretary, Richard Bellings. This proposal may well have been connected with the earlier dispute over the council withholding information from assembly members. 87 Another financial reform, forbidding the payment of rent to neutrals or enemies of the confederates, would have hit Ormond hard. Between September 1643, when the first truce came into effect, until the collapse of the peace treaty in late 1646, Ormond received over £12,000 for mortgaging his estates in confederate territory. The surviving records indicate he was only receiving about £600 in annual rents from other lands (NLI Calendar of Ormond deeds D.3951-4384). 88 Lowe's suggestion that Rinuccini supported the move to reduce the size of the supreme council is not an improbable one considering the nuncio's complaint about the size of the previous council. Lowe, "Negotiations between Charles and the confederates" p. 460; Report on the state of Ireland, 1 March 1646 (Aiazza [ed.], *Embassy* p. 133). 89 The report by the anonymous assembly member (known only by the initials R.J.) concludes, however, that an element of self-interest may also have been involved in Plunkett's behaviour. R.J. to Clanricarde, 11 Feb. 1646 (Lowe [ed.], *Clanricarde letter-book* pp 208-10). Shortly after his arrival in Ireland, Rinuccini criticised the lack of a confederate "council of war" to direct the military campaign. He lobbied unsuccessfully for such a council, but eventually in April 1646 the supreme council created a sub-committee to liaise with the nuncio on military matters, consisting of Bishop MacMahon, Lucas Dillon, Donough O'Callaghan and Nicholas Plunkett. The committee quickly lapsed as the peace crisis unfolded during the course of the summer, but may have provided a further opportunity for

measures was the first indication of an alliance which would transform confeder-ate politics in September 1646.

For the present, however, factional conflict overshadowed all else, as the com-promise agreed between the nuncio and his opponents quickly began to unravel. Rinuccini had no intention of allowing the Ormond treaty to be published in May. In a report on the state of Ireland written at the end of the assembly, the nuncio speculated that the defeat of Charles might actually help the Irish cause, uniting all catholics in opposition to the English parliament. He believed that the confederates should try to gain possession of the entire kingdom through aggres-sive military campaigns.[90] For their part, the peace faction remained determined to press ahead with a peace settlement, even without the nuncio's consent.

On 12 March the confederate commissioners returned to Dublin to complete the negotiations with Ormond, while preparations continued to transport 3,000 Irish troops to Chester.[91] Confederate anxiety to conclude a treaty before the lord lieutenant's authorisation expired on 1 April forced them to moderate their demands. The king's denunciation of Glamorgan and the fall of Chester to the forces of the English parliament, news of which finally reached Ireland in mid-March, failed to delay proceedings.[92] On 28 March 1646, almost three years to the day since the presentation of the remonstrance at Trim, the two sides signed a peace treaty and left the document in the safe keeping of Clanricarde.[93]

Ormond refused the supreme council's pleadings to join forces against the Scots, but gave assurances to the committee of treaty that if any hostile forces attacked the confederates he would appear in arms against them.[94] The signato-ries agreed to postpone publication of the terms until confederate troops reached England. This delay suited the confederate commissioners, who had agreed with the nuncio not to conclude any deals until 1 May.[95] They subsequently failed to

Plunkett to acquaint himself with the views of the clergy. O'Ferrall and O'Connell (eds), *Commentarius*, ii, pp 192-3; Report on the state of Ireland, 1 March 1646; Rinuccini to Pamphili, 11 April 1646 (Aiazza [ed.], *Embassy* pp 139-40, 159). **90** Report on the state of Ireland, 1 March 1646 (Aiazza [ed.], *Embassy* pp 133-147). **91** Confederate preparations to transport troops to England (PRO SP Ire. 261/12 f.76, 261/15 f.80 etc.). Rinuccini presumed the confederate com-missioners had gone to Dublin to conclude the treaty, which again strongly suggests that the clerical faction did not dispute the commissioners' authority. Rinuccini to Pamphili, 12 March 1646 (Aiazza [ed.], *Embassy* p. 148). **92** Charles to Ormond, 30 Jan. 1646 (Bodl. Clarendon Mss 98 f.112). The arrival of parliamentary commissioners to Dublin at the beginning of March, although they left for Belfast shortly afterwards, would have further increased the anxiety of the council for a speedy settlement. Ormond to Arthur Annesley, 2 March 1646 (Bodl. Carte Mss 16 f.573). **93** Treaty articles, 28 March 1646 (Bodl. Carte Mss 176 ff 205-8). See also Gilbert (ed.), *Irish confederation*, v, pp 286-310. **94** Glamorgan to Ormond, 18 March 1646 (Bodl. Carte Mss 16 f.666), Ormond to Muskerry, 30 March 1646 (Bodl. Carte Mss 17 f.28). This assurance was published two weeks later much to Ormond's irritation, although the supreme council protest-ed their innocence on the matter (Bodl. Carte Mss 17 f.135). **95** By delaying publication of the treaty until 1 May, the commissioners could at least argue they had maintained the spirit of their

inform Rinuccini that the treaty had been signed, although the conclusion of the talks appears to have been common knowledge in Dublin.[96]

Subterfuge and deceit characterised the following four months until the publication of the treaty, as each faction tried to outmanoeuvre the other. The total collapse of the royalist position in England during 1646 made the confederates understandably reluctant to transport troops across the Irish Sea, while the seizure of Bunratty castle early in the year by a force of 2,000 English parliamentarians provided additional justification for postponing the expedition. The supreme council could not ignore the threat posed to the Munster heartland, and on 3 April, just six days after the signing ceremony, Viscount Muskerry notified Ormond of the council's decision to use the troops on the domestic front.[97]

Throughout April and May, the council sought clarification from Ormond on the sensitive issue of religious concessions. Nicholas Plunkett travelled to Dublin and informed the lord lieutenant that if he published the civil articles in May, the confederates believed it wise to proclaim Glamorgan's religious concessions at the same time. Not to do so, he continued, would result in the loss of foreign aid "and endanger a rupture in the kingdom" (most probably within confederate ranks). Ormond replied that the articles could not be published as the troops had not yet been sent, adding that if the confederates insisted on Glamorgan's terms, he would disown them, "his majesty having already by declaration so done".[98]

Ormond's refusal to compromise presented the council with a serious dilemma. Should they push ahead with the publication of Glamorgan's terms, and risk having them denounced by the lord lieutenant, or alternatively omit the religious articles and hazard a complete rupture with the clerical faction? At the beginning of June, the existing supreme council, along with former council members and the committee of instruction, assembled in Limerick (where the nuncio had already taken up residence) to discuss the crisis. Plunkett, recently returned from Dublin, informed the meeting of the king's surrender to the Scottish army near Newark. The confederate leadership decided immediately to halt any further transport of troops to Scotland (frustrating Antrim's hopes of re-

agreement with the nuncio. **96** On 2 April 1646, a Dublin resident, Valentine Savage, informed Edmund Smith that the articles of peace had been signed the previous Saturday, and would be published when the confederate troops reached England. *HMC, Egmont*, vol. 1, Part 1, pp 284-5. It is clear, however, from Rinuccini's letter to Cardinal Pamphili on 6 April that he was unaware that the treaty had already been signed. Aiazza (ed.), *Embassy* pp 156-7. **97** Muskerry to Ormond, 3 April, 1646 (Bodl. Carte Mss 17 f.49). This decision also caused problems for Antrim who was trying to raise a levy for Scotland. Ohlmeyer, *Civil War and Restoration* pp 169-73. **98** Instructions of the supreme council to Nicholas Plunkett, 16 April 1646 (Bodl. Carte Mss 17 f.160); Ormond's answer, April 1646 (Gilbert [ed.], *Irish confederation*, v, pp 332-3). **99** Bellings to Ormond, 2 June 1646 (Bodl. Carte Mss 17 f.440). This was clearly an informal gathering, as Plunkett wrote to Ormond that the supreme council had "called hither sundry of the

enforcing Alasdair MacColla in the Western Isles).[99]

The marquis of Clanricarde, in a letter to Patrick Darcy (who attended the meeting), warned against expecting Glamorgan's concessions to be proclaimed considering the king's present position. He argued that if the confederates dropped that demand, the lord lieutenant would "proclaim the peace immediately upon his own articles". Moreover, the marquis advised them not to insist on maintaining their association until peace terms had been settled in a parliament, but instead put all government in the hands of the lord lieutenant.[100] The prospect of an immediate publication of the treaty, resulting in a full reconciliation with the royalists, greatly appealed to the peace faction, but appalled the nuncio.

This dispute went to the core of the dilemma facing Kilkenny throughout the 1640s. Anxious for an speedy resolution of their conflict with the king, the confederate leadership failed to develop an alternative strategy, even as the royalist position collapsed in England. Rinuccini alone appears to have identified the weakness in their position, and he advocated instead a complete conquest of the kingdom. The nuncio's aggressive military strategy in 1646 was not "extremist", but rather constituted a pragmatic assessment of developments in the three Stuart kingdoms. Only with the royalist revival in 1648 did the peace faction policy of an alliance with the king once again become a feasible option.[101]

Controversially, the meeting in Limerick agreed not to publish the Glamorgan treaty, given the impossibility of the king granting religious concessions in public at this time.[102] The personal intervention of Rinuccini, however, provoked a tense debate as he counselled in favour of waiting for papal aid. News of the king's surrender and Owen Roe O'Neill's stunning victory over Monro at Benburb on 5 June strengthened his position. Council members favouring an immediate conclusion of the peace treaty argued that accommodation with the royalists remained the only option for the confederate association. Rinuccini (furious on discovering that the treaty had already been signed) produced a declaration, signed by a majority of bishops on 6 February, warning against a peace without the consent of the nuncio.[103]

nobility and others". Plunkett to Ormond, 3 June 1646 (Bodl. Carte Mss 17 f.445). **100** Clanricarde to Darcy, 6 June 1646 (Lowe [ed.], *Clanricarde letter-book* pp 257-61). Considering that the king had just surrendered to the Scots presbyterians, implacable enemies of Irish catholics, this was at best very dubious advice. **101** The royalist revival in 1648 is examined in chapters 5 and 6. **102** According to Bellings, the meeting in Limerick was conducted without rancour as "there was no great contrariety of opinions in the debate". This was obviously prior to the nuncio's intervention. Bellings' History in Gilbert (ed.), *Irish confederation*, vi, pp 3-6. **103** Again, according to Bellings, the council greatly resented the interference of the bishops, as by signing such a document they did "single themselves out of the body of the confederate catholics". Bellings' History in Gilbert (ed.), *Irish confederation*, vi, pp 3-6; Rinuccini to Pamphili, 20 June 1646 (Aiazza [ed.], *Embassy* p. 180).

In a conciliatory gesture before the meeting at Limerick dispersed, the council assured a sceptical nuncio that until the king's wishes were known, the treaty could not be concluded.[104] The crucial decision, however, not to publish the Glamorgan terms alongside the political settlement remained in place, and on 12 June, Nicholas Plunkett and Geoffrey Browne received instructions to this effect from Thomas Tyrrell, chairman of the committee of instructions, to convey to Ormond.[105] The confederates left the publication date, therefore, entirely at the discretion of the lord lieutenant.

Before departing to Dublin, Plunkett and Browne visited Rinuccini to seek his blessing, but the nuncio instead fell into "a violent passion", leaving the two agents in no doubt as to the strength of his opposition to the peace.[106] Nonetheless, the peace faction seriously underestimated their principal opponent, believing he required authorisation from Innocent X before taking any action. By that time the Ormond treaty would have been well established and the confederates fully reconciled with the king. The council's complacency appeared justified when Rinuccini raised no objections to the missions of Edward Tyrrell (Paris) and Bernard Davetty (Rome). Their instructions made it clear that the confederates intended to publish Ormond's treaty on its own, but without waiving the concessions agreed with Glamorgan.[107]

In all probability Rinuccini had already started to plan an alternative strategy, after realising the futility of further arguments with the council. On the military front, both Owen Roe O'Neill and Thomas Preston pledged their support to the nuncio, who declined their offers to march on Dublin for the moment "lest it should be said I had superseded Ormond without the consent of the supreme council".[108] The two generals, however, played a central role as the crisis developed. On the political front Rinuccini decided to summon the ecclesiastical congregation to Waterford, to deliberate on the pending treaty, and allow the nuncio to acquaint himself with clerical opinion. More importantly, opposition to the peace would now be identified with the clergy as a whole, rather than the nuncio as an individual.[109]

---

**104** Rinuccini to Pamphili, 20 June 1646 (Aiazza [ed.], *Embassy* p. 180). **105** The committee of instructions, having fulfilled its primary function, then disbanded. Instructions by committee, 12 June 1646 (Bodl. Carte Mss 17 f.492); Bellings' History in Gilbert (ed.), *Irish confederation*, vi, p. 6. **106** This encounter deeply upset Plunkett, and may well have further undermined his conviction regarding the desirability of the peace treaty. Ibid. p. 5; Cregan, D.F., "Confederation of Kilkenny" (PhD thesis) pp 228-30. **107** Bellings' History in Gilbert (ed.), *Irish confederation*, vi, pp 13-16. Tyrrell was coadjutor to the archbishop of Dublin, and brother of Thomas, chairman of the committee of instruction. Davetty was a Jesuit priest who died on the return journey from Rome in September 1648. O'Ferrall and O'Connell (eds), *Commentarius*, iii, pp 658-65. **108** Rinuccini to Pamphili, 17 July 1646 (Aiazza [ed.], *Embassy* p. 189). Although less spectacular than O'Neill's successes in Ulster, Preston's campaign in Connacht made good progress during the summer, leading to the capture of Roscommon in July. **109** Rinuccini to Pamphili, 3 Aug. 1646 (Aiazza [ed.], *Embassy* p. 193).

Meanwhile, the arrival of the king's secretary of state, George Digby, in Dublin early in July hastened the process towards publishing the treaty. He brought news that Charles had conveyed to Queen Henrietta Maria in Paris his approval of a peace with the confederates, and publicly declared that the king's orders to the lord lieutenant on 11 June to cease negotiations had been "contrary to his free judgement".[110] In addition, the envoy du Moulin announced the French state's willingness to act as arbiter in the agreement between Ormond and the confederates. In return the French hoped to recruit large numbers of troops in Ireland for service abroad.[111]

Confident of his support both in Ireland and on the continent, Ormond finally published the treaty on 30 July, in the presence of a confederate delegation led by Viscount Muskerry. Almost three years after the first cessation came into effect, the negotiating process had at last borne fruit. On 3 August the supreme council also proclaimed the treaty, and prepared to hand over power to the lord lieutenant. Crucially, they ignored previous promises to maintain the structures of confederate government until the terms of a settlement had been ratified in the Irish parliament. Instead, as soon as Ormond reached Kilkenny "the supreme council received him with all due respect and surrendered their government to him".[112]

The treaty itself contained 30 articles, the first of which declared that catholics, on taking office, need only subscribe to the oath of allegiance rather than of the oath of supremacy. The document, however, simply referred the repeal of the penal laws "to his Majesties gracious favour and further concessions", leaving all matters of religion to be dealt with elsewhere.[113] As the Glamorgan treaty had already been denounced by the king (and the Roman treaty remained unverified), the lack of religious concessions in the treaty with Ormond represented a major gamble by the confederate delegation after years of negotiation. The peace faction, however, clearly accepted private assurances concerning freedom of religion, once the impediments to royal service had been removed.

**110** Statement by Lord Digby, 28 July 1646 (Gilbert (ed.), *Irish confederation*, vi, pp 55-7). Charles, a prisoner of the Scottish army at Newcastle, ordered Ormond "to proceed no further in treaty with the rebels nor to engage us upon any condition with them after sight hereof". *The lord marquess of Argyle's speech to a grand committee of both houses of parliament, 25 June 1646 ... also his majesty's letter to the marquess of Ormond*, London 1646 (BL Thomason Tracts E341 f.25); Carte, *Ormond*, vi, p. 392. The king's letter reached Dublin on 26 June. Armstrong, "Protestant Ireland" p. 226. **111** Du Moulin to Ormond, 2 July 1646 (Bodl. Carte Mss 65 f.313). Rinuccini was unimpressed by this French intervention, believing it nothing more than a royalist ploy. Ó hAnnracháin, "Far from terra firma" pp 260-1. **112** Declaration of Ormond, 29 July 1646 (Bodl. Carte Mss 18 f.121); Declaration of the supreme council, 3 Aug. 1646 (Bodl. Carte Mss 18 f.237); Tuchet, *Castlehaven's memoirs* p. 120. **113** After the appointment of catholics to certain governmental positions, no further distinction was to be made on the grounds of religion. Treaty articles, 1646 (Gilbert [ed.], *Irish confederation*, v, pp 286-310).

The second article stipulated that a new Irish parliament be convened before 1 November 1646, to ratify the treaty terms. Residential and property qualifications were introduced for the Commons and Lords, but the settlement contained nothing about Poynings' law. All bills had to be transmitted to England according to the existing practice, although Ormond guaranteed they would not be altered there in any way. On the issue of independence, another clause allowed that the Irish parliament "make such declaration therein as shall be agreeable to the laws of the kingdom of Ireland", with no provision, however, for a declaratory act.[114] The concessions represented no significant gains on those offered to the Irish parliamentary delegation by Charles in 1641.

On the positive side, the treaty included a clause to vacate all attainders and indictments enacted since 7 August 1641, at least 40 days before the next parliament. This measure effectively removed any impediments on catholics voting or sitting in parliament. The treaty terms gave no indication as to whether the franchise in the forthcoming elections extended to those catholics actually in possession of the land, or the original freeholders prior to the revolt. The balance of probabilities, however, favours the latter group, which fact (along with the large number of protestant boroughs) would ensure the catholics did not control parliament. Further reforms dealt with residency issues and the use of proxy votes, in an attempt to eradicate the worst abuses prevalent before 1641.[115]

A further concession by the royalists provided for an act of oblivion for all acts committed since 23 October 1641. For particularly "barbarous" crimes the confederates favoured trial by parliament rather than suspect courts, but eventually agreed on a commission to deal with the problem.[116] The majority of the other articles centred on issues dating back to the Graces in 1628 or the innovations introduced by Thomas Wentworth. The reforms included overturning the Connacht plantation, introducing an act of limitation on royal titles, removing all incapacities on natives, and giving catholics permission to erect schools, a university and inns of court. The court of wards was to be replaced by a yearly payment of £12,000 to the crown, and limits placed on the jurisdiction of the chief governor, the council board and the court of castle chamber.[117] Despite the

114 The relevant clause on Poynings declared that "his Majesty is graciously pleased to call a new parliament to be held in this kingdom, on or before the last day of November next ensuing, and that all matters agreed on by these articles to be passed in parliament, shall be transmitted into England, according to the usual form, to be passed in the said parliament, and that the said acts so to be agreed upon, and so to be passed, shall receive no alteration or diminution here or in England". Idem. 115 Idem. The large number of new Ulster boroughs in effect guaranteed a protestant majority in any Irish parliament. See map 2 for the distribution of parliamentary seats. 116 Armstrong, "Protestant Ireland" p. 162 117 The income derived from the court of wards during Wentworth's tenure of office averaged around £7,000 per annum, so Ormond had struck a good deal for the king on this issue. Kearney, *Strafford in Ireland* p. 80.

importance of these concessions, dealing with many of the long term grievances of Irish catholics, they represented a poor return on almost four years of war.

Disturbing reports, emanating from Waterford, of clerical opposition to the treaty soon shook peace faction complacency. The clergy had framed a new oath of association, whereby confederates swore to oppose any peace not approved by the ecclesiastical congregation.[118] The supreme council decided to send Nicholas Plunkett and Patrick Darcy to Waterford with copies of the treaty, to persuade sceptics of the advantages of peace. At the same time the council urged Ormond to deploy troops "towards the parts from whence most danger is to be expected".[119]

The choice of Plunkett and Darcy, two distinguished lawyers capable of explaining the complexities of the treaty, made perfect sense. Both men had been directly involved in the negotiating process, but had also helped broker the religious compromise between clergy and council in June 1645.[120] On arriving in Waterford they tried, at least at first, to defend the treaty, drawing attention to a secret pledge of the supreme council to summon a general assembly and fight if the religious concessions ultimately proved unacceptable.[121] The arrival of an aggressive letter from Bellings, questioning the competence of the ecclesiastical congregation to oppose an agreement of the secular government, destroyed any prospect of a reconciliation between the two factions. A counter charge by the clerical faction accused their opponents of misleading the assembly, as a number of articles read to that body did not appear in the treaty itself.[122]

On 12 August the ecclesiastical congregation declared unanimously ("none contradicting") that the peace violated the oath of association, principally because of the lack of religious concessions. Four days later, the congregation dispersed, giving full authority to a committee, comprised of Rinuccini and eight others, to act on its behalf.[123] Conflict now seemed unavoidable. Rinuccini in a letter to Rome reported that the lords of Munster and Ulster, aggrieved at their exclusion from office, and "the most zealous towns in the kingdom" supported the clergy.[124] Uncertainty over the stance of Thomas Preston and Owen

---

118 Form of oath prescribed by ecclesiastical congregation at Waterford, [Aug.] 1646 (Bodl. Carte Mss 18 f.327). 119 Mountgarret to Ormond, 11 Aug. 1646 (Bodl. Carte Mss 18 f.242). He simply replied that the council should deploy their own forces to counter any internal threat. Gilbert (ed.), *Irish confederation*, vi, p. 92. 120 This compromise is discussed earlier in the chapter. Both Plunkett and Darcy signed the supreme council's declaration on 3 August announcing the peace treaty (Bodl. Carte Mss 18 f.237). 121 Report on peace, 16 Aug. 1646 (Aiazza [ed.], *Embassy* pp 195-200). 122 Ó hAnnracháin, "Far from terra firma" pp 214-15. The clerical charge is discussed earlier in the chapter. 123 Declaration of ecclesiastical congregation against peace, 12 Aug. 1646 (Bodl. Carte Mss 18 ff 250-1). See also Gilbert (ed.), *Irish confederation*, vi, pp 71-2. 124 Report on peace, 16 Aug. 1646 (Aiazza [ed.], *Embassy* pp 195-200). Strong opposition to the treaty emerged in a number of confederate towns and cities. Bellings criticised Clonmel, for example, as "the rendezvous of all the turbulent spirits in the

Roe O'Neill may have tempered the clergy's demands, and they produced a more conciliatory statement after "serious debate" with Plunkett and Darcy, who had returned a second time from Kilkenny.[125]

The new document criticised the supreme council for failing to publish the concessions agreed with Glamorgan, and for not honouring the commitment to maintain confederate authority until the settlement had been ratified by the Irish parliament. The clerics also observed that the parliament in Dublin had recently dispersed, before taking any steps to void the records of indictments and attainders against individual confederates. Moreover, neither Preston nor O'Neill had been allocated positions in the new military structure, a staggering miscalculation by the council. This fact, indicative of the suspicion with which the peace faction viewed all military exiles, further alienated potential support in the provincial armies for the peace treaties.[126]

The clerical faction demanded the immediate publication of Glamorgan's treaty, and the maintenance of confederate government until the meeting of a new Irish parliament. They also sought the repeal of penal legislation against catholics, the suspension of Poynings' law, and the appointment of Preston and O'Neill as general of horse and sergeant major general of the field respectively.[127] Providing these terms proved acceptable, the clerical faction expressed a desire to see the present confederate government remain in power, and form an alliance with the royalists against the king's enemies. Otherwise the clerics insisted on a meeting of the general assembly.[128] It is hardly a coincidence that the demand for an assembly emerged shortly after Nicholas Plunkett, chairman of the previous six assemblies, arrived back in Waterford.

The supreme council promised to seek further concessions from Ormond, but continued to make preparations to receive the lord lieutenant and his forces into Kilkenny. When news of Ormond's departure from Dublin reached Waterford Rinuccini authorised the publication of the decree of excommunication, a move which finally drove Plunkett and Darcy into the nuncio's camp.[129]

province". Burke, W.P. , *History of Clonmel*, pp 63-4. **125** Declaration of the ecclesiastical congregation to the supreme council, 24 Aug. 1646 (PRO SP Ire. 261/51 ff 207-10). Plunkett and Darcy were in effect acting as mediators between Waterford and Kilkenny. Mountgarret to [Bishop Ferns], 26 Aug. 1646 (Bodl. Clarendon Mss 28 f.191). **126** Declaration of ecclesiastical congregation, 24 Aug. 1646 (PRO SP Ire. 261/51 ff 207-10). **127** The failure to obtain (at the very least) a suspension of Poynings' law constituted one of the main accusations levelled by the clerical faction against the architects of the peace treaty. Walter Enos accused the treaty commissioners of perjury (breaking the oath of association) having rejected the king's offer to suspend Poynings' law. He added that nothing had been done to dissolve the new corporations in Ulster, "as were unjustly erected to gain voices in the parliament". Enos also expressed outrage that noblemen without estates in Ireland were still permitted to sit in parliament. Enos "Survey" in Gilbert (ed.), *Irish confederation*, vi, p. 337. **128** Declaration of ecclesiastical congregation, 24 Aug. 1646 (PRO SP Ire. 261/51 ff 207-10).   **129** Mountgarret to [Bishop Ferns], 26 Aug. 1646 (Bodl. Clarendon Mss 28 f.191); Castlehaven to Ormond, 28 Aug. 1646

Considering the leading role both men played in negotiating the treaty, their dramatic switch of allegiance excited little critical comment at the time. Their colleague on the council, Richard Bellings, simply noted in his memoirs that fearing clerical sanctions, Plunkett and Darcy "returned no more to those that sent them". Other peace faction members failed to comment at all.[130]

Both men appear to have been motivated by a combination of personal, political and religious considerations. As Rinuccini reported to Rome, the clerical faction received support from a broad spectrum of confederate opinion, with "some drawn by fear of censure, some from private hatred to the council and some also by the common habit of joining the winning side".[131] This final comment appears particularly appropriate in the case of Patrick Darcy, who acquired a reputation during the 1640s as something of a political chameleon. Rinuccini's second-in-command, Dionysius Massari, dean of Fermo, claimed that no one "more frequently turned his coat" than Darcy. The anonymous author of the *Aphorismical discovery* described him as "a perfidious member to his nation", while John Walsh of Tipperary in a deposition given in 1653 commented starkly that Darcy was "sometimes against the said [clerical] party and sometimes very violently for them".[132]

Darcy's switch of allegiance, on realising the full extent of clerical opposition to the treaty, proved a shrewd act of political expediency. Interestingly, his name does not appear in the treaty among those nominated for office, even in the judiciary. This omission, deliberate or otherwise, would hardly have endeared him to the new royalist regime.[133] Although an experienced politician, Darcy may well have been influenced by Rinuccini's spiritual authority, particularly on the matter of excommunication. Thomas Wentworth once described him as "earnest in the way of his own religion", and the combined voice of the Irish clergy, led by a papal nuncio, could not easily be ignored.[134]

(Bodl. Carte Mss 18 f.356). The decree of excommunication was published on 1 September (Bodl. Carte Mss 18 f.414). Ormond left Dublin with Clanricarde, Digby and a small band of troops. Cregan, D.F., "Confederation of Kilkenny" (PhD thesis) p. 232. **130** Bellings' History in Gilbert (ed.), *Irish confederation*, vi, p. 17. One possible reason for the lack of criticism from the peace faction is that most accounts were written years later, by which time both men had changed sides again, actively supporting the second Ormond peace. The one exception is the Plunkett manuscript in the National Library, where the author describes Nicholas Plunkett as one "who in his bigotry was a while of the nuncio's party". NLI Plunkett Mss 345 (A treatise or account of the war and rebellion in Ireland since the year 1641) f.57, 559. **131** Report of the affairs of Ireland, 1649 (Aiazza [ed.], *Embassy* p. 499). **132** Deposition of John Walsh, Co. Tipperary, 14 Feb. 1653 (TCD Mss 830 f.249a); Massari, Dionysius, "My Irish campaign", *Catholic bulletin*, vol. 8 (1918) p. 478; *Aphorismical discovery* in Gilbert (ed.), *Contemporary history*, i, p. 40. **133** He was appointed, however, as one of the commissioners to oversee the implementation of the treaty. The full list of those appointed to office is included in item 8 of the peace treaty. Gilbert (ed.), *Irish confederation*, v, pp 286-310. **134** Kearney, *Strafford in Ireland* p. 92.

As for Nicholas Plunkett, religion undoubtedly proved an important motivating factor. Plunkett, a remarkably talented lawyer, and popular assembly chairman, also appears to have been an extremely devout catholic. One royalist source, late in 1644, described him as "wholly Jesuited".[135] In April 1646 Gerald Fennell informed Ormond that he had full confidence in Plunkett, with one exception. If the dispute arose about religion, Fennell feared "that he will not take his own way". Viscount Muskerry also warned Ormond that Plunkett was "a zealous catholic and violent that way", but added "he is fallen of much in that of late".[136]

This reputation for religious zeal appealed greatly to Rinuccini, unimpressed by the secular attitudes of many leading confederates. In December 1645, shortly after his arrival in Ireland, the nuncio described the assembly chairman as "one of our most honoured members of council and perhaps the man of all others best affected to the catholic religion to be found at present in this kingdom". As the crisis began to unfold in August 1646, Rinuccini informed Rome that Plunkett had "sustained to the utmost the catholic party in the supreme council". Later, in his report of the mission written after returning to the continent in 1649, the nuncio praised Plunkett and his ally Nicholas French, bishop of Ferns, as "good catholics certainly but at the same time not bad politicians".[137]

This last comment captures the essence of Nicholas Plunkett. A reluctant rebel, he had remained neutral in the early days of the uprising, supporting Clanricarde's compromise initiative in March 1642, and attracting criticism from Viscount Gormanston as a result. Accusations of self-interest surfaced early in 1646 when one of Clanricarde's correspondents agreed with the earl that forces other than religious zeal drove Plunkett. "Interest is the thing", he declared emphatically.[138] Certainly, Plunkett's actions in the years leading up to the peace do not give the impression of a man motivated by religious fervour. Late in 1644, for example, he joined Muskerry and Geoffrey Browne in recommending a compromise on the religious question to the king. In return for secret guarantees to repeal the penal laws, they expressed a willingness to moderate their religious demands in the peace negotiations with Ormond.[139]

Divisions in confederate ranks over the treaty emerged publicly during the course of the 1645 general assembly, chaired by Plunkett. It is difficult to gauge

135 [Sir William Usher to Sir Philip Percivall], 4 Oct. 1644 in *HMC, Egmont*, vol. 1, part 1, pp 237-40. Religious devotion clearly ran in the family, as his brother, Patrick, was consecrated bishop of Ardagh on 19 March 1648. Cregan, "Counter-reformation episcopate" p. 87. 136 Muskerry to Ormond, 18 April 1646 (Bodl. Carte MSS 17 f. 180); Fennell to Ormond, 14 April 1646 (Gilbert [ed.], *Irish confederation*, v, pp 329-30). For Plunkett's involvement in the Clanricarde peace initiative see chapter 1 pp 36-8. 137 See Aiazza (ed.), *Embassy* pp 105-7, 193-5, 509-11. 138 Gormanston to Clanricarde,14 April 1642 (Bourke, *Clanricarde memoirs* p. 123); R.J. to Clanricarde, 11 Feb. 1646 (Lowe [ed.], *Clanricarde letter-book* pp 208-10). 139 The other two delegates were Viscount Muskerry and Geoffrey Browne. Charles I to Ormond, [15 Dec.] 1644 (Gilbert [ed.], *Irish confederation*, iv, pp 104-5). See chapter 2 pp 80-2.

how these factional disputes affected him, but the arrival of a papal nuncio a few months later undoubtedly influenced his thinking. Nonetheless, Plunkett remained active in the peace negotiations throughout the summer, and supported the treaty as published by Ormond.[140] His defection a short time later to the clerical faction was most likely due to a well-developed political acumen (sensing that the pendulum of popular support had swung against the treaty), underpinned by religious devotion and a desire to reform confederate government. The marquis of Clanricarde (and George Digby), however, did suspect a degree of premeditation in the actions of the leading moderates, such as Plunkett and Darcy, during August 1646.[141]

As the peace faction's authority disintegrated, Ormond's procession through confederate territory encountered increasing difficulties. Facing armed opposition in Munster, and with O'Neill's army rapidly approaching from the north, the marquis retreated back to Dublin, only escaping across the Barrow river with the assistance of the confederate commander Walter Bagenal.[142] Ormond's humiliating flight and the subsequent confirmation of Preston's rejection of the treaty emboldened the clerical faction, who issued a fresh declaration. They proclaimed their loyalty to Charles, but vowed to unite all catholics against the common enemy and rejected the peace "concluded by a few interested persons".[143]

140 Plunkett, however, did not sign the peace treaty with Ormond on 28 March 1646. There is no evidence to suggest he opposed the signing, but his absence is puzzling nonetheless and indicated perhaps an attempt to maintain some degree of independence. Treaty articles, 1646 (Gilbert [ed.], *Irish confederation*, v, pp 286-310). 141 Clanricarde wrote that some confederates (unfortunately not named) "purposely to take occasion to quarrel with the peace and raise new distempers, they would need have all the concessions concerning religion quite left out of the articles and referred to his majesty's future grace and favour". Lowe (ed.), *Clanricarde letter-book* p. 325. The complete absence of religious articles from the Ormond treaty was indeed startling, and Digby claimed they were left out "by the subtlety of some of their own party who intended to found this late mischief upon it". Digby to Ormond, 18 Nov. 1646 (Carte, *Ormond*, vi, pp 457-60). This would certainly help explain Plunkett's involvement in negotiating the treaty before subsequently denouncing the settlement. Clanricarde appears to have distrusted Plunkett and the other moderates, and condemned the "mischievous practices of some few persons hiding their private guilt under the spurious pretence of zeal to religion". Clanricarde to Sir John Winter, 20 Feb. 1647 (Lowe [ed.], *Clanricarde letter-book* p. 358). At a later stage, he commented on Geoffrey Barron, Nicholas Plunkett "and their mischievous associates". Clanricard to Ormond, 8 Jan. 1647 (Carte, *Ormond*, vi, pp 489-90). As with so many conspiracy theories during the 1640s, it is impossible to verify or dismiss Clanricarde's claims entirely. The balance of evidence, however, indicates that Plunkett and Darcy simply took advantage of developments as they occurred. 142 Without Bagenal's intervention at Leighlin Bridge Ormond's small force would probably have been intercepted by the Ulster army. Bagenal was imprisoned by Rinuccini as a result of his actions. Prendergast Papers, King's Inns, Mss 2 f.994. 143 The supreme council had made serious attempts to ensure the loyalty of Preston, writing to him on a number of occasions in early August 1646 (PRO SP Ire.

The supreme council, with few options remaining, reopened negotiations with the papal nuncio. Lucas Dillon and Gerald Fennell arrived in Waterford on 8 September, with expectations fluctuating "betwixt hopes and despairs". On 10 September the peace faction agreed to all clerical demands, except on the repeal of penal legislation and the suspension of Poynings' law, insisting that the clergy had already consented to the first article of the Ormond treaty. All outstanding issues would be addressed in the next parliament, leaving catholics in the meantime unmolested in their ecclesiastical possessions, or in the practice of their religion.[144]

On 15 September the clergy rejected these terms, and imprisoned the proponents of peace, including Muskerry, Fennell and Bellings.[145] They established a new government on 26 September 1646, "until a general assembly shall either confirm our proceedings therein or establish another course".[146] Strictly speaking clerical actions did not constitute a *coup d'état*, as the previous supreme council had voluntarily renounced its authority to Ormond, creating a power vacuum when he retreated to Dublin. The clergy, therefore, simply filled the void, "all face of government being amongst us dissolved", as the earl of Castlehaven explained.[147]

The clerical faction nominated a new supreme council of 17 members, with Rinuccini as president. It included among others the three provincial generals, Thomas Preston, Owen Roe O'Neill, and the earl of Glamorgan, who had replaced the discredited Muskerry in Munster, as well as the bishop of Ferns and Nicholas Plunkett.[148] Patrick Darcy accepted a judicial position along with Hugh Rochford and William Hore of Cork. In a significant development, the new council ruled in association with the ecclesiastical congregation, ensuring a direct clerical input into the new regime, but otherwise all confederate officials received orders to proceed "according to the model of government".[149]

261/37 f.137, 261/42 f.191). Finally, however, the notoriously indecisive general wrote to the bishops that he would "never do or consent to do any act entrenching thereon or [on] my religion". Preston to [Bishop Ferns], 24 Aug. 1646 (PRO SP Ire. 261/52 f.211). The clerical declaration was issued on 10 September (PRO SP Ire. 262/3 ff 4-5). **144** Dillon and Fennell to Ormond, 11 Sept. 1646 (Bodl. Carte Mss 18 f.492); Presumably, when talking of prior clerical consent, the supreme council are referring to the previous general assembly in February 1646. The dispute over what exactly assembly members discussed at this meeting is covered earlier in the chapter. Answers of supreme council to congregations demands, 10 Sept. 1646 (Gilbert [ed.], *Irish confederation*, vi, pp 132-4). **145** Declaration of congregation, 15 Sept. 1646 (Bodl. Carte Mss 18 f.513); Bellings' History in Gilbert (ed.), *Irish confederation*, vi, p. 21. **146** Order by ecclesiastical congregation, 26 Sept. 1646 in Moran (ed.), *Spicilegium Ossoriense*, ii, pp 27-9. **147** Castlehaven to Ormond, 28 Aug. 1646 (Bodl. Carte Mss 18 f.356). **148** The clerical faction may well have selected Glamorgan, a neutral figure in some respects, in the hope of reconciling the various factions in Munster. Ó hAnnracháin, "Far from terra firma" pp 309-11. **149** Order by ecclesiastical congregation, 26 Sept. 1646 in Moran (ed.), *Spicilegium Ossoriense*, ii, pp 27-9.

Rinuccini, hoping to achieve his goal of outright military victory, immediately began to organise an assault on Dublin.

In the space of two months the nuncio had succeeded in overthrowing the Ormond peace, arresting his enemies, and assuming control of confederate government. Major miscalculations on the part of the peace faction facilitated his success. Muskerrt and his allies totally underestimated the extent of clerical opposition to their actions and as such made no contingency plans. The failure to find positions for commanders such as Preston and O'Neill deprived them of crucial military support, while the immediate recognition of Ormond's leadership further negated whatever influence they retained among the confederates.

The lord lieutenant's delay in leaving Dublin enabled the clerical faction to organise themselves and fill the power vacuum in confederate territory. The nuncio's personal authority as papal representative, combined with the powerful weapon of excommunication (fully supported by the clergy), seriously undermined the authority of the peace faction. The defection of Plunkett and Darcy also proved a crucial, if not decisive, factor. Both men had been closely involved in the peace process, and their switch of allegiance gave substantial credibility to the clerical opposition. The broad support the nuncio received, during August and September 1646, would not otherwise have been forthcoming.

# An uneasy compromise

෴

## SEPTEMBER 1646–APRIL 1647

> You Irish which doe boast and say
> 'Tis for the king you fight and pray
> Tell me now I crave
> Wherefore doe you a peace deny
> "On the breach of the peace", 1646[1]

The confederate assault on Dublin was a complete fiasco from start to finish. Bad timing, mistrust, treason and sheer incompetence combined to thwart Rinuccini's grand strategy. The nuncio had believed for quite some time that only a complete conquest of the island could safeguard confederate interests, while also allowing them to come to the assistance of the king and English catholics.[2] Despite the undeniable logic of Rinuccini's argument, in practical terms his plan proved extremely difficult to implement. The string of confederate victories had given the nuncio a distorted sense of their military capacity. The royalists, parliamentarians and Scots still controlled three distinct territorial blocs (north-east Ulster, Dublin and Cork), as well as numerous outposts, each of which could only be reduced by a lengthy and costly siege.

Even after his crushing victory at Benburb in June 1646, Owen Roe O'Neill made little headway in Ulster. This failure is usually blamed on the nuncio's intervention, insisting on summoning O'Neill southwards as the peace crisis unfolded, but that did not occur until two months later.[3] In fact the Ulster forces dispersed during the summer months, as the soldiers returned home with the spoils of battle and to gather in the harvest. O'Neill did not have the troops,

---

1 Contemporary poem in *HMC*, 14th Report, appendix, part 7, p. 109. 2 Shortly after the general assembly dispersed in March 1646, the nuncio wrote of the confederates' need to gain possession of the entire kingdom. Rinuccini to Pamphili, 22 March 1646 (Aiazza [ed.], *Embassy* p. 153). 3 See for example Hollick, Clive, "Owen Roe O'Neill's Ulster army of the confederacy, May-August 1646", *Irish sword*, vol. 18 (1991) p. 224. Cregan also argues that O'Neill could have gained control of the entire province after Benburb. Cregan, D.F., "Confederation of Kilkenny" (PhD thesis) p. 221.

equipment or supplies to undertake a determined assault on the Scots heartland around Belfast and Carrickfergus, and by August General Monro had returned to the field "with a good number of men".[4]

In Connacht, Preston's original orders stressed the importance of recapturing Sligo, a parliamentarian stronghold, "the taking of which place only will give the lord nuncio more satisfaction and draw more help from his holiness".[5] Preston made good progress and by July had taken the town of Roscommon. This constituted an important breakthrough in itself, but as long as Sligo was in enemy hands, the confederate position in Connacht remained vulnerable.[6] In Munster, Viscount Muskerry took the castle of Bunratty in July, but Inchiquin's forces in Cork retained an offensive capability. The viscount's army scattered shortly afterwards, angry over arrears of pay and rife with internal divisions, leaving the confederate heartland of Tipperary and Limerick inadequately protected.[7]

On the other hand, the royalists in Leinster appeared to be in total disarray, which in itself may have justified the nuncio's decision to launch an offensive in that province. The first problem to beset the confederates, however, concerned the timing of the campaign itself. Instead of moving against Dublin in mid-September (before the on-set of winter), their forces only reached the outskirts of the city by early November, when poor weather and the dearth of supplies made a prolonged siege extremely difficult. The nuncio's moves to consolidate his authority in Kilkenny preoccupied the confederates during most of September and delayed the campaign.[8] Moreover, whereas Rinuccini wanted to

---

**4** Stevenson, *Covenanters and confederates* p. 234; Massari, Dionysius, "My Irish campaign", p. 249; Casway, J., *Owen Roe O'Neill and the struggle for catholic Ireland* (Philadelphia 1984) pp 137-8. Even in early September, O'Neill's intentions were unclear to both confederates and royalists. Daniel O'Neill to Roscommon, 1 Sept. 1646 (Bodl. Carte Mss 22 f.190). **5** Supreme council to Preston; instructions for Connacht expedition, 11 April 1646 (Bodl. Clarendon Mss 27 ff 125-6). The death of the much respected Malachy O'Queely, archbishop of Tuam, in a skirmish outside the town the previous year, provided another incentive to capture Sligo. **6** Massari claims that after publishing the peace treaty, the supreme council recalled Preston from Roscommon, thus preventing him from attacking Sligo. Massari, Dionysius, "My Irish campaign", p. 301. Preston was in close contact with the supreme council during the first weeks in August, and probably needed no encouragement to halt his offensive and monitor developments in Waterford and Kilkenny (PRO SP Ire. 261/37 f.183, 261/42 f.191, 261/46 f.198). **7** Bellings' History in Gilbert (ed.), *Irish confederation*, v, pp 16-8. The dispute in the Munster army, and its effect on confederate fortunes in the province, is examined in the next chapter. **8** The clerical faction only established their new supreme council on 26 September . Order by the ecclesiastical congregation, 26 Sept. 1646 (Gilbert [ed.], *Irish confederation*, vi, pp 144-6). Rinuccini had tried to divert O'Neill's forces to Dublin to take advantage of the lord lieutenant's military disarray. The Ulster general, however, marched to Kilkenny, on the pretext that he lacked cannon for a siege. Rinuccini to Pamphili, 21 Sept. 1646 (Aiazza [ed.], *Embassy* p. 204). Whatever the reason, O'Neill would hardly have undertaken an assault on Dublin with the confederate government still in a state of upheaval.

rely on Owen Roe O'Neill alone, "the less resolute" (meaning Bishop French) insisted on Thomas Preston's involvement.[9]

Although the tensions associated with this dual command undoubtedly contributed to the shambles which followed, it is difficult to envisage an alternative strategy.[10] Neither general possessed sufficient strength on his own to undertake the campaign with any degree of confidence. In any event, having already summoned O'Neill southwards to assist the clerical faction Rinuccini could hardly now exclude the Ulster general in favour of Preston. Employing O'Neill alone, however, would have caused widespread revulsion among Leinster confederates, with the possibility of defections to the lord lieutenant. The problem lay in provincial and historic rivalries, but the foraging tactics of the Ulstermen also gave rise to much resentment.[11]

Finally, the new regime in Kilkenny may have been concerned by the threat posed to their authority by a hostile and inactive Leinster army. Preston welcomed the peace at first, and only confirmed his loyalty to the clerical faction on hearing of the actions of the ecclesiastical congregation in Waterford. Involving the Leinster general in the campaign, therefore, made sense, if only to ensure his continued support and to occupy his troops.[12] Appointing both men also promoted the idea of confederate unity, a policy pursued with great vigour by Bishop French and others over the next twelve months.

The conspiratorial activities of a number of confederates seriously undermined the Dublin campaign. Preston, while accepting command of the expedition, balked at the prospect of confronting the lord lieutenant. He viewed with concern the rapid growth of O'Neill's forces, describing them as "an unlimited multitude of licentious caterpillars".[13] The Leinster general opened private chan-

9 Report on the affairs of Ireland, 1649 (Aiazza [ed.], *Embassy* pp 500-1). The bishop's connection with Preston went as far back as 1635, when both men were present at the siege of Louvain. Bindon, S.H. (ed.), *The historical works of the right reverend Nicholas French D.D* (Dublin 1846), vol. 1, p. xxx. Scarampi, who was on good personal terms with the Leinster general, also lobbied for his inclusion. Ó hAnnracháin, "Far from terra firma" pp 280, 438-46. 10 Corish, *NHI*, iii, pp 321-2; Wheeler, Scott, "Four armies in Ireland", *Independence to Occupation* pp 55-6. 11 Efforts were made as early as 1644 to control the activities of O'Neill's troops and camp followers. "Propositions touching the present government, 1644" (Marsh's Library, Mss z 3.1.3); O'Ferrall and O'Connell (eds) *Commentarius*, i, pp 573-7. For examples of the resentment aroused by the Ulster forces see Robert Preston to Thomas Preston, 18 April 1647 (PRO SP Ire. 263/105 f.176 ), Patrick Darcy to Thomas Preston, 20 April 1647 (PRO SP Ire. 263/108 f.180 ), Leinster Committee to Thomas Preston, 21 April 1647 (PRO SP Ire. 263/109 f.182 ). 12 Preston to Ormond, 12 Aug. 1646 (Bodl. Carte Mss 18 f.257); Preston to [Ferns], 24 Aug. 1646 (PRO SP Ire. 261/52 f.211). 13 The Leinster general informed Clanricarde that the threat posed by the Ulster forces required "the application of some speedy antidote to prevent the infallible destruction thereby like to ensue". Preston to Clanricarde, 14 Oct. 1646 (Lowe [ed.], *Clanricarde letter-book* pp 292-3).

nels of communication with Ormond, offering military support in return for assurances on the issue of religion.[14]

Meanwhile, discontent began to manifest itself in the ranks of the Leinster forces, with both the earl of Westmeath and Thomas Nugent returning home, vowing never to serve with O'Neill. These developments merely intensified Preston's notorious indecisiveness. The supreme council, aware of the dangers, insisted that the Leinster general take a new oath to assist O'Neill and "use and exercise all acts of hostility against the lord Marquis of Ormond and his party".[15] That council members deemed such an oath necessary is an extraordinary comment on the perceived loyalty of a leading confederate general.

The council's suspicions proved well warranted, as Preston continued to correspond with the enemy. The Leinster general proposed that the marquis of Clanricarde join with him, "that we may fix on resolutions for preventing the ensuing evils". Clanricarde declined this offer and pursued an alternative strategy, tentatively suggesting to the supreme council that he act as an intermediary between Dublin and Kilkenny. The council responded cautiously, pressing ahead with their military offensive, while at the same time exploring possibilities for a political settlement.[16]

In an unusual development, council members decided to accompany the confederate forces on the campaign, rather than attempting to direct events from Kilkenny. Rinuccini often complained about the lack of a confederate council of war, as once a military campaign began the input of the political leaders diminished, while the generals enjoyed total autonomy in the field.[17] Considering the importance of the campaign against Dublin, and the potential

14 Colonel Fitzwilliam to Ormond, 22 Sept.1646 (Bodl. Carte Mss 18 f.553). George Digby requested at meeting with the supreme council early in October to discuss a possible settlement. His subsequent assessment of the confederate position noted that Preston, in return for religious guarantees, would almost certainly join forces with the lord lieutenant. Digby to Ormond, 13 Oct. 1646 (Bodl. Carte Mss 19 f.170). Preston's duplicitous behaviour (often using Digby as an intermediary) was a constant feature in confederate politics over the next 12 months, and contributed greatly to the disasters which followed. 15 Cadogan to Ormond, 17 Oct. 1646 (Bodl. Carte Mss 19 f.206); Copy of an oath taken by Thomas Preston, 21 Oct. 1646 (Bodl. Carte Mss 65 f.331). 16 Preston to Clanricarde, 14 Oct. 1646; Clanricarde to Rinuccini, 20 October 1646; Supreme council to Clanricarde, 25 Oct. 1646 (Lowe [ed.], *Clanricarde letter-book* pp 292-300). Clanricarde had of course been acting as just such an intermediary since the first cessation in September 1643, attending a number of assemblies and maintaining close contact with the confederate leadership. 17 Letters of the supreme council from various camps along the route to Dublin (Harristown, Sigginstown, Lucan) outline its movements at this time. PRO SP Ire. 262/14 f.14, 262/19 f.174; Bodl. Carte Mss 19 ff 369-70. Ironically, Rinuccini complained in early 1646 that the supreme council, although inexperienced in military affairs, took all the decisions. Once he became president of the council, however, the nuncio immediately began to dictate military strategy. Report on the state of Ireland, 1 March 1646 (Aiazza [ed.], *Embassy* pp 139-40).

for conflict between O'Neill and Preston, the nuncio was anxious to ensure that the council retained ultimate authority.

As the Clanricarde initiative began to take shape, the confederate forces reached Lucan on the outskirts of Dublin, before indecision and internal divisions prevented any further advance. On 2 November, Preston and O'Neill issued a joint proclamation, calling on Ormond to guarantee freedom of religion and to join the confederates against the forces of the English parliament. The lord lieutenant equivocated, stalling for time by demanding to know from whom the generals derived their authority.[18] With negotiations set to drag on until the confederate armies ran out of supplies, Clanricarde finally presented his proposals to the supreme council on 14 November. These included a revocation in the Irish parliament of all laws against the free exercise of the catholic religion, and a guarantee that no one would be disturbed in their ecclesiastical possessions until the king made his wishes known in parliament.[19]

A second paper recommended a catholic lieutenant-general for the royalist army (a post Clanricarde no doubt coveted for himself), appointments for confederate military leaders, and a promise in the meantime that catholic forces "be drawn into all the chief garrisons under his majesty's obedience". The marquis undertook to gain these concessions from the king as soon as the confederates agreed a peace treaty with Ormond.[20] It remains unclear if this initiative constituted a sincere attempt to broker a compromise, or was specifically designed to split the confederate ranks. Prior to this, Clanricarde's interventions tended to be in good faith. The religious concessions offered by Ormond failed to impress him, while the stipulation for a catholic lieutenant-general suggests an element of self-interest in the whole affair.[21]

The arrival of a parliamentary fleet into Dublin Bay dramatically altered the political and military situation. As the prospect of a successful siege receded, O'Neill, already suspicious of Preston, withdrew his army from the confederate camp. The supreme council refused to contemplate a settlement with the royalists as long as parliamentarian troops remained in the area, and eventually severed all contact with Clanricarde.[22] The nuncio returned to Kilkenny with the

18 Preston and O'Neill to Ormond, 2 Nov. 1646 (Bodl. Carte Mss 19 f.313). Ormond's answer, 4 Nov. 1646 (Bodl. Clarendon Mss 28 ff 281-2). With the royalist army of 4,000 men outnumbered 2 to 1 by the combined confederate forces, there was little else Ormond could do at this time. Wheeler, "Four armies in Ireland", *Independence to Occupation* p. 55. 19 Clanricarde to supreme council, 14 Nov. 1646 (Lowe [ed.], *Clanricarde letter-book* pp 309-11). 20 Ibid. pp 313-14. Without any official support, it is highly unlikely Clanricarde could have obtained the consent of the king (or more importantly Ormond) to any of these concessions, a fact pointed out by the supreme council at a later stage. Supreme council to Preston, 24 Nov. 1646 (PRO SP Ire. 262/31 f.193-4). 21 With Preston and O'Neill to be appointed to other posts, there is no question but that Clanricarde hoped to obtain the position of lieutenant-general for himself. 22 Supreme council to Clanricarde, 15 Nov. 1646 (Bodl. Carte Mss 19 ff 369-70).

rest of the council, but Preston maintained contact with the royalists for another month. By early December, however, the threat of clerical sanctions, combined with Ormond's refusal to allow confederate troops into Dublin, shattered the Leinster general's dream of a broad alliance.[23]

Developments in late 1646, after the retreat to Kilkenny, are the subject of some controversy. Lowe argues that the nuncio lost control of events (albeit only temporarily), while other accounts detect no shift in the balance of power away from the clerical faction.[24] There is no question, however, that the nuncio's scheme of military conquest lay in ruins, and for the moment, he had no strategy beyond the continuance of an unpopular war. The peace faction was similarly in disarray, their leaders under arrest and the marquis of Ormond negotiating with commissioners from the English parliament. The possibility of a settlement with the royalists, or of providing effective opposition to the nuncio, appeared remote.

At this critical juncture, with both confederate factions foundering, the supreme council decided to summon a general assembly, and to release the supporters of the peace treaty, who had been in jail since the middle of September. The impetus for this fundamental shift in policy (essentially a decision to seek a middle ground between the extremes of war and peace) came from Bishop French and Nicholas Plunkett. On 23 November a hastily convened meeting of the council issued election writs and signed the release orders for Muskerry and his allies.[25] It is unclear when exactly Rinuccini arrived back in Kilkenny, although the balance of evidence suggests he attended this crucial meeting. The nuncio, however, specifically ascribed this new policy to Plunkett and French.[26]

In fact, the harsh political and military realities of the time forced the moderates to act. With O'Neill's army retiring to winter quarters, and Preston's attitude

---

23 Preston and his officers in the Leinster army informed Clanricarde of their support for his initiative on 19 November, entering into a formal engagement. Intense negotiations followed, but on 10 December Preston conceded that in the face of clerical threats his army was not "excommunication proof", while Theobald Butler wrote that Ormond's decision not to admit a confederate garrison to Dublin "did change the whole frame of their former resolutions". Lowe (ed.) *Clanricarde letter-book* pp 316-17, 343-4; Theobald Butler to Ormond, Dec. 1646 (Gilbert [ed.], *Irish confederation*, vi, pp 164-5). 24 Lowe, "Negotiations between Charles and the confederates" p. 589. 25 The electoral return for the city of Cork refers to the writ "bearing the date at Kilkenny the 23 of November". Bodl. Clarendon Mss 29 f.8. As the nuncio always mentions the decision to call an assembly and release prisoners together, they were probably both taken at the same meeting. Report on the affairs of Ireland, 1649 (Aiazza [ed.], *Embassy* pp 509-11). 26 Rinuccini was certainly present at the council on 24 November, and may well have been there the previous day. Despite his retrospective condemnation of the decisions, at the time he was enthusiastic in particular about the prospects for an assembly. Supreme council to Preston, 24 Nov. 1646 (PRO SP Ire. 262/31 ff 193-4); Rinuccini to Pamphili, 28 Nov. 1646; Considerations upon the future assembly, 30 Dec. 1646, and Report on the affairs of Ireland, 1649 (Aiazza [ed.], *Embassy* pp 219, 238, 509-11).

at best ambiguous, the position of the ruling clerical faction had become increasingly vulnerable and isolated. Plunkett and French calculated that the calling of the assembly would deflect criticism from the supreme council by showing a willingness to submit to a "higher authority", while the release of Viscount Muskerry and others would (temporarily at least) mollify the peace faction. The objectives of the moderates hinged primarily on preserving confederate unity, and they presented themselves, according to the nuncio at least, as "advocates of equality for all".[27]

Apart from dealing with internal divisions, the moderates had also to decide whether to continue the war, increasingly unpopular after the Dublin fiasco, or attempt another reconciliation with the royalists. With the king a prisoner of the Scots covenanters and Ormond apparently ready to surrender Dublin to the English parliament, the latter option appeared anything but straightforward. Moreover, to be acceptable to a majority of confederates, any new treaty would have to show significant improvement on the previous one, particularly in the crucial area of religious concessions.

Although Nicholas Plunkett spear-headed this drive for a political compromise, he relied heavily on the support of the bishop of Ferns. Nicholas French, born in 1604 of old English extraction, hailed from the confederate stronghold of Wexford and attended the first assemblies as a representative of the town. Appointed bishop of Ferns early in 1645 (before the arrival of Rinuccini), his consecration took place in December of that year.[28] French, and his colleagues the bishops of Clogher, Clonfert, Limerick and Leighlin, belonged to a new generation of young, dynamic, politically active clergy. Gradually during the 1640s, and more noticeably after 1646, these men replaced the older generation, represented by Armagh, Ossory and Meath, as the most influential prelates.[29]

At the general assembly in June 1645, French rose to prominence when he helped Nicholas Plunkett and Patrick Darcy forge a compromise on the contentious issue of retaining churches.[30] Despite his high political profile at this time, the bishop did not feature prominently in the nuncio's early reports to Rome. As the peace crisis began to unfold during the course of 1646, however, Rinuccini and French began to co-operate closely. After the publication of the treaty in August 1646, the bishop acted as a spokesman for the ecclesiastical congregation, in which capacity he negotiated once again with both Nicholas Plunkett and Patrick Darcy.[31]

27 Report on the affairs of Ireland, 1649 (Aiazza [ed], *Embassy* pp 509-11). 28 Bindon (ed.), *Historical works*, vol. I, p. xxxvii; Cregan, "Counter-reformation episcopate" p. 87. 29 Bishop O'Dempsey of Leighlin emerged as a leading opponent of the Ormond peace treaty, while Clogher, Clonfert (later archbishop of Tuam) and Limerick were the most active clerical representatives on the supreme council throughout the 1640s. Bellings' History in Gilbert (ed.), *Irish confederation*, vii, p. 5; For a full list of council members see appendix 2 (table 13). 30 O'Ferrall and O'Connell (eds), *Commentarius*, i, pp 524-42. The negotiations in 1645 are discussed in chapter 3 pp 89-91. 31 Rinuccini to Pamphili, 31 Dec. 1646 (Aiazza [ed], *Embassy* pp

Bishop French's outlook on developments during the 1640s coincided very closely with that of Plunkett. The bishop felt unable to justify the initial uprising, which he described as "an inconsiderate attempt by some northern gentlemen", but he blamed the violent response of the lords justices for forcing the king's loyal subjects into "desperate courses". He argued that the war which followed was essentially "just", fought by Irish catholics to defend their rights, rather than to usurp royal authority. Nonetheless, he dismissed the first Ormond treaty as "not secure for the chief concerns of the catholics", and claimed that the committee of treaty had ignored the rules and instructions given them by the assembly.[32]

For French the strength of the confederates' association lay in unity and co-operation, which he described as "our only bulwark". The bishop later coined what might well have served as the motto of moderate confederates – "that commonwealth doth prosper whose citizens are of one accord".[33] From November 1645 onwards both French and Plunkett worked closely together on the supreme council, promoting a policy of compromise and conciliation. Whereas the general assembly acted as Plunkett's power-base, French commanded respect among the rank and file of the clergy. Between them, therefore, the two men successfully mobilised moderate confederate opinion across the factional divide, and in the process developed a new political strategy.

In retrospect, Rinuccini claimed that the decision to call the general assembly, taken during his tenure as president of the supreme council, caused "all the misfortunes that followed". At the time, however, the nuncio displayed no hostility towards the idea, writing in a letter to Rome of his intention to transfer all authority to the assembly as soon as it met, by resigning as head of government.[34] From the early days of the crisis in August 1646, the clerical faction stressed the temporary nature of their actions. The ecclesiastical congregation claimed that only a general assembly possessed sufficient authority to decide on the major issues of peace and war. Nonetheless, a number of clerical supporters opposed the moderates' strategy, as they believed that such a meeting might allow the peace faction to regain the initiative.[35]

No evidence survives to indicate that Rinuccini shared such fears. In fact, he believed that all important measures "would receive a more ready obedience if they

105-7); Declaration of the ecclesiastical congregation to the supreme council, 24 Aug. 1646 (PRO SP Ire. 261/51 ff 207-10). **32** Bindon (ed.), *Historical works*, vol. 1, pp 35-40, 120; vol. 2, pp 44-52. The background to French's historical works is discussed in appendix 3. **33** Ibid., vol. 2, p. 151. **34** Rinuccini to Pamphili, 30 Dec. 1646; Report on the affairs of Ireland, 1649 (Aiazza [ed.], *Embassy* pp 236, 509-11). **35** Although reserving the right to interpret the confederate oath, the clergy never claimed temporal jurisdiction during the crisis. Declaration of the ecclesiastical congregation to the supreme council, 24 Aug. 1646 (PRO SP Ire. 261/51 ff 207-10); Order by the ecclesiastical congregation etc., 26 Sept. 1646 (Gilbert [ed.], *Irish confederation*, vi, pp 144-6).

were concerted in common by all than if they proceeded from a magistrate elected exclusively by the clergy".[36] In a letter to Cardinal Pamphili on 30 December the nuncio reflected on the prospects for the forthcoming assembly, confident that the "Ormondist and Clanricarde" factions would be defeated in any debates. For the nuncio, however, war weariness presented a far greater threat to his military strategy. He recognised the abhorrence felt by all classes towards the extortion of soldiers and conceded that this issue, rather than any religious question, preoccupied the vast majority of people. Even in the absence of a satisfactory peace, he believed it would prove difficult to persuade the assembly to pursue an active war.[37]

The second crucial decision taken by the supreme council, releasing all the prisoners arrested in September, prompted Richard Bellings to declare dramatically that "the flood was turned". Again with the benefit of hindsight, Rinuccini argued that the opposite policy "if it had been carried out with the requisite firmness might have been the salvation both of religion and of the kingdom".[38] This statement credited Muskerry and his allies with a far greater influence than they actually possessed at this time.

In fact the council had little option but to release the men. Their continued imprisonment proved an acute source of embarrassment to the confederate government, and would certainly have caused bitter divisions in the general assembly. By setting the men free, on condition that they did not attempt anything in favour of the rejected treaty until that assembly met, the moderates diffused a potentially explosive political crisis.[39] The peace faction actively supported the calling of this assembly, viewing the meeting as an ideal opportunity to vindicate themselves personally, and to curtail what they saw as the worst excesses of their clerical rivals.

The greatest opposition to an assembly came from royalists such as Clanricarde, who wanted the peace treaty accepted as it stood. In his correspondence with the confederate commander, Thomas Preston, Clanricarde questioned the general's judgement in deferring to an assembly which would "certainly prove very prejudicial to the king's service and the peace and quiet of this kingdom".[40] He seriously doubted whether the forthcoming elections would be

36 Report on the affairs of Ireland, 1649 (Aiazza [ed.], *Embassy* pp 509-11). 37 Considerations upon the future assembly, 30 Dec. 1646 (Aiazza [ed.], *Embassy* p. 238). The term "Clanricarde faction" was only used once before, by the clerical ambassador Matthew O'Hartegan in a letter to the supreme council in late 1644. O'Hartegan complained "that Ormond, Clanricarde and Castlehaven's factions are strong about your board", and that the Church's interests were neglected as a result. O'Hartegan to the supreme council, Nov. 1644 (Gilbert [ed.], *Irish confederation*, iv, pp 61-2). Both Rinuccini and O'Hartegan were probably referring to those individuals (like Patrick Darcy) close to Clanricarde, rather than a distinct group such as the clerical or peace factions. 38 Bellings was one of those to be released from prison. Bellings' History in Gilbert (ed.), *Irish confederation*, vi, pp 46-7; Report on the affairs of Ireland, 1649 (Aiazza [ed.], *Embassy* p. 503). 39 Bellings' History in Gilbert (ed.), *Irish confederation*, vi, pp 46-7. 40 Clanricarde to

free in the face of clerical threats, while Ormond also expected little comfort from the assembly's proceedings. The lord lieutenant, preparing for the worst, issued a compulsory work order in Dublin to help strengthen the city's defences.[41]

The seventh general assembly met in the city of Kilkenny from 10 January until 4 April 1647, with the confederates at the height of their power militarily. They remained seriously divided, however, on the question of a settlement with Charles I, at a time when the king's freedom of action continued to diminish.[42] Sessions were well attended, and debates fiercely contested, as both sides sought to justify their record over the previous twelve months.[43] Although fire destroyed the vast bulk of assembly records in the eighteenth century, two vivid eye-witness accounts of this meeting, by Richard Bellings and Giovanni Battista Rinuccini, still survive.[44]

Before embarking on a reconstruction of events, however, it is important to draw attention to the emergence of a new factor in the dynamics of confederate politics. All previous accounts of this assembly have examined developments solely in the context of factional conflict (peace faction versus clerical faction). This narrow framework, however, fails to answer a number of crucial questions. Why, for instance, did an assembly supposedly dominated by the clerical faction insist on adding so many conditions to the religious articles favoured by Rinuccini and the bishops? And why, despite their so called "revival", did the peace party only succeed in having four of their number elected to the new and expanded supreme council? The answers lie in the exploitation of the balance of power by a small group of pragmatic moderates, led by Nicholas Plunkett, who successfully dictated confederate policy for most of 1647.

Without neglecting the political activities of certain individuals, it is equally important to focus on certain crucial themes which engaged the attention of

Preston, 10 Dec. 1646 (Lowe [ed.], *Clanricarde letter-book* pp 341-2). **41** The compulsory order directed that all men and women over 15 years of age (estimated to number 24,000 people) work to complete the city's defences. *HMC Calendar of the manuscripts of the marquess of Ormonde,* new series, vol. 1 (London 1902) p. 113. **42** In February 1647, the Scots handed Charles over to the custody of the English parliament, although this news did not reach Kilkenny until after the assembly had rejected the peace treaty. Bellings' History in Gilbert (ed.), *Irish confederation,* vii, pp 15-7. **43** This assembly is one of only four for which a full list of members is available. The manuscript copies are as follows: BL Add Mss 4,781 ff 12-34, 35,850 ff 12-34; Bodl. Carte Mss 70 ff 64-85; RIA Mss H.V.1; Dublin City Library (Gilbert Collection) Mss 219. Two printed versions also exist in Gilbert (ed.), *Irish confederation,* ii, pp 212-19 (mistakenly dated 1643),and in Bourke, T., *Hibernia Dominicana siue historia provinciae Hiberniae ordinis praedicatorum* (Supplementum 1772) pp 883-5. See appendix 1 for further information. **44** Bellings' History in Gilbert (ed.), *Irish confederation,* vii, pp 1-12; various letters, January-April 1647 (Aiazza [ed.], *Embassy* pp 241-4). Apart from political rivalry, both men appeared to harbour a strong personal dislike for one another. During this assembly, for example, Rinuccini wrote of Bellings that "no one speaks or writes more discreditably than he does". Rinuccini to Pamphili, 23 Feb. 1647 (Aiazza [ed.], *Embassy* pp 251-2).

assembly members during that period. Four major issues dominated proceedings – the Ormond peace treaty, the confederate oath of association, the election of a new supreme council, and negotiations with the royalists. The decision on the treaty, the oath and supreme council elections were taken sequentially in that order. Negotiations with Ormond continued, in one form or another, in parallel with these developments.

A logical starting point for discussing the assembly is the election which determined its membership, held in mid-winter during the month of December 1646. The confederates controlled a greater expanse of territory than ever before, ensuring a high return to the assembly, although the pattern of provincial representation remained unchanged from earlier meetings.[45] With so much at stake, elections were fiercely contested and tension remained high throughout the campaign. Clanricarde and others complained bitterly of electoral malpractice and physical intimidation of both candidates and voters by supporters of the clerical faction. Such reports must be treated with caution, but warrant investigation nonetheless.[46]

Bellings, a leading proponent of peace, noted that from the beginning of the election campaign the supreme council, with the co-operation of the clergy "made it their study" to make sure the assembly rejected the Ormond treaty. The tactics used, according to his account, varied from oaths against the settlement administered by priests, to physical violence perpetrated by the Ulster army.[47] More specifically he charged that certain individuals, drawn out of the creaghts planted by Owen Roe O'Neill in the Midlands, illegally filled vacant places in the Ulster returns. Subsequent attempts to have these "supernumeraries", or "prime men", removed from the assembly proved too difficult and tedious.[48]

The royalists, although obviously not participating directly in the elections, also claimed that the clerical faction intended to dominate the proceedings by fair means or foul. In early December, just as the campaign got underway, Clanricarde wrote that, with the help of the clergy, "the enemies of peace will have great advantage in elections". Charles Lambert, based in Dublin, informed

---

45 Recent victories in Connacht and Ulster greatly increased the confederate presence in both provinces. See chapter 7 (table 2) for provincial representation at assembly meetings. 46 Those making complaints included the earl of Clanricarde, Charles Lambert in Dublin and the French agent in Kilkenny, monsieur Du Moulin. Clanricarde to Preston, 10 Dec. 1646 (Lowe [ed.], *Clanricarde letter-book* p. 342); Lambert to Ormond, 25 Dec. 1646 (Bodl. Carte Mss 19 ff 699–700); Du Moulin to Ormond, 30 Jan. 1647 (Bodl. Carte Mss 20 ff 218–9). 47 The importance of the oath can be gauged from the statement of Roebuck Lynch, a leading confederate from Connacht, who announced in the assembly that he would not "forswear himself, and that most of his province had taken an oath to reject it [the treaty]". Bellings' History in Gilbert (ed.), *Irish confederation*, vii, p. 8. 48 Again according to Bellings, the assembly included "such an overcharge of supernumeraries, as for some boroughs, three have been returned and actually voted". Ibid., vi, pp 47–8; vii, p. 1.

the lord lieutenant that those opposed to peace planned to order an army to Kilkenny to keep "moderate and well affected men" from attending the assembly.[49] The target of all these accusations, the clerical faction, remained silent on the issue of electoral malpractice, except for one incidental reference. Rinuccini believed that poor attendance at previous assemblies had allowed the ruling clique to control the sessions. The election of a large number of candidates, the nuncio hoped, would prevent such manipulation.[50]

Statistical evidence suggests that the accusations of Bellings and others can be dismissed as campaign rhetoric, or sour grapes at having lost out to the clerical faction. The seventh general assembly (despite Rinuccini's hopes) does not appear to have been unusually well attended, while the percentage of members from Ulster remained virtually unchanged from earlier meetings. Moreover, almost three quarters of the assembly members in 1647 had sat at previous meetings, undermining claims of a huge influx of new faces.[51] On the question of clerical interference, no examples of oaths issued specifically for this election campaign have survived, although Bellings may have been referring to the new oath of association framed by the clergy back in August 1646.[52]

As for complaints of intimidation by the Ulster army, it seems highly unlikely that O'Neill made any pact with the clerical faction. The earl of Clanricarde observed in his memoirs that the Ulster forces "no further obeyed the orders of assemblies or councils than did best agree with their own designs".[53] By December 1646 O'Neill's army had dispersed for the winter, and as such could hardly have engaged in a systematic campaign against the supporters of the peace treaty. The Ulster general also quarrelled with Rinuccini at this time. He refused to hand over Athlone castle to Viscount Dillon, who had recently converted back to catholicism much to the nuncio's delight. Rinuccini denounced O'Neill as being "insubordinate" and "inflexible", while describing his troops as "barbarous" – hardly a picture of two men in close alliance.[54]

The French agent (and supporter of the peace faction) Du Moulin claimed that northerners residing in the city of Kilkenny selected five people to speak for

49 Although Clanricarde had many friends in the confederate ranks, the source of Lambert's information is unclear. Dublin, however, was undoubtedly awash with rumours at this time as to the intentions of the clerical faction and Owen Roe O'Neill's Ulster forces. Clanricarde to Preston, 10 Dec. 1646 (Lowe [ed.], *Clanricarde letter-book* p. 342); Lambert to Ormond, 25 Dec. 1646 (Bodl. Carte Mss 19 ff 699-700). 50 Considerations upon the future assembly, 30 Dec. 1646 (Aiazza [ed.], *Embassy* p. 238). 51 300 members attended the assembly in early 1647, compared to over 400 in 1645, although that year was probably exceptional. See appendix 1. 52 By this oath, confederates swore to oppose any peace that did not have the consent of the ecclesiastical congregation. Bodl. Carte Mss 19 ff 309. 53 Lowe (ed.), *Clanricarde letter-book* p. 377. 54 What really upset the nuncio was the fact that the Ulster forces styled themselves "the army of the Pope and the Church", which led many confederates to blame the clergy, and Rinuccini in particular, for the excesses committed by these troops. Report of the proceedings of Owen O'Neill, April 1647 (Aiazza [ed.], *Embassy* pp 281-4).

them at the assembly. These representatives, according to Du Moulin, sat as deputies for places recently won by the confederates in Ulster. Rinuccini had observed the peace faction making similar appointments in January 1646, and this appears to have been standard practice throughout the 1640s.[55] Abuses undoubtedly occurred as the electoral system adapted to the realities of war, and improvisation (or malpractice) proved inevitable in such circumstances. The tactics employed in December 1646, however, were probably no worse than those used by the peace faction in earlier elections.

Nicholas Plunkett, as chairman of the assembly, took steps to protect the meeting from outside interference. In a letter to Preston, requiring his presence in Kilkenny, Plunkett informed the general that nothing was "more requisite than full and absolute freedom unto the several members returned from the several places of the kingdom to be of the general assembly". Assembly members experienced great difficulties in finding accommodation for themselves, and they issued an order prohibiting anybody travelling to the city from bringing more than the "necessary" number of attendants.[56] This policy not only eased the congestion problems in Kilkenny, but also prevented the military commanders from intimidating the meeting with a large retinue of armed supporters.

Although Plunkett and other moderates on the supreme council increasingly dictated confederate policy, the two main factions still secured significant representation at the assembly. Clanricarde reported that Viscount Muskerry had returned to Munster in December, "looking to the elections for this assembly", and his adherents predominated in the ranks of temporal peers.[57] The exceptional unity of this group enabled it to exert a disproportionate influence on assembly proceedings, without ever enjoying majority support. The clerical faction, centred around the bishops, also campaigned energetically throughout the country. The hostility, however, felt by many confederates towards its perceived principal supporter, the Ulster army of Owen Roe O'Neill, created problems for Rinuccini and his supporters.

---

55 Du Moulin to Ormond, 30 Jan. 1647 (Bodl. Carte Mss 20 ff 218-9); Rinuccini to Pamphili, 13 Feb. 1646 (Aiazza [ed.], *Embassy* p. 116). 56 Plunkett informed Preston of a general assembly order limiting the number of people entering Kilkenny to prevent assembly members being distracted by the "multitudes". Plunkett to Preston, 13 Jan. 1647 (PRO SP Ire. 263/31 ff 48-50). The extent of overcrowding in Kilkenny is illustrated by the petition of the inhabitants of the St John's street to the general assembly. They were seeking relief as "a great and considerable part of the said street is inhabited by gentlemen who lost their estates by the distempers of these times, and do not contribute to the payment of any public charge accrued in the said street". PRO SP Ire 261/48 f.201. 57 Clanricarde to Ormond, 8 Jan. 1647 (Carte, *Ormond*, vi, pp 489-90). The large number of Butler peers alone (Mountgarret, Cahir, Dunboyne, Galmoy) ensured that the lord lieutenant received a sympathetic hearing from the confederate nobility. Piers Butler, Viscount Ikerrin, however, does not appear to have supported the peace treaty.

In the absence of detailed records, it is extremely difficult to identify the political allegiances of each individual at the assembly, but subsequent developments clearly illustrate that neither the peace or clerical factions dominated the session. The vast majority of members probably remained uncommitted to any faction, and appeared ready to be swayed by the arguments of the day. This fact enabled a small group of moderates, whose composition will be discussed later in the chapter, to exploit the balance of power, and assert their own authority. Plunkett's policies of compromise, and his advocacy of the primacy of the legislature, proved a popular combination.[58]

On the first day of proceedings the ecclesiastical congregation, meeting in simultaneous session with the general assembly, issued a series of proposals deemed necessary to ensure the security of religion in any future treaty. These included the free and public exercise of religion in Ireland and the retention of all church buildings and church livings by the catholic clergy. Furthermore, the Irish parliament, functioning independently of its English counterpart, had to revoke all the penal laws. Finally and most crucially, the clergy called on assembly members to frame a new oath of association, which would incorporate all of these demands.[59]

The general assembly itself focused first on the core issue of the Ormond peace treaty. In a rare display of consensus politics, all members unanimously agreed that ultimate authority in this matter lay with the assembly. For the peace faction this gathering represented an immediate opportunity to overturn the policies of their clerical opponents, and Bellings in a burst of populist enthusiasm wrote that "notwithstanding any thing the prelates had determined, that certainly the nation by their representatives there met were the only competent judges of war and peace, and the grounds of either of them".[60]

The clerical faction echoed these sentiments, hoping the legislative body would vindicate its actions over the previous six months and legitimise what many regarded as an illegal usurpation of power. Rinuccini indicated the willingness of the bishops and clergy to lay down their authority to the assembly, "all power being now vested in that body".[61] This sudden interest in, and respect for, repre-

---

58 Plunkett had been instrumental in getting the clerical faction to summon an assembly in late 1646. Declaration of the ecclesiastical congregation to the supreme council, 24 Aug. 1646 (PRO SP Ire. 261/51 ff 207-10); Report on the affairs of Ireland, 1649 (Aiazza [ed.], *Embassy* pp 509-11). 59 The clerical faction adopted an uncompromising position on constitutional issues, calling for "a free parliament independent of the parliament of England. Propositions of the ecclesiastical congregation to the general assembly at Kilkenny, 10 Jan. 1647 (Bodl. Carte Mss 20 ff 100-1). See also Gilbert (ed.), *Irish confederation*, vi, pp 171-2. 60 Bellings' History in Gilbert (ed.), *Irish confederation*, vii, p. 3. This statement came from the same man who was forced to apologise to the assembly in 1644, for having ignored its instructions in his capacity as secretary to the supreme council. Ibid., iii, p. 10. 61 Report of the speech delivered by the nuncio in the assembly, Feb. 1647 (Aiazza [ed.], *Embassy* p. 244).

sentative government was nothing more than a charade, driven purely by self-interest. By agreeing to let the assembly have the final word on the peace treaty, however, the extremists unwittingly played into the hands of the moderates who sought a compromise settlement in order to preserve confederate unity.

The main point of contention in the ensuing debate centred on whether the committee of treaty and the supreme council possessed the authority to conclude a peace deal without referring the matter to an assembly. The confederate "model of government" proved sufficiently vague to be open to various interpretations. Not surprisingly, the peace faction and the clergy adopted widely divergent positions, and fiercely contested each point of discussion. The main protagonists included Rinuccini and Edmund O'Dempsey, bishop of Leighlin, on the anti-treaty side, and Richard Bellings, Walter Bagenal and the resident French agent, Du Moulin, on the pro-treaty side. According to the nuncio, the meeting was conducted with "much acrimony in public", while Bellings referred to heated debates "as vexed the souls of some composed men".[62] A plot by Robert Talbot (a recent prisoner of the clerical faction) to seize his opponents and incarcerate them in Carlow Castle, came to nothing, but the threat of violence persisted throughout the following weeks.[63]

The session began with Rinuccini resigning his position as president of the supreme council, a shrewd move politically, and one which temporarily silenced those critical of his seizure of power. The nuncio, however, had no intention of taking a back seat in the peace debate, and in a forceful address to the assembly argued that the clergy had organised a government only from necessity and "not because they considered that temporal things belonged to their jurisdiction". He pointed out that the bishops willingly acknowledged the supremacy of the assembly, in stark contrast to the previous supreme council dominated by the peace faction. Rinuccini sensed the overwhelming desire for peace, with a clear majority favouring a compromise "to annul the peace and pardon the contumacious". In such circumstances, the clergy could not appear as an obstacle to peace, or the cause of any internal strife.[64]

The pro-treaty side conceded that the religious guarantees in the Ormond treaty appeared limited, but pointed to the possibility of further concessions outlined in the first article. They argued that the supreme council members had at all times acted with the full consent and knowledge of the general assembly. The signatories of the treaty further demanded "that it might be instanced where they varied from their instructions". According to Bellings, nobody could deny

62 Report on the public rejection of the peace by the assembly, 4 Feb. 1647 (Aiazza [ed.], *Embassy* p. 244); Bellings' History in Gilbert (ed.), *Irish confederation*, vii, p. 2. 63 Notes on Sir Robert Talbot, 1660s (Prendergast Papers, King's Inns, Mss vi ff 710-16). Little information survives on Talbot's plot, which was probably one of many in circulation at this time. 64 One of the first acts of the assembly had been to cease all acts of hostility against the royalists to allow time, as Plunkett informed Ormond, to clear up any "misunderstandings". Plunkett to

"the public and solemn direction given by the president of the general assembly met at Kilkenny [March 1646], to the council and commissioners, to conclude this very peace read to them in the same terms, with some little alteration in words, but no way in substance".[65] The clerical faction hotly denied the assertion that the treaty terms (without alteration) had been read to the assembly, and urged members to unequivocally reject the terms on offer.[66]

The debate then shifted ground with both factions claiming that the foreign courts supported their position. Bellings declared that during his visit to Italy in 1645 Innocent X had recognised the need for Irish catholics to steer a prudent and cautious course. Rinuccini immediately interjected that as papal nuncio he alone could speak for Rome.[67] In a speech to the assembly, the French agent Du Moulin, anxious for a settlement that would enable him to export troops to the continent, hinted at the French king's unease with confederate opposition to the Ormond treaty. Geoffrey Barron, recently returned from Paris, challenged this assertion, while Du Moulin's close association with the peace faction further undermined his credibility.[68]

The assembly next heard an impassioned plea from Colonel Walter Bagenal, addressed to the bishops, warning of the vengeance exacted against those who broke solemn treaties, and he pleaded with them to avoid a similar fate.[69] Unable to reach a decision, the assembly issued a decree ordering a stated number from the two main factions to seek a compromise formula.[70] The promotion of con-

Ormond, 15 Jan. 1647 (Bodl. Carte Mss 20 f.133); Rinuccini's assistant, Scarampi, favoured a hard-line approach, but this was rejected unanimously by the bishops, with the nuncio's support. Report on public rejection of the peace by the assembly, 4 Feb. 1647 (Aiazza [ed.], *Embassy* pp 244-9). **65** In Bellings' view, once the Roman treaty failed to arrive by 1 May 1646, the commissioners were perfectly entitled to conclude the treaty. This interpretation conveniently ignores the fact that the treaty was actually signed on 31 March. Bellings' History in Gilbert (ed.), *Irish confederation*, vii, p. 8. **66** The argument over reading the treaty terms to the general assembly in February 1646 is examined in chapter 3 pp 100-103. **67** Bellings visited Rome during his mission to the continent in 1645, which presumably enabled him to provide some insight into papal thinking. O'Ferrall and O'Connell (eds), *Commentarius*, ii, p. 508; Bellings' History in Gilbert (ed.), *Irish confederation*, vii, p. 3. **68** Barron returned to Ireland in early 1647, having spent almost two years in France, as confederate envoy to the court of Louis XIV. Paper presented by Du Moulin to the general assembly, 19 Jan. 1647 (Bodl. Carte Mss 20 ff 160-1); Dr Tyrrel to council of confederates, 30 Jan. 1647 (Bodl. Carte Mss 67 f.140); Rinuccini to Pamphili, 23 Feb. 1647 (Aiazza [ed.], *Embassy* pp 249-51); O'Ferrall and O'Connell (eds), *Commentarius*, ii, p. 509. **69** Bellings' History in Gilbert (ed.), *Irish confederation*, vii, p. 10. Bagenal cited the example of the king of Hungary, illustrating once more the confederates' interest in mainstream European affairs. Bagenal was a fervent supporter of the peace treaty, and the previous September had allowed Ormond to escape back to Dublin over Leighlin Bridge, suffering imprisonment as a result. Notes on Colonel Walter Bagenal, Feb. 1661 (Prendergast Papers, Kings Inns, Mss 2 f.994). **70** Report on the public rejection of the peace by the assembly, 4 Feb. 1647 (Aiazza [ed.], *Embassy* pp 244-9). Unfortunately, Rinuccini neglects to name those chosen to reach this compromise agreement.

sensus through committees became a favourite tactic of the moderates as they tried to prevent a potentially ruinous split in confederate ranks.

This particular working party recommended a rejection of the peace and, according to Nicholas French, the assembly passed an appropriate resolution by unanimous consent on 2 February. Rinuccini, however, recorded 12 votes (out of the 300 cast) against the decision, and certainly a few die-hard clerical opponents refused to concede defeat. According to Bellings, the vote was "far from being unanimous in the public acclamation and very far from finding a tacit consent in the minds of men", while Robert Talbot, in a letter to Clanricarde, complained that the supporters of peace had been "overborne with vote and not weight or strength of reason".[71]

After the vote assembly members issued a lengthy official statement explaining their decision. The peace faction, they argued, had relied totally on Glamorgan's treaty for religious concessions "though by reason of many accidents happened since" this agreement was no longer secure. As a result, the assembly had little option but to reject the Ormond peace, which it declared "invalid and of no force". In principle, therefore, the members vindicated the actions of the clerical faction, but in reality an astute and politically vital compromise had been reached, as the statement continued that "this assembly do likewise declare that the said council, committee of instructions and commissioners of treaty, have faithfully and sincerely carried and demeaned themselves in their said negotiations pursuant and according to the trust reposed in them, and gave thereof a due acceptable account to this assembly".[72]

This formula of rejecting the peace but exonerating its creators from any blame, found widespread approval and prevented a permanent split in confederate ranks. Rinuccini expressed his displeasure at the partial exoneration of his opponents, but there appears to be no substance to claims by the authors of the *Commentarius* that the deal originated with the peace faction.[73] Compromise proved the order of the day and even though the assembly rejected the treaty favoured by Viscount Muskerry and his supporters, their political careers had been salvaged. The vote signalled the triumph of consensus over faction, consolidating the strategy of the moderates, who emerged as the leading force in confederate politics.

---

71 Talbot was convinced that "the most active in that design will as soon rue it as the opposers thereof". Talbot to Clanricarde, 20 March 1647 (Lowe [ed.], *Clanricarde letter-book* pp 369-71); Bindon (ed.), *Historical works*, vol. 2, p. 174; Report on the public rejection of the peace by the assembly, 4 Feb. 1647 (Aiazza [ed.], *Embassy* pp 244-9); Bellings' History in Gilbert (ed.), *Irish confederation*, vii, p. 11. 72 Declaration of the general assembly against the peace, 2 Feb. 1647 (Bodl. Carte Mss 65 f.364). See also Gilbert (ed.), *Irish confederation*, vi, pp 177-8. 73 Rinuccini did not challenge the agreement as he feared an open breach precipitated by the clergy. Report on the public rejection of the peace by the assembly, 4 Feb. 1647 (Aiazza [ed.], *Embassy* pp 244-9); O'Ferrall and O'Connell (eds), *Commentarius*, ii, pp 511-15.

The final part of the debate dealt with the shape of any future peace agreement, and in particular the demands raised by the clergy at the beginning of the session. Events during the previous six months had brought the confederate organisation to the brink of collapse. The assembly now set out to restore unity by assuming total control of the talks process, replacing factional interest groups. The oath of association emerged as the instrument for developing this process which had manifested itself for the first time in June 1644, with the presentation of the reform package proclaiming the primacy of the assembly in the confederate power structure.[74]

The clergy sought to amend the oath to include the religious demands of the ecclesiastical congregation. According to Bellings (no friend of the clergy) the additional clauses caused little or no contention, but other accounts present a different picture. Supporters of the peace faction bitterly opposed the amendments, and Clanricarde argued that the new oath would be grounded "upon impossible undertakings". Rinuccini wrote that the "general compact was refused by none", but that disputes arose over particular details. These led to prolonged and heated discussions with "dissensions raging more bitterly than ever". The "unwearied [peace] faction" he noted ruefully "constantly meets in secret and turn everything to their own ends".[75]

Despite this concerted opposition, assembly members voted for the following amendments to the confederate oath of association – the free and public exercise of the catholic religion as in the reign of Henry VII; secular clergy to enjoy all manner of jurisdictions, privileges and immunities as in the reign of Henry VII; the revocation by parliament of all penal acts against catholics passed since the reign of Henry VIII; secular clergy to enjoy all churches and church livings in confederate controlled areas.[76] The victory of the clerical faction seemed assured, except for the addition of two crucial conditions by the following day. The first made clear that the final amendment concerning churches and church livings should not preclude the possibility of reaching an accommodation with the royalists. In the second, the assembly assumed the sole "power of declaring the kingdom unable to carry out these proposals".[77]

Assembly members, therefore, rather than the clergy as the nuncio had hoped, would act as final arbiters of any future agreement with the king. Rinuccini, although angered by these late additions, believed that "in a full assembly there is no fear of the well-disposed not prevailing".[78] Claims that

---

**74** The reform proposals in June 1644 are discussed in chapter 2 pp 83-6.  **75** Rinuccini to Pamphili, 15 Feb. 1647 and 6 March 1647 (Aiazza [ed.], *Embassy* pp 251, 258); Bellings' History in Gilbert (ed.), *Irish confederation*, vii, p. 12; Clanricarde to Sir Luke Fitzgerald, 15 March 1647 (Lowe [ed.], *Clanricarde letter-book* p. 365).  **76** The oath is written in at the top of the 1647 assembly list, a fact discussed in more detail in appendix 1.  **77** Rinuccini to Pamphili, 4 March 1647 (Aiazza [ed.], *Embassy* p. 257).  **78** Idem.

Muskerry and his allies engineered this outcome are contradicted by their subsequent failure during elections to the supreme council. They simply did not command sufficient support on the assembly floor to force through any changes.[79] The compromise nature of the final settlement strongly suggests that the proposals originated with moderates hoping to ensure an acceptable peace deal, untarnished by factional interests.[80]

Although the assembly emphatically rejected the Ormond treaty, the confederates still wished to reach an accommodation with the lord lieutenant. They never felt comfortable opposing their monarch, and according to Rinuccini, if satisfactory terms could be arranged, the vast majority favoured peace.[81] On 15 January 1647, therefore, a full two weeks before the vote on the peace treaty, Nicholas Plunkett wrote to Ormond informing him of the assembly order to cease attacks on royalist positions. Plunkett believed that the forthcoming debate would "quiet the distractions of the kingdom and clear all misunderstandings for the advancement of his majesty's service".[82]

Expecting another confederate attack, this news caught Ormond completely unawares. Unsure how to respond, he waited ten days before sending a detailed reply, in which he outlined his disappointment at the overturning of the peace settlement the previous September.[83] The confederate commissioners (in his opinion) possessed sufficient authority to conclude this treaty and the ecclesiastical congregation had no right to contravene the work of the secular government. Despite his misgivings, Ormond instructed Lord Taaffe and Colonel Barry to travel to Kilkenny, and explore the possibilities of arranging a fresh settlement. They could agree to a cessation of hostilities for a month in return for £1,000 sterling in cash, and extend the deadline for another month at the same price.[84]

---

79 The authors of the *Commentarius* claim that the peace faction changed the oath to facilitate a deal with the lord lieutenant. O'Ferrall and O'Connell (eds), *Commentarius*, ii, pp 511-15. Robert Talbot notes in a letter to Clanricarde that only 3 out of the 24 members on the new council belonged to the peace faction. Talbot to Clanricarde, 20 March 1647 (Lowe [ed.], *Clanricarde letter-book* p. 370). 80 This declaration by the general assembly mirrored efforts at Westminster to ensure that the English parliament, and not the executive Committee of Both Kingdoms, acted as final arbiter in any peace settlement with the king. Gardiner, S.R., *History of the civil war* (New York 1965), vol. 1, pp 305-6. 81 Rinuccini to the nuncio of France, 27 April 1647 (Aiazza [ed.], *Embassy* p. 276). 82 Plunkett to Ormond, 15 Jan. 1647 (Bodl. Carte Mss 20 f. 133). Plunkett wrote frequently to the lord lieutenant at this time in his capacity as chairman of the general assembly. No evidence survives of any private correspondence between the two men, which strongly suggests that Plunkett did not belong to Ormond's inner circle of friends and clients. 83 Ormond to Nicholas Plunkett, 25 Jan. 1647 (Lowe [ed.], *Clanricarde letter-book* pp 348-53). 84 Instructions [by Ormond] to Taaffe and Barry, 25 Jan. 1647 (Bodl. Carte Mss 20 f.190). these instructions illustrate Ormond's desperate need for hard currency at this time, considering that at one stage of the conflict his monthly military expenditure was over £50,000. Gillespie, "Economy at war", *Independence to occupation* p. 171.

The lord lieutenant disliked negotiating directly with the general assembly and held out little hope of reaching a mutually acceptable agreement. Events in England during the early months of 1647 vastly reduced his room for manoeuvre. On 30 January the Scots handed the king over to the English parliament, and shortly afterwards parliamentary commissioners left for Dublin to negotiate the city's surrender.[85] Ormond's position, caught between the confederates and parliament, was becoming increasingly perilous, but by negotiating with both sides he sought to gain some valuable time. Three days after despatching Taaffe and Barry to Kilkenny the lord lieutenant contacted the parliamentary delegation seeking a safe pass to parley.[86]

Ormond's agents arrived in Kilkenny during the crucial debate on the peace treaty, but shortly after the final vote the assembly formed a committee, chaired by Hugh Rochford, to conclude a truce with the royalists. Rochford, an old English lawyer and former parliamentarian from Wexford, supported the clerical faction in denouncing the peace treaty in September 1646. That same month Rinuccini appointed him to the judicature, but this involvement in the cease-fire arrangements suggests a switch to the moderate camp, alongside his former parliamentary colleague, Nicholas Plunkett.[87]

The confederate committee signed a four-week truce with the royalists on 17 February, although Rinuccini continued to argue for a immediate military strike, complaining bitterly that truces "have been the ruin of the whole affair".[88] The nuncio eventually relented in his opposition to the cease-fire, however, to ensure the passage of the clerical amendments through the assembly. Plunkett hoped that Ormond might consider reopening full peace negotiations as a result of this agreement. Despite repeated overtures from the moderates in Kilkenny, however, the lord lieutenant despaired of the prospects of a permanent settlement with the confederates and he decided instead to hand Dublin over to the forces of parliament.[89]

---

85 Parliamentary commissioners had visited Dublin the previous year, in March 1646. Ormond received the delegation but refused to negotiate at that time. Ormond to Annesley, 2 March 1646 (Bodl. Carte Mss 16 f.573). With the king now in parliamentary custody, however, this fresh approach was difficult to ignore. 86 The three parliamentary agents were Robert Meredith, Robert King and John Clotworthy, the Antrim planter who had played a leading role in Strafford's downfall. Ormond to Meredith, King and Clotworthy, 28 Jan. 1647 (TCP vol. 20 p. 126). 87 Rochford sat as MP for the borough of Fethard in the 1640-1 parliament, and was identified by Perceval-Maxwell as one of the catholic "leaders". Perceval-Maxwell, *Irish rebellion* pp 136-7. According to Castlehaven, Rochford travelled to France as an accredited confederate after the first general assembly, but he did not assume a central role until the peace crisis of August 1646. Tuchet, *Castlehaven review* pp 59-60. 88 Articles of agreement for cessation between Colonel Barry and Hugh Rochford, 17 Feb. 1647 (Bodl. Carte Mss 20 f.315); Rinuccini to the nuncio of Spain, 26 April 1647 (Aiazza [ed.], *Embassy* p. 275). 89 Ormond offered to surrender on 6 February, almost two weeks before agreeing to a truce with the confederates. At the end of February, Parliament accepted his

Unaware of this development, on 28 February the assembly appointed Gerald Fennell, a leading associate of Viscount Muskerry, and Geoffrey Barron, "an ardent nuncioist" (according to Bellings at least), to present the lord lieutenant with a new offer.[90] By selecting individuals from each faction the moderate leadership sought to bind both sides in advance to any subsequent peace deal. By the terms of the agreement the confederates and royalists would continue with separate governments until the signing of a treaty, and in the meantime prosecute a joint war against the forces of the English parliament and the Scots. Ormond promised to examine the proposals carefully and make a reply within a few days. Encouraged by his reaction, Fennell and Barron returned to Kilkenny and persuaded a sympathetic assembly to extend the truce until 10 April.[91]

By 18 March however, the situation had become critical, with rumours circulating of an agreement between Ormond and the English parliament, and no reply from the lord lieutenant to the assembly's offer. In desperation, Plunkett instructed Theobald Butler, a confederate officer, to go to Dublin and discover Ormond's true intentions. Butler warned the marquis "not to conclude with any but the general assembly", a body which could not be kept together indefinitely. Forced to declare his position publicly the lord lieutenant announced that he could not assent to the confederate propositions "in the manner as they are framed". This reply confirmed suspicions in Kilkenny that Ormond had struck a deal with parliament, and the assembly decided that further talks at this time would serve no purpose.[92]

Rinuccini reported that even Ormond's close friends expressed outrage at his answer, and that as a result "a stricter union has already become visible between

offer, although some tough bargaining needed to be done before Ormond would agree to hand over the city. Parliamentary acceptance of Ormond's offer to surrender, 27 Feb. 1647 (TCP vol. 20 p. 228). The timing of this undermines Adamson's argument that it was only at the end of March 1647, when the reappointment of his enemy Lord Lisle as parliamentarian lord lieutenant of Ireland was looking increasingly unlikely, that Ormond took definite steps to surrender Dublin. Adamson, "Strafford's ghost", *Independence to occupation* p. 146. Ormond's letter to the king on 17 March 1647, before Lisle's fall from favour, confirms that he was prepared to surrender Dublin to parliament regardless of which faction predominated at Westminster. Bodl. Clarendon Mss 29 f.153. **90** Plunkett to Ormond, 28 Feb. 1647 (Bodl. Carte Mss 20 ff 372-4); Bellings' History in Gilbert (ed.), *Irish confederation*, vii, p. 7. Although a nephew of Luke Wadding, the confederate agent in Rome, his actions during the 1648 crisis suggest that he was a moderate rather than an adherent of the clerical faction. **91** For cessation terms and ensuing correspondence see Bodl. Carte Mss 20 f.386, 420 and Gilbert (ed.), *Irish confederation*, vi, pp 185-6. **92** Cessation negotiations in Bodl. Carte Mss 20 f.405, 497, 501, 519 and Gilbert (ed.), *Irish confederation*, vi, pp 191-2. The supreme council wrote to a number of leading catholic neutrals (Nicholas White, Henry Talbot and Andrew Aylmer among others) at the end of March, inviting them to join the confederates as Ormond intended to surrender Dublin to the English parliament. Bodl. Carte Mss 20 f.556, 558, 560.

the different parties but everyone allows that necessity alone can cement it entirely".[93] In desperation, the confederates began to re-examine the idea of a foreign protector for the kingdom. Prior to the assembly meeting, a rumour in circulation (around Dublin at least) suggested that the nuncio and his supporters intended to declare for Spain "and that they first give it out to see how it will take".[94] Indeed, by March 1647, some assembly members agreed that an approach should be made to the Spanish monarch seeking his protection. Others favoured the French king, while the clergy naturally enough looked to the pope. Rinuccini, with no recent instructions on the issue, adopted a neutral stance and wrote to Rome seeking guidance.[95] Unable to reach a consensus decision, the assembly dropped the proposals for the moment.

In early February the introduction of articles by the clerical faction condemning Thomas Preston, clearly exposed the fragility of confederate unity. The articles accused the Leinster general of obstructing the Dublin expedition, and of agreeing secretly not to attack Ormond. They further alleged that he disobeyed direct orders from the supreme council, and plotted to seize Duncannon and Kilkenny. The final and most damning charge claimed that Preston continued to correspond directly with Ormond even after his formal reconciliation with the council on 8 December 1646.[96]

Despite Preston's duplicitous behaviour during the Dublin campaign, he did appear content by early 1647 to allow the assembly to decide on the fate of the Ormond peace treaty.[97] The timing of these accusations convinced his supporters that "the clergy sought only to aggrandise O'Neill", and both sides almost came to blows on the assembly floor. Plunkett and Rinuccini, the latter once again displaying a moderation which belied his extremist reputation, successfully interposed in the row, and the Leinster general retained command of the army.[98] For the moment at least, a semblance of confederate unity was restored.

---

**93** Rinuccini to Pamphili, 25 March 1647 (Aiazza [ed.], *Embassy* pp 266-7).   **94** Lambert to Ormond, 25 Dec. 1646 (Bodl. Carte Mss 19 ff 699-700).   **95** Rinuccini to Pamphili, 25 March 1647 (Aiazza [ed.], *Embassy* pp 266-7).   Rinuccini's instructions prior to his arrival in Ireland, however, advised him to maintain a strict neutrality between France and Spain. Ibid. p. xlix. The activities of the French agent Du Moulin at the assembly in support of the Ormond treaty might have inclined the nuncio more towards Spain at this time.   **96** The articles against Preston are printed in Gilbert (ed.), *Irish confederation*, vii, pp 336-8, with a latin manuscript form in Bodl. Carte Mss 118 f.29.   **97** Preston did continue to correspond with Clanricarde after 8 December, but by 12 December informed the marquis that the threat of clerical censure would force "a protracting of our agreements until the assembly now at hand, the composure whereof being legal and free will settle such an understanding between us as will unite the nation in acceptance of these conditions". Preston to Clanricarde, 12 Dec. 1646 (Lowe [ed.], *Clanricarde letter-book* pp 343-4).   **98** O'Ferrall and O'Connell (eds), *Commentarius*, ii, p. 557; Rinuccini to Pamphili, 7 April 1647 (Aiazza [ed.], *Embassy* pp 270-2). Admittedly, Rinuccini in his own version of events to Rome, was anxious to portray himself in the best possible light. The author of the Plunkett manuscript in the National Library blamed

One of the final and most important acts of the assembly involved electing a new supreme council to implement confederate policy over the following months. Its composition would also give a good indication of the shifting balance of power within the confederate ranks. The previous council had not been elected but rather appointed by the clerical faction after the rejection of the peace treaty. As he promised in a letter to Rome, Rinuccini resigned as president as soon as the assembly met on 10 January 1647. The rest of the council, however, continued to work, dealing mainly with routine administrative matters.

On 8 March, the nuncio recommended that fresh elections take place immediately. With the assembly still well attended, Rinuccini believed an opportunity existed for the return of councillors favourable to the clerical position. The longer the session continued the more members drifted home, with the consequent danger of leaving the peace faction, based around the Butler heartland of Kilkenny and Tipperary, with a majority.[99] The assembly accepted Rinuccini's suggestion and announced the results of the ensuing elections just over a week later on 17 March.

The new council consisted of 24 members, chosen equally from the four provinces, 12 of whom would be based permanently in Kilkenny city. Surviving manuscripts provide us with the names of all the members.[100] From the previous council, 11 out of 17 secured re-election, principal among them Nicholas Plunkett, and Bishop French. As for the other six, Rinuccini and two of the provincial generals, Preston (Leinster) and Glamorgan (Munster) did not stand again. Archbishop Walsh, Phelim O'Neill, and Viscount Roche, therefore, failed to retain their seats or did not put their names forward. The council had 13 new members, including a number from the peace faction.[101]

Robert Talbot, one of those imprisoned after the rejection of the peace treaty, explained in a letter to the marquis of Clanricarde that the clerics could not prevent the election of Viscount Muskerry, Richard Everard and John Dillon, "unless they did put in such as were as averse to their manner of proceedings as they". Rinuccini refers to four of the successful candidates being hostile to the clergy's interests. The extra man was almost certainly Lord Athenry, as the cleri-

Nicholas French for introducing the articles, which were then suppressed by Nicholas Plunkett in his capacity as chairman of the general assembly. NLI Mss 345 f.63. French may well have felt personally betrayed by Preston, as the bishop had insisted on his involvement in the Dublin campaign. **99** Plunkett, towards the end of the session, reported difficulties preventing assembly members from returning home. Plunkett to Ormond, March 1647 (Bodl. Carte Mss 20 f.501). Rinuccini always believed that in a full assembly there was "no fear of the well-disposed not prevailing". Rinuccini to Pamphili, 4 March 1647 (Aiazza [ed.], *Embassy* p. 257). **100** For supreme council documents signed by various members see Bodl. Carte Mss 20 f.556, 21 f.571; PRO SP Ire. 264/46 f.108, 265/19 f.68; Bodl. Tanner Mss 58/2 f.529, 533 etc. **101** See appendix 2 (table 13) for the full list of those elected.

cal faction vigorously opposed his return to the council table at the next assembly in December 1647.[102]

The election of Muskerry and his allies marked something of a revival for the peace faction, though on a very minor scale, with only four representatives on a supreme council of 24 members. Moreover, according to Rinuccini, Muskerry owed his election to the direct intervention of Nicholas Plunkett, acting in a spirit of reconciliation.[103] The clerical faction, however, also had to contend with a number of leading moderates on the council. Apart from Plunkett and French, these included Patrick Darcy, Roebuck Lynch, Richard Blake (all from Galway), Hugh Rochford, the marquis of Antrim and his brother Alexander MacDonnell. This group never constituted a majority, but instead skilfully manipulated the balance of power between the two main factions.

Surviving evidence suggests that the marquis of Antrim served as president of the new council, and he certainly claimed as much during the Restoration period.[104] Antrim had returned from Scotland early in January 1647, to an enthusiastic welcome in Kilkenny, due largely to the spectacular victories of his kinsman Alasdair MacColla against the covenanters. An ardent opponent of the Ormond peace treaty, the marquis nonetheless maintained good personal relationships with many of the peace faction leaders. An experienced, though somewhat enigmatic, politician his election as president proved a popular choice, and provided the moderates with an ideal compromise candidate.[105]

The seventh general assembly finally dispersed on 4 April 1647 after almost three months in continuous session, with restless members anxious to return to their homes. The decisive rejection of the Ormond treaty and the revising of the oath of association to include four religious articles appeared to vindicate the actions of Rinuccini and the clerical faction in opposing the peace, but their triumph could hardly be described as absolute. The assembly attached a number of

---

**102** Talbot to Clanricarde, 20 March 1647 (Lowe [ed.], *Clanricarde letter-book* pp 369-71); Rinuccini to Pamphili, 24 March 1647 (Aiazza [ed.], *Embassy* p. 264). The nuncio attempted to veto the nomination of Athenry in December 1647, as well as those of Richard Bellings, Lucas Dillon and Gerald Fennell. Ó hAnnracháin, "Far from terra firma" pp 319-25. **103** Report on the affairs of Ireland, 1649 (Aiazza [ed.], *Embassy* p. 511). **104** In the months following the assembly's dispersal his signature is at the top of supreme council documents, indicating that he held a position of prominence on the council. See PRO SP Ire 263/98 f.163, 264/12 f.22; Bodl. Carte Mss 20 f.556 etc. Moreover, George Leyburn in the report on his mission to Ireland, refers directly to Antrim as president of the supreme council. Ohlmeyer, *Civil war and restoration* pp 188-90. Ohlmeyer is correct in identifying Antrim as the president, but mistakenly believes that the council was dominated by the clerical faction. **105** Shortly after arriving back in Ireland in January, Antrim received permission from the general assembly to raise 5,000 men, and was promised £5,000 to transport them to Scotland. Antrim's involvement with the confederates often proved secondary to his Scottish interests. Supreme council order, June 1647 (PRO SP Ire 265/19 ff 101-2); Ohlmeyer, *Civil war and restoration* pp 183-4.

important conditions to the clerical amendments, while their enemies retained important positions in the confederate government.

The assembly exonerated Viscount Muskerry and his supporters from any blame for concluding the peace treaty and elected four of them (including Muskerry) to the new supreme council. Rinuccini wrote later that the peace faction emerged from this assembly triumphant", while other accounts refer to a "revival", although it is difficult to justify either description.[106] True the supporters of the peace had avoided total political annihilation but they no longer controlled the council. Moreover, the prospects for an accommodation with the royalists seemed particularly bleak as the lord lieutenant entered into negotiations with commissioners from the English parliament.

Rinuccini recorded proudly in a letter to Rome the common habit at the time of referring to the confederate executive supreme council as the "council of the clergy".[107] The reality, however, was very different, and in any event the general assembly increasingly dominated confederate politics at the expense of the council. A mere eighteen months after Glamorgan's refusal to negotiate directly with assembly members, the legislature had assumed total control of the negotiating process, and no peace could now be concluded without its prior approval.

During the course of 1647-8 the assembly developed a more independent identity, and its power was (according to Richard Bellings) "unlimited".[108] The experiences of George Leyburn, the royalist agent sent to Ireland by Queen Henrietta Maria, confirmed this fact. He arrived in Kilkenny a few hours after the dispersal of the assembly, and commented ruefully, "indeed it was very unfortunate for the assembly had both the power and the means to do or undo what they had done in order to treaty which the supreme council, limited within bonds by the assembly, afterwards had not".[109]

The emergence of the general assembly to the forefront of confederate politics actually marked the growing influence of a group of moderates led by Nicholas Plunkett. Advocating consensus politics, the primacy of the legislature, and the need for a more balanced peace treaty, these moderates mobilised enough support on the assembly floor to gain a controlling influence on the supreme council. For the remainder of 1647 they dictated confederate political and military policy with notable consequences for the association and the royalists both in Ireland and England.

---

106 Report on the affairs of Ireland, 1649 (Aiazza [ed.], *Embassy* p. 511); Lowe, "Negotiations between Charles I and confederates" p. 599. 107 Rinuccini to Pamphili, 24 March 1647 (Aiazza [ed.], *Embassy* p. 264). 108 Bellings' History in Gilbert (ed.), *Irish confederation*, vii, p. 12. 109 Bindon (ed.), *Historical works*, vol. 2, p. 163.

# CHAPTER 5

# The middle course

## APRIL 1647–MAY 1648

> The new council, to whom the assembly remitted the whole regulation of affairs, took as usual a middle course, which is always pernicious in state affairs.
>
> Rinuccini to Cardinal Panzirolo, 22 August 1647[1]

Throughout much of 1647, Nicholas Plunkett dictated confederate political, military and diplomatic policy, ably assisted by Nicholas French and Patrick Darcy. These moderates chose a middle course, seeking to find a compromise between the irreconcilable extremes of peace and war. The main threat to their authority emerged, not from the previously dominant clerical faction, but from a resurgent peace faction, marshalled by Viscount Muskerry. No longer the majority voice on the council, or in the assembly, the peace faction sought to regain power through the provincial armies, concentrating their attentions on Munster.

In contrast to Leinster, the province of Munster had experienced great difficulties financing and maintaining an army after the initial months of the uprising. Successive defeats at Liscarroll (August 1642) and Bandonbridge (November 1642) consolidated protestant control of Cork, while personal rivalry between the leading nobles, Viscounts Roche and Muskerry, created further problems. The cessation agreement in September 1643 established an uneasy peace in the province, which only lasted until July 1644 when the royalist commander of Cork, Lord Inchiquin, declared for the English parliament. The confederates, anxious to deny the parliamentarians a bridgehead on the southern coast, launched a major offensive against Inchiquin the following year. In the aftermath of this failed campaign, the Munster army started to disintegrate, due to lack of pay and internal disputes.[2]

In March 1646, following the seizure of Bunratty castle by 2,000 parliamentarian troops, the confederate forces organising the siege had to be supplemented

---

1 Aiazza (ed.), *Embassy* p. 302. 2 Bellings' History in Gilbert (ed.), *Irish confederation*, v, pp 16-18. The first general assembly appointed the continental veteran Garret Barry as commander of the Munster forces. In 1641, Barry was one of eight colonels who received commissions to trans-

by regiments from outside the province. The Munster provincial council nominated Viscount Muskerry to lead this army, which eventually captured the strategic castle.[3] The rejection of Ormond's peace treaty resulted in further upheaval, with Muskerry imprisoned and replaced as Munster general by the royalist earl of Glamorgan, who, despite his support for the clerical faction, had little interest beyond recruiting troops for England. In early 1647, the marquis of Clanricarde commented on the "strong parties out [in Munster] that paid no obedience to any side".[4] The confederate position in the province was threatened with imminent collapse.

A number of the Munster delegates at the seventh general assembly demanded Muskerry's reinstatement as general of the provincial forces.[5] The assembly delegated the final decision to the new supreme council, which imposed a compromise agreement, reflecting the strategy of the moderates. Glamorgan remained as commander of the army, but in association with a council of commissioners dominated by Muskerry's adherents. This arrangement resolved nothing, only temporarily defusing an increasingly explosive dispute. A significant number of officers began to desert their posts, hoping to gain employment on the continent with either France or Spain. Rinuccini condemned the settlement, alleging that commissioners supportive of the peace faction failed to levy sufficient taxes to maintain the army, and colluded with Lord Inchiquin.[6]

port regiments of Strafford's army to the continent. His appointment by the assembly probably represented a compromise between the main factions in the province. Perceval-Maxwell, *Irish rebellion* p. 326 n. 29; Richard Martin to Clanricarde, 2 Dec. 1642 (Bourke, *Clanricarde memoirs* pp 296-8). A competent (if uninspired) general, he proved no match for the young, energetic Lord Inchiquin. Barry's successor Castlehaven, a cavalry commander, lacked experience in the field. Lenihan, "Catholic confederacy" pp 189-90. **3** Troops initially intended to relieve the siege of Chester were diverted "against the insulting enemy at home". Muskerry to Ormond, 3 April 1646 (Bodl. Carte Mss 17 f.49). Bellings reported that Muskerry was reluctant to assume the command of the Munster forces, and only relented after the provincial council agreed to provide adequate supplies for the troops. Bellings' History in Gilbert (ed.), *Irish confederation*, v, p. 19. **4** Lowe (ed.), *Clanricarde letter-book* p. 377. The earl of Glamorgan does not appear to have had any practical military experience either in England or Ireland, and was almost certainly appointed because of his close relationship with the nuncio. **5** Muskerry faced considerable opposition from elements of the Munster nobility (principally Roche, Kilmallock, Ikerrin, Dunboyne and Castleconnell), who felt excluded from the provincial government under the viscount's leadership. *Aphorismical discovery* in Gilbert (ed.), *Contemporary history*, i, p. 207. **6** Rinuccini to Panzirolo, 22 Aug. 1647 (Aiazza [ed.], *Embassy* p. 302). Inchiquin monitored these developments with great interest, observing on one occasion that Glamorgan was a general without an army. He also noted in May the large number of confederate officers secretly flocking to the French agent in Waterford. Inchiquin to Percivall, 5 and 18 May 1647 in *HMC, Egmont* vol. 1, part 2, pp 398-9, 407; *Two letters sent from the lord Inchiquin unto the speaker of the honourable House of Commons ...,* London 1647 (Thomason tracts E389 f.1). In May 500 men, under James Preston, left Waterford for Spain but were diverted to France. Stradling. R.A., *The Spanish monarchy and Irish mercenaries: The wild geese in Spain, 1618-68* (Dublin 1994) p. 59.

Whatever the basis of such allegations, Muskerry clearly had not been molli-fied by the supreme council's intervention. He bided his time until early June, at which time, with Inchiquin already on the offensive in Tipperary, he dramatical-ly left Kilkenny for the Munster army's camp. On arriving, sympathetic officers declared him as general in place of the earl of Glamorgan, a move which rein-stated the viscount as a major player in confederate politics. In a letter to Clanricarde, Muskerry explained the necessity of his actions to protect himself and his friends, "deemed to be at the mercy and disposal of General Owen O'Neill".[7]

This military coup constituted a major challenge to the authority of the council, and the moderates in particular. The clerical faction urged immediate action against Muskerry, but Plunkett, French and Darcy had no desire to pre-cipitate a confederate civil war. They accepted the viscount as Munster general, perhaps hoping he would organise effective opposition to the parliamentarians in that vital province. Rinuccini reflected shortly afterwards that the council had "lost both credit and power by this weakness, and their authority is no longer respected".[8] Although the nuncio may have overstated the case, the whole affair unquestionably placed the moderates' policy of unity under strain.

Developments in Leinster during the winter of 1646-7 further eroded the authority of the supreme council. Owen Roe O'Neill continued to defy orders to remove Ulster troops from the vicinity of Kilkenny, and to hand over Athlone castle to Viscount Dillon. Rinuccini expressed frustration at O'Neill's behaviour, particularly as his forces styled themselves "the army of the pope and the church". In a report to Rome, he denounced the Ulstermen's behaviour as "bar-barous", while conceding that the general's help remained "only too necessary" to the confederate cause.[9] The nuncio, conscious of O'Neill's crucial role during the recent peace crisis, opposed any moves to disband the general's forces. O'Neill, a tough disciplinarian, might well have controlled his soldiers, but mutual suspicion and hostility increasingly defined the relationship between the supreme council and the Ulster army.

Thomas Preston's brother Robert wrote angrily (in terms which echoed the nuncio's own criticism of recent developments in Munster) that unless the coun-cil and assembly punished abuses by Ulster troops their authority would be severely compromised.[10] For the council, Patrick Darcy expressed his outrage at

7 Muskerry to Clanricarde, 17 June 1647 (Lowe [ed.], *Clanricarde letter-book* pp 448-9). Muskerry complained to Preston that the supreme council had given him no satisfaction on the issue of the Munster command, but nonetheless pledged to "maintain the authority of the council". Muskerry to Preston, 14 June 1647 (PRO SP Ire. 264/88 f.263). **8** Rinuccini to Panzirolo, 30 June 1647 (Aiazza [ed.], *Embassy* p. 296). **9** Report on the proceedings of Owen Roe O'Neill, April 1647 (Aiazza [ed.], *Embassy* pp 281-4). The assembly ordered the retaking of Athlone, but lacked the military muscle to achieve this. Order of the general assembly, 23 March 1647 (PRO SP Ire. 263/91 f.153). **10** Robert Preston to Thomas Preston, 18 April 1647

the conduct of the Ulstermen, while Nicholas Plunkett agreed that they had committed "much evil". Bishop French wrote that Kilkenny felt like a city under siege because of the Ulstermen's presence, but the council seemed powerless (as in Muskerry's case) to counter such determined disobedience.[11]

The peace faction benefited most from all this, cleverly exploiting widespread confederate dissatisfaction with O'Neill's army. Viscount Mountgarret encouraged the women of Kilkenny to protest against the Ulster troops outside the city, by throwing stones at the windows of council members and the nuncio.[12] Eventually in June, the supreme council ordered O'Neill northwards into Connacht to attack the strategic stronghold of Sligo, a task which Thomas Preston had failed to perform the previous year. More importantly, the Connacht campaign removed the Ulster forces out of Leinster, thus helping to ease internal confederate tensions.[13]

The moderates' twin track strategy depended for success on complementary progress in both the military and diplomatic spheres. On the military side, the minimum requirement involved retaining the initiative against the Scots and parliamentarians; on the diplomatic side, evident gains in the negotiations with Ormond were essential to hold together the confederate alliance. Internal disputes continued to undermine the military strategy in all provinces, while Ormond's bad faith in his dealings with the supreme council now vitiated the diplomatic plan.

The confederates' erratic military manoeuvres continued against a backdrop of renewed negotiations between the confederates and the marquis of Ormond, prompted by the arrival of the royalist agent George Leyburn (using the pseudonym Winter Grant). Leyburn had been sent to Ireland by Queen Henrietta Maria at the end of 1645 to frustrate the ambitions of the newly arrived papal nuncio, but he left for France a few months later without achieving much.[14]

---

(PRO SP Ire. 263/105 f.176). **11** Patrick Darcy to Thomas Preston, 20 April 1647 (PRO SP Ire. 263/108 f.180), Nicholas Plunkett to Thomas Preston, 27 April 1647 (PRO SP Ire. 263/124 f.209 ), Bishop French to Thomas Preston, 28 April 1647 (PRO SP Ire. 263/126 f.213 ). **12** Report on the proceedings of Owen O'Neill, April 1647 (Aiazza [ed.], *Embassy* pp 281-4). Viscount Mountgarret kept a low profile after the peace crisis of August 1646. Despite his close association with the Ormond treaty, the viscount escaped imprisonment by the clerical faction, and attended the assembly in January 1647. Apart from organising the women's demonstration in Kilkenny, he disappeared again from the national stage until the Inchiquin truce crisis the following year. This absence may well have been for health reasons (Mountgarret was almost 70 years old), as even after resuming his seat on the council board in 1648, he did not play a leading role in confederate affairs. **13** O'Neill to Clanricarde, 15 Aug. 1647, "Unpublished letters and papers of Owen Roe O'Neill", presented by J. Casway, *Analecta Hibernica*, no. 29 (1980) pp 241-2; Theobald Butler to Preston, 4 June 1647 (PRO SP Ire. 264/63 f.219). According to the authors of the *Commentarius*, Plunkett and French supported the campaign against Sligo in order to prevent the Scots taking the offensive in Leinster. O'Ferrall and O'Connell (eds), *Commentarius*, ii, p. 663. **14** O'Ferrall and

Returning in April 1647, he hoped to encourage a reconciliation between the royalists and confederates, leading to a new treaty and vital assistance for the king in England. The queen instructed Leyburn to apply himself "to such persons amongst the Irish, as you shall find to have credit and power amongst them and inclination to conclude a peace upon more moderate conditions".[15]

His private instructions included the delivery of 14 blank letters (as well as 12 signed by the queen) to Ormond, authorising him to fill them as best "for the advancement of peace in Ireland".[16] These letters effectively presented the lord lieutenant with a *carte blanche* to conclude a treaty with the confederates on whatever terms he deemed necessary. Ormond, however, appeared intent on surrendering Dublin to the English parliament, and refused to be diverted by yet another royalist initiative from overseas.

In a heated exchange (illustrating the gap between Irish protestant thinking and attitudes at the exiled royal court in Paris), the lord lieutenant confided to Leyburn that if necessary he would "give up those places under his command rather to the English rebels than the Irish rebels, of which opinion he thought every good Englishman was". Leyburn, horrified by Ormond's attitude, replied that nothing would please the queen more than a treaty with the confederates, while nothing would be more grievous to the royalist cause than the relinquishing of Dublin to the English parliament.[17] He repeated this statement in a letter to the marquis of Clanricarde, and concluded that the surrender of Dublin to parliament would not please the queen and prince "and least of all the king".[18] Ormond can have been in no doubt, therefore, as to the evolving royalist strategy, and yet he chose to ignore Leyburn's advice and pursue his own goals.

In a report to the king, written after his flight to England in late July 1647, Ormond blamed the confederates for the collapse of the peace talks, claiming that the addition of four religious articles to the confederate oath marked "a full period to all our hopes from the Irish". The lord lieutenant acknowledged that the instructions brought by Leyburn from the queen all tended towards "a reconciliation of the differences", but insisted that confederate obduracy frustrated

O'Connell (eds), *Commentarius*, i, p. 712; Queen Henrietta Maria to Clanricarde, May 1645 (Lowe [ed.], *Clanricarde letter-book* p. 196). **15** Leyburn later wrote a detailed account of his mission, an invaluable source for the period April-August 1647. Leyburn, George, "Memoirs of George Leyburn, 1722", *Clarendon historical society's reprints*, series 2 (1884-86) pp 273-354. **16** Ibid. pp 307-11. **17** Ibid. p. 317; Winter Grant to Ormond, 13 May 1647 (Gilbert [ed.], *Irish confederation*, vi, pp 197-8). Ormond had already written to the king expressing this conviction. The lord-lieutenant blamed the "perfidy of the Irish" for forcing him to deal with Westminster, adding that he preferred to surrender Dublin to the English parliament "than to the Irish rebels". Ormond to Charles I, 17 March 1647 (Bodl. Clarendon Mss 29 f.153). **18** Leyburn to Clanricarde, 10 May 1647 (Lowe [ed.], *Clanricarde letter-book* pp 436-7). Clanricarde, prevented by the confederates from corresponding with Dublin, wrote back strongly defending Ormond's loyalty and criticising the supreme council. Ibid. pp 438-9.

his best efforts. Ormond undoubtedly felt concerned at the prospect of putting Dublin's protestants under "the tyranny of those that then ruled amongst the Irish". Having recently suffered a humiliating defeat at the hands of the clerical faction, and with accounts of the massacres of 1641 still fresh in his mind, the lord lieutenant's reluctance was at least understandable.[19]

A number of other factors, apart from religious issues, influenced Ormond at this time, including political developments in England. The handing over of Charles I to the Westminster parliament by the Scots on 30 January 1647 convinced the lord lieutenant of the need for a rapprochement with the victors of the English civil war. A week later Ormond offered to surrender Dublin to parliament, and talks continued for a number of months.[20] A parallel set of negotiations contributed towards his reluctance to conclude a settlement with the confederates. Three French agents in Ireland (De la Monnerie, Du Talon and Du Moulin) hoped to encourage a new treaty between Kilkenny and Dublin, as a means of facilitating the recruitment of troops for service on the continent. The supreme council authorised them to enlist 1,000 troops in confederate territory, but their primary interest at the beginning of the year centred on the royalist administration in Dublin. Using George Digby as an intermediary, Ormond began to explore the possibility of exporting the soldiers under his command, as well as some confederate regiments, into French service.[21]

From March until July 1647, Ormond directed his energies into organising the French expedition, keeping the confederates occupied with another round of pointless negotiations, and offering Dublin to the parliamentarians in return for a licence to transport troops abroad.[22] His surrender of the city in July contributed greatly to the ultimate destruction of royalist hopes in Ireland, providing the English parliament with a second strategic beachhead for an invasion of the country, and delaying the final peace treaty with Kilkenny by almost two years. Ormond's duplicity in his dealings with the confederates also undermined the authority of the moderates, who desperately needed to show some dividends

**19** The lord lieutenant presented this report to the king at Hampton Court. BL Egerton Mss 2541 ff 377–81. Ormond clearly believed that the clerical faction still dominated affairs in Kilkenny, or at least used this as an excuse for failing to conclude a new settlement with the confederates. **20** These developments are discussed in chapter 4 pp 137–8. **21** Du Moulin to Ormond, 26 March 1647 (Bodl. Carte Mss 20 f.549). On 19 February, while he was negotiating the surrender of Dublin to parliament, Ormond commissioned George Digby to treat with any foreign minister for the military employment of the marquis and over 5,000 troops. Commission by Ormond to Digby, 19 Feb. 1647 (Bodl. Carte Mss 20 f.326). **22** Ormond, despite having rejected the assembly's peace overtures in March, offered another cessation in mid-April. This was declined by the supreme council because of the arrival of more parliamentarian troops from England. Bodl. Carte Mss 20 f.627, 646. Right up until his departure from Dublin in July, Ormond anxiously petitioned Westminster to allow the transfer of troops to the continent, but without success. Manchester etc. to Ormond, 31 July 1647 (Bodl. Carte Mss 21 f.366).

from negotiations (as well as military success) in order to hold the association together.

During this period, the supreme council made every effort to accommodate the royalists (despite Ormond's unwillingness to make a deal), but in April, following the admittance of a regiment from Chester into Dublin, the confederates retaliated by ordering Preston to take the offensive in Leinster.[23] The town of Carlow, the sole surviving royalist stronghold in the south of the province, fell to the confederates after a short siege at the end of that month. Preston's progress delighted Nicholas Plunkett, and even the nuncio admitted this success was "much to his credit".[24] Leyburn's return to Kilkenny from Dublin shortly afterwards, however, resurrected hopes of a peace settlement. The council repeated the offer, delivered by Gerald Fennell and Geoffrey Barron on 3 March, that the two sides retain separate governments but unite against the king's enemies. The confederates would pay Ormond's costs, who in return would ensure that catholics in royalist areas enjoyed their religion, lives, estates and liberties without hindrance.[25]

Throughout these negotiations, the lord lieutenant bitterly criticised the confederates' resolve "to insist positively upon the votes of the late assembly, which, as we [Ormond] understand them, are inconsistent with those grounds, on which there can be any hope of settling any peace in this kingdom". Nicholas Plunkett must have been confused by such attacks, convinced just two months earlier of the lord lieutenant's determination "not to conclude with any but the general assembly".[26] Despite their anxiety for a settlement, Plunkett refused to be intimidated by Ormond's demands that the supreme council decide on the peace issue. A central part of the moderates' strategy involved the primacy of the assembly, the final arbiter in any deal with the royalists. Ormond failed to fully understand this fundamental shift in confederate politics until his return to Ireland in September 1648.[27]

23 Captain Matthew Wood to Lenthall, 24 April 1647 (Bodl. Carte Mss 20 f.646). A number of these newly arrived troops from England, presumably not all catholics, actually fled to the confederate side, who were never sure how to deal with protestant deserters. Later that same year Rinuccini rebuked the supreme council for encouraging protestants to join their ranks. Rinuccini to Panzirolo, 3 Nov. 1647 (Aiazza [ed.], *Embassy* p. 327). Why any protestants would wish to join the association of confederate catholics of Ireland is another matter entirely! 24 Plunkett to Preston, 27 April 1647 (PRO SP Ire. 263/124 f.209); Rinuccini to Panzirolo, 3 May 1647 (Aiazza [ed.], *Embassy* p. 285). 25 Declaration of the supreme council, 10 May 1647 (Bodl. Carte Mss 21 f.42). The terms, rejected earlier by Ormond on 22 March, are listed in Bodl. Carte Mss 20 f.386. The mission of Barron and Fennell is discussed in chapter 4 p. 138f. 26 During the negotiations in March, Plunkett purposely kept the assembly in session for this very reason, "with great sufferance and much expense of time and otherwise". Leyburn, "Memoirs" p. 323; Plunkett to Ormond, 20 March 1647 (Gilbert [ed.], *Irish confederation*, vi, pp 191-2). 27 After his return to Ireland in September 1648, Ormond informed Inchiquin that no treaty "can be so valid or effectual as that which shall be transacted immediately with a general assembly of them". There was no question at that stage as to where the ultimate

By the middle of May, George Leyburn, frustrated by the lack of progress in the talks, attempted to broker a deal on his own initiative. He solicited the support of George Digby, whose primary interest in peace concerned the recruitment of soldiers (confederate and royalist) for France. On 18 May, Leyburn returned to the supreme council at Clonmel with fresh proposals, and requested that a committee be appointed to examine his offer. The council agreed, nominating Viscount Muskerry and Bishop O'Dwyer of Limerick to represent the two principal factions, with Nicholas Plunkett acting as chairman.[28]

Leyburn offered a month-by-month cessation for six months, but insisted on using the last treaty as the basis for any future settlement. He claimed that before granting any further religious concessions Ormond would require a fresh commission from the queen. By limiting the duration of the cease-fire, and playing down the extent of the lord lieutenant's powers, Leyburn hoped to moderate confederate demands, while also providing Digby with enough time and space to organise the export of troops. Plunkett remained unconvinced, explaining that the previous assembly had already rejected the peace terms. Leyburn argued that this decision could easily be reversed, adding that "if you be not enabled of your own selves to go through with a peace, you will, when it shall be seasonably proposed, accord to the calling of an assembly".[29]

Sensing that the real obstacle to peace lay with the clerical faction, Leyburn travelled to Kilkenny, with the bishop of Clogher, to confront the nuncio. Rinuccini made clear his preference for a new peace treaty over a renewed cease-fire, as "cessations had been the reason why the Irish affairs had no better progress". Leyburn believed, however, that in reality the nuncio objected to any new agreement. Nonetheless, the royalist agent endorsed the idea (which he claimed originated with Rinuccini) of a clerical convocation to discuss the matter, particularly in light of the council's reluctance to take any decision on its own. Digby approved of this development, writing that he was "very glad of the assembly of the clergy at Limerick and should be gladder of a general assembly".[30]

Rinuccini's account of these events differed in one crucial area. The nuncio insisted that the idea of a clerical convocation arose as part of the supreme council's response to his objections to yet another cease-fire. Certainly, in a letter to Rome at the end of May, the nuncio expressed grave doubts about the possible consequences of such a meeting, convinced "that the general timidity, and hostility of the laity to the clergy will outweigh my opinion".[31] Taking the nuncio's

authority lay within the confederate association. Ormond to Inchiquin, [13 Nov. 1648] (Carte, *Ormond*, vi, pp 581-3). **28** The royalist agent made no comment on the composition of the committee, but the principle of balance was clearly being invoked. Leyburn, "Memoirs" pp 324-30. **29** Idem. **30** The meeting eventually took place in Clonmel where the supreme council was already in residence. Idem. **31** Rinuccini was also acutely aware of the fact that the support of Owen Roe O'Neill had "produced an indescribable hatred towards him, still more

reservations into consideration, it seems more probable that the council first proposed the meeting of the clerical convocation. This suggests, therefore, that Rinuccini did not in fact command unconditional support among the bishops.

The clerics assembled in early June and reaffirmed their opposition to the Ormond peace treaty. On the question of a cease-fire with the royalists, however, they adopted the middle course so despised by the nuncio, deciding to leave the matter to the discretion of the council "without offering either assent or dissent".[32] The confederate leadership could now arrange a truce without fear of clerical opposition. Even at this late stage, the moderates, with some assistance from Leyburn (and a degree of flexibility by the bishops), won majority support for a policy of compromise, but time was not on their side.

The arrival of 2,000 parliamentarian soldiers, led by Colonel Michael Jones, outside Dublin on 7 June 1647, added a sense of urgency to the situation. On 11 June the confederates, desperate for an agreement to prevent the surrender of the city to Jones, concluded a two month truce with Leyburn. The day before this, however, Ormond signed letters-patent ordering the Leinster garrisons under his command to admit parliamentarian troops.[33] This agreement signalled the total collapse of the royalist position in Ireland, with Dublin the sole remaining centre under the control of the lord lieutenant.

The picture becomes even more confused at this stage, with a multitude of plots and sub-plots unfolding during the course of that summer. It was at this critical juncture (the beginning of June), that Muskerry seized control of the Munster army on the pretext of some unspecified threat from Owen Roe O'Neill. The viscount contacted Thomas Preston seeking his support, while still proclaiming his loyalty to the supreme council. Despite his recent military success, capturing the town of Carlow, the Leinster general still harboured a deep resentment over the attempts to censure him in the assembly. As a result, he proved susceptible to fresh approaches from the peace faction.

Sensing an opportunity to exploit confederate tensions, George Digby devised a new plan, which involved Preston moving his army towards Dublin to increase the pressure on the parliamentary forces.[34] This would have the dual purpose of strengthening Ormond's hand in his negotiations with Westminster, while also bringing into the vicinity of the capital a large body of troops ready for export to France. Preston, however, proved unwilling to advance without support, and pleaded with the supreme council to order O'Neill's army from

towards the clergy, he being considered their champion". Rinuccini to Panzirolo, [29 May] 1647 (Aiazza [ed.], *Embassy* p. 289). **32** Rinuccini to Panzirolo, 18 June 1647 (Aiazza [ed.], *Embassy* p. 295). **33** Leyburn, "Memoirs" pp 332-6. The Leinster garrisons were to admit troops with a patent from the parliamentary commissioners Arthur Annesley and Robert King. Letters-patent of Ormond, 10 June 1647 (Bodl. Carte Mss 21 f.194). **34** Certainly Edward Walsingham, Digby's secretary, encouraged Preston to advance towards Dublin on 16 June (PRO SP Ire. 264/98 f.279) and again on 3 July (PRO SP Ire. 265/1 f.1).

Connacht to assist him in attacking Dublin.[35] This astonishing *volte face* by Preston on the issue of working with O'Neill strongly suggests that the Ulster general (or more likely certain of his officers) had indicated a desire to serve abroad. Rumours to this effect were certainly in circulation after O'Neill halted his advance on Sligo to monitor developments elsewhere.[36]

The supreme council kept its nerve and resisted demands to divert Owen Roe O'Neill into Leinster. Leyburn ascribed this refusal to the council's "hatred" of the native Irish, and certainly Plunkett, French and Darcy had been horrified by the behaviour of the Ulster troops the previous winter.[37] The moderates, however, also suspected Preston's motives, and their decision made perfect military sense, "holding it sufficient if the lord lieutenant means well, having a party of his own, wherewith, together with the Leinster forces, he may be able to oppose and suppress the insolency of those newly landed". Reinforcements would be provided if necessary, and in the meantime the council authorised Preston to recruit new soldiers and incorporate any irregular forces into the weaker regiments of the regular army.[38]

On 18 June, Ormond finally concluded a deal with the parliamentary commissioners, surrendering control of the city of Dublin to Colonel Jones. The lord lieutenant retained possession of the castle, but only until he verified bills of exchange worth almost £11,000, given him by the commissioners to offset his expenses.[39] In many respects Ormond had little alternative, with the parliamen-

---

35 The supreme council, while favouring an attack on the parliamentarians, was almost certainly unaware of Preston's dealings with Digby. 36 Supreme council to Leinster committee, 14 June 1647 (PRO SP Ire. 264/87 f.262); Leinster committee to Preston, 17 June 1647 (PRO SP Ire. 264/105 f.293). After all the complaints about Ulster troops, the supreme council must have been extremely suspicious of Preston's request, and that efforts were being made to "direct General O'Neill's forces from Connacht until the Scots had been better provided". Pa[trick] N[etterville] to [Preston], 18 June 1647 (Bodl. Carte Mss 21 f.234). These developments might also explain the appearance of Daniel O'Neill before the supreme council with a proposal from the Ulster army for a truce with Ormond. For reasons that remain unclear, the council imprisoned O'Neill on the spurious grounds that he had travelled without a proper pass. Cregan, D.F., "An Irish cavalier: Daniel O'Neill in the civil wars 1642-51", *Studia Hibernica*, no. 5 (1965) p. 125; Leyburn, "Memoirs" pp 330-1. Later that year Phelim O'Neill, Alexander MacDonnell and others left Owen Roe's army, an incident which could well be related with Digby's plot to export troops to France. Casway describes these developments in his biography of Owen Roe O'Neill but makes no mention of any French connection. Casway, *Owen Roe O'Neill* p. 193. Finally, the rumours about Owen Roe wishing to transport troops to the continent were mentioned by the French agent De la Monnerie in a report to Mazarin in August but cannot be confirmed or refuted. De la Monnerie to Mazarin, 25 Aug. 1647 (Gilbert [ed.], *Irish confederation*, vi, pp 329-35). 37 Leyburn, "Memoirs" p. 343. The moderates' concern at the behaviour of the Ulster troops is discussed earlier in this chapter. 38 Supreme council to Leinster committee, 14 June 1647 (PRO SP Ire. 264/87 f.62), Supreme Council to Preston, 14 June 1647 (PRO SP Ire. 264/89 f.265 ); Supreme council to Leinster committee, 14 June 1647 (PRO SP Ire. 264/91 f.268). 39 Declaration of Ormond, 18 June

tarian army camped on his doorstep controlling all the royalist garrisons in Leinster. Nonetheless, when news of the surrender reached Kilkenny, Leyburn recorded the supreme council's bitter comment "that my lord [Ormond] had never meant in good earnest".[40]

The fact that, for the moment at least, the lord lieutenant remained in Dublin castle encouraged the various conspirators to persist with their plans. Although the council warned Preston not to expect any help from Ormond, the Leinster general still entertained plans of a grand alliance with the royalists.[41] Digby and his cohorts viewed the brief mutiny among parliamentarian troops in Dublin at the beginning of July, over pay and conditions, as a missed opportunity. Walsingham wrote to Preston that "if your army had been in these parts you might have carried the whole business [be]fore you". The Leinster general, as ever, favoured a more cautious approach, waiting for further reinforcements before proceeding with his campaign.[42]

By mid-July, as Ormond prepared to abandon Dublin castle, Digby urged him to delay his departure until ships for the transport of troops arrived from France. Digby believed that this deal with the French government would eventually facilitate "the restitution of Ireland to the crown of England". He claimed that within one month the "Irish shall be more broken and weakened by art, than they can hope to do in twelve months of war". This argument appealed greatly to Ormond, who had already explained to the parliamentary commissioners in April that by exporting 5,000 troops to the continent, he would take the best of the Irish out of the country, thereby "weakening them exceedingly".[43]

A week later, Digby changed his tactics, informing Ormond of a meeting with two representatives of the Leinster army, Robert Talbot and Richard Bellings. If the lord lieutenant postponed his departure by just one month "they make no doubt but that this army [Leinster] and that of the lord Munster [Muskerry] shall so awe the council, as to prevent the destruction which they see

1647 (PRO SP Ire. 264/109 f.300); *Articles of agreement made, concluded and agreed on at Dublin the eighteenth day of June 1647 ...*, Dublin 1647 (BL Thomason Tracts E394 f.14). Ormond, beset by financial difficulties, was obsessed with money; after the restoration of Charles II he submitted a detailed account of debts accrued by him on behalf of the royalist administration. TCD Mss 1181 (Miscellaneous documents). **40** Leyburn, "Memoirs" p. 349. In fairness to Ormond, he at least made some provisions for those catholics who had remained loyal to his administration. The articles concluded that those catholics not adhering to the rebels "may be encouraged to continue in their habitations, and in enjoyment of their estates with confidence". *Articles of agreement, June 1647* (BL Thomason Tracts E394 f.14). **41** Plunkett to Preston, 21 June 1647 (PRO SP Ire. 264/117 f.313). **42** Preston wrote to Walsingham that "as soon as monies come I shall march hence into them quarters. I wait, however, 'till I am strong enough, which is the wise plan". Preston to Walsingham, [July] 1647 (PRO SP Ire. 265/1 f.1). **43** Digby to Ormond, 17 July 1647 (Carte, *Ormond*, vi, pp 525-6); Ormond to Dudley Loftus, 9 April 1647 (Gilbert [ed.], *Irish confederation*, vii, pp 325-6). Neither Ormond nor Digby specified exactly the source of these troops.

visible before them by the council and Owen O'Neill".[44] If the council did not back down these royalist sympathisers were prepared to serve in France. Ormond expressed no interest in the prospect of a new alliance, and with no sign of parliamentary permission to transport any soldiers, he decided to leave Dublin.

Digby's disclosures (if true) reveal an astonishing degree of treachery within the confederate ranks. But are they credible? Muskerry allegedly committed himself in writing to the export of troops; but no evidence survives to support Digby's story, other than his own letters, and reports of his statements by the French agents.[45] It seems altogether more plausible that both Muskerry and Preston harboured ambitions to regain control of the supreme council (with royalist support if necessary) and to conclude a peace settlement with Ormond. The possibility of exporting troops to France would never have been anything more than a last-ditch alternative in the event of failure.[46]

With the peace faction actively plotting the overthrow of the supreme council, the moderates staked everything on a military break-through in Leinster. They urged Preston forward, fully realising how crucial the following six months would be for the confederate association. Bishop French exclaimed dramatically that everything would be "lost or won this very summer".[47] Convinced by this time of the futility of further talks with Ormond, they adopted an aggressive strategy to counter the threat of the English parliamentarians. The transfer of

**44** Digby to Ormond, 22 July 1647 (Carte, *Ormond*, vi, pp 526-9). The "lord Munster" in this context is almost certainly Viscount Muskerry, general of the confederate forces in that province. **45** Certainly, both Plunkett and French later denied that Leinster confederate soldiers were willing to depart to France. O'Ferrall and O'Connell (eds), *Commentarius*, iii, pp 700-16. There is no doubting, however, the close links between the Preston family and the French at this time. Thomas Preston's son, Colonel Robert Preston, had been employed by French agents to levy troops in 1646-7, and the following year, the Leinster general accepted an annual French pension of £125. Ohlmeyer, "Ireland Independent", *Independence to occupation* p. 104. None of this confirms of course that Thomas Preston would (or could) export the entire Leinster army to the continent. **46** It is true that following the confederate defeat at Dungan's Hill in August, Digby bemoaned the destruction of the Leinster forces, "having so great a part of Preston's army sure for foreign employment". Digby to Ormond, 19 Sept. 1647 (Carte, *Ormond*, vi, pp 543-8). But had Preston won that battle it is highly improbable that he would have agreed to the transport of the bulk of his victorious troops abroad. They would surely have been used by the peace faction in an attempt to overthrow the supreme council. Digby, moving in the shadowy world of intrigue and espionage, had come to believe his own propaganda. See also Ó hAnnracháin, "Far from terra firma" pp 298-300. **47** Both Plunkett and French urged Preston forward. Plunkett to Preston, 27 April 1647 (PRO SP 263/124 f.209); French to Plunkett, 28 April 1647 (PRO SP Ire. 263/126 f.213 ). French believed the approaching summer campaign was "made by God to try the hearts and resolutions of Ireland", concluding that both he and Preston would "stand or fall together in God's service". Ferns to Preston, 12 May 1647 (PRO SP Ire. 264/21 f.35). How Preston felt about all this talk of death or glory is not recorded!

power in Dublin presented the confederates with an ideal opportunity to consolidate their position in the province, through a scorched earth policy rather than
a direct assault on the city.[48]

In a significant move (reminiscent of the 1646 Dublin campaign), the council dispatched two members to Preston's camp, to encourage the general forward.
Bishop French departed for the front line in the middle of July and Nicholas
Plunkett joined him a few weeks later. Both men demanded decisive action "laying before the officers the little hope there was of the armies being supplied with
any further means in a long time".[49] Preston's initial advance culminated in the
capture of Naas, Sigginstown and Harristown. Digby made one last attempt to
forge a settlement, instructing Leyburn to arrange a meeting with Plunkett and
French "about laying a new foundation on our business". They agreed to talks,
but news of the parliamentarian army marching out of Dublin prevented any
further discussions from taking place. Leyburn desperately tried to convince
Preston not to fight but Ormond's departure had rendered the general "distrust-
ful".[50]

In early August Preston, having earlier refused battle in a more advantageous
situation, now inexplicably left a secure camp at Portlester and began to march
towards Dublin. Although running short of supplies, Colonel Jones managed to
intercept and decisively defeat him at Dungan's Hill, near Trim on 8 August.[51]
Jones proved himself an able and effective commander, but Preston's inept display of generalship during the battle contributed to the parliamentarian victory.
The Leinster army, the best trained and equipped confederate force, was totally

---

**48** On 13 July the council ordered Preston to destroy the enemy's harvest, an action they hoped
would end all resistance. Council members feared that further supplies reaching Dublin from
England the following Spring would prove fatal to the confederate cause. Supreme council to
Preston, 13 July 1647 (Bodl. Carte Mss 21 f.296). The Leinster army commissioners were also
ordered to gather up provisions. Leinster committee to Ferns and Plunkett, 4 Aug. 1647 (PRO
SP Ire. 265/25 f.151). **49** On 13 July the council informed Preston of French's imminent arrival.
Bodl. Carte Mss 21 f.296. Plunkett was still in Kilkenny a few days later, but had reached the
Leinster army's camp by the beginning of August. Order of the supreme council, 17 July 1647
(PRO SP Ire 265/19 f.122). Payments to the army of Leinster, 5 Aug. 1647 (Gilbert [ed.], *Irish
confederation*, vii, p. 348). According to Lenihan, this story (recounted by Bellings) is implausi-
ble, but Plunkett and French, desperate for gains in Leinster, may well have raised fears about
future supplies. Lenihan, "Catholic confederacy" p. 401. **50** Leyburn's observation must cast
doubts on Digby's assurances that the Leinster troops were ready for export to France. Leyburn
"Memoirs" pp 352-3; Preston to -, 15 July 1647 (PRO SP Ire. 265/7 f.13). **51** A parliamentarian
officer, Patrick Wemys, wrote that Jones "was forced to fight Preston, as he had got between us
and Dublin and meant to have stormed it". Sir Patrick Wemys to Percivall, 10 Aug. 1647 in
*HMC Egmont*, vol. 1, part 2, p. 447. Another officer, Matthew Rowe, also reported that
Preston intended to seize the city. *An exact and full relation of the great victory obtained against
the rebels at Dungan's Hill in Ireland 8 Aug. 1647 ...*, London 1647 (NLI Thorpe IV. no. 447).
Bellings, for his part, believed that Jones fought "but for bread and elbow-room about
Dublin". Bellings' History in Gilbert (ed.), *Irish confederation*, vii, p. 33.

destroyed in one afternoon's folly. The defeat, Digby reported, caused "a great consternation in all the old English and more moderate party of the Irish".[52]

The moderates also shared some of the responsibility, having urged a more active policy on a cautious general of limited abilities. Perhaps the temptation to capture the city proved irresistible to those confederates anxious to utilise the Leinster army, assembled and maintained at such a great cost. Edmund Borlase suggested that Preston may have received word from somebody in Leixlip (presumably Digby) to march on Dublin, but it is clear from Leyburn's account, that the royalists had temporarily lost all influence as a result of Ormond's departure.[53] Whatever the cause, confederate ambitions lay in ruins, leaving the council no alternative but to recall Owen Roe O'Neill from Connacht.[54]

The arrival of Ulster troops prevented a total collapse of the confederate position in Leinster. Preston's army, however, never recovered from the loss of so many seasoned veterans and any prospect of capturing Dublin faded entirely. Preston, temporarily appointed governor of Waterford and Kilkenny, began the slow process of recruiting and training new volunteers.[55] Despite Owen Roe O'Neill's timely intervention in Leinster, his own reputation had also suffered, due to his failure to capture the strategic town of Sligo, followed by a near mutiny in his army.[56] Many in Leinster were unhappy at the return of Ulster

---

52 Digby to Ormond, 19 Sept. 1647 (Carte, *Ormond*, vi, pp 543-8). Preston was undoubtedly an effective administrator and siege commander. He captured the vital fortress at Duncannon in March 1645, and the town of Roscommon during the Connacht campaign the following year. By 1647, the Leinster army under his command was the best equipped (and paid) of the confederate forces. Lenihan, "Catholic confederacy" p. 396. Preston, however, was never comfortable leading his troops in the field. As Bellings shrewdly observed, many of the Irish officers possessed "such a temper of abilities and parts as moved excellently by direction, but irregularly when they were the balance upon which their own motion depended". Bellings' History in Gilbert (ed.), *Irish confederation*, i, p. 74. Both of Preston's battlefield forays (at Old Ross in March 1643 and at Dungan's Hill, Aug. 1647) proved disastrous. According to Pádraig Lenihan the latter defeat was the single most important reason why the confederate association ultimately collapsed, as the trained and experienced troops of the Leinster army could not easily be replaced. Lenihan, "Catholic confederacy" p. 554. 53 The author of the *Aphorismical discovery* states that Preston, when questioned about the poor positioning for the battle, "did acknowledge the fact, but said that he was persuaded thereunto by the bishop of Ferns". Gilbert (ed.), *Contemporary history*, i, p. 157. See also Lenihan, "Catholic confederacy" pp 401-2. 54 The council sent Patrick Darcy and Piers Butler to inform O'Neill of the crisis in Leinster, allowing Darcy an opportunity to assess the damage caused by the Ulster troops in Connacht at first hand. O'Neill to Clanricarde, 15 Aug. 1647, "Unpublished Letters", *Analecta Hibernica*, no. 29 (1980) p. 243. 55 According to one report, Preston had recruited 4,000 men by the end of November. Cavan to Ormond, 20 Nov. 1647 (Bodl. Carte Mss 21 f.526). Colonel Michael Jones in Dublin was particularly well informed about the deployment of the confederates' Leinster troops. Michael Jones to Speaker at Westminster, 29 Sept. 1647 (Bodl. Carte Mss 118 f.42). 56 Casway asserts that lack of pay was the principal cause of the unrest in the Ulster ranks. Casway, *Owen Roe O'Neill* p. 193. According to one of O'Neill's officers,

troops (however necessary), who faced the usual problem of finding winter quarters.[57] Mutual suspicion and distrust threatened once more to plunge the confederates into violent internal conflict.

Thwarted in Leinster, George Digby shifted his attentions to the confederate army of Munster. Muskerry, despondent at Ormond's surrender of Dublin, relinquished command of this force to his close friend and ally Viscount Taaffe at the end of July. The supreme council confirmed the appointment even though the viscount had only taken the confederate oath after Ormond's departure from Ireland. In close contact with Digby and the French agents since April 1647, Taaffe nonetheless proved reluctant to commit himself to any particular plot.[58] On 31 August Digby informed the Munster general that he hoped to "succeed in drawing the party you are now engaged with under his majesty's power", or else assist in the export of troops. Repeating the strategy he employed in Leinster, Digby pleaded with Taaffe not to engage the enemy as royalist plans "depend upon your preserving that army".[59]

Taaffe heeded Digby's advice, and the Munster army remained inactive for the next two months, while he monitored events in Dublin and Kilkenny. As a result, Lord Inchiquin raided unchallenged throughout the province during the autumn, destroying much of County Tipperary. Rinuccini feared a royalist plot, with Taaffe preserving his army "that it may serve as a counter-poise to that of Ulster and force the assembly to pass resolutions".[60] Inchiquin also learned of these plans, when a confederate officer captured by the parliamentarians informed him that Taaffe intended to use his forces to overthrow the supreme council. The council, although suspicious, took no action against the lieutenant-general other than urging him to take the offensive against Inchiquin, and threatening to send for Owen Roe O'Neill.[61]

Henry McTully O'Neill, a general dissatisfaction with the supreme council contributed to the unrest. "A journal of the memorable transactions of General Owen O'Neill", *Desiderata curiosa Hibernica*, vol. 2, pp 507-9.  **57** Munster confederates also opposed the quartering of Ulster troops in their province. Rinuccini to Panzirolo, 28 Dec. 1647 (Aiazza [ed.], *Embassy* pp 352-5). **58** On 8 April, Valentine Savage observed a meeting in Dublin between Taaffe, Digby and a French agent. By late August, De la Monnerie informed Mazarin that he had received a written promise of troops from Muskerry, and a verbal one from Taaffe, who was evidently too shrewd to commit anything to paper. Savage to Percivall, 8 April 1647 in *HMC, Egmont*, vol. 1, part 2, p. 388; De la Monnerie to Mazarin, 25 Aug. 1647 (Gilbert [ed.], *Irish confederation*, vi, pp 329-35); Rinuccini to Panzirolo, 14 Aug. 1647 (Aiazza [ed.], *Embassy* p. 300).  **59** *Two letters of the lord Digby to the lord Taaffe, the rebels general in Munster, taken in the said general's cabinet in the late battle between him and the lord Inchiquin …*, London 1647 (BL Thomason Tracts E419 f.8). **60** Rinuccini to Panzirolo, 5 Nov. 1647 (Aiazza [ed.], *Embassy* pp 328-9).  **61** Supreme council to Taaffe, 23/25 Sept. 1647 (Bodl. Tanner Mss 58/2 f.529, 533); Supreme council to Taaffe, 8 Oct. 1647 (Bodl. Carte Mss 21 f.486); Inchiquin to Lenthall, 18 Nov. 1647, *Tanner letters* pp 274-8. Inchiquin's informant claimed the supreme council became suspicious of Taaffe when he recommended a truce with the parliamentarians in Munster. Indeed, rumours of such a truce

On 27 September 1647, the supreme council informed Muskerry that the previous assembly "by order of the 3 April last adjourned to the 12 November next, and then to meet at such place as we should think fit to direct".[62] This meeting of the eighth general assembly took place in Kilkenny against the backdrop of military reversals, internal tensions and treacherous intrigue. The day after the session began on 12 November, another military disaster brought the confederates to the brink of ruin. Viscount Taaffe, under pressure from the council, and worried by the prospect of O'Neill marching into Munster, finally engaged the parliamentarian forces. Lord Inchiquin, desperately short of supplies, had no alternative but "to starve or fight".[63]

At Knocknanuss, near Mallow in county Cork, Taaffe failed to exploit the initial breakthrough achieved by Alasdair MacColla and his Highland troops, allowing Inchiquin the opportunity to inflict a crushing defeat on the confederate Munster army. Considering the viscount's strenuous efforts during the previous six months to keep this force intact, either for export to France or to help overthrow the council, the disaster at Knocknanuss presumably resulted from Taaffe's sheer incompetence (and Inchiquin's military talent) rather than any possible treachery on his part.[64]

The confederates now faced their most severe crisis since the establishment of the association. It would take time, and more importantly money, to rebuild their shattered forces, both of which were in short supply. Inchiquin now controlled most of Munster (including the vital wheat growing region of Tipperary), except for the towns of Limerick, Clonmel and Waterford. In Leinster, although

were current at this time. Henry Jones, the protestant bishop of Clogher, informed Michael Jones on 6 October that there was "talk in Munster of a cessation offered by lord Taaffe to lord Inchiquin". Bodl. Carte Mss 118 f.41. **62** Supreme council to Muskerry, 27 Sept. 1647 (Bodl. Carte Mss 21 f.468). Taaffe to supreme council [Oct. 1647] (Bodl. Tanner Mss 58/2 f.711). Viscount Taaffe (and presumably all the confederate noblemen) received similar writs of summons. **63** Inchiquin believed that criticisms of Taaffe forced the viscount, for the sake of his honour, to take the offensive against "my lord Digby's advice, who forbid him to engage upon any terms against us, lest it should overthrow all his other designs". Inchiquin to Lenthall, 18 Nov. 1647, *Tanner letters* pp 274-8; Hodder to Percivall, 16 Nov. 1647, *HMC, Egmont* vol. 1, part 2 p. 483. **64** Parliamentary propaganda claimed that the enemy had lost over 4,000 men. *A mighty victory in Ireland obtained by the lord Inchiquin near Englishman's Hill* …, London 1647 (BL Thomason Tracts E417 f.14). Another report, clearly anxious to minimise the extent of the disaster, estimated confederate losses as low as 1,500 men. "Account of battle of Knockmoness [*sic*], 1647" (Aiazza [ed.], *Embassy* pp 335-7). A few days after the battle, Inchiquin wrote that as the fighting did not last long, he believed the number slain could not have exceeded 3,000. *A true relation of a great victory obtained by the forces under the command of the lord Inchiquin in Munster in Ireland* …, London 1647 (BL Thomason Tracts E418 f.6). Certainly fewer were killed at Knocknanuss than Dungan's Hill, as the majority of confederate troops fled the battlefield. In a generous assessment, Lenihan argues that Taaffe lost because he was leading a scratch army. Lenihan, "Catholic confederacy" p. 552.

O'Neill successfully implemented the scorched earth policy originally entrusted to Preston, the attendant destruction left the Ulster army with no winter quarters.[65] Much of Ulster and Connacht remained disputed with the Scots and parliamentarians, and contributed little or nothing to the confederate cause.

Money from Rome, promised by Rinuccini earlier in the year, had also failed to arrive, further undermining the nuncio's influence. He wrote despairingly that the country was "not only divided but full of suspicion and treachery without a chief ruler capable of cutting the knot of difficulty", and predicted as "inevitable" a confederate civil war. According to Rinuccini, those who favoured peace could be divided into two groups, one "longing for quiet", the other "more malignant". The latter sought not only to revive the old peace treaty, but at the same time to disgrace the clergy, Owen Roe O'Neill and the Ulstermen.[66]

A general assembly, held in such an atmosphere of distrust and potential violence, represented a major challenge to the moderates, whose aggressive military strategy had clearly failed. They urgently needed to re-examine their options, but the general mood at the meeting favoured a renewed attempt at a settlement with the royalists. The low attendance (due to the onset of winter and military pressures) undoubtedly influenced proceedings, as the peace faction supporters in the Butler heartland of south Leinster and east Munster enjoyed relatively easy access to Kilkenny. Rinuccini claimed "the mob of Leinster, many of them minions of Muskerry" dominated the assembly. In the absence of any returns, however, his accusations of electoral malpractice must be treated with caution.[67]

For whatever reasons, only nine Ulster representatives travelled to Kilkenny. They demanded proxy votes for the entire province, much to the chagrin of the peace faction, who successfully opposed the move. The Ulster delegates responded that as a result they would not be bound by any decisions taken in the assembly. With Owen Roe O'Neill's army lurking menacingly outside the city, unable to secure winter quarters, the prospects for consensus appeared remote.[68]

---

65 In November, Michael Jones reported O'Neill's advance to within 5 miles of Dublin to the English parliament. Jones to the Speaker at Westminster, 10 Nov. 1647 (Bodl. Carte Mss 118 f.41). Again according to Inchiquin, the supreme council, suspicious of Taaffe's intentions, ordered O'Neill not to engage the parliamentarians "until they had established their own power in the assembly by the countenance of it". Inchiquin to Lenthall, 18 Nov. 1647, *Tanner letters* pp 274-8. **66** Rinuccini to Panzirolo, 6 Oct. 1647 (Aiazza [ed.], *Embassy* pp 323-7). The dean of Fermo, Dionysius Massari, did not return from Rome until early 1648, and only brought a fraction of the sum sought by Rinuccini. Massari, "Irish campaign" p. 743. **67** The nuncio claimed that Muskerry's supporters prevented their opponents from attending the assembly. Rinuccini to Panzirolo, 24 Dec. 1647 (Aiazza [ed.], *Embassy* pp 343-6); O'Ferrall and O'Connell (eds), *Commentarius*, ii, p. 789. Similar accusations at the previous assembly, directed at the clerical family, proved grossly exaggerated. See chapter 4 pp 128-31. **68** Rinuccini wrote that Ulster only sent 9 instead of 73 representatives to the assembly. Rinuccini to Panzirolo, 24 Dec. 1647 (Aiazza [ed.], *Embassy* pp 343-6). 1640 parliamentary

Viscount Muskerry and his colleagues made a further attempt to weaken their opponents by objecting to the presence of unconsecrated bishops at the assembly. They had been summoned by the supreme council, but those termed "lawyers and malignants" by the nuncio challenged this ruling. The case against the bishops centred on the fact that according to English law (which the confederates swore to uphold) unconsecrated bishops had no temporal possessions, and therefore did not qualify as barons of the kingdom. Muskerry added that Boetius MacEgan, bishop-elect of Ross, should also be excluded on the grounds that his appointment by the pope, without the prior consent of the supreme council, directly contravened an earlier agreement with Rome.[69]

Despite the merits of the peace faction's argument, the practice until then had been to admit unconsecrated bishops to the assembly. Clogher, Ardfert and Ferns all attended previous, less contentious, assemblies before their consecrations.[70] The dispute over the bishop-elect of Ross, however, raised the potentially explosive issue of foreign jurisdiction. Rinuccini, while content to obtain the council's approval for his choice of bishop, firmly believed the final word lay with the papacy.[71] The issue remained unresolved for the moment, and all the unconsecrated bishops (including MacEgan) continued to sit in the assembly.

The moderates also suffered a severe setback with the defection of one of their leading figures Patrick Darcy. A key supporter of Nicholas Plunkett during the treaty crisis in August 1646, Darcy subsequently helped to formulate the new confederate policy. At the assembly in March 1647, his election to the council (along with Plunkett and French) confirmed the growing ascendancy of the moderates.[72] During the course of that year, however, the Galway lawyer became increasingly disillusioned with political and military developments, declaring

returns, however, list only 66 seats for the province. Clarke, *Old English* p. 255. According to the nuncio, O'Neill cast a long shadow over the proceedings of the assembly. Account of what happened to the bishop of Clogher, 18 Dec. 1647 (Aiazza [ed.], *Embassy* pp 339–42). **69** Rinuccini to Panzirolo, 4 Dec. 1647 (Aiazza [ed.], *Embassy* pp 337–8); O'Ferrall and O'Connell (eds), *Commentarius*, ii, pp 787–8. **70** One of the first assembly lists contains the names of Richard O'Connell (described as bishop-elect of Ardfert) and Heber MacMahon (described as bishop-elect of Down and Connor). Dublin City Library, Gilbert Collection Mss 219 (roll 2). Nicholas French sat in the 1645 assembly as bishop-elect of Ferns. Dublin City Library, Gilbert Collection Mss 219 (roll 3). The dates of consecration are contained in Cregan, "Counter-reformation episcopate" p. 87. **71** Shortly after his arrival, Rinuccini was presented by the supreme council with a list of 13 nominees to vacant bishoprics. At the time the papal nuncio had no objection to any of them, although he was careful to change the term "election" in the document to "recommendation". Rinuccini to Pamphili, 31 Dec. 1645 (Aiazza [ed.], *Embassy* p. 106). **72** Order by the ecclesiastical congregation, 26 Sept. 1646 (Gilbert [ed.], *Irish confederation*, vi, pp 144–6). Darcy is not included in one list of council members for 1647, but was certainly elected by the assembly in March of that year as his name appears on most council documents. The list is in Bodl. Carte Mss 21 f.571, Darcy's name appears on the following documents: Bodl. Carte Mss 20 f.556, 21 f.296; PRO SP Ire. 264/12 f.22, 264/46 f.108, 265/19 f.102 etc.

himself particularly shocked at the behaviour of the Ulster troops. He returned to Connacht in the autumn determined "never to intermeddle in public affairs".[73]

On witnessing at first hand the devastation of his native province (which he blamed on the abuses of the clergy and Ulstermen), Darcy contacted Viscount Muskerry to offer his services in the forthcoming assembly. He urged decisive action to prevent the total destruction of confederate government by unruly elements. Lucas Dillon wrote to Viscount Taaffe that the celebrated lawyer had "converted beyond belief and promises to perform many good acts in this next assembly".[74] Darcy had provided a vital link between the moderates and influential representatives from Galway, including Roebuck Lynch and Richard Blake among others. Together with Nicholas Plunkett (Pale gentry), and Bishop French (moderate clergy), he formed a powerful triumvirate which increasingly controlled affairs in Kilkenny after the collapse of the first Ormond peace treaty. Without his support the influence of the moderates at the assembly declined significantly, with serious implications for confederate unity.

The appointment of agents to travel to the continent provided the catalyst for renewed factional conflict. After their recent military disasters the confederates desperately needed money and supplies from abroad. Anthony Martin of Galway formally proposed "that they should call in some foreign prince for protection", with France, Spain and the papacy as the most likely candidates.[75] Assembly members supported Martin's idea, but only in the context of renewed plans to form an alliance with the exiled English court in Paris. The detailed instructions given to the various agents are examined later in the chapter, as during the assembly itself the main controversy centred on the process of selection.

The assembly nominated the two leading moderates, Nicholas Plunkett and Bishop French for the vital mission to the papacy, a move which aroused little controversy. According to the nuncio, a motion by Richard Bellings to prevent any bishop travelling to Rome was laughed out of the chamber. Despite the military and political failures of the previous eight months, Plunkett and French retained their popularity with the confederate rank and file, the result no doubt of both men's "desire to stand well with everybody".[76]

---

**73** Darcy to Muskerry, 6 Nov. 1647 (Bodl. Carte Mss 21 f.517). Darcy was one of the most active members on the supreme council until August 1647, when after the confederate defeat at Dungan's Hill he was sent to order O'Neill from Connacht into Leinster. O'Neill to Clanricarde, 15 Aug. 1647, "Unpublished letters and papers of Owen Roe O'Neill", *Analecta Hibernica*, no. 29 p. 243. **74** Darcy to Muskerry, 6 Nov. 1647 (Bodl. Carte Mss 21 f.517); Dillon to Taaffe, 6 Nov. 1647 in *HMC, Manuscripts of the duke of Portland*, vol. 1,13th report, appendix part 1 p. 440. **75** Martin's proposal, Nov. 1647 (BL Stowe 82 f.155). The idea of a foreign protector had been raised at the previous assembly, early in 1647. See chapter 4 p. 139. **76** Supreme council instructions to Plunkett and Ferns (BL Stowe Mss 82 f.155-6); Rinuccini to Panzirolo, 24 and 28 Dec. 1647 (Aiazza [ed.], *Embassy* pp 348-9, 352-5).

Another moderate, Richard Blake of Galway agreed to accompany the bishop-elect of Ross, considered by many an ally of Owen Roe O'Neill, to Spain. Blake's inclusion had been at the insistence of the Spanish envoy, De la Torre, who argued that Spain, like Rome, deserved two agents. With the Spanish monarchy virtually bankrupt and facing revolts in Portugal, Catalonia and Naples, the confederates expected little from that quarter. No evidence survives to show whether Blake or Ross ever left the country, although a copy of the instructions given to the French delegation, included a note that similar instructions be given to those travelling to Spain.[77]

Serious trouble erupted between the factions, however, over the selection of the delegation for Paris.[78] The assembly nominated Viscount Muskerry and Geoffrey Browne, both of the peace faction, with the bishop of Clogher, a close associate of Owen Roe O'Neill and the nuncio, providing an element of political balance. Clogher, however, declined the appointment on the grounds that he spoke neither English nor French, and was hated by Queen Henrietta Maria and her advisers. In reality, the bishop's reluctance stemmed more from political considerations, than any linguistic deficiencies. Rinuccini claimed assembly members (dominated by the peace faction) chose Clogher as part of a concerted strategy to clear the country of "all suspected persons", though this accusation is difficult to reconcile with the selection of Muskerry and Browne.[79]

Whatever the truth, the nuncio and ecclesiastical congregation supported the bishop's stance. The assembly, however, insisted that Clogher accept its orders, and his refusal led to a walk-out by over fifty members. Viscount Muskerry, eager to take advantage of the clerical faction's discomfiture, demanded the bishop's arrest. The following day assembly members, determined to enforce the supreme authority of the legislature, ordered Clogher to leave the chamber.[80] A

77 The balance of probabilities, given that the missions to Rome and Paris are well documented, suggests the Spanish mission never left Ireland. In fact, De la Torre, had already been informed from Spain that there was no money available for Ireland. Instructions for France (BL Stowe Mss 82 f.157); Letters from De la Torre, *Wild Geese in Spanish Flanders, 1582-1700*, ed. Brendan Jennings (Dublin 1964) p. 381; Cregan, D.F., "Confederation of Kilkenny" (PhD thesis) p. 260. 78 Inchiquin, whose intelligence network provided a stream of excellent information, reported a "great contention" between the factions, with Viscount Muskerry eventually emerging victorious. Inchiquin to Ormond, 19 Jan. 1648 (Bodl. Carte Mss 22 f.5). 79 Account of what happened to the bishop of Clogher, 18 Dec. 1647; Report on the affairs of Ireland, 1649 (Aiazza [ed.], *Embassy* pp 339-42, 519-21). MacMahon was educated in the religious colleges at Douai and Louvain, and therefore almost certainly spoke Latin and Spanish, apart from his native Irish. In May 1647 the bishop also acted as an interpreter for the nuncio in his dealings with the royalist agent, George Leyburn. It seems improbable that MacMahon would have undertaken this task if he could not speak English, Leyburn's native tongue. Given that the bishop sat on all nine supreme councils, it is almost certain he possessed some knowledge of the English language, however imperfect. Leyburn, "Memoirs" pp 327-8. For the educational background of the Irish bishops see Cregan, "Counter-reformation episcopate" pp 112-13. 80 Account of what happened to the bishop of Clogher, 18 Dec. 1647 (Aiazza

direct clash between the civil and religious powers within the confederate association appeared inevitable.

Muskerry argued that the "customs and the decrees of the king who was represented by the assembly" countenanced the incarceration of a bishop. The assembly, therefore, issued a decree forbidding Clogher to leave the city, which in Rinuccini's opinion, represented an outrageous breach of clerical immunity. Owen Roe O'Neill, sensing an opportunity for the clerical faction to regain control of the central administration, offered his services to the nuncio. With the Leinster and Munster forces in total disarray, there was little to prevent the Ulster army staging a *coup d'état*. Rinuccini resisted the temptation, anxious not to be blamed yet again for the collapse of confederate unity, and worried that hostility towards the Ulster troops might "possibly change the feelings of the half-hearted".[81]

The crisis was eventually defused through the intervention of Nicholas Plunkett, using his authority as assembly chairman to enforce a compromise. The assembly suspended its decree prohibiting Clogher from leaving Kilkenny, with Plunkett merely advising the bishop not to quit the city. The removal of Clogher from the delegation, to be replaced by the marquis of Antrim, a moderate (if somewhat maverick) figure, further eased the tension between the various factions.[82] For the moment at least, Plunkett had successfully restored a semblance of confederate unity, without resolving any of the underlying problems threatening to destroy the association.

Although the controversy over Clogher's appointment to the Paris mission dominated assembly proceedings, the meeting also witnessed one final attempt to reform the confederate system of government. The proposals concentrated on the functions and practices of the supreme council, and on the issue of accountability in particular.[83] The reformers hoped to curb increasing level of disorders, "occasioned by the neglect of putting the orders of the several assemblies, and the supreme council, in execution". This failure had resulted in a breakdown of

[ed.], *Embassy* pp 339-42). **81** Idem; Rinuccini to Panzirolo, 24 Dec. 1647 (Aiazza [ed.], *Embassy* pp 339-42, 346-7). The defeats of Preston and Taaffe increased, rather than moderated, the militancy and demands of their supporters. The more Leinster and Munster confederates relied on Owen Roe O'Neill, the more they resented the Ulster troops and their clerical allies. **82** The French agent De la Monnerie reported that Antrim was delighted with his appointment "hoping it would serve to replace him in the good opinion of their majesties". The confederates hoped to exploit his connections at court, but Rinuccini feared Antrim would be dominated by Muskerry and Browne. The nuncio insisted, therefore, that Antrim's mentor, Patrick Crelly, abbot of Newry, accompany the marquis "to temper his excessive good nature and bring it about that he remain firm in the midst of the plots of the other two envoys". Ohlmeyer, *Civil war and restoration* pp 203-4. **83** The reforms are printed in Gilbert (ed.), *Irish confederation*, vi, pp 208-33. The accountability of the confederate executive had been a major concern of reformers in both 1644 and 1646. See chapter 2 pp 83-6 and chapter 3 pp 103-4.

central authority, described as "a general contempt of government". The thrust of these reforms was similar to those implemented by the assembly two years earlier, although expanded in a number of crucial areas.[84] The growing frustration at the inefficiency and ineffectiveness of confederate rule, by whatever faction, ensured these proposals received widespread support.

Changes in the structure of the supreme council reflected the desire for a more streamlined and efficient administration. The assembly reduced the council by half, from 24 to 12 resident members, three from each province, and established a committee to try to come up with an agreed list of councillors. This committee consisted of Viscount Muskerry and Geoffrey Browne of the peace faction, with Nicholas Plunkett and Bishop French, representing the views of the clergy.[85] It soon became apparent, however, that Plunkett and French had their own agenda, effectively excluding the voice of the clerical faction from the decision process.

Rinuccini had attempted to veto the election of four particular individuals (Lord Athenry, Lucas Dillon, Gerald Fennell and Richard Bellings), but much to his disgust they all appeared on the agreed list. In order to avoid further disputes, the committee declined to appoint anybody to the crucial post of council secretary, announcing instead that the nomination "should be as yet suspended".[86] On the final day of the assembly, the peace faction tried to replace the council with a new body consisting of 48 members "and among these were all of their own party who were not of the council". A last minute compromise resulted in the extra nominees becoming supernumeraries (or alternates) to replace absentee members. The nuncio commented that "although some satisfaction was accorded to the ecclesiastics on this matter also, nevertheless their feeling was embittered by the abruptness of the measure and the suspicions it excited".[87]

Rinuccini could not understand why Bishop French had supported the actions of the election committee and signed the decree. The moderates, such as Plunkett and French, having earlier supported the clergy in rejecting the peace, appeared now to be leaning more towards the peace faction. The composition of the new council reflected changes in the confederate balance of power. Inchiquin welcomed the election of Ormond's close associate, Gerald Fennell "with diverse others whom they term moderate men". Equally good news, from Inchiquin's perspective, concerned the ejection of Dermot O'Brien "with diverse others

**84** The 1646 reforms are listed in Bodl. Carte Mss 16 ff 470-80. **85** Ó hAnnracháin, "Far from terra firma" pp 320-5. **86** Orders of the assembly, 12 Nov. 1647 (Gilbert [ed.], *Irish confederation*, vi, pp 208-33). It is unclear who had acted as secretary on the previous council, but Richard Bellings, one of the Leinster residents, had occupied that position from 1642 until the rejection of the Ormond peace treaty in August 1646. Bellings, however, was despised by the clerical faction, who would have bitterly opposed his candidature. **87** Rinuccini to Panzirolo, 24 Dec. 1647 (Aiazza [ed.], *Embassy* pp 343-6); Orders of the assembly, 12 Nov. 1647 (Gilbert [ed.], *Irish confederation*, vi, pp 208-33); Ó hAnnracháin, "Far from terra firma" pp 320-5.

whom they account violent", meaning in effect the supporters of the clerical faction.[88]

Despite the revival of the peace faction, marked by the return of such familiar figures as Viscount Mountgarret, Richard Bellings and Lucas Dillon, it still faced significant opposition at the council table. The names of seven bishops appear on the final list, and the entire Ulster contingent had opposed the first Ormond peace treaty back in 1646. Although the allegiances of certain individuals remains unclear, the moderates may well have controlled the balance of power as before. The departure of Plunkett and French for the continent, however, deprived this group of effective leadership, and their allies on the council (such as Roebuck Lynch and Geoffrey Barron) became increasingly marginalised as the factional strife intensified.[89]

Having restructured the council, the assembly next turned its attention to the crucial question of accountability. The major problem (identified as far back as 1644) centred not only on a general contempt for authority, but also on the failure of the supreme council to enforce various decrees issued by the assembly. To combat this, the reform proposals recommended that a resident member from each province personally oversee the implementation of orders. Rotating the duties on a monthly basis, each one of them would provide regular written reports to the council, and to the assembly at its next meeting. Moreover, the task of publishing and distributing orders would also be delegated to council members, with the assembly kept informed on their progress.[90]

The reform proposals stated unequivocally, however, "that the whole members of the council residents shall have a general care of execution of orders as they shall answer to the contrary at their extremist peril". To ensure compliance with this directive, the assembly enunciated the doctrine of collective responsibility. The council would continue to function according to the principle of majority rule, but with all members, regardless of how they voted, accepting responsibility for the council's actions. The only exception to this rule involved matters of faith or clerical immunity, presumably to prevent a bishop being forced to support a decision contrary to the teachings of the Catholic Church.[91]

All these measures not only ensured that individual council members became actively involved in the governmental process, but were also specifically designed to facilitate more efficient administrative practices and to help eliminate the blight of factionalism which threatened to destroy the confederate association. As such these policies illustrate a remarkable degree of political sophistication,

---

**88** Inchiquin to Ormond, 19 Jan. 1648 (Bodl. Carte Mss 22 f.5). Even after leaving Ireland, Rinuccini still found it difficult to understand French's behaviour at this assembly. Report on the affairs of Ireland, 1649 (Aiazza [ed.], *Embassy* pp 519-21). **89** The seven bishops elected to the council, including supernumeraries, were Dublin, Tuam, Cashel, Ferns, Limerick, Killala and Down/Connor. The full council list is in appendix 2 (table 13). **90** Orders of the assembly, 12 Nov. 1647 (Gilbert [ed.], *Irish confederation*, vi, pp 208-33). **91** Idem.

particularly at a time of severe crisis. The reforming measures advocated by the moderate members of the general assembly, clearly contradict the argument that the confederates never developed a political philosophy.[92]

The reformers also directed their attention at abuses in the national electoral process. They argued that a number of assembly meetings had been composed "of serving men, and men uninterested in the kingdom, procuring returns within the city of Kilkenny, or by some other private ways or practice". The destruction and dislocation caused by war undoubtedly disrupted the system of elections, and both the clerical and peace factions exploited this fact to their own advantage. Rinuccini observed, shortly after his arrival, the practice of electing people resident in Kilkenny for boroughs and counties under enemy control. In late 1646, with the clerics in the ascendancy, their opponents complained of the assembly being packed with northerners from the creaghts accompanying the army of Owen Roe O'Neill.[93]

The assembly now ordered the council to take appropriate steps to ensure that future meetings would be composed of "genuine, apt and natural members … men estated and of fortune … and that no such serving men, uninterested in the kingdom be admitted thereto". To this end, they recommended the close supervision of the electoral process itself, with sheriffs and magistrates appointing suitable venues voting to take place, to provide "the greatest freedom and security of the people against any attempts of the enemy". Again this concern for free and fair elections is truly remarkable so soon after the destruction of two confederate armies, and with enemy forces only a few miles from the confederate capital.[94]

Returning to more mundane administrative matters, assembly members ordered that sheriffs and justices of the peace take greater care to observe the commands of the supreme council. They also introduced general military training for all men between the ages of 16 and 60, to be maintained by a yearly charge on each county, in a desperate attempt to replenish confederate forces. Moreover, in future the supreme council would directly farm the excise to ensure a greater revenue for the central exchequer, with lay officials assisting the clergy to collect money due from ecclesiastical lands for the same reason.[95]

---

92 This claim is made by Patrick Corish, who denies that the confederates were ever concerned with the concept of executive responsibility to the legislature. Corish, *NHI*, iii, pp 300-1. 93 Orders of the assembly, 12 Nov. 1647 (Gilbert [ed.], *Irish confederation*, vi, pp 208-33); Du Moulin to Ormond, 30 Jan. 1647 (Bodl. Carte Mss 20 ff 218-9); Rinuccini to Pamphili, 13 Feb. 1646 (Aiazza [ed.], *Embassy* p. 116); Bellings' History in Gilbert (ed.), *Irish confederation*, vi, p. 46. 94 Orders of the assembly, 12 Nov. 1647 (Gilbert [ed.], *Irish confederation*, vi, pp 208-33). By early February 1648, Inchiquin had captured the town of Callan, eight miles from Kilkenny. Inchiquin to Lenthall, 17 Feb. 1648, *Tanner letters* p. 287. 95 Orders of the assembly, 12 Nov. 1647 (Gilbert [ed.], *Irish confederation*, vi, pp 208-33). This implicit criticism of the clergy strongly suggests that (unlike 1646) the clerical faction did not support the reforms.

The final order concerned the creaghts which accompanied the forces of Owen Roe O'Neill. The presence (and practices) of these herdsmen had generated numerous complaints throughout Munster, Leinster and Connacht for a number of years. Both old English and native Irish land owners viewed these wandering bands as a threat to the existing social order, their lifestyle as barbaric and backward.[96] Even allowing for exaggerations in the reports of damage and destruction, the creaghts undoubtedly aroused deep hostility within confederate ranks. With O'Neill and his army camped outside Kilkenny, resentful at the failure to provide them with winter quarters, any move against the Ulstermen risked provoking a violent response. Nonetheless, the assembly ordered that the creaghts be assigned to waste lands in the various provinces until they could return to their former homes.[97]

The reforms envisaged by the eighth general assembly of the confederate catholics proved both elaborate in scope and ambitious in design. By espousing the principles of executive accountability, collective responsibility, and free elections, assembly members displayed a remarkable degree of political sophistication, as well as admirable concern for truly representative government (at least in the context of the seventeenth century). They hoped to create a more effective and efficient central government, preserve confederate unity and uphold the existing social order. These policies, most closely associated with moderates such as Nicholas Plunkett, emerged triumphant at the assembly but were subsequently undermined by the collapse into internecine warfare.

On 18 January 1648, over three weeks after the dissolution of the assembly, the new supreme council, together with the bishops, finally issued instructions for confederate agents travelling to the continent. Despite the growing influence of the peace faction, the council made every effort to secure clerical support for the peace initiative. The confederates decided to offer the government of the country to Queen Henrietta Maria and the prince of Wales, but only if a treaty could be agreed which included religious terms approved by the pope.[98] This compromise, satisfying the demands for a settlement with the king while at the same time providing certain religious guarantees, bears all the hallmarks of the moderates' policy of consensus.[99]

**96** The Ulster Irish were criticised (and sometimes physically attacked) by both native Irish and old English. See PRO SP Ire, 263/105 f.176, 263/119 f.200; Clanricarde to Taaffe, 23 Feb. 1644; Clanricarde to Ormond, 5 July 1647 (Lowe [ed.], *Clanricarde letter-book* pp 46, 459-60); Report on the proceedings of Owen O'Neill, April 1647 (Aiazza [ed.], *Embassy* pp 281-4) etc. **97** Orders of the assembly, 12 Nov. 1647 (Gilbert [ed.], *Irish confederation*, vi, pp 208-33). **98** According to Rinuccini, the agents travelling to France could "neither begin nor conclude anything, nor accept a peace or change in government until the terms have been proposed in Rome and approved of by his Holiness". Rinuccini to nuncio of France, 9 Jan. 1648 (Aiazza [ed.], *Embassy* pp 363-4). **99** As with previous missions, the assembly probably decided on the terms, but left it to the council to issue the actual commission. Supreme council instructions to agents travelling abroad, 1648 (BL Stowe Mss 82 f.155-7); Corish, *NHI*, iii, pp 325-6;

The mission to Rome provided the best opportunity to save the confederate association from financial collapse and political disintegration. After the rejection of the Ormond treaty, Rinuccini had promised massive financial aid, but nothing arrived during the course of 1647. Without a significant influx of papal cash it would prove difficult (if not impossible) for the confederates to maintain the war on all fronts.[100] Moreover, religious issues remained the single biggest obstacle to a new peace settlement, with the clergy seemingly determined to insist on conditions wholly unacceptable to Charles I. A direct appeal to the pope offered the best prospect of breaking the stalemate, by-passing Rinuccini in the same way the king used Glamorgan in 1645 to overcome Ormond's opposition to religious concessions. The Irish clergy could hardly refuse to accept a deal sanctioned by Innocent X.[101]

Rinuccini interpreted the mission differently, and believed that Plunkett and French were being "exiled under colour of doing them honour".[102] Far from being dupes of the peace faction, however, both men hoped their negotiations with the papacy would facilitate an acceptable peace agreement. They had nothing to gain by staying in Ireland, particularly as internal confederate tensions intensified. Any outbreak of violence between the various factions would force all moderates to take sides before the full range of options had been explored. Accepting the mission to Rome provided Plunkett and French with one final opportunity to dictate confederate policy; it proved a shrewd political move in the circumstances.

The council instructed the two agents to inform Innocent X about the state of the country and seek his mediation in attempts to broker a peace between Kilkenny and the exiled English court in Paris. While assuring the pope of the confederate leadership's determination to obtain religious concessions, they also had to stress the necessity to be practical. The agents in Paris received authorisation to waive demands for religious articles to be published alongside political ones, and for a catholic lord lieutenant, but only if the pope agreed. Finally, the confederates committed themselves to retaining a separate government until the publication of religious articles, in order to ensure the royalists upheld their side of the agreement. If Innocent X refused to make any religious concessions the agents would ask for military aid, and failing that offer him the protectorship of the kingdom.[103]

Ohlmeyer, *Civil war and restoration* pp 201-5. **100** Gillespie, "Irish economy at war", *Independence to occupation* pp 176-7. Rinuccini recognised the shortage of hard currency as one of the biggest problems facing the confederates at this time. Rinuccini to Panzirolo, 7 Jan. 1648 (Aiazza [ed.], *Embassy* pp 358-62). **101** As Innocent X had already agreed a treaty with Kenelm Digby on behalf of Queen Henrietta Maria, the confederates must have been confident another deal was possible. The "Roman" treaty of Nov. 1645 is discussed in chapter 3 p. 99f. **102** Rinuccini, despite his misgivings about some of their policies, still believed that both men supported the clerical faction. Rinuccini to Panzirolo, 24 Dec. 1647 (Aiazza [ed.], *Embassy* pp 343-6). **103** If the pope declined the protectorship the French were to be

These instructions clearly prioritised the various options open to the confederates at this time. The council sought an agreement with the royalists, but only after obtaining papal approval for the crucial religious clauses. Unfortunately for Plunkett and his moderate allies, a revival in royalist fortunes during 1648 encouraged the peace faction to support an alternative strategy, undermining all efforts at consensus. Once again, secret plots and negotiations dominated the Irish political landscape, with the marquis of Ormond (as ever) providing the focus for discontented elements in the confederate ranks.

The period from February 1648, when the missions to Rome and Paris finally departed, until the outbreak of factional warfare three months later, is relatively poorly documented.[104] With the marquis of Ormond moving between England and France, a gap appears in the Carte collection until his return to Ireland in September 1648. The third volume of the marquis of Clanricarde's letters (covering the years 1647 until 1650) is missing, while the state papers contain little of interest after August 1647. As a result the historian must rely almost exclusively on Rinuccini for details of events, supplemented by the memoirs of Richard Bellings written over twenty years later.[105]

Early in January 1648 Rinuccini wrote a detailed report on the state of the kingdom to Cardinal Panzirolo in Rome. According to the nuncio, the confederates were in a desperate state due to the lack of money, internal conflicts, the loss of Munster towns to Inchiquin, and the general devastation of the country by enemy forces. On the positive side, significant gains had been made in Ulster, while in Connacht only Sligo remained under enemy control. Moreover, the departure of Ormond from Ireland removed any obstacles to an attack on Dublin. For Rinuccini, the key to recovery involved the expeditious arrival of papal subsidies to rebuild Taaffe's army, who would then launch an offensive against Inchiquin in Munster, while O'Neill marched into the heartland of

approached. Supreme council instructions to agents, 1648 (BL Stowe Mss 82 f.155-7). The clause about the protectorship would come back to haunt Nicholas Plunkett after the restoration of Charles II. In 1661, Plunkett was representing former catholic land-owners who hoped to be restored to their lands when a copy of these instructions was shown to the king and his council. The king banished Plunkett from court, and refused to accept any further petitions as a result. Banishment of Plunkett, 14 March 1662 (BL Add Mss 4,781 f.146); Letter of John Davies, 15 March 1662 (BL Stowe Mss 82 f.324). **104** Both delegations had departed from Ireland by the end of February, although bad weather delayed the arrival of Muskerry and Browne in Paris until the middle of March. Carte, *Ormond*, iii, pp 348-50; Ohlmeyer, *Civil war and restoration* p. 205. **105** This unsatisfactory situation is only mitigated by the fact that the two surviving accounts come from totally contrasting perspectives. Volume 22 of the Carte collection contains some material for the early part of 1648, but it is only after Ormond's return to Ireland in September that the number of relevant documents increases significantly. The last entry in the Clanricarde letter-book for this period is a note addressed to Bishop French on 5 September 1647. Lowe (ed.) *Clanricarde letter-book* (1983). Nothing then survives until 1650.

Ulster. The nuncio still hoped to conquer the entire kingdom before invading Scotland and England to assist catholics there, and of course the king.[106]

Despite his bellicose assessment of confederate options, the nuncio nonetheless favoured a temporary alliance with one of the protestant groups in Ireland, preferring the Scots in Ulster over Lord Inchiquin in Munster. Inchiquin, a notorious anti-catholic, was responsible for the sack of Cashel in September 1647, and had displayed a particular hatred of Ulstermen.[107] The nuncio's strategy, however, failed to take into account confederate weaknesses in Munster following the disastrous defeat at Knocknanuss, as well as a general war weariness throughout the country.

The supreme council strongly supported the idea of a truce with Inchiquin.[108] From a military point of view this made perfect sense, as the Munster parliamentarians (in alliance with Michael Jones), threatened to overwhelm confederate resistance in the province. Indeed, before dispersing, the general assembly ordered a meeting of the Munster provincial assembly to discuss possible solutions.[109] At this assembly the dispute between Muskerry and his opponents in the Munster army, which had been simmering since the previous summer, erupted once again.

Rinuccini reported that the supreme council travelled to Clonmel in an attempt to resolve the quarrel.[110] Meanwhile, Jones and Inchiquin moved about unchallenged in Leinster and Munster respectively. The situation looked grim for the confederates, but on 13 February Owen Roe O'Neill repulsed an attempt by the two parliamentarian commanders to link up their forces. A subsequent meeting of confederate generals and the supreme council decided, despite this success, against attacking Inchiquin, but left open the possibility of a northern offensive. O'Neill may well have been influenced by the provincial council of Ulster, which ordered him not to make peace with the Scots.[111] The Ulster Irish,

---

**106** Rinuccini to Panzirolo, 7 Jan. 1648 (Aiazza [ed.], *Embassy* pp 358-62). **107** Bellings admitted as much, but claimed (somewhat disingenuously) that the supreme council would protect the interests of the northerners "being by the oath of association bound to stand for and protect one the other". Bellings' History in Gilbert (ed.), *Irish confederation*, vii, p. 65. Rinuccini had proposed a truce with Inchiquin in late 1646, while preparing to attack Dublin, but the massacre at Cashel seems to have changed his mind. Cregan, D.F., "Confederation of Kilkenny" (PhD thesis) p. 267. **108** Bellings' History in Gilbert (ed.), *Irish confederation*, vii, p. 37. **109** The city of Limerick, displaying an independent streak characteristic of its actions prior to 1646, refused to host this assembly, which met in Clonmel instead on 20 January 1648. Inchiquin to Ormond, 19 Jan. 1648 (Bodl. Carte 22 Mss f.5); Rinuccini to Panzirolo, 29 Jan. 1648 (Aiazza [ed.], *Embassy* pp 366-7); O'Ferrall and O'Connell (eds), *Commentarius*, iii, pp 126-33. **110** The Munster assembly agreed to raise an army, and delegated the business to a committee before disbanding. O'Ferrall and O'Connell (eds), *Commentarius*, iii, pp 129-32; Rinuccini to Panzirolo, 29 Jan. 1648 (Aiazza [ed.], *Embassy* pp 366-7). **111** O'Ferrall and O'Connell (eds), *Commentarius*, iii, pp 73-5; Rinuccini to Panzirolo, 13 Feb. 1648 (Aiazza [ed.], *Embassy* p. 370); Bellings' History in Gilbert (ed.), *Irish confederation*, vii, pp 56-7.

anxious to regain their estates and consolidate the gains of the previous two years, did not want their objectives frustrated by a truce in the province.

Despite the obvious military threat posed by Inchiquin in Munster, elements on the council had very different motives for supporting a truce with the parliamentarian general. In early October 1647 Sir Maurice Eustace, a leading figure in Ormond's royalist administration, received a letter from a number of confederates, including Muskerry, Mountgarret and Taaffe. They declared a desire to "come and submit" to the lord lieutenant, in return for a "moderate exercise of their religion".[112] Nothing came of this offer at first, but subsequent events in England soon created fresh possibilities for a royalist revival in the three Stuart kingdoms.

On 26 December 1647 (two days after the dissolution of the assembly in Kilkenny), Charles signed an "engagement" with the Scots.[113] Together with the duke of Hamilton and the marquis of Ormond, the king set about creating a powerful royalist alliance to challenge the English parliament. Ormond's role involved re-establishing himself in Ireland with the help of confederate allies and disillusioned supporters of parliament, principal among them being Lord Inchiquin.[114] By January 1648 Ormond had contacted Inchiquin who promised to assist his plans. Ormond's agent, Colonel John Barry arrived in Cork shortly afterwards to continue the negotiations before travelling on to Viscount Taaffe's headquarters. On 3 March, Barry wrote to the marquis of Clanricarde confidently predicting that a considerable party of the confederates would appear for the king. This evidence appears to confirm Rinuccini's suspicions that the Inchiquin truce formed part of a wider plot to invite Ormond back to the country.[115]

Meanwhile, Ormond successfully undermined the confederates' own peace initiative. Shortly after arriving in Paris in March, he advised Queen Henrietta Maria not to give any detailed answers to the delegation from Kilkenny, but instead "preacquaint some of the best affected" with royalist plans. Although the marquis of Antrim officially acted as the confederates' chief negotiator, the royal-

---

112 Eustace to Ormond, 8 Oct. 1647 (Gilbert [ed.], *Irish confederation*, vi, pp 206-8). 113 Ormond's involvement in these negotiations with the Scots is outlined in Gardner, W., *The life of James first duke of Ormond, 1610-1688*, vol. 1, pp 333-7. 114 The Scottish army in Ireland was informed about the treaty, and instructed to give diversions to Owen Roe O'Neill, presumably to assist Ormond's confederate allies. Lauderdale etc. to Ormond, 28 March 1648 (Bodl. Carte Mss 22 f.51). Adamson suggests that Inchiquin's disillusionment stemmed from political developments at Westminster, in particular the growing threat posed by the Independents. Adamson, "Strafford's ghost", *Independence to occupation* p. 157. 115 Inchiquin to Ormond, 19 Jan. 1648 (Bodl. Carte Mss 22 f.5); Colonel John Barry to Clanricarde, 3 March 1648 (Bodl. Carte Mss 22 ff 37-8). Rinuccini wrote that the real problem lay not with the coming of the prince of Wales to Ireland, "but the hidden evil of it is, that many efforts will be made to restore Ormond". Rinuccini to Panzirolo, 24 Dec. 1647 (Aiazza [ed.], *Embassy* pp 343-6).

ists excluded him from discussions, preferring to deal with Viscount Muskerry and Geoffrey Browne.[116] The queen fully supported Ormond's strategy, and after two months of inconclusive talks announced her intention to "speedily give power to some such as we shall think fit to receive, there upon the place, more particulars and full propositions from you".[117]

The royalists received a significant boost when, on 3 April, Lord Inchiquin changed sides for a second time during the war, and declared for the king.[118] The news was a bitter blow to the nuncio, who still hoped for an alliance with the Scots in Ulster. The supreme council (increasingly dominated by the peace faction) had initiated contact with Inchiquin at the beginning of March, but negotiations on a truce only started in earnest after his public declaration. The two sides arranged a meeting for 22 April in Dungarvan, with John Walsh, Patrick Gough and Sir Richard Everard appointed to represent the confederates.[119] Council members urgently requested the nuncio's presence in Kilkenny, promising not to make any decisions without his approval.[120] Their concern may have been prompted by fears of the nuncio taking a unilateral decision to oppose the truce, but also by the return from Rome of Dean Massari with papal funds. Unknown to the council, however, Massari only brought a fraction of the money promised by Rinuccini.[121]

With negotiations about to begin, the lines of communication between the council and the nuncio became dangerously crossed, as happened during the summer of 1646.[122] Bellings claimed that the council made every effort to keep

116 Muskerry and Browne had arrived with private instructions signed by Preston and Taaffe, announcing as their primary aim "the re-establishment of the king's authority in all his dominions". They requested that the prince of Wales come to Ireland "with a considerable proportion of money and arms, and with a resolution to condescend to the requests of his moderate and well-affected subjects". In return, the two generals would provide troops to help settle Ireland and England. Carte, *Ormond*, iii, pp 350-1. 117 Memorial by Ormond, 26 March 1648 (Bodl. Carte Mss 22 f.58-9); Queen Consort and Prince to Antrim, 13 May 1648 (Bodl. Carte Mss 63 f.541). 118 Colonel Barry wrote to Ormond that Inchiquin had been forced by circumstances to declare for the king sooner than was expedient. Barry assured Ormond that if he arrived in Ireland he would be "safe". Colonel John Barry to Ormond, 6 April 1648 (Bodl. Carte Mss 22 f.60); Inchiquin's declaration, 3 April 1648 (Bodl. Carte Mss 117 f.151); *Papers presented to the parliament against the Lord Inchiquin ...*, London 1648 (BL Thomason Tracts E435 f.33). 119 On 15 March, a council member, Geoffrey Barron, had been sent to ascertain Rinuccini's attitude towards a truce with Inchiquin. The nuncio, perhaps unwilling to reveal his hand, answered in a non-committal fashion. Cregan, D.F., "Confederation of Kilkenny" (PhD thesis) pp 268-75. 120 Rinuccini confided to Panzirolo his fear (based on past experiences) that the council would not adhere to this pledge to consult him. Rinuccini to Panzirolo, 8 April 1647 (Aiazza [ed.], *Embassy* pp 376-81). 121 The dean eventually collected £16,000, but was forced to leave half the money in France before Mazarin would allow him travel to Ireland. Nonetheless, any cash would provide a major boost to the confederate war effort. Massari, "Irish campaign", p. 743; Ó hAnnracháin, "Far from terra firma" pp 289-91. 122 The talks started on 22 April, and by 6 May, a protestant officer in

Rinuccini informed on the progress of talks, and that the nuncio supported the idea of a cease-fire (or at least did not object). Rinuccini, however, insisted he only discovered about the negotiations after forcing the bishop of Limerick to divulge council secrets.[123] Of course the possibility exists of a simple misunderstanding, but it seems more likely that both sides were already preparing for conflict.

As the threat of civil war loomed, the two factions sought to obtain majority confederate support. The council summoned the nobles and bishops of Munster to Kilkenny, where the Leinster provincial assembly was already in session, to debate the cease-fire before the delegation departed to Dungarvan on 20 April. A number of the supernumerary members appointed to the council by the previous general assembly also attended the meeting. The assembled confederates supported the Inchiquin truce, although according to the clerical apologist, Walter Enos, the decision proved far from unanimous.[124]

To counter these moves, Rinuccini, after his arrival in the confederate capital, brought together 14 bishops, who signed a declaration against the truce. The nuncio had obtained similar documents in November 1645 and February 1646, but on this occasion divisions existed among the bishops themselves. Bellings wrote that the declaration "notwithstanding that six of the number did dissent in opinion, was sent to the supreme council as the unanimous sense of the bishops".[125] Rinuccini admitted in a letter to Panzirolo that the archbishop of Tuam and the bishop of Limerick had expressed serious doubts about signing the document. The subsequent defection of these two men seriously undermined clerical opposition to the truce, but for the present, the clerics maintained a facade of unity.[126]

Kinsale reported that the truce was agreed "though not yet proclaimed". *Tanner letters* pp 290-1. Bellings maintained that the council was unaware of the full extent of the Rinuccini's opposition to the truce, but this hardly appears credible considering the nuncio's stated position on the issue. The council, as in the summer of 1646, was probably attempting to present Rinuccini with a *fait accompli*. Bellings' History in Gilbert (ed.), *Irish confederation*, vii, pp 45-7. **123** Bellings "History" in Gilbert (ed.), *Irish confederation*, vii, pp 44-9. Bellings' version is supported by a document entitled "An abstract of the proceedings concerning the cessation with the right honourable the lord baron of Inchiquin" (TCD Mss 844 f.71). Rinuccini's account is in Aiazza (ed.), *Embassy* pp 408-17. **124** The authors of *Commentarius* complained that at a properly constituted meeting, 200 people would have been in attendance instead of the 44 who appeared, which suggests that it was the provincial assemblies rather than councils that were summoned. O'Ferrall and O'Connell (eds), *Commentarius*, iii, pp 111-12, 126-33. Bellings interchanged the words "assembly" and "council" so it is unclear which exactly he was referring to in this instance. Bellings' History in Gilbert (ed.), *Irish confederation*, vii, p. 68. **125** Bellings' History in Gilbert (ed.), *Irish confederation*, vii, p. 59. Corish suspects that the rumoured dissenters (who signed nonetheless) were Dublin, Cashel, Tuam, Killala, Limerick and Kilfenora. Corish, P.J., "Rinuccini's censure of May 22 1648", *Irish theological quarterly*, vol. 18 (Oct. 1951) pp 325-7. **126** Rinuccini remarked in this letter that Bishop O'Dwyer of Limerick had joined the peace faction 18 months earlier, while Tuam's hostility dated as far

Council members replied to the bishops that they possessed full authority to conclude a truce, "the like being the course taken in all former cessations". They accepted that Inchiquin displayed a particular aversion to Ulstermen, but claimed the oath of association ensured that all confederates would "protect one another". Clerical opposition, however, unnerved the supreme council, which was reported to be "confused and perhaps divided", suggesting significant opposition to the peace faction strategy.[127] On 4 May, before dispersing, the bishops empowered the nuncio and four of their number (Dublin, Limerick, Clogher and Killala) to act on their behalf.[128]

On 9 May, Rinuccini confronted the bishop of Limerick, a member of the supreme council, about the negotiations with Inchiquin. The bishop, despite his oath of office which bound him to secrecy, confirmed an agreement was imminent. At the same time, a Carmelite priest informed the nuncio of an alleged plan to assassinate him. No evidence has ever emerged of a plot against the nuncio, but the peace party leaders may well have been contemplating a pre-emptive strike against their greatest adversary.[129] In any event, Rinuccini left Kilkenny that night and fled northwards to Owen Roe O'Neill's camp at Maryborough, in what more or less amounted to a declaration of war on the supreme council.

The following day, the bishop of Clogher joined him as the council began to fragment. Only five of the twelve resident members publicly favoured the Inchiquin truce, while the others either opposed it or adopted a neutral position.[130] With the supernumerary council members already in Kilkenny, however, the peace faction simply replaced anybody who left the council board with their own supporters, just as the nuncio had predicted back in December. It soon proved impossible for the moderate members to any sort of middle ground.

---

back as August 1647. In his report to Rome after leaving Ireland, Rinuccini noted that Tuam later explained his signature on the document by "declaring it was the money [from Rome] only which moved him to do it". Rinuccini to Panzirolo, 3 May 1647; Report on the affairs of Ireland, 1649 (Aiazza [ed.], *Embassy* pp 381-3, 526). O'Dwyer of Limerick and Bourke of Tuam were among a number of clerics uncomfortable with the extreme tactics adopted by the nuncio. Nonetheless, they still favoured major religious concessions, and as such were potential allies of the moderates. **127** Bellings' History in Gilbert (ed.), *Irish confederation*, vii, pp 62-5; Rinuccini to Panzirolo, 3 May 1647 (Aiazza [ed.], *Embassy* pp 381-3). **128** Delegation of authority to the nuncio and four bishops, 4 May 1648 (Jesuit Archives Mss B f.25). **129** Corish believes that the plot "seems to have been without any real foundation". Corish, *NHI*, iii, p. 329. The question of whether the nuncio knew of the talks with Inchiquin before his encounter with O'Dwyer remains unanswered. Report on the affairs of Ireland, 1649 (Aiazza [ed.], *Embassy* pp 524-6). **130** Inchiquin to Ormond, 29 May 1648 (Carte, *Ormond*, vi, pp 549-53). Inchiquin informed Ormond that only five of the council could be "relied upon". These were Richard Bellings, Gerald Fennell, Lucas Dillon, Lord Athenry and probably Robert Devereux. Walter Enos in the *Commentarius* also names Roebuck Lynch and Patrick Bryan, but they were almost certainly moderates. O'Ferrall and O'Connell (eds), *Commentarius*, iii, pp 531-4.

At this crucial juncture, Thomas Preston, anxious to restore his reputation after the disaster at Dungan's Hill, pledged his support to the peace faction. Described by Rinuccini as "a most unsteady man, unfit to take council with, and easily dictated to by the evil minded", the Leinster general had taken great offence at the pope's gift to Owen Roe of Hugh O'Neill's sword, brought back to Ireland by Massari. Rumours circulating in confederate territory described the swords as an "emblem of royalty", which signified that Owen Roe wished to become king of Ireland.[131]

The previous winter, a book entitled *Disputatio apologetica*, by an Irish Jesuit (Conor O'Mahony) resident in Lisbon, appeared in towns and cities controlled by the confederates. O'Mahony, contrary to the ideals of the confederate association, called on the Irish to expel all English from Ireland and elect a native king. Although the authorities in Kilkenny, Galway and elsewhere promptly condemned the author, the book, along with O'Neill's sword, greatly increased tension within confederate ranks.[132] Rinuccini, by openly joining Owen Roe O'Neill in Maryborough, firmly cemented the alliance between the clergy and the Ulster Irish, but also succeeded in alienating potential moderate supporters.

In the week following Rinuccini's flight from Kilkenny, the supreme council, superficially at least, expressed an interest in reconciliation. Patrick Bryan and Geoffrey Barron, two moderate council members, travelled to Maryborough with an offer from the Leinster assembly to unite with its Munster counterpart and attack Dublin, if they received a £10,000 sterling loan from the nuncio.[133] Rinuccini rejected this crude attempt to elicit papal funds, and further overtures from Miles O'Reilly, a supernumerary council member from Ulster. The council's sincerity in these negotiations must be questioned, as O'Reilly also tried to draw moderate officers from the Ulster army. In any event, the publication of the Inchiquin truce on 20 May, and rumours that

---

**131** Rinuccini to Panzirolo, 4 May 1648 (Aiazza [ed.], *Embassy* p. 385). **132** Condemnation of *Disputatio*, 1647 (Galway corporation records, book A f.191b). The sheriff of Galway ordered that all copies of the book be handed in to the authorities. Walsh, Peter, *The history and vindication …* (1674) pp 736-9. Walsh, a bitter enemy of the clerical faction, preached against the book for five consecutive weeks in Kilkenny. He also blamed the nuncio for protecting John Bane, the man on whom the first copy was discovered. Rinuccini expressed no sympathy with O'Mahony's ideas and merely commented that the appearance of the book had been exploited by his enemies to discredit him. Rinuccini to Panzirolo, 1 Oct. 1647 (Aiazza [ed.], *Embassy* pp 321-2). The king of Portugal also issued two orders in 1647 censuring the book, under pressure from the English royalist ambassador. Bodl. Clarendon Mss 30 f.198. **133** Bellings' History in Gilbert (ed.), *Irish confederation*, vii, pp 71-2. Bellings earlier described Barron as an "ardent nuncioist", but this seems unlikely. After the rejection of the peace treaty by the assembly in February 1647, Barron had been sent with Gerald Fennell to reopen negotiations with Ormond. As a man who appealed to both sides, Barron was more probably a moderate. Ibid. p. 12.

Preston intended marching against O'Neill, brought all communications to an abrupt end.[134]

The duplicity of the marquis of Ormond in peace negotiations, and the subsequent catastrophic confederate defeats at Dungan's Hill and Knocknanuss, effectively undermined Plunkett's dual strategy during the course of 1647. Forced by circumstances to seek urgent assistance from abroad, Plunkett and his associate, Bishop French, gambled everything on the mission to Rome. In their absence civil war erupted in the confederate association, precipitated by peace faction plotting with Ormond and the supreme council's inept handling of the truce with Inchiquin. By May 1648, the factional divide, aggravated by the lack of an effective moderating influence, ran so deep that armed conflict proved inevitable.

134 Bellings' History in Gilbert (ed.), *Irish confederation*, vii, p. 77; Articles of agreement, 20 May 1648 (Bodl. Carte Mss 22 f.99); Ó hAnnracháin, "Far from terra firma" p. 337.

CHAPTER 6

# War and peace

ℰℑ

MAY 1648–JANUARY 1649

What really surprises the majority of those who contemplate the affairs of Ireland is to see that the people of the same nation and of the same religion – who are well aware that the resolution to exterminate them totally has already been taken – should differ so strongly in their private hostilities; that their zeal for religion, the preservation of their country and their own self interest are not sufficient to make them lay down – at least, for a short time – the passions which divide them one from the other.

Monsieur Bellièvre, French ambassador to London, 3 November 1648[1]

The final phase of confederate Ireland witnessed a collapse into civil war, as the papal nuncio and Owen Roe O'Neill orchestrated opposition to renewed efforts at a peace settlement with the royalists. With Nicholas Plunkett and Bishop French absent in Rome, the political middle ground gradually disappeared, the growing divisions forcing all confederates to take sides. Throughout the summer of 1648 the clerical and peace factions battled for supremacy, while the English parliament prepared for a major offensive in Ireland. It was only after the calling of the general assembly in September, and the return of Plunkett and French to Ireland, that the moderates regained some authority.

The publication of the cease-fire agreement with Inchiquin, on 20 May 1648, destroyed whatever hope remained of a reconciliation between Rinuccini and the supreme council. Exactly one week later the nuncio excommunicated all supporters of the truce.[2] This dramatic response, however predictable, constitut-

1 Ohlmeyer, J., "A failed revolution?", *Independence to occupation* p. 20. 2 The truce articles were signed for the confederates by Richard Everard, Patrick Gough and John Walsh, three supernumerary members of the supreme council for the province of Munster. Articles of agreement, 20 May 1648 (Bodl. Carte Mss 22 f.99). The bishops had delegated their authority to a committee consisting of Rinuccini, Clogher, Limerick, Killala and Dublin. Instead, the nuncio, along with Clogher, co-opted Cork, Ross and Down without contacting the other bishops. This suggests that Rinuccini already suspected that Limerick and Killala (and maybe even Dublin) would oppose the excommunication. Report on Inchiquin truce, 1648 (Aiazza [ed.], *Embassy* pp 408-17); Corish, "The crisis in Ireland in 1648" pp 234-5; Corish,

ed nonetheless a powerful challenge to the authority of the council. The rumour (false as it transpired) that Preston intended marching on O'Neill's headquarters at Maryborough influenced the exact timing of the declaration, but the nuncio had already decided on this course of action after seeing the terms of the truce.[3]

Ó hAnnracháin describes the nuncio's reaction to the unfolding crisis as panicky and largely defensive in nature. Although circumstances at the time may well have affected his tactics, for the most part Rinuccini implemented a carefully planned strategy, in a deliberate re-enactment of the clergy's successful 1646 campaign. Indeed on his return to Rome he wrote how it seemed "most fitting to follow in this second controversy precisely the same course which was held in the first".[4] By 1648, however, his opponents proved better prepared for the challenge, and for the next three months a bitter struggle developed as both sides sought to impose their supremacy on the confederate rank and file. In such a polarised environment, the moderates, particularly in the absence of Nicholas Plunkett, could exert little influence.

Rinuccini's failure to repeat his earlier victory could not have been predicted, despite a number of factors working against him during this latest crisis. Most importantly, divisions existed among the bishops over the Inchiquin truce and the subsequent excommunications. Differences of opinion had permeated clerical ranks from the very beginning of the uprising. Dissension from the majority position, however, remained confined to a few aged prelates, like Thomas Dease, bishop of Meath, unable (or unwilling) to challenge the authority of the papal nuncio.[5] Rinuccini's opponents in 1648, based around a younger more active group of clerics, led by John Bourke, the ambitious archbishop of Tuam, were not so easily intimidated. Clerical censures proved far less effective when publicly opposed by such men.[6]

Rinuccini's clerical opponents in 1648 could be divided into two distinct groups. Firstly the Connacht (or to be more precise the Galway) bishops consisting of John Bourke of Tuam, Francis Kirwan of Killala and Andrew Lynch of Kilfenora. Bourke, a supreme council member and judge, emerged after 1642 as a

"Rinuccini's censure" pp 325-31; Declaration against the cessation, 27 May 1648 (Jesuits Mss B f.25). The excommunication order was translated from Latin into English two days later, on 29 May, by the bishop of Ossory (Bodl. Carte Mss 22 ff 111-12). **3** Claims that Rinuccini, reluctant to resort to excommunication, was worn down by the arguments of others at the camp, are contradicted by the nuncio's own account of events. Report on the Inchiquin truce, 1648 (Aiazza [ed.], *Embassy* pp 408-17); Corish, "Rinuccini's censure" p. 329. **4** Ó hAnnracháin, "Far from terra firma" p. 337; Report on the affairs of Ireland, 1649 (Aiazza [ed.], *Embassy* p. 524). Admittedly, the nuncio's report was written a year later, with a view to self-justification, but the parallels between the two crises (1646 and 1648) are striking. **5** In March 1642, the synod of the province of Armagh censured Dease for his criticisms of the rebels. Synod at Kells, 22 March 1642 (Gilbert [ed.], *Irish confederation*, i, pp 290-2). **6** Ó hAnnracháin, "Far from terra firma" pp 132-3.

central figure in confederate politics. An enthusiastic supporter of the nuncio during the first peace crisis, he gradually began to drift from Rinuccini as the war turned against the confederates. The nuncio later accused the Connacht bishops of committing the greatest evil "under the pretext of following a middle course".[7]

The second group consisted of Thomas Dease of Meath, Oliver Darcy of Dromore, Patrick Plunkett of Ardagh and David Rothe of Ossory, all from important Pale families. Rinuccini despised Dease, and wrote after receiving (premature) news of his death, that it was "to the great blessing of the country". In another report, the nuncio described Bishop Darcy (no relation of the lawyer Patrick) as "the most open contemner of my authority". Patrick Plunkett owed his advancement to his more famous brother, Nicholas, and appears to have adopted a moderate position throughout 1648. Rothe, an old and respected prelate, vacillated during the first days of the Inchiquin crisis before declaring for the supreme council.[8]

Subsequent events revealed the nuncio's clerical opponents in 1648 more as supporters of Nicholas Plunkett and Nicholas French, rather than mere hirelings of the peace faction. They opposed Rinuccini's excommunication decree, recognising the need for some form of settlement with the royalists. Nonetheless, Bourke and his associates insisted on significant religious concessions, including the "free and public exercise of the Roman Catholic religion", with the Catholic Church restored to its "full liberty and splendour".[9] These bishops provided the core around which a number of confederate moderates now gathered, and together they successfully set the agenda for the subsequent peace negotiations with the marquis of Ormond.

In 1648 the general mood in the country also worked against the nuncio's campaign. During the first crisis in 1646, confederate fortunes reached their peak,

7 Report on the Inchiquin truce, 1648 (Aiazza [ed.], *Embassy* pp 408-17). Bourke sat on the first three supreme councils, before his appointment to the new confederate judicature in 1644, replacing Patrick Darcy as lord chancellor. Order by the commissioners of the general assembly, 30 Aug. 1644 (Gilbert [ed.], *Irish confederation*, iii, pp 266-7). He returned to the council after the seizure of power by the clerical faction, and was rewarded for his loyalty with a transfer from Clonfert to Tuam the following year. Cregan, "Counter-reformation episcopate" p. 87. The Connacht group was reinforced in late 1648 by the return from Spain of Hugh Bourke, bishop of Kilmacduagh, and a brother of John Bourke. 8 Rinuccini to Panzirolo, 4 and 11 July 1648 (Aiazza [ed.], *Embassy* pp 402-5). Dease belonged to an old gentry family in Meath, and was closely related to the Nugents and other Pale nobility. The Darcys of Platten were one of the most important landed families in Meath, while Plunkett's nephew Christopher was the earl of Fingal. The Rothes of Kilkenny were one of the most distinguished families in the city. Cregan, "Counter-reformation episcopate" pp 95-9; Cokayne, *Complete peerage*, vol. 5 (1926) p. 386. Bishop Edmund O'Dwyer of Limerick, although not strictly belonging to either group, was closely allied to them. 9 This demand was included in the confederate propositions to the marquis of Ormond on 17 October 1648 (Gilbert [ed.], *Irish confederation*, vi, pp 290-3).

following a string of military victories in Ulster, Connacht and Munster. Emboldened by the influx of papal money and the prospect of further successes, most confederates backed the nuncio's aggressive war policy. By early 1648, however, the situation had changed dramatically. The defeats at Dungan's Hill and Knocknanuss exposed the limits of confederate military capability in dramatic fashion. With money in short supply, and the confederate heartland threatened by the armies of Michael Jones and Lord Inchiquin, the majority now favoured a peace settlement and proved reluctant to support Rinuccini a second time.[10]

Finally, the peace faction were better organised on this occasion, having absorbed the lessons from their rout eighteen months earlier. Rather than proceed with the Inchiquin truce on its own authority, the supreme council summoned the provincial assemblies of Munster and Leinster to endorse the decision. A general assembly meeting at this time might well have presented clerical supporters in Ulster and elsewhere with an opportunity to block the moves towards peace.[11] With the guaranteed backing of confederates in at least two provinces, as well as a number of dissident bishops, the council felt more confident about confronting the nuncio.

Yet, despite all these disadvantages, the nuncio's cause was by no means hopeless. Excommunication remained a powerful weapon, although damaged by divisions among the clergy, and nobody could predict with any confidence the reaction of the catholic population at large to clerical condemnations. Inchiquin reported that "in many parts of the country the people do greedily embrace the infusions of their disaffected clergy, so that in the greatest probability the generality of the people will be drawn blindfold along with that party who vehemently contend against the re-establishing of his Majesty's authority in this kingdom or the settlement of any accord with those of the protestant profession".[12]

Moreover, Rinuccini could also rely on the active support of the most effective confederate provincial army. Owen Roe O'Neill and his Ulster troops, alienated by the hostility of successive councils, denounced the "factionists" in Kilkenny and prepared to confront their former colleagues.[13]

---

10 By 1647, the confederates noted "our exchequer empty and altogether hopeless to get in moneys from a country so totally exhausted and so lamentable ruined; our expectation of great sums and help beyond the seas being turned into wind and smoke and despair". Gillespie, "Irish economy at war", *Independence to occupation* p. 177. Even Rinuccini acknowledged a growing war weariness in confederate controlled areas towards the end of 1647. Rinuccini to Panzirolo, 24 Dec. 1647 (Aiazza [ed.], *Embassy* pp 346-7).  11 From their experience in January 1647, the peace faction was keenly aware of the enormous influence wielded by the bishops at assembly meetings. The meeting of the two assemblies is discussed in chapter 5 p. 173.  12 Inchiquin to Ormond, 12 Aug. 1648 (Bodl. Carte Mss 22 ff 165-6). Preston's experience at the end of 1646 is a perfect example of the power of clerical censures, with the exasperated Leinster general writing in December that his troops were not "excommunication proof". Preston to Clanricarde, 12 Dec. 1646 (Lowe [ed.], *Clanricarde letter-book* pp 343-4).  13 Ohlmeyer credits the marquis of Antrim with devising a plan, after his return to Ireland in

Disunity affected the supreme council as well as the bishops. As previously mentioned, Rinuccini noted in a report to Rome that after the declaration of the Inchiquin truce only five of the original twelve resident council members remained in Kilkenny, with the other places filled by supernumeraries appointed at the last assembly. Later in May, Inchiquin confirmed these figures, informing Ormond that only five of the twelve council members could be relied upon to support a new peace settlement. Neither man identifies the five in question, but the group almost certainly consisted of Richard Bellings, Lucas Dillon, Gerald Fennell, Lord Athenry and Robert Devereux, each of whom had attracted particular criticism from the clerical faction.[14]

The nuncio claimed that no bishops remained at the council board after the declaration of the Inchiquin truce. Bishop O'Dwyer probably returned to his home base in Limerick city, although his movements at this time remain unclear. Bishop MacMahon actually joined the nuncio in Maryborough, while the two other Ulster delegates on the council, Henry Óg O'Neill and Turlough O'Boyle, also sided with the clerical faction. Inchiquin, however, reported a split in the Ulster ranks, after hearing that Phelim O'Neill, Alexander MacDonnell and Viscount Iveagh had deserted Owen Roe O'Neill's army.[15]

Tensions had existed in the ranks of the Ulster forces ever since the declaration of the first Ormond peace, with Phelim O'Neill declaring on 9 December 1646 that "be it war or peace I will never obey him [Owen Roe]". The compromise settlement at the next assembly in early 1647 temporarily restored provincial unity, but conflict erupted again during the subsequent Connacht campaign.[16] Colonel Henry McTully O'Neill identified the officers who deserted the general's command after the Inchiquin truce as those "possessed of their estates in 1641". Anxious to retain the lands they had held prior to the rebellion, Phelim O'Neill and his associates abandoned the dispossessed exiles to their fate, and joined forces with the supreme council.[17]

The remaining three resident members of the council, Patrick Bryan of Leinster, Geoffrey Barron of Munster and Roebuck Lynch of Connacht, could

late July, to capture the seat of confederate government at Kilkenny, using Ulster troops. O'Neill, however, appears to have been operating to a personal agenda, which above all else involved keeping his army intact. Ohlmeyer, *Civil war and restoration* p. 211. **14** Inchiquin to Ormond, 29 May 1648 (Carte, *Ormond*, vi, pp 549-53); Report on the Inchiquin truce, 1648 (Aiazza [ed.], *Embassy* pp 408-17). Clerical criticisms of particular individuals are mentioned in chapter 5 p. 164f. **15** Inchiquin to Ormond, 29 May 1648 (Carte, *Ormond*, vi, pp 549-53). **16** Phelim O'Neill to Father Oliver D'Arcy, 9 Dec. 1646 (PRO SP Ire 262/77 f.259). The tensions in the ranks of the Ulster army during the Connacht campaign in 1647 are described in chapter 5 p. 156f. **17** Apart from Phelim O'Neill, Colonel Henry McTully O'Neill also lists Alexander MacDonnell, Viscount Iveagh, Brian MacMahon and Myles O'Reilly among those Ulster officers who supported the supreme council. "Journal of Colonel Henry McTully O'Neill", *Desiderata curiosa Hibernica*, vol. 2, p. 511.

best be classified as moderates, advocating confederate unity above all else. Both Bryan and Barron had been involved in last minute negotiations to avoid a breach with the nuncio, but after the outbreak of civil war, Bryan firmly allied himself with the peace faction. He took an active part throughout the summer in the council's sustained campaign against the clerical faction. Barron, however, dismissed by Bellings as an "ardent nuncioist", disappeared from public view for a time.[18]

Roebuck Lynch had sat on the council throughout 1647, supporting his former parliamentary colleagues, Nicholas Plunkett and Patrick Darcy. The gradual disillusionment of Darcy (a fellow Galwayman) probably affected Lynch's own political outlook, and in the early days of the excommunication crisis he co-operated with the peace faction. During the summer, however, Lynch became involved in attempts to bring about a confederate reconciliation, before returning home as political and military tensions escalated. Lynch did not attend the final assembly in September, although he kept in touch with his Galway colleagues who travelled to Kilkenny.[19]

Despite numerous desertions, the council responded quickly to the nuncio's excommunication decree, issuing an appeal to Rome just four days later. The document stressed the legitimacy of the council's authority, having been "duly and rightly chosen in the general assembly". As for the agreement with Lord Inchiquin, the council explained how the assemblies of Munster and Leinster both voted in favour of the truce, "though we could have concluded it without them".[20] The peace party hoped an appeal would suspend the excommunication until the papacy resolved the dispute, thus clearing the biggest obstacle in the path of a new treaty with the royalists. Rinuccini, however, insisted the censures remain in place despite the council's actions, a decision which further increased the bitterness between the two sides.[21]

---

**18** Bryan's signature appears on most of the supreme council documents during the summer. See Bodl. Carte Mss 22 ff 115-20, Bodl. Tanner Mss 57/1 f.137, 151, 155. Bellings' dislike of Barron may well have resulted from the latter's role in conveying word of French support for rejecting the Ormond treaty to the general assembly in early 1647. Bellings' History in Gilbert (ed.), *Irish confederation*, vii, p. 7. According to Giblin, Barron seceded from the council rather than accept the Inchiquin truce. Giblin, A., "Geoffrey Baron, 1607-51", *The commemoration of the siege of Limerick* (Limerick 1951) pp 51-7. **19** Lynch was one of the signatories of a council declaration on 7 July, seeking a reconciliation with the clerical faction. Declaration by the supreme council, 7 July 1648 (Bodl. Tanner Mss 57/1 ff.151). Richard Blake, chairman of the last general assembly was one of those who kept in touch with Lynch in late 1648. Richard Blake to Sir Rob. Lynch, 25 Nov. 1648 (Bodl. Carte Mss 22 f.685). **20** Appeal of supreme council to Rome, 31 May 1648 (Bodl. Carte Mss 22 ff 115-20). A second declaration shortly afterwards appealed to the bishops not to harass supporters of the truce. Declaration by the supreme council, 3 June 1648 (Bodl. Tanner Mss 57/1 f.137). **21** Whether Rinuccini was entitled to do this was the subject of a protracted debate. Corish, "Rinuccini's censure of May 22 1648" pp 336-7.

Previous accounts of this period have concentrated almost exclusively on the excommunication issue, ignoring another decisive move by the council which impacted greatly on the nature of the ensuing factional struggle. On 28 May, the council secretary (most probably Richard Bellings) commandeered the Jesuit printing press in Kilkenny.[22] The Jesuit order later dismissed an accusation that it had complied with this move as "a mere calumny". Whatever the truth, two days later, on 30 May, when Dean Massari sought to print the nuncio's decree of excommunication, those in charge of the press denied his request. By this pre-emptive strike the council assumed total control over all material printed in confederate territory, "to the incredible injury of the ecclesiastical party which was never afterwards able to print its ordinations and necessary answers".[23]

This was in sharp contrast with the 1646 crisis, when the clerical controlled printing press published all the major declarations of the ecclesiastical congregation, distributing them to confederate urban centres. The peace faction simply could not compete on the same level, a fact which greatly damaged their cause. In 1648, however, as Rinuccini ruefully observed, the clergy were obliged to make copies of everything in writing, while the supreme council printed a large number of documents explaining their policies.[24] In the propaganda war, the peace faction had already gained the upper hand.

Immediately after receiving news of the excommunication, the council published an order demanding obedience from all confederates, claiming that Rinuccini was being manipulated "by the suggestions of a few persons, for their private ends".[25] Three weeks later, the printing press produced copies of the new oath of association which pledged loyalty to the council. This latter document, signed by 11 lords and 34 "prime gentlemen", who had been summoned to Kilkenny "in nature of a grand council", publicly demonstrated the extent of support for the peace faction. Peter Walsh, a clerical opponent of the nuncio, entitled this body the "Grand Extraordinary Council of the Four Provinces", consisting of the council "together with those others called then by them to their

22 The Jesuits moved their printing press from Waterford to Kilkenny in 1646, probably after the clerical faction seized control in September. The original press in Waterford, run by Thomas Bourke, appears to have been operating in Cork by 1648, brought there by another printer. Sessions, W.K., *The first printers in Waterford, Cork and Kilkenny pre-1700* (York 1990) pp 186-9. The assembly in late 1647 deferred a decision on the appointment of a council secretary, but once the split occurred, Bellings, with all his experience, almost certainly assumed the position. Orders of the general assembly, 12 Nov. 1647 (Gilbert [ed.], *Irish confederation*, vi, pp 208-33). 23 Sessions, *First printers* pp 186-9. 24 Declaration of ecclesiastical congregation against peace,12 August 1646 (Bodl. Carte Mss 18 f.414); Solemn protestation of loyalty and oath of association, 10 September 1646 (Bodl. Carte Mss 113 f.486) and so on. None of the clerical declarations in 1648 were published. Report on the Inchiquin truce, 1648 (Aiazza [ed.], *Embassy* pp 408-17). 25 Sessions, *First printers* p. 242. Mountgarret's signature starts to appear at the head of supreme council documents from this time on, suggesting he was once again acting as council president.

assistance out of the four provinces". In fact, no Ulster and only four Connacht names appear on the list.[26]

The nuncio counter-attacked, claiming the council merely intended to resurrect the peace treaty already rejected by the general assembly. This charge (if true) would have seriously damaged the credibility of the peace faction, which once again made maximum use of the printing press to repudiate such "slanders". The council promised not to "bring in any peace but that which by the orders of the last assembly was directed and committed to the agents sent for Rome, France and Spain to be by them obtained, until the general assembly of the confederate catholics shall otherwise determine". This declaration, strongly reminiscent of those issued by the ecclesiastical congregation in August and September 1646, confirmed the primacy of the legislature within the confederate association, a policy largely inspired by Nicholas Plunkett.[27] To avoid being outflanked by their opponents and maintain public support, the peace faction increasingly had to adopt a more moderate political position.

Rinuccini, outmanoeuvred and dispirited, decided on drastic action to revive the fortunes of the clerical faction. On 11 July he informed Panzirolo of his intention to summon a national synod in Galway, where he had recently moved, to unite the clergy in opposition to the truce.[28] Unfortunately for the nuncio, clerical unity remained an elusive goal, while the council took immediate steps to prevent a synod undermining its authority, as had happened in August 1646. On 28 July a declaration published in Kilkenny denounced the meeting; Clanricarde, joint royalist/confederate commander in Connacht, proceeded to block the roads to Galway.[29] With the nuncio a virtual prisoner in the city, the peace faction continued to consolidate its power.

---

**26** The four Connacht names on the list were Roebuck Lynch, Lucas Dillon, Geoffrey Browne and Lord Athenry. Oath of association, 27 June 1648 (Gilbert [ed.], *Irish confederation*, vii, p. 80). See also Walsh, *Irish remonstrance* p. xlvi. The council was clearly taking the necessary steps to avoid the isolation which led to its downfall in September 1646. **27** Declaration by the supreme council, 7 July 1648 (Bodl. Tanner Mss 57/1 f.151). In 1646 the ecclesiastical congregation declared that "forthwith a general assembly of men and members of integrity be convented and called upon to accept or reject the foresaid peace". Declaration of the ecclesiastical congregation, 24 August 1646 (PRO SP Ire. 261/51 ff 207-10). The clerical faction, on 15 September 1646, talked of the need for the consent of the confederates gathered at an assembly to confirm or reject the peace. Bodl. Carte Mss 18 f.513. **28** With south Leinster and most of Munster controlled by the peace faction, Galway was one of the few remaining cities where clerics could gather with the minimum of interference. Rinuccini to Panzirolo, 11 July 1648 (Aiazza [ed.], *Embassy* p. 405). **29** Declaration by the supreme council, 28 July 1648 (Bodl. Tanner Mss 57/1 f.155). Much to the fury of the nuncio, three Connacht bishops (Tuam, Killala and Kilfenora) openly supported the council's declaration, and Clanricarde's blockade. Report on the Inchiquin truce, 1648 (Aiazza [ed.], *Embassy* pp 408-17). Although the diocese of Kilfenora is north Clare, in the province of Munster, Lynch himself was from Connacht.

Prior to all this, Muskerry and Browne, contrary to their instructions, had returned to Ireland without waiting for any communication from Rome. The peace talks in Paris had been totally overshadowed by news of Ormond's impending return to Ireland, as part of a grand royalist strategy incorporating the three Stuart kingdoms.[30] In April 1648, the counter-attack against the parliamentarians began when forces loyal to the king captured the strategic towns of Berwick and Carlisle, and localised uprisings broke out across England and Wales. Two months later on 8 July, the duke of Hamilton crossed the Scottish border into Cumberland at the head of a large army.

In Ireland, Inchiquin (now acting as royalist commander in Ireland) received word that the committee of estates of the parliament of Scotland had agreed to support Ormond. Royalists, covenanters and confederates appeared poised to secure control of the entire kingdom, with only Michael Jones in Dublin and Owen Roe O'Neill providing any serious opposition.[31] Plans continued apace for a fresh peace settlement between Kilkenny and the marquis of Ormond, with Muskerry and his associates determined to ensure a successful conclusion on this occasion. The final part of the peace faction's strategy, therefore, involved summoning a general assembly to meet on 4 September. The supreme council announced solemnly that the final decision on the truce with Inchiquin, and any future peace, resided with the assembly as "the highest authority among the confederate catholics".[32] This statement, primarily directed against clerical interference, inadvertently provided an opening for the moderates to reassert some authority in Kilkenny.

The marquis of Ormond returned to Ireland on 30 September 1648, over a year after his surrender of Dublin to the English parliament, receiving an enthusiastic welcome from his loyal supporters in the confederate ranks.[33] The defeat of Hamilton's army at Preston the previous month had shattered royalist hopes in England and Scotland, thus increasing the importance of Ormond's mission. With the clerical faction on the defensive, and in the absence of any credible alternative strategy, the peace party confidently expected to secure a speedy set-

30 The "engagement" between the Scots and the king is discussed in chapter 5 p. 171f. Queen Henrietta Maria announced her intention to send Ormond to Ireland in early May. Queen consort and prince to Antrim, 13 May 1648 (Bodl. Carte Mss 63 f.541). 31 The committee of estates was particularly damning in its assessment of O'Neill, a man "guilty of the shedding of so much blood of the protestants there". Answers of the committee of estates of the parliament of Scotland to desires sent from Inchiquin, 28 June 1648 (Bodl. Carte Mss 67 ff 161-2). The Ulster general had threatened Kilkenny in late July before being driven off by Preston and Inchiquin. Casway, *Owen Roe O'Neill* pp 220-1. 32 The council believed that above all else (including a synod of bishops) the general assembly "should be first consulted with in so great an affair". Declaration of the supreme council, 7 July 1648 (Bodl. Tanner Mss 57/1 f.151). 33 The list of those sending congratulations on his safe arrival includes Gerald Fennell, John Walsh, Edmund Butler, Edward Comerford and James Preston. See Bodl. Carte Mss 22 f.304, 308, 310, 341, 380.

tlement with the lord lieutenant. Nonetheless, two months of bitter negotiations brought the marquis to the brink of despair once more. If by mid-1648 the peace party dominated confederate politics, why did an agreement prove so difficult to reach? The answer to this questions lies in the alignment of forces within the general assembly itself.

While reports from hostile sources must be treated with caution, there seems little doubt that the majority of members who attended the meeting came from the south Leinster-east Munster axis, the main block of territory still under confederate control. Elsewhere, particularly in Ulster and Connacht, the clerical boycott of the assembly and the continuing civil war seriously diminished the numbers travelling to Kilkenny. On 14 September the poor attendance forced the assembly to issue a general summons, which does not appear to have improved matters greatly as by mid-October Rinuccini boasted of a significant absentee rate. Ironically, the small outcome actually favoured the peace faction.[34]

Nonetheless, the assembly had displayed an increasingly independent streak since 1645, seeking to reform confederate government and assume a more direct role in the peace negotiations. By 1648, the earl of Castlehaven noted that "the assembly used all means to be rightly informed of their condition", determined not to allow any one faction to dominate the proceedings.[35] Those who threatened confederate unity or the prospect for peace would be severely dealt with, but Ormond would also be expected to make significant concessions in return for a new treaty. In short, by striving to preserve the confederate association while at the same time advocating a more balanced settlement with the royalists, the 1648 assembly adopted the classic middle course.

Nicholas Plunkett and Bishop French, the two leading moderates did not, however, return to Ireland until the end of November, almost three months after the assembly began. So who orchestrated this strategy in their absence, and how did the moderates exert any influence in a sparsely attended assembly, packed with supporters of the peace faction?[36] Eight bishops defied Rinuccini and travelled to the assembly; by the end of the session three more had arrived.[37] Although opposed to Rinuccini's more extreme policies, they still insisted on the

---

34 Rinuccini to Panzirolo, 10 Oct. 1648 (Aiazza [ed.], *Embassy* pp 422-3); Cregan, D.F., "Confederation of Kilkenny" (PhD thesis) p. 278. 35 Tuchet, *Castlehaven review* p. 133. 36 According to Rinuccini the assembly "wants half its usual number no true adherent of the Church party having attended it". He went on to state that some provinces (presumably Ulster and Connacht) had no representatives. Rinuccini to Panzirolo, 10 Oct. 1648 (Aiazza [ed.], *Embassy* pp 422-3). Richard Bellings reported that the nuncio sent an agent to Rome to discredit the peace by stating "there was scarce any in the assembly", a claim he vigorously denied. Bellings' History in Gilbert (ed.), *Irish confederation*, vii, p. 112. 37 They were Tuam, Kilfenora, Killala, Dromore, Ardagh, Meath, Ossory, Limerick. Ferns arrived back from Rome in November, while the archbishop of Cashel and the bishop of Waterford also arrived during the session. Reports of peace and Roman envoys, 30 March 1649 (Aiazza [ed.], *Embassy* pp 457-64). All these bishops signed a declaration welcoming the second Ormond treaty.

restoration of the Catholic Church to "full liberty and splendour". These prelates, led by the archbishop of Tuam (ably supported by Bishop French after his return from the continent), exercised a powerful influence in the assembly, and presented a serious obstacle to a speedy peace settlement.[38]

The landowners of Ulster, although small in number, also pressed for significant concessions. They expressed particular dissatisfaction with the provisions for Ulster (or lack of them) in the original peace treaty. Apart from general guarantees for their existing estates, men such as Phelim O'Neill and Miles O'Reilly sought a review of the plantation process in the hope of recovering lost lands. Such a re-examination would also encourage some of Owen Roe O'Neill's supporters back into the confederate fold.[39] Finally, a number of Plunkett's legal and parliamentary colleagues (including Patrick Darcy) attended the assembly, providing another possible source of opposition to the more extreme policies of the peace faction.[40]

Inchiquin noted with disgust the "indulgence and awful respect" shown by the supreme council to the clergy. Edmund Butler hoped the lord lieutenant would grant religious concessions, as due to the influence of the bishops "all honest men were driven to undertake insisting on it".[41] Even Ormond's staunchest allies in Kilkenny, such as Richard Bellings and Viscount Taaffe, recognised the need for changes in the peace treaty to make it palatable to the majority of confederates.[42] Refusal to compromise on the issues of religion and plantations risked driving potential supporters into the arms of the nuncio and

Declaration of the Roman Catholic bishops, 17 January 1649 (Bodl Clarendon Mss 34 f.76). **38** Propositions of the confederates, 17 Oct. 1648 (Gilbert [ed.], *Irish confederation*, vi, pp 290-3). **39** On 23 October 1648, Viscount Taaffe informed Ormond that the confederates demanded the entire plantation process to be "reviewed and determined in the next free parliament". Taaffe to Ormond, 23 Oct. 1648 (Gilbert [ed.], *Irish confederation*, vi, pp 302-3). This review, conducted by existing landholders, would of course have protected their interests rather than those of the dispossessed. Inchiquin was also told by Taaffe that there were many people in the assembly "that are earnest to have Owen O'Neill fairly invited to conform himself to the council". Inchiquin to Ormond, 10 Oct. 1648 (Bodl. Clarendon Mss 31 ff 274-5). **40** Darcy was particularly active on the supreme council and various committees after September 1648. With the Ulster army severely censured, and not represented at the assembly, the Galway lawyer probably reverted to a more moderate political position. Supreme council documents, 1648 (Bodl. Carte Mss 22 f.448, 547). See also order of the general assembly, 19 Dec. 1648 (Gilbert [ed.], *Irish confederation*, vii, pp 154-5). **41** Inchiquin was particularly incensed at the council's obsequious attitude, given that many of the clergy continued to spread dissent. Inchiquin to Ormond, 12 Aug. 1648 (Bodl. Carte Mss 22 ff 165-6). Butler assured Ormond that the bishops, by defying the nuncio and attending the assembly, clearly did not intend to introduce a jurisdiction which "might prejudice the king's prerogative". Sir Edmund Butler to Ormond, 5 Oct. 1648 (Bodl. Carte Mss 22 f.308). **42** Taaffe swore to Inchiquin that the confederates would insist on holding onto churches "or at least most of those now in their own quarters". Inchiquin to Ormond, 10 Oct. 1648 (Bodl. Clarendon Mss 31 ff 274-5). Bellings believed that without religious concessions "Ireland cannot be quieted". Bellings to Ormond, 25 Nov. 1648 (Bodl. Carte Mss 22 f.687).

Owen Roe O'Neill. These considerations meant in effect that the moderates set the agenda for the negotiations with the lord lieutenant, re-emerging as a significant force in confederate politics once more.[43]

This influence is clearly evident in the process by which the assembly established a new committee of treaty. During the period 1644-6, the peace faction's control of the first committee of treaty enabled it to by-pass the assembly (and opponents on the supreme council as well) in agreeing terms with the royalists. In October 1648, however, the assembly simply instructed the commissioners to present Ormond with the confederate proposals rather than enter into any negotiations. The terms could not be altered in any way until they returned to the assembly with Ormond's answers, thus preventing any secret deals.[44]

Apart from a strong peace faction representation on the committee (including such figures as Robert Talbot, John Walsh and Geoffrey Browne), two Ulster members (Phelim O'Neill and Miles O'Reilly) ensured neither side ignored the plantation issue in the subsequent negotiations.[45] Moreover, the assembly, although fully aware of the lord lieutenant's antipathy towards catholic clergymen, insisted on appointing a bishop to the talks team. Viscount Taaffe opposed the move but according to his own account, was "cried down with much violence". Anticipating his objection, Taaffe assured Ormond that it would be easier for the confederates to accept a treaty with a bishop present to sanction the religious terms.[46] On this occasion, unlike 1644 when the aged archbishop of Dublin nominally sat on the committee of treaty, the assembly chose the archbishop of Tuam, the most senior and powerful cleric in the chamber.[47] Although an opponent of Rinuccini, Tuam proved a stubborn advocate of major religious concessions in the ensuing negotiations.

The limits to peace faction control became apparent shortly after Ormond's return to Ireland. The debate on a motion brought before the assembly to begin talks with the lord lieutenant had to be adjourned after a number of members successfully argued that the confederates possessed no proof of Ormond's authority to conclude a treaty. Although the marquis provided the necessary guarantees the following day (after a hurried letter from Viscount Taaffe explaining the situation), the episode did not augur well for those who hoped to secure a speedy settlement.[48]

---

43 Similarly, Smith notes the re-emergence of the moderates during the Newport negotiations in September 1648 which followed the end of the second English civil war. Smith, *Constitutional royalism* p. 138.  44 Taaffe to Ormond, 11 Oct. 1648 (Bodl. Carte Mss 22 f.347). 45 For the full list of committee members see chapter 7 (table 6). 46 Taaffe to Ormond, 11 Oct. 1648 (Bodl. Carte Mss 22 f.347).  47 Richard Blake, chairman of the assembly, informed Ormond of the appointment of the commissioners. Blake to Ormond, 16 Oct. 1648 (Bodl. Carte Mss 22 f.389). The 1644 committee of treaty is discussed in chapter 2 p. 74. 48 Ormond requested that the assembly send a delegation to meet him in Carrick, County Tipperary. Ormond to Sir Richard Blake, 4 Oct. 1648 (Bodl. Carte Mss 22 f.298). Unfortunately, Taaffe,

The peace treaty agreed with the marquis of Ormond in 1646 provided the starting point for the new negotiations which finally began in mid-October 1648. The confederates sought major amendments to the original document, based primarily on the religious clauses added to the oath of association in early 1647, and the instructions given to the three agents travelling to Paris the following year.[49] Both the oath and the instructions had already been approved by the assembly, whose central role in the political process was now recognised by the lord lieutenant. In contrast to his dismissive attitude during earlier talks, Ormond proved anxious in 1648 to deal directly with the assembly, explaining in a letter to Inchiquin that no treaty could be "so valid or effectual as that which shall be transacted immediately with a general assembly".[50]

The commissioners, in accordance with the terms of the oath of association, demanded "the free and public exercise of the Roman Catholic Religion". They also sought the removal of all penal laws, with the catholic clergy retaining the church buildings already in their possession and the right to exercise their ecclesiastical jurisdiction. Taaffe reported to the lord lieutenant that "there was not two there [in the general assembly] that would decline the propositions for churches", further evidence that even supporters of the peace faction had radically shifted their position on religious matters.[51]

Ormond must have found it difficult to conceal his dismay as he listened to this particular submission. His instructions from Queen Henrietta Maria in Paris merely authorised him to grant anything already conceded in earlier negotiations, even though the confederates had already rejected these terms. In case of difficulties, the queen advised the lord lieutenant to assure the confederates that catholics would not be disturbed in the possession of property "until such time as his Majesty upon a full consideration of their desires in a free parliament, shall declare his further pleasure". This concession did not imply royal consent for catholic occupation of ecclesiastical property "but only a sufferance of their present profession".[52] An acceptable religious deal would clearly require major compromises on both sides.

along with most confederates, rarely identified the source of opposition in the assemblies. Taaffe to Ormond, 3 Oct. 1648 (Bodl. Carte Mss 22 f.294). **49** Propositions presented by the confederate commissioners to Ormond, 17 Oct. 1648 (Bodl. Carte Mss 22 ff 394-6); Gilbert (ed.), *Irish confederation*, vi, pp 290-3. **50** Ormond to Inchiquin, [13 Nov.]1648 (Carte, *Ormond*, vi, pp 581-3). Ormond's earlier opposition to the assembly's involvement in the peace negotiations is discussed in chapter 5 p. 149f. **51** Taaffe also noted the determination of some assembly members to have "a catholic government". Inchiquin to Ormond, 10 Oct. 1648 (Bodl. Clarendon Mss 31 ff 274-5). Confederate demands are outlined in the propositions presented by the confederate commissioners to Ormond, 17 Oct. 1648 (Bodl. Carte Mss 22 ff 394-6). See also Gilbert (ed.), *Irish confederation*, vi, pp 290-3. **52** The queen stressed that any concessions did in no way imply "a consent in his Majesty of giving away of the churches or church livings from the protestants to them [the catholics] or the settling of them in the same for a perpetuity". Instructions of the Queen and Prince concerning religion, [1648] (Bodl. Carte Mss 63 f.568).

On constitutional matters, the lord lieutenant pledged to defend the privileges of parliament and the liberty of subjects, but offered no guidelines as to how this could be achieved.[53] Confederate proposals called for a parliament within six months, or failing that a general assembly within two years, for "settling the affairs of the kingdom, without any transmission into England, and that an act shall pass in the next parliament enacting, establishing and confirming the peace to be concluded, and all the articles thereof; and Poynings' Act to be repealed".[54] With the king a prisoner of the English parliament (implacable enemies of Irish catholics), transmission to England no longer appeared a feasible option.

On the issue of the independence of the Irish parliament, however, the confederates simply requested that the king would "leave both houses of parliament in this kingdom to make such declaration therein as shall be agreeable to the laws of the kingdom of Ireland".[55] This decision, not to insist on a declaratory act, is difficult to explain, considering the ever increasing threat from Westminster. Perhaps the confederates finally accepted the royalist argument that such a demand would prove of no immediate use to them, delay the conclusion of the treaty unnecessarily, and cause severe problems for Charles I in England.

Ormond readily agreed to a declaration by the Irish parliament, but despite the desperate plight of the king, he still refused to concede on the crucial issue of transmission. He declared emphatically that "we do not understand nor conceive there can be any way found by an act of parliament to establish and confirm the peace to be concluded, and all the articles thereof, without transmission into England, nor that Poynings' act can be suspended or repealed until a bill for the same be first agreed on in a session of parliament to be held in this kingdom and then transmitted".[56] The lord lieutenant, however, singularly failed to explain how (and to whom) these bills were to be transmitted.

Apart from religious and constitutional matters, the committee of treaty also demanded significant concessions in the area of plantations, particularly in the province of Ulster. In order to prevent a repeat of the abuses perpetrated by Thomas Wentworth during the 1630s, they sought to remove the Irish council's jurisdiction over the whole process. Moreover, confederates reoccupying plantation lands were to retain possession, and be recognised as the legal owners, until challenged in law. Those who failed to recover their estates would be granted permission to petition the next parliament, dominated, in theory at least, by sympathetic catholic landowners.[57]

53 Declaration by Ormond, 6 Oct. 1648, *HMC, Report on the manuscripts of the marquis of Ormonde* (1899), vol. 2, p. 81. Ormond made this declaration to Inchiquin's troops at Cork, illustrating once again the convergence of protestant and catholic interests on the issue of parliamentary privileges. 54 Propositions from the confederates, 17 Nov. 1648 (Gilbert [ed.], *Irish confederation*, vii, pp 134-6). 55 Idem. 56 Ormond to Richard Blake, 21 Dec. 1648 (Gilbert [ed.], *Irish confederation*, vii, pp 161-2). 57 Propositions presented by the confederate commis-

These new terms clearly show that the 1646 treaty, so painstakingly constructed by the peace faction, remained totally unacceptable to the general assembly. On 23 October, a week after talks began, the commissioners informed a dismayed lord lieutenant that they had no authority to recede from any of the original propositions.[58] With the negotiations stalled, Richard Blake (chairman of the assembly in Nicholas Plunkett's absence) invited the lord lieutenant to travel to Kilkenny to facilitate a breakthrough. The marquis eagerly accepted the offer, arriving in the city some time before 8 November. Ormond hoped that his presence might have a moderating influence on the assembly, which he believed was "as well composed for us, and in as good temper as we can expect any assembly will ever be".[59]

These talks progressed against a background of increasing tension in both confederate and royalist ranks. The general assembly declared Owen Roe O'Neill a traitor on 30 September and gave his followers until 25 October to submit. Nonetheless, O'Neill maintained contact with Kilkenny, exploring the possibility of a compromise.[60] In a letter to the lord lieutenant, O'Neill expressed his support for a settlement, claiming the rupture with his former colleagues resulted only from his desire to protect the nuncio from "the violence and indiscretion of some of the council that were at Kilkenny". He would accept any treaty which satisfied the clergy on religion, the assembly on other matters, and took care of the interests of his own province.[61] For the present, however, O'Neill and his allies remained outside the confederate fold.

The breach between the nuncio and Kilkenny widened when on 19 October, Richard Blake notified Rinuccini of a protestation prepared by the assembly for Innocent X, and recommended that the nuncio travel to Rome to defend himself. The assembly accused Rinuccini of failing to provide adequate financial support to the confederates (despite repeated promises), issuing warrants to dis-

sioners to Ormond, 17 Oct. 1648 (Bodl. Carte Mss 22 ff 394-6). See also Gilbert (ed.), *Irish confederation*, vi, pp 290-3. This last point addressed one of the two major grievances of the Ulster Irish with the first peace treaty, at least according to Daniel O'Neill. The other grievance concerned the failure to assign any positions to Ulstermen in the new regime. Daniel O'Neill to Ormond, 3 Sept. 1646 (Gilbert [ed.], *Contemporary history*, i, p. 702). **58** The only exception involved the plantations issue, where the confederates expressed a desire to have the whole process examined in the next parliament, rather than delay the treaty trying to resolve the complexities of the issue. Taaffe to Ormond, 23 Oct. 1648 (Gilbert [ed.], *Irish confederation*, vi, pp 302-3). **59** Blake to Ormond, 28 Oct. 1648 (Bodl. Carte Mss 22 f.453). Ormond to Prince of Wales, [2 Nov.]1648 (Carte, *Ormond*, vi, pp 578-9). Ormond's assessment of the assembly was undoubtedly accurate in this regard. **60** O'Neill to Blake, 6 Nov. 1649 (Bodl. Carte Mss 44 f.349). O'Neill was joined around this time by the marquis of Antrim, who had organised an abortive uprising in Wexford shortly after Ormond's arrival in Ireland. Antrim refused the offer of a safe conduct to Kilkenny and developed contacts with the English parliament instead. Ohlmeyer, *Civil war and restoration* p. 208; Cregan, D.F., "Confederation of Kilkenny" (PhD thesis) p. 289. **61** O'Neill to Ormond, 6 Dec. 1648 (Bodl. Carte Mss 23 f.6).

possess confederates of church lands, and ignoring the council on the question of ecclesiastical appointments. The most serious allegation concerned the nuncio's attempts to undermine the solidarity of the confederates, who prior to his arrival had been "all united and prone to a settlement [with the king]".[62]

Although clearly exaggerated, the accusations about the nuncio's disruptive influence carried some substance, particularly after the signing of the Inchiquin truce. Assembly members realised that Innocent X would hardly support them against his own representative, but hoped that forcing Rinuccini out of the country might possibly bring the confederate civil war to an end. The nuncio's continued presence posed the most serious obstacle to a reconciliation with Owen Roe O'Neill, as well as hindering the prospects of a settlement with the royalists. The protest, therefore, constituted yet another attempt to reconstruct a semblance of confederate unity, rather than a vindictive swipe at a weakened opponent.

While internal confederate conflicts threatened a peace deal, the situation in the royalist camp proved equally volatile. During October and November, Inchiquin experienced increasing difficulties with the troops under his command and warned the lord lieutenant of a possible mutiny.[63] Until early 1648 the Munster parliamentarians had been the confederates' most effective opponents, and many actively disliked their leader's new alliance. Shortly after arriving in Cork, Ormond tried to assuage any fears by declaring his determination to defend the protestant religion and the royal prerogative, although he neglected to explain exactly how this could be achieved in direct negotiations with Irish catholics.[64]

The initial demands from Kilkenny increased Ormond's pessimism on the prospects of reaching a settlement capable of satisfying the confederates and Inchiquin's troops. The lord lieutenant realised, nonetheless, that an open breach in royalist ranks would prove fatal to the king's interests in Ireland. On receiving Inchiquin's warning therefore, he decided immediately to suspend peace negotiations, and travel to Cork to quell the disquiet. The assembly, recognising the urgency of the situation, agreed to postpone the talks on 20 November, and promised not to disperse before Ormond's return.[65]

---

62 Rinuccini's divisive tactics (according to the assembly), included using Owen Roe O'Neill to intimidate his opponents, and persisting with ecclesiastical censures despite the supreme council's appeal to Rome. Blake to Rinuccini, 19 Oct. 1648 (Gilbert [ed.], *Irish confederation*, vi, pp 294-300). Confederate divisions prior to Rinuccini's arrival are examined in chapter 3. 63 On 14 November Inchiquin informed Ormond that he could not travel to Kilkenny to participate in the negotiations as planned because of "disaffection" among his troops. Bodl. Carte Mss 22 f.615. 64 Declaration by Ormond, 6 Oct. 1648 in *HMC, Report on the manuscripts of the marquess of Ormond*, vol. 2, p. 81. 65 Resolution of the general assembly, 20 Nov. 1648 (Bodl. Carte Mss 22 f.660). On 21 November, Ormond and Richard Blake agreed to extend the cessation between royalist and confederate troops until 1 January 1649. Bodl. Carte Mss 22 f.670.

Meanwhile, royalists and confederates awaited the return of Nicholas Plunkett and Bishop French with various degrees of expectation and trepidation.[66] Substantial financial aid from Rome would have enabled the confederates to pursue an independent military strategy. A successful mission, therefore, threatened to undermine the royalist strategy of creating a broad alliance in Ireland to challenge the English parliament. Moreover, the agents' report on the papal attitude towards religious concessions would prove crucial in determining, not only clerical attitudes, but those of the vast majority of Irish catholics, towards a peace settlement. In the confederate civil war both sides desperately needed the support of Plunkett, French and their moderate allies to bolster their respective positions.

The two agents heard news of the confederate split during their stay in Rome. With no real prospect of direct assistance from Innocent X, they faced a stark choice – to support Rinuccini's war strategy, despite the internal divisions and lack of finances, or attempt to extract a better deal from the lord lieutenant and unite with the royalists against the parliamentarians. The nuncio's military ambitions, however attractive in late 1646, no longer seemed viable in the changed circumstances two years later, while the calling of a general assembly must have strongly influenced Plunkett's thinking. Both men appear to have decided before leaving Rome to actively explore the possibility of a new peace settlement.[67]

Neither agent appears to have informed anyone in Ireland of their decision, preferring to reserve final judgement until they could view the situation at first hand.[68] They arrived back in Kilkenny shortly after Ormond's departure to Cork, and presented a report of the mission to the assembly on 25 November 1648, in a move interpreted by Rinuccini as a gross betrayal. The nuncio believed that after visiting Rome, they should have reported directly to him as the pope's representative. Both men, however, had received their commissions as confederate agents from the assembly, which was once again in session.[69] The decision to travel first to Kilkenny, rather than Galway, effectively proclaimed their political preference.

**66** Abbot Crelly wrote to Rinuccini from the continent in September that the two men would be back in Ireland shortly. This letter was intercepted, probably by the supreme council. Bodl. Carte Mss 22 ff 217-18. See also Ohlmeyer, *Civil war and restoration* p. 213 n.70. **67** Father Bernard Davetty reported from Rome that the two men had openly gone over to the nuncio's opponents. It is not clear if anybody in Kilkenny received this information before the agents' return to Ireland. O'Ferrall and O'Connell (eds), *Commentarius*, iii, pp 658-65. Richard Blake later claimed that the two men only heard of the confederate split after taking leave of the pope. Richard Blake to Rob. Lynch, 25 Nov. 1648 (Bodl. Carte Mss f.685). See also Corish, *NHI*, iii, pp 332-3. **68** This can be inferred from the fact that neither the peace or clerical factions knew what to expect from the papacy until the return of the two agents. **69** Rinuccini to Panzirolo, 23 Dec. 1648 (Aiazza [ed.], *Embassy* pp 443-6). Although the agents were appointed by the assembly, the issuing of instructions was left to the supreme council and bishops. Instructions to Plunkett and Ferns, 18 Jan. 1648 (BL Stowe Mss ff 155-6).

Plunkett and French informed assembly members that Innocent X refused to endorse any settlement with a protestant monarch, or to commit further funds to the confederate cause. Although, publicly at least, the papacy supported Rinuccini's actions in the excommunication crisis, French hinted that letters brought from Cardinal Roma (a member of the congregation of Irish affairs in Rome) disapproved of the nuncio's censures. French's speech, therefore, implied that Rinuccini no longer enjoyed the total support of his superiors. Moreover, the bishop failed to inform Rinuccini that the pope had left the handling of the excommunication entirely to his own discretion.[70]

The failure of the mission to Rome had an immediate and electrifying impact on the assembly. Bellings immediately sought to expose false hopes of papal aid, as "until that pretence be taken away from such as have other interests, Ireland cannot be quieted". The report of Plunkett and French, according to Bellings at least, left the confederates "at liberty to proceed as best suits with the good of the kingdom".[71] The peace faction confidently prepared for another round of negotiations, while Rinuccini's only hope of preventing a treaty lay in ruins, destroyed by the two confederates he admired most.

The talks made little progress, however, in the weeks following these dramatic events, with Ormond proving as stubborn as ever. On 15 December, the assembly appointed a delegation of six members, including Nicholas Plunkett, to bring additional proposals to the royalists, and to threaten a dispersal of the assembly before the conclusion of a treaty unless the lord lieutenant responded straight away. Ormond could hardly afford to ignore such a warning, as without confederate support, the king's cause was lost. As before, religion provided the main obstacle to a settlement, and the lord lieutenant admitted in a letter to Inchiquin that the two sides remained as far apart as ever on the issue.[72]

In many ways Ormond occupied an unenviable position, trying to quell the disquiet among Inchiquin's troops on the one hand, while meeting the expectations of the assembly on the other. He complained bitterly to Inchiquin of the confederates' insistence on pressing for "concessions beyond my instructions".[73] The varied and often contradictory orders he received from England (and Paris)

70 Reports of peace and Roman envoys, 30 March 1649 (Aiazza [ed.], *Embassy* pp 457-64); Ó hAnnracháin, "Far from terra firma" pp 345-7; Corish, P. J, "Bishop Nicholas French" pp 89-90. 71 Bellings to Ormond, 25 Nov. 1648 (Bodl. Carte Mss. 22 f.687); Gilbert (ed.) *Irish confederation*, vii, pp 148-9. Richard Blake sent a similar message to Roebuck Lynch in Galway. Richard Blake to Rob. Lynch, 25 Nov. 1648 (Bodl. Carte Mss 22 f.685). According to the Plunkett manuscript in the National Library, the agents return from Rome "did so clearly open the eyes of such as formerly wavered". NLI Mss 345 p. 557. 72 Order of the general assembly, 15 Dec. 1648 (Bodl. Carte Mss 23 f.48); Gilbert (ed.) *Irish confederation*, vii, p. 154. Ormond still hoped, even at this late stage, to keep the religious concessions out of the treaty. Ormond to Inchiquin, 18 Dec. 1648 (Bodl. Carte Mss 23 f.54). 73 Ormond to Inchiquin, 18 Dec. 1648 (Bodl. Carte Mss 23 f.54).

provided a further obstacle to progress, and with the king's denunciation of Glamorgan still fresh in his memory, Ormond proved reluctant to take any risks. Nonetheless, the desperate nature of the royalist position demanded decisiveness and flexibility.[74] The marquis appeared to lack the political will, or courage, to make the necessary concessions; as a result he almost irrevocably destroyed royalist hopes in Ireland.

On 19 December, under tremendous pressure, he finally answered the confederate proposals, agreeing to abolish by act of parliament all penalties "concerning the free exercise of their religion". The marquis refused, however, to concede ground on the issues of church property, or the exercise of clerical jurisdiction, pleading that he did not possess sufficient authority from the king. Instead, he promised that catholics would not be molested in their possessions until the next parliament examined the whole question. This response, basically restating his previous position, infuriated the confederates, increasingly frustrated at the lack of progress in the negotiations.[75]

The assembly debated Ormond's reply, objecting strongly to the lack of religious concessions, and established yet another committee in one final attempt to forge a settlement. The membership of this task force consisted of all the bishops present at the assembly and twelve laymen, including Nicholas Plunkett.[76] Failure to reach an agreement would almost certainly have further split the confederate association, leading to an escalation of the civil war. Plunkett, French and the other moderates, desperate to avoid such an outcome, had little alternative but to persist with the negotiations.

Between 20 and 23 December the confederates made frantic efforts to save the peace process. Their treaty committee prepared a number of documents outlining a possible compromise. One draft suggested that the confederates would be satisfied with the free exercise of religion, the revocation of penal laws and the replacement of the oath of supremacy with the oath of allegiance. Catholics would retain all churches already in their possession until the next parliament,

74 Further negotiations took place between the king and the English parliament following the royalist defeat in the second civil war. On 25 November, Charles informed Ormond of an agreement to "entrust the prosecution and management of the war in Ireland to the guidance and advice of our two Houses", and ordered the lord lieutenant to desist from any further dealings with the confederates. Charles to Ormond, 25 Nov. 1648 (Bodl. Tanner Mss 57/2 f.426). A week later, the army occupied Westminster and purged the parliament, effectively signalling the end of efforts to each an accommodation with the king. It is unclear if Ormond ever received this letter from Charles. 75 Treaty negotiations, Dec. 1648 (Bodl. Carte Mss 23 f.60, 66). 76 The full list of lay members was as follows; Nicholas Plunkett, Lucas Dillon, Geoffrey Browne, Patrick Byran, Donough O'Callaghan, John Haly, Gerrald FitzGerald, John Walsh, Thomas Tyrrell, Patrick Darcy, James Cusack, Bartholomew Stackpole. Order of the general assembly, 19 Dec. 1648 (Gilbert [ed.], *Irish confederation*, vii, pp 154-5). The bishops present were Tuam, Kilfenora, Killala, Dromore, Ardagh, Meath, Ossory, Limerick, Ferns, Cashel and Waterford.

with all other religious matters deferred to "his majesty's gracious favour and further concessions". The lord lieutenant readily agreed to these terms, but the assembly, determined to keep control of the negotiations, demanded further concessions. Ormond, however, refused to budge on the issues of churches and clerical jurisdiction, and the stalemate continued.[77]

On 24 December, Ormond wrote in desperation to Inchiquin that the treaty negotiations had reached such a point that they "must immediately determine in an agreement or rupture".[78] Inchiquin's decisive intervention at this moment undoubtedly prevented the collapse of the entire talks process. News had just arrived in Cork from England of the king's impending trial and Inchiquin decided to publish the information. He disseminated news-sheets among the confederate delegates at Kilkenny with dramatic results. On 28 December, Richard Blake informed Ormond that the assembly, "upon consideration of his majesty's present condition" unanimously accepted the terms on offer.[79]

Blake's statement appears hard to reconcile with the obvious reluctance of the bishops to concede on the issue of church jurisdiction. On this occasion, however, the clergy proved incapable of blocking the settlement or forcing any further concessions. On 29 December (the day following Blake's dramatic announcement), the assembly issued an unequivocal declaration on the religious amendments contained in the oath of association. The confederates were "not obliged to insist on the said propositions but may and are at liberty to descend to such an agreement and conditions as *this Assembly* shall judge necessary and reasonable".[80]

The contrast with events in 1646 could hardly be more striking. In March of that year, the supreme council and committee of treaty alone acted as arbiters of the peace terms. Following the rejection of the Ormond peace in August 1646, the clergy replaced the council and committee as the self-proclaimed guardians of confederate aspirations. Clerical ascendancy proved short-lived, as Nicholas Plunkett and his associates orchestrated a compromise in early 1647 which saw the assembly emerge as the dominant force in confederate politics. Confederates embraced the doctrine of legislative supremacy, allowing assembly members in future to have the final say on any treaty terms with the royalists. The declara-

---

77 The content of the drafts suggest that the bishops were not involved in the committee's discussions. Treaty negotiations, Dec. 1648 (Bodl. Carte Mss 23 f.70, 96); Gilbert (ed.), *Irish confederation*, vii, pp 157-8, 160-1, 165-6. **78** Ormond to Inchiquin, 24 Dec. 1648 (Bodl. Carte Mss 23 f.108). **79** Apparently the news from England also silenced the complaints of Inchiquin's protestant troops. Carte, *Ormond*, iii, p. 407. On 28 December, Blake informed Ormond of the assembly members' desires "to expand their lives and fortunes in maintaining his [the king] rights and interests". Bodl. Carte Mss 23 f.123. **80** Declaration of the general assembly in respect of the oath of association, 29 Dec. 1648 (Bodl. Carte Mss 23 f.131). The emphasis in the quotation is my own. See also Corish, "Bishop Nicholas French" pp 98-9; Lowe, "Negotiations between Charles I and confederates" p. 681.

tion of 29 December 1648 confirmed this fact and clearly marked the limits of factional power.

The same day as the assembly declaration the bishops held a meeting, addressed by Nicholas French, to debate the religious concessions on offer. French urged the prelates to accept the treaty, citing the example of the treaty of Westphalia, signed two months earlier, despite the opposition of the papal nuncio to the clause on ecclesiastical jurisdiction.[81] The bishops reluctantly agreed to accept the terms of the proposed settlement with the royalists, but only (as Ormond noted) because they observed the assembly's determination "to rest satisfied however they should declare".[82] The only alternative involved condemning the treaty and joining forces with the nuncio and O'Neill, an unpalatable prospect for the moderate bishops at this late stage.

The sole outstanding issue centred on the question of "interval government", as Ormond termed it, or how to govern the country until the Irish parliament confirmed the treaty. The confederates sought to retain as much of their existing governmental structures as possible until the parliament met, while Ormond hoped to assume overall military and civil control immediately after signing the peace deal. The lord lieutenant confided to Inchiquin that the confederates had "much reason on their side". He believed it would prove difficult "to bring them to consent to waive what they needs must waive if the English are to be satisfied too".[83]

The solution to this problem, first mooted in the 1646 treaty, involved appointing leading confederates to govern in association with the lord lieutenant until a parliament or assembly met. These "commissioners of trust" would assist Ormond in judging particularly "barbarous" crimes excluded from the act of oblivion, oversee the supply of military forces, and select transitional commanders for confederate controlled areas.[84] The proposals in 1648, however, differed from those in 1646 in that the assembly rather than the committee of treaty chose the commissioners, which resulted in the selection of a more representative body. Ulster, for example, enjoyed equal status with the other provinces, and although Ormond refused to govern with any members of the clergy, he agreed that the archbishop of Tuam and the bishop of Ferns be associated as "secondary assessors", as long as they did not use their ecclesiastical titles in subscribing public acts.[85]

---

**81** The fact that the Westphalia settlement featured in this debate demonstrates the extent to which the confederates kept themselves informed of recent developments on the continent. **82** Corish, "Bishop Nicholas French" p. 99. Ormond was convinced that the assembly had forced the bishops to accept the religious terms. Ormond to Inchiquin, 29 Dec. 1648 (Bodl. Carte Mss 23 f.141). **83** This statement illustrates the dual pressure under which Ormond operated at all times in trying to reach a settlement. Ormond to Inchiquin, 29 Dec. 1648 (Bodl. Carte Mss 23 f.141); Ormond to Inchiquin, 12 Dec. 1648 (Carte, *Ormond*, vi, pp 589-90). **84** Details of the commissions are contained in the two peace treaties. Gilbert (ed.) *Irish confederation*, v, pp 286-310 (1646); Gilbert (ed.) *Irish confederation*, vii, pp 184-211 (1648). **85** O'Ferrall and O'Connell (eds), *Commentarius*, iv, pp 37-45. Rinuccini noted with dismay the

The greater involvement of the Ulstermen, and the inclusion of the bishops, ensured that the commissioners enjoyed a greater degree of support than might otherwise have been the case.[86] Finally, the general assembly sought to reassure the sceptics by declaring that the proclamation of the 28 August 1645 would remain in full force, even after the signing of the peace treaty. Assembly members therefore, reaffirmed "the union and association of the said catholics and the obligation of the said oath" until the Irish parliament ratified the treaty terms.[87] By these various actions, the advocates of peace hoped to persuade the majority of their supporters to accept the new regime.

Despite the importance of the 1646 and 1649 peace treaties in confederate Ireland, no detailed study exists of the two documents, or an assessment of how they compare. The traditional assumption that the terms of the second treaty did not significantly differ from those on offer in 1646 has largely gone unchallenged. Rinuccini, when he finally saw the 1649 peace treaty, commented mournfully "it is in fact no other than that concluded before my arrival". According to this line of argument, the upheavals which followed the rejection of the settlement in 1646 proved totally unnecessary. They had no impact on the eventual outcome, other than to postpone for two years the forming of an alliance against the English parliament, with fatal consequences for catholic Ireland.[88] But was this really the case? What changes, if any, appeared in the second agreement?

The peace treaty of August 1646 is a long document, containing 30 clauses of various lengths dealing with religious, civil and military matters. The later agreement consists of 35 clauses, 22 of which are unchanged from 1646, seven have been modified in some way, and six are completely new items. The 1649 treaty also omitted three of the original clauses, though none of major importance.[89] Some of the amendments and additions simply reflected the changed military and political circumstances pertaining at the end of the English civil wars, but a

involvement of the bishop of Ferns on the commission, and the need to restrict himself to the title "Nicholas". Report on the affairs of Ireland, 1649 (Aiazza [ed.], *Embassy* p. 542). In 1646 only two of the twelve commissioners came from Ulster. Gilbert (ed.) *Irish confederation*, v, pp 286-310. **86** The council consisted of lords Dillon, Muskerry and Athenry, Lucas Dillon, Richard Barnewall, Geoffrey Browne, Donough O'Callaghan, Gerald Fennell, Nicholas Plunkett, Alexander MacDonnell, Turlough O'Neill, and Myles O'Reilly, all of whom had served on confederate supreme councils. See appendix 2 (table 13). **87** The proclamation of 1645 was made shortly after the signing of the secret Glamorgan treaty which confederates hoped would be ratified in the next parliament. Declaration of the general assembly, 28 Aug. 1645 (Bodl. Carte Mss 15 ff 558-9); Order of the general assembly, 12 Jan. 1649 (Bodl. Carte Mss 23 f.252). **88** Rinuccini to Panzirolo, May 1649 (Aiazza [ed.], *Embassy* p. 473). The most recent study of the nuncio accepts his assessment uncritically. Ó hAnnracháin, "Far from terra firma" p. 420. **89** Gilbert (ed.), *Irish confederation*, v, pp 286-310 (1646); Gilbert (ed.), *Irish confederation*, vii, pp 184-211 (1648).

number marked significant confederate gains, particularly on religious and constitutional issues.

In 1646, the first article of the treaty, dealing with the vexed question of religion, unquestionably proved the most contentious. On appointment to any office of government, Irish catholics were no longer obliged to take the oath of supremacy, and a straight-forward oath of allegiance would henceforth suffice. All other religious matters, including the repeal of anti-catholic laws were simply "referred to his Majesties gracious favour and further concessions". The absence of safeguards for the free exercise of religion, the exercise of ecclesiastical jurisdiction by catholic clergy or their retention of church property, infuriated the clerical faction. The opposition to the treaty centred mainly, though by no means exclusively, around these particular issues.[90]

Significant alterations appeared in the crucial religious clause of the 1649 agreement. The first article granted individual catholics the free exercise of religion, security of tenure and exemption from recusancy fines, but the official position of the Catholic Church remained unclear. The treaty deferred the controversial issue of church property to the next meeting of parliament, which (because of other concessions in the treaty) confederates hoped would be dominated by the catholic interest. In the meantime, catholic clergy retained possession of church buildings and property. Although these terms fell short of the demands made in the 1647 assembly, and during the subsequent negotiations, they still represented a major advance on the original concessions.

The 1649 settlement contained a clause for the holding of a parliament within six months or an assembly within two years. The articles of treaty would be "transmitted into England, according to the usual form, to be passed in the said parliament, and that the said acts so agreed upon, and so to be passed shall receive no disjunction or alteration here or in England". The formula appeared almost identical to that used in 1646, except for an amendment declaring that "both houses of parliament may consider what they shall think convenient touching the repeal or suspension of the statute commonly called Poynings' Act".[91] This in fact guaranteed very little, as the king retained the power to veto any future act of the Irish parliament calling for a repeal of Poynings' law. Charles, however, would certainly have found it difficult to ignore repeated demands from parliament on this issue.

With a declaratory act no longer on the agenda, the royalists (as in 1646) recognised the right of the Irish parliament to make any declaration regarding the independence of that parliament "as shall be agreeable to the laws of the

90 See declarations by ecclesiastical congregation against the peace 12 August 1646 (Bodl. Carte Mss 18 ff 250-1), 24 August 1646 (PRO SP Ire. 261/51 ff 207-10), 10 September 1646 (PRO SP Ire. 262/3 ff 4-5), and Enos "Survey" in Gilbert (ed.), *Irish confederation*, vi, pp 307-433. 91 Articles of peace, 17 Jan. 1649 (Gilbert [ed.], *Irish confederation*, vii, pp 184-211).

kingdom of Ireland".[92] The 1649 treaty also retained the original clauses from
1646 requiring lords to be estated, and members of the House of Commons to
be estated and resident, in the kingdom. Regarding the elections, "all impediments which may hinder the said Roman Catholics to sit or vote in the next
intended parliament, or to choose, or be chosen knights and burgesses to sit or
vote there, shall be removed, and that before the said parliament".[93] These measures would ensure the return of significant numbers of catholics to the next parliament, although without the guarantee of a majority.

Another notable addition in 1649 concerned those in Ulster and elsewhere
affected by attainders and forfeitures since the succession if James I to the
English throne in 1603. The treaty granted them the right to petition parliament
for redress, although the final decision on any claim remained with the king.
This may have been an attempt to entice Owen Roe O'Neill back into the con-
federate fold, or at the very least to encourage further defections from his camp.
Additional clauses contained a list of individuals, as well as the towns of Cork,
Youghal and Dungarvan, who could petition parliament for compensation.

Both agreements contained a provision for an act of oblivion, but whereas
the 1646 version only covered the period after the outbreak of the uprising in
Ulster, the later one extended to all acts committed before, on or since 23
October 1641, provided the individual in question had not already been convict-
ed before that date. This extension, therefore, not only exonerated those
involved since the very beginning of the uprising, such as Phelim O'Neill, but
also anybody who had taken part in the various plots during the course of that
year, including a number of the Pale leadership.

The final major difference between the two treaties centred on the future
deployment of the confederate armed forces. In 1646 the confederates agreed to
send 10,000 men to England, to provide Charles I with a field army. In the
changed circumstances of 1649 the two sides agreed on a standing army of
15,000 foot and 2,500 horse, to be maintained until a full settlement had been
reached in the next Irish parliament. This overwhelmingly catholic force, while
primarily intended to protect the country from the expected invasion from
England, would also ensure that the royalists did not renege on their promises.
Moreover, whereas delays in the publication of the 1646 treaty allowed the opponents of peace to organise resistance, both sides published the 1649 version
immediately, to deny the clerical faction any such opportunity.

In conclusion, it is clear that the second peace treaty of 1649 incorporated
major changes on religious, constitutional, plantation and military matters,

---

**92** This represented no gain on the position prior to the revolt. In July 1641, the Irish parliament had issued a similar declaration without royal authority. Clarke, "Colonial constitutional attitudes", p. 359. **93** Articles of peace, 17 Jan. 1649 (Gilbert [ed.], *Irish confederation*, vii, pp
184-211).

with religion in particular being dealt with in a far more comprehensive manner. The agreement included specific concessions, with other points left to be resolved in the Irish parliament rather than by royal discretion. This approach helped mollify a significant number of clerics, despite the nuncio's continued opposition to a royalist alliance. Concessions to the Ulster Irish, allowing the plantation settlement to be challenged in parliament and enforcing a more equitable policy of appointments to committees and army posts, resolved many of their difficulties with the initial treaty. Both these groups, under the leadership of Plunkett and French, represented the core of moderate opinion in the final assembly.

The peace negotiations were finally concluded on 17 January 1649 at a lavish ceremony in Kilkenny castle. Richard Blake, chairman of the assembly, which he described as "the representative body of the Roman catholics of this kingdom", formally presented the articles to Ormond. In an eloquent speech, Blake hoped that the agreement would "restore this nation in its former lustre". The lord lieutenant for his part, outlined the benefits of the settlement, and in an attempt to placate the sceptics, hinted at the possibility of further gains. "There are no bounds to your hopes", he announced in a dramatic flourish. Ormond concluded by pleading with those present to forget the wounds of what he termed a civil war, and to create instead a new "bond of unity".[94]

The reality, however, proved very different, as the reconciliation between confederates and royalists simply exacerbated existing tensions within catholic Ireland. For the moment, the weakness of the clerical faction undermined efforts to oppose the treaty. Without the unified support of Irish bishops, clerical censures lacked sufficient authority to overcome the widespread desire for a settlement with the royalists and a quick end to the war. Rinuccini could do little except monitor the course of events from Galway and plan his return to Rome, embittered at the failure of his mission.[95] Nicholas Plunkett and Nicholas French still hoped to appease the nuncio, but he departed from Galway at the end of February 1649 without meeting his former allies.[96] The censures remained in place, although Rinuccini agreed that certain bishops could grant absolutions to anybody who sought forgiveness.[97]

94 *The marquesse of Ormond's proclamation concerning the peace concluded with the Irish rebels ... with a speech delivered by Sir Richard Blake ... also a speech delivered by the marquesse of Ormond ...,* London 1649 (BL Thomason Tracts E545 f.12). 95 On 31 October 1648, two weeks after the assembly's declaration against him, Rinuccini informed Rome of his intention to leave Ireland. Although the peace treaty negotiations were far from complete, with the bishops in Kilkenny driving a hard bargain, Rinuccini had decided that nothing more could be achieved by his continued presence in the country. Rinuccini to Panzirolo, 31 Oct. 1648 (Aiazza [ed.], *Embassy* p. 424). 96 One account suggested that the two men in fact deliberately delayed their journey so as to avoid a potentially heated encounter. O'Ferrall and O'Connell (eds), *Commentarius,* iv, pp 93-9. Indeed, it is difficult to see what they could have achieved by such a meeting, except perhaps an easing of the clerical censures. 97 The contro-

The other leading opponent of the peace treaty, Owen Roe O'Neill, spent most of 1649 skirmishing with the combined royalist/confederate forces. During the course of the year he formed a series of pragmatic alliances, culminating in the rescue of the parliamentarian Charles Coote at the siege of Derry. Plunkett and French tried to broker a peace with O'Neill, but reconciliation only occurred after Ormond's catastrophic defeat at Rathmines on 2 August, and the subsequent arrival in Dublin of Oliver Cromwell. The great Ulster general, however, did not have long to live; he died in November 1649 while marching south to confront the parliamentarians. Ironically, eight months later, Charles Coote wiped out the Ulster army, led by O'Neill's great friend and ally Bishop MacMahon, at Scarrifhollis in County Donegal.[98]

Despite the weakness of his clerical and Ulster Irish opponents, Ormond proved incapable of uniting catholic opinion in the kingdom.[99] His protestant allies also gradually deserted him or fled to the continent, while Cromwell's military onslaught progressed relentlessly across the country. Unable to assemble an effective field army, Ormond had little choice but to garrison various towns and strongholds. Drogheda and Wexford, however, fell in quick succession, and when protesant officers loyal to Lord Broghill seized control of Cork, Youghal, Kinsale and Bandon for the parliamentarians, the future looked bleak for the royalist alliance.

In desperation, the catholic bishops met at Clonmacnoise in early December 1649, and issued a declaration calling for a united opposition against the parliamentarians, condemning "all such divisions between either provinces or families, or between old English and old Irish, or any of the English or Scots adhering to his majesty".[100] The fall of Kilkenny in March 1650, followed by crushing defeats in both Munster and Ulster, shattered any hopes of a recovery. Internal dissension persisted and the strategic cities of Limerick and Galway refused to admit royalist garrisons. Exasperated by this catalogue of defeat and incompetence, the

versy over the censures raged with intense ferocity for decades and left a legacy of bitterness which is apparent in the various personal accounts written after the restoration of the monarchy in 1660. This is particularly evident in the works of Bellings, Castlehaven, French, and the anonymous author of the *Aphorismical discovery*. **98** Casway, *Owen Roe O'Neill* pp 241-64. In May 1650 (a month before Scarrifhollis) at the siege of Clonmel, a detachment of the Ulster army under the leadership of Hugh Dubh O'Neill inflicted the heaviest losses ever suffered by the New Model Army, who lost over 2,000 killed. Corish, *NHI*, iii, p. 347. **99** Corish, P.J., "The Cromwellian conquest, 1649-53", *NHI*, iii, pp 336-53 provides the best summary of the Cromwellian conquest, and what follows is largely based on his work. Further information can be found in Cregan, D.F, "Confederation of Kilkenny" (PhD thesis) pp 292-318. Clanricarde's memoirs, which stop abruptly in 1647, restart in 1650, and provide a first hand account of this period. See Ulick Bourke, *Memoirs* (1747). Both O'Ferrall and O'Connell (eds), *Commentarius* (1932-49) and Gilbert, J.T., *Contemporary history* (1879) contain valuable source material. **100** Decree of the bishops at Clonmacnoise, 13 Dec. 1649 (Moran [ed.], *Spicilegium Ossoriense*, vol. 2, pp 41-3).

bishops assembled once again, this time at Jamestown on 6 August. A declaration six days later rejected Ormond's leadership, and they issued a decree excommunicating his supporters the following month.

Charles II's declaration at Dunfermline on 16 August 1650 further undermined Ormond's authority. In return for Scottish support the king rejected the 1649 peace treaty and denounced any terms with Irish catholics. As the crisis deepened, Ormond and the commissioners of trust summoned an assembly which met in Loughrea towards the end of November. This assembly, chaired by Richard Blake, was bitterly divided, with the marquis of Clanricarde, Richard Bellings, Walter Bagenal, Richard Barnewall supporting the lord lieutenant, while Nicholas Plunkett joined the bishops in leading the opposition. Although the majority of the assembly sympathised with Ormond, the members nonetheless agreed on the necessity of a change of leadership to boost their war effort. Deprived of Irish catholic support, Ormond once again fled into exile on 11 December 1650, just two years after his triumphant return.

Ormond's replacement, the marquis of Clanricarde, personified in many ways the hopes and ambitions of the confederate moderates. A catholic nobleman, intensely loyal to the king, Clanricarde provided a unifying focus for the confederates in a way the marquis of Ormond never did. Throughout the 1640s he acted as a valuable moderating influence on the royalist side, mirroring, to some extent, the work done in confederate ranks by Plunkett and French. By the time he assumed the leadership, however, the war in Ireland was all but lost. Galway, the last major catholic stronghold, surrendered in April 1652, while Clanricarde, Plunkett and French all fled into exile. Clanricarde died in England in 1658, while Bishop French lived another twenty years on the continent in lonely, bitter isolation. Of the three, only Nicholas Plunkett, the great survivor, returned to Ireland to play a leading role in the restoration settlement.[101]

Overall, events during the 1640s and 1650s proved disastrous for catholic interests in Ireland. Catholic land ownership declined from almost two-thirds of the total in 1641 to around one-fifth in 1688, even after decades of slow recovery during the reign of Charles II.[102] The resident hierarchy suffered hardship, death or exile; by 1653 only the aged bishop of Kilmore remained in the country, while the extensive administrative infrastructure assembled during the confederate period had been totally dismantled.[103] Finally, all hopes of overturning the Ulster plantation disappeared with the annihilation of the Ulster army at

---

**101** Plunkett was the legal representative of Irish catholics at the court of Charles II who sought to regain their estates. Papers relating to the act of settlement 1660-2 (BL Add Mss 4,781). French's writings have been collected together in Bindon (ed.), *Historical works*, 2 vols (1846). See appendix 3. **102** See the two maps by J.G Simms in *NHI*, iii, p. 428. **103** Jesuit Archives, MSS B f.24 contains information on the dispersal of Irish catholic bishops around Europe in 1653. See also Corish, *NHI*, iii, pp 380-5.

Scarrifhollis, a battle which re-established the dominance of the protestant interest in that province.[104]

104 After 1660, the earl of Antrim was the only major catholic land-holder in the entire province. McKenny, K., "The seventeenth-century land settlement in Ireland: towards a statistical interpretation", *Independence to occupation* pp 181-200.

# CHAPTER 7

# The workings of confederate government

In all the kingdom our affairs mighty declined, for neither civil or martial government was extant, but everyone running a particular score which caused confusion.

*Aphorismical discovery of treasonable faction* (1650s)[1]

This chapter examines the structures, procedures and personnel of confederate government, between 1642 and 1649. Despite the increasing number of studies of confederate Ireland, there has been comparatively little research on its political institutions.[2] Without this detailed information, the decisions and actions of the administration in Kilkenny are, at times, almost impossible to fathom. While military, diplomatic and economic pressures may have been the primary factors driving confederate policy, the impact of internal power structures, and of certain individuals also proved crucial. Three institutions dominated confederate politics – the legislative general assembly, the executive supreme council, and the committee (or committees) negotiating a peace deal with the royalists.

### The general assembly, 1642–1649

The general assembly functioned as a legislative body, at the apex of the confederate political structure. It was summoned on nine occasions between 1642 and 1648, to debate the major issues of peace and war, with at least one meeting each year. This record compares favourably with the Irish parliament which only met on three occasions under the Stuarts (1613-5, 1634-5 and 1640-1) prior to the outbreak of the uprising in Ulster.[3] In total, the assembly sat for 69 weeks during

1 Gilbert (ed.), *Contemporary history*, i, p. 36. 2 The only exception to this is the pioneering research carried out by Dónal Cregan, starting in the 1940s (see bibliography). A summary of his work recently appeared in *Irish Historical Studies*. Cregan, D.F., "The confederate catholics of Ireland: The personnel of the confederation, 1642-9", *IHS*, vol. 29, no. 116 (Nov. 1995) pp 490-512. 3 It also compares favourably with the Scottish parliament (and conven-

*Table 1: General assembly meetings*[4]

| Year | Venue | Opening | Closing | Main business |
|------|-------|---------|---------|---------------|
| 1642 | Kilkenny | 24 Oct. | 21 Nov. | Create structures of government |
| 1643 | Kilkenny | 20 May | 19 June | Appoint commissioners for cessation |
| 1643 | Waterford | 7 Nov. | 1 Dec. | Elect agents to go to Oxford |
| 1644 | Kilkenny | 20 July | 31 Aug. | Establish committee of treaty |
| 1645 | Kilkenny | 15 May | 1 Sept. | Discuss peace terms/2 sessions |
| 1646 | Kilkenny | 5 Feb | 4 March | Review of talks process |
| 1647 | Kilkenny | 10 Jan. | 3 April | Debate on Ormond treaty |
| 1647 | Kilkenny | 12 Nov. | 24 Dec. | Appoint envoys for abroad |
| 1648-9 | Kilkenny | 4 Sept. | 17 Jan. | Negotiate new treaty with Ormond |

this six year period, with an average session lasting four weeks.[5] All meetings took place in Kilkenny, either in the house of Robert Shee, one of the city's leading merchants and a nephew of Viscount Mountgarret, or in the castle, principal residence of the Butlers of Ormond. The only exception was the third assembly, held in Waterford in late 1643.

The city of Kilkenny, the confederate capital, was chosen for practical, political and historical reasons. Royalists, parliamentarians or Scots covenanters controlled Dublin, Cork and most of the Ulster towns throughout the 1640s. Limerick proved problematic for the confederates, displaying strong neutralist tendencies, while Galway city remained within the royalist sphere of influence until 1643, due to the close proximity of the earl of Clanricarde. The only viable

tion of estates), which met for around 90 weeks between 1642 and 1648. Young, J.R., *The Scottish parliament 1639-1661: A political and constitutional analysis* (Edinburgh 1996). The Dublin parliament, after expelling its catholic members, continued to meet sporadically throughout the 1640s. **4** This table is based on a similar model which appeared in Dónal Cregan's thesis, though with slight modifications. Cregan, D.F., "Confederation of Kilkenny" (PhD thesis) pp 75-6. **5** On three occasions, 1645, 1647 and 1648, assembly delegates extended the session to accommodate negotiations with the royalists on a peace treaty. In 1645, the assembly started in May and finished in September, with a one month break in July. Controversy over the treaty terms on offer from the marquis of Ormond, and the arrival of the earl of Glamorgan with the offer of religious concessions, were the principal reasons for the extension. In early 1647, the bitter debate over the first Ormond peace treaty, followed by a determined effort to engage the lord lieutenant in fresh negotiations, prolonged the assembly session from mid-January until the beginning of April. The final confederate general assembly lasted four and a half months, until mid-January 1649, while the terms of the second Ormond treaty were debated.

alternatives (Wexford, Waterford, New Ross, Clonmel and Kilkenny) were clustered around the confederate heartland in the south-east. Kilkenny received the final vote presumably in view of its relative accessibility to other parts of the kingdom. The fact that the Irish parliament had met there on occasion also provided an important historical precedent for the confederates, desperately seeking to legitimise their actions.[6]

The confederates favoured a unicameral structure for the assembly, with lords, bishops and commons all sharing the same chamber, although at the first meeting in 1642 the nobility insisted on a separate room for private deliberations. Corish suggests that the failure to create an upper chamber constituted a deliberate attempt by opponents of the Catholic Church to limit clerical influence. There is no evidence, however, to support such an assumption, and in any case the bishops' influence arguably proved greater in the general arena than among the nobility.[7] Each member of the assembly, regardless of social status, exercised a single vote of equal weight, but during debates lords and bishops enjoyed precedence in the speaking order.[8]

The confederates deliberately avoided establishing an exact replica of the Irish parliament in Dublin, to avoid charges of usurping the royal prerogative. They always refrained from using the term "parliament", and described the assembly as a temporary expedient, forced upon them by events.[9] In keeping with this policy, the speaker of the assembly was simply entitled "the chairman", and addressed by his proper name.[10] By virtue of numbers alone the assembly in Kilkenny might well have claimed to be the legitimate representative body of the kingdom. James Ware recorded in June 1642 how the parliament in Dublin, with only 30 members present (6 lords, 24 commons), had expelled 41 catholic MPs for joining the confederate association.[11]

6 The choice of Kilkenny appeared all the more appropriate as Ormond's relations and associates (Muskerry, Mountgarret, Fennell etc.) increasingly assumed control of confederate government after 1643. Shee's house, with its large hall, proved an ideal venue for the assembly. See Cregan, "Confederation of Kilkenny" (PhD thesis) p. 72. 7 Corish, *NHI*, iii, p. 301. For example, during the first assembly in 1647, Bellings reported that Edmund O'Dempsey, the bishop of Leighlin, could raise a storm on the assembly floor, simply by waving his hat. Bellings' History in Gilbert (ed.), *Irish confederation*, vi, p. 2. 8 Both Richard Bellings and Richard Martin described assembly structures in some detail. Bellings' History in Gilbert (ed.), *Irish confederation*, i, pp 110-15; Richard Martin to Clanricarde, 2 Dec. 1642 (Bourke, *Clanricarde memoirs* pp 296-8). See also Cregan, "Confederation of Kilkenny" (PhD thesis) pp 66-70. 9 In a petition to the king, in late 1642, the confederates assured Charles "that we intended not this assembly to be a parliament, or to have the power of it". Bourke, *Clanricarde memoirs* p. 299. 10 Bellings actually refers to Nicholas Plunkett (chairman of every assembly, bar the final one) as "prolocutor". Bellings' History in Gilbert (ed.), *Irish confederation*, i, pp 110-15. Walter Bagenal addressed the chairman as "Mister Plunkett" in a speech delivered during the debate over the first Ormond treaty. Ibid., vii, p. 10. Philip Kearney acted as the clerk in each general assembly. Cregan, D.F., "Confederation of Kilkenny" (PhD thesis) p. 71. 11 TCD Mss 6404 (Ware Manuscript) f.128.

Whatever their scruples about the name and structure of the new legislative body, the confederates followed existing parliamentary procedure as much as possible, even in the case of elections. Despite the upheavals of war, they issued writs in the usual manner, a month or so before an assembly, with candidates returned on the basis of existing borough and county constituencies.[12] Little is known about the electorate, but the confederate leadership almost certainly restricted the franchise to freeholders of 40 shillings and upwards in the counties (excluding the protestants), with the boroughs retaining their own voting systems.[13] As a result, catholic landowners dominated the assembly, leaving the vast majority of confederates without the vote or direct representation. This ensured that the legislature favoured the existing social order, and adopted a conservative position on most issues, with the important exception of religion.[14]

The 1634 parliament consisted of 256 members elected from 128 two-seat constituencies (32 counties, 95 boroughs, as well as Trinity College Dublin). The lord deputy, Thomas Wentworth, however, disenfranchised seven "catholic" boroughs during his term of office.[15] In 1640, therefore, only 240 MPs attended parliament at first, but as Wentworth's influence declined, six of the seven disenfranchised boroughs held elections. Presuming that the confederates premitted representatives from these six boroughs to attend the assembly, and excluding Trinity College (a protestant university), a total of 250 commoners would have gathered in Kilkenny.

Contradictory evidence survives as to whether all constituencies were indeed represented at the assemblies. The royalist agent, George Leyburn, reported that

---

**12** Unfortunately, information on particular constituencies is scarce. One of the surviving assembly lists (Bodl. Carte Mss 70 ff 64-85) includes the members' place of origin, which does not necessarily correspond with their constituency. Further information on electoral procedures survives in the evidence presented to the court of claims in 1663. Documents refer to the return of burgesses and knights of the shire for various constituencies, with sheriffs supervising the elections. Talon, Geraldine (ed.), *Act of settlement* pp 53, 65, 92, 102, 318, 419. **13** The 40-shilling freehold threshold was established by the 1542 franchise act. Only one example of a confederate electoral return still exists, with the names of the voters attached. Electoral return for the city of Cork, 14 Dec. 1646 (Bodl. Clarendon Mss 29 f.8). Material from the court of claims in the 1660s provides more names, covering 14 counties throughout the country, all claimants seeking to recover their estates. Talon, Geraldine (ed.), *Act of settlement* pp 53, 131, 159, 163. The list of voters in appendix 1 (table 11), however inadequate, probably fairly illustrates the restricted nature of the franchise. Multiple voting also appears to have taken place, with James Walsh of Waterford, Christopher Archbold of Kildare, and others taking part in elections in several corporations. Ibid. p. 199, 413, 528. **14** Cregan estimated that the average landholding of assembly members (outside of peers) was 7,000 acres. Cregan, D.F., "Confederation of Kilkenny" (PhD thesis) p. 106. He did not, however, have access to all the assembly lists (see appendix 1), and in light of the new evidence his figures seem inflated. **15** Moreover, two seats permanently disappeared when the county of the cross of Tipperary was united with Tipperary County by letters patent in 1637. Electoral representation during this period is discussed in Kearney, *Strafford in Ireland* pp 223-63 and Clarke, *Old English in Ireland* pp 255-61.

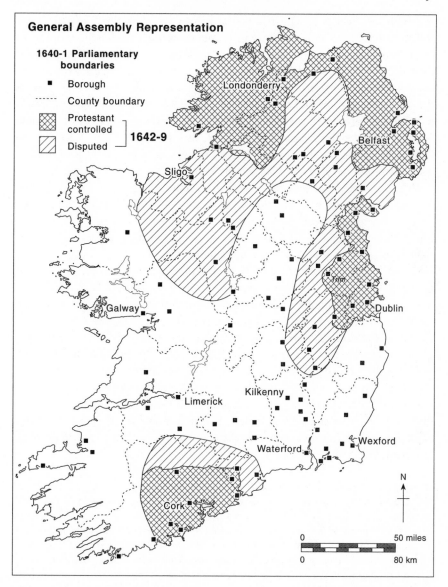

*Map 2: General assembly representation* The confederates based their assembly
representation on existing parliamentary boundaries (boroughs and counties).
Over half the parliamentary seats, however, remained in areas controlled by (or
disputed with) their enemies. The usual practice, in the absence of elections,
appears to have been for the supreme council to appoint representatives. This
ensured that the dominant group on the council always enjoyed significant
support in the general assembly.

the confederates only elected representatives from areas within their sphere of influence, but Rinuccini observed the supreme council in 1646 appointing *ex officio* persons for boroughs in royalist and parliamentarian territory.[16] The dominant faction on the supreme council, therefore, could easily manipulate assembly attendance, as just over half the parliamentary constituencies lay in parts of the country outside of direct confederate control.[17] Even in such cases, the council may well have attempted to consult the legitimate electorate, as happened with the aldermen and councillors of Cork. Living as refugees in Kilkenny, following their expulsion from their native city by Lord Inchiquin, they nonetheless elected two members to the assembly in January 1647.[18]

Most surviving assembly lists, however, contain well in excess of 250 names. A possible explanation is that records of membership, also listed anybody who took the confederate oath during that particular meeting. This included locals in both Kilkenny and Waterford, where the assemblies took place, as well as prominent individuals present in a non-representative capacity.[19]

In the Irish parliament of 1640-1, 41% of the representatives came from Leinster, 26% from Ulster, 22% from Munster and only 11% from Connacht. The corresponding figures in confederate assemblies were as follows – 47% from Leinster, 32% from Munster, 11% from Connacht and only 10% from Ulster.[20] On the surface this appears to confirm the accusations of prejudice against the Ulster Irish made by Rinuccini and others, but these figures contained a certain rationale. In parliament, Ulster had became increasingly over-represented, due to the government policy of establishing new boroughs to ensure a protestant majority. Furthermore, a large section of the 1641 Ulster population, the protestant planter community, were excluded from confederate assemblies. Finally, throughout the 1640s, large tracts of Ulster remained under the control of royalists, parliamentarians or Scots.[21]

---

16 Leyburn, "Memoirs" p. 287; Rinuccini to Pamphili, 13 Feb. 1646 (Aiazza [ed.], *Embassy* p. 116). Moreover, the French agent Du Moulin reported in early 1647 that many of the Ulster contingent at the assembly had been selected from among people resident in Kilkenny. Du Moulin to Ormond, 30 Jan. 1647 (Bodl. Carte Mss 20 ff 218-9). Numerous complaints exist of attempts by both the peace and clerical factions to influence the elections and pack the assemblies. Rinuccini frequently protested about his opponents manipulating elections, as did Richard Bellings when the peace faction were ousted from the supreme council in late 1646. See Aiazza (ed.), *Embassy* pp 116, 343-6, 519-21; Bellings' History in Gilbert (ed.), *Irish confederation*, vi, p. 48; vii, p. 1. 17 See map 2. 18 William Hore and Captain John Gould were elected "in the name and behalf of the said city of Cork and the corporation thereof". Electoral return for the city of Cork, 14 Dec. 1646 (Bodl. Clarendon Mss 29 f.8). 19 1642/3 (318); 1644 (197); 1645 (396); 1647 (292). See appendix 1 for an explanation of the various surviving assembly lists. Lacking the electoral returns, it is impossible to distinguish representatives from observers. 20 These figures are analysed in appendix 1. Using information from the assembly lists, and a multitude of other evidence, scattered over many collections, it is possible to give approximate figures for provincial representation. 21 See map 1. Even after Owen Roe

Table 2: General assembly: provincial representation

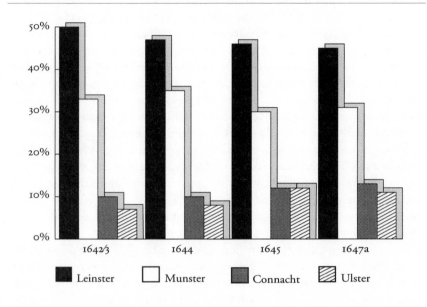

It appears likely that successive supreme councils, in order to redress the parliamentary imbalance, appointed people from Munster and Leinster to represent those Ulster constituencies outside of confederate control.[22] This practice created a more equitable provincial balance, at least in terms of population distribution. Despite the turbulence of internal confederate politics, the provincial figures at the assemblies remained remarkably consistent throughout the 1640s, a fact which refutes the charge (for example) that the clerical faction packed the assem-

O'Neill's victory at Benburb in June 1646, the confederates failed to capture any major town or stronghold in Ulster. Most of the northern province remained disputed territory throughout the 1640s. **22** Although confederate electoral returns no longer survive, we know for example that Nicholas Darcy of Plattin, County Meath represented the borough of Limavady, County Derry, while John Baggott of Limerick and Terence Coughlan of Queen's County were returned as burgesses for several places. Talon, Geraldine (ed.), *Act of settlement* pp 275, 312, 367. Furthermore, a number of important urban centres were clearly over-represented. In January 1647, the town and county of Galway, which before 1641 returned eight members of parliament (two county, six borough), had at least 14 representatives in Kilkenny: Geoffrey Browne, Roebuck Lynch, Patrick Darcy, Robert Blake, John Bermingham, Christopher French, Patrick Kirwan, Nicholas Lynch, Anthony Martin, Christopher Lynch, James French, Francis Blake, Edward Browne, Dominick Bodkin. The extra Galwaymen may well have been returned for Ulster constituencies. See assembly list in Dublin City Library, Gilbert Collection Mss 219 (roll 1).

bly in January 1647 with Ulstermen from the creaghts accompanying Owen Roe O'Neill's army. There are quite a number of new Ulster names on that particular list, but the percentage of Ulstermen is actually slightly less than in 1645.[23]

With only four assembly lists surviving, it is difficult to assess continuity in assembly membership, but as they extend from 1642/3 to 1647, some observations can be made. In the first instance, the names of over 140 people appear on three or more lists. These individuals constituted the core of confederate government, including most of the prominent leaders. Some, however, rarely appear elsewhere on confederate documents, despite these members active participation in the legislature throughout the 1640s. Reflecting the provincial distribution in the assembly, Leinster and Munster confederates predominated among the regulars, whereas Ulster remained poorly represented. The vast majority also came from old English backgrounds, which is hardly surprising given the ascendancy of that group in previous Irish parliaments.[24]

Dónal Cregan did some excellent work on the constituent elements in the general assemblies, but he inexplicably ignored the largest (and probably most influential) interest group, namely former members of the Irish parliament. Irish catholics had a long tradition of parliamentary involvement, and they had been particularly active in the sessions just before the uprising in October 1641, assisting in the overthrow of Wentworth while, at the same time, seeking constitutional and political reforms. The list of commons "leaders" (as Perceval-Maxwell terms them) included Nicholas Plunkett, Geoffrey Browne, James Cusack and Richard Blake.[25] All of these men became central players within the confederate association, both at the executive and legislative levels.

Of the 183 catholics who sat in the 1634 and 1640 parliaments, almost half attended at least one or more assembly meeting. In the surviving lists, former parliamentarians on average constituted 20% of total assembly membership.[26] They provided the confederates with a wealth of legislative and political experience, and featured strongly on all major councils and committees. The confederate passion for retaining parliamentary procedure reflected their influence, and ensured that these men continued to play a leading role throughout the 1640s. A certain commonality of political interest is suggested in that a number of leading

23 This charge was made by Richard Bellings, and the French agent Du Moulin, both supporters of the peace faction and enemies of Owen Roe O'Neill. Bellings' History in Gilbert (ed.), *Irish confederation*, vi, p. 48; Du Moulin to Ormond, 30 Jan. 1647 (Bodl. Carte Mss 22 ff 218-19). 24 The lists of those with parliamentary experience and of those who attended on a regular basis are contained in appendix 1 (tables 8 and 10). 25 The term leader is used to denote those members who sat on large number of parliamentary committees in 1640-1. Perceval-Maxwell, *Irish rebellion* pp 75, 136-7. 26 Other prominent ex-parliamentarians in confederate ranks, apart from those already mentioned, were Viscount Muskerry, Viscount Gormanston, Viscount Mountgarret, Geoffrey Barron, Richard Bellings, Phelim O'Neill and Robert Talbot.

confederates, Patrick Darcy, Roebuck Lynch, Hugh Rochford among others, supported the moderate policies of their former parliamentary colleague, Nicholas Plunkett.

Another influential group consisted of people with legal training, many of whom also had parliamentary experience. An average of 20% of assembly members had attended inns of court in England, although this by no means guaranteed an expert knowledge of the law.[27] The inns frequently provided only a veneer of education for the children of wealthy families, who concentrated mainly on property law.[28] Nonetheless, many graduates from Ireland became renowned constitutional lawyers, and later joined the confederate association. This list included not only Plunkett, Darcy and Cusack, but also Adam Cusack, Geoffrey Browne and John Dillon.[29]

With most of the 1640s taken up with complex legal negotiations on constitutional matters, the lawyers played a central role in confederate politics, a fact reported on by many contemporary commentators, and not always in a complimentary manner. At the 1645 assembly, for example, Clanricarde noted the intimidation of ordinary members by "the sages of the law, who have a prevailing power to pervert the best ways and means of persuasion to a false and mischievous construction of their own".[30] Trained lawyers from each of the four provinces invariably dominated not only assembly meetings but almost all confederate councils and committees.

Compared to lawyers and former parliamentarians, the lords and bishops constituted numerically insignificant groups in terms of assembly membership (averaging around 3% each). Nonetheless, the combination of high social standing and an extensive network of contacts enabled them to wield considerable authority. The names of 17 bishops appear on the surviving lists, although a number of others attended an assembly on at least one occasion.[31] A clerical convocation usually met in Kilkenny at the same time as the general assembly, to

---

**27** See appendix 1 (table 9). **28** Morrill, *Revolt of the provinces* p. 23. Cregan argued, however, that most of Irish students frequented the inns with the express purpose of entering the legal profession. Cregan, D.F., "Confederate catholics" (PhD thesis) pp 499–500. **29** Plunkett, Darcy and others were employed by both catholic and protestants before 1641, as professional ability, for once, seemed to outweigh sectarian considerations. See appendix 1 (table 9) for the full list of those with legal training. **30** Clanricarde to Ormond, 21 Aug. 1645 (Lowe [ed.], *Clanricarde letter-book* p. 174). **31** Those bishops whose names appear on assembly lists are for Leinster: Fleming (Dublin), Dease (Meath), Rothe (Ossory), Dempsey (Leighlin), French (Ferns); Munster: Walsh (Cashel), O'Connell (Ardfert), Comerford (Waterford), O'Molloney (Killaloe), O'Dwyer (Limerick), Tirry (Cork); Connacht: O'Queely (Tuam), Bourke (Clonfert and later Tuam), MacEgan (Elphin); Ulster: O'Reilly (Armagh), MacMahon (Clogher), Magennis (Down/Connor). A number of other bishops attended the final assembly and signed a declaration in favour of the peace treaty. They were Darcy (Dromore), Lynch (Kilfenora) and Kirwan (Killala). Bishops declaration to the general assembly, 17 Jan. 1649 (Bodl. Clarendon Mss 34 f.76). Bishop Plunkett of Ardagh was also present and active at the

*Table 3: General assembly: representative profile*[32]

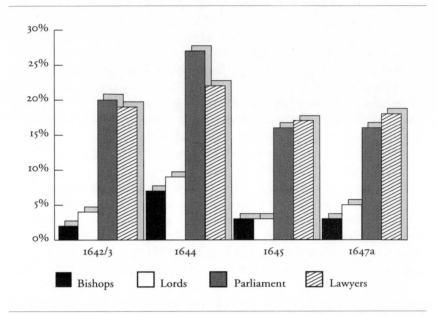

monitor developments and provide informal advice on religious matters. As the clerics increasingly found themselves at odds with confederate policy from 1644 onwards, the convocation adopted a more vocal role, directly intervening in assembly affairs.

Whereas the bishops received an automatic entitlement to sit in the assembly, this did not apply to abbots or the heads of religious orders. The clerics blamed the peace faction for this exclusion, but the confederates, in this case as elsewhere, simply adhered to existing Irish parliamentary practice.[33] It appears that nothing prevented clerics from standing in national elections, and a number were returned as ordinary assembly members, including Nicholas French (before his promotion to the see of Ferns).[34] The position of unconsecrated bishops emerged as a controversial issue in late 1647, when Viscount Muskerry

final assembly but did not sign the declaration. Hynes, *Mission of Rinuccini* p. 246. Bishop O'Brien of Emly came to Kilkenny at this time, but fled when he discovered the nuncio's opposition to proceedings. Reports of peace and Roman envoys, 30 March 1649 (Aiazza [ed.], *Embassy* pp 457-64). **32** "Parliament" refers to those assembly members who sat in previous parliaments in Dublin. "Lawyers" refers to those assembly members who attended inns of court in London. **33** Admittedly, the Irish parliament in this instance did not provide an ideal comparison, as the protestant clergy, who sat in the House of Lords, had no equivalent religious orders. **34** O'Ferrall and O'Connell (eds), *Commentarius*, i, pp 524-36; Bindon (ed.), *Historical works*, vol. 1, p. xxxvi.

questioned their right to sit in the assembly, but in the end they retained their seats.[35]

There were 28 catholic peers in 1642, 19 (66%) of whom appear on confederate lists at some time or other. Of those missing, two lived in England (Viscount Fitzwilliam and Lord Glanmullen), and two more were prisoners of the administration in Dublin (Lords Dunsany and Maguire). Lord de Courcy of Kinsale remained on his estates, and appears to have maintained a strict neutrality throughout the 1640s. Viscount Clanmorris died in September 1642 shortly after joining the rebels, while Lord Curraghmore had been declared a lunatic in the 1630s. A further two peers (the earl of Westmeath and Lord Athenry) did not join the confederates, but were succeeded by sons who did, Westmeath in 1642, and Athenry in 1645. During the course of the 1640s, four peers (Castleconnell, Costello-Gallen, Iveagh and Mayo), educated as protestants, reverted to catholicism and attended confederate assemblies. Finally, the king raised two Irish catholics to the peerage in August 1646 – Viscount Galmoy who sat in later assemblies, and Viscount Kingsland, who fled to Wales in the early stages of the uprising, and took no part in Irish affairs.[36]

The leaders of the peace faction, Mountgarret, Muskerry and Castlehaven, supplanted the Pale nobility as the dominant aristocratic influence in the confederate association after the deaths of Slane and Gormanston.[37] The surviving Pale lords concentrated more on military activity, and except for Louth, supported the peace faction. Muskerry could also rely on the Butler lords (Dunboyne, Cahir and after 1646 Galmoy as well) in a crisis. Pierce Butler, 1st Viscount Ikerrin, however, proved the exception in this case and may well have sided with

---

**35** This dispute is described in chapter 5 p. 160f above. **36** See Cokayne, *Complete peerage*, 12 volumes; Valentine Savage to [Percivall], 31 Aug. 1646 in *HMC, Egmont*, vol. 1, part 1, p. 310; Names of lords and others now assembled in the assembly [Oct. 1648] (Bodl. Carte Mss 22 f.339); Perceval-Maxwell, *Irish rebellion* p. 342 n. 87. Patrick de Courcy, 15th Lord Kinsale, somehow managed to remain neutral in the chaos which surrounded him in Munster during the 1640s, although he must have had some dealings with both the confederates and the parliamentary forces led by Lord Inchiquin. In early 1645, Ormond had suggested to the king's secretary, George Digby, that it might be possible to gain "many considerable persons of the Irish" by raising them to the peerage. This could well explain the promotions of Edward Butler (Galmoy) and Nicholas Barnewall (Kingsland) the following year. Ormond to Digby, 28 March 1645 (Carte, *Ormond*, vi, pp 272-5). **37** The exact date of Slane's death is unclear, although James Ware (usually an accurate source) records it as sometime in November 1642, during the first general assembly. He was certainly present during the session in Kilkenny, according to the testimony of John Purcell on 15 November 1642. NLI Ormonde Mss 2307 f.359. A November death would certainly explain his absence from the supreme council elected at the end of the meeting. TCD Mss 6404 (Ware Manuscript) f.130. Gormanston died at the end of July 1643, shortly after he had begun to negotiate a truce with Ormond. Will of Nicholas, Viscount Gormanston, 27 July 1643, *Analecta Hibernica*, no. 25 (1967), Gormanston papers pp 157-8.

the nuncio in rejecting the first Ormond treaty. His son Richard certainly emerged as a major opponent of the peace faction in Munster.[38]

Serious friction existed among the nobility of Munster and south Leinster from the early days of the uprising. Viscount Roche quarrelled with Mountgarret on the issue of precedence, the former probably having the stronger case, although Mountgarret's age and experience gave him considerable authority. Roche's kinsmen, Castleconnell and Brittas supported their relative throughout the 1640s, although they do not appear to have adopted any agenda other than opposition to Mountgarret. Viscount Bourke of Mayo remained something of a maverick figure, unwilling at first to accept confederate authority in north Connacht. Arrested in 1644, he made his peace with Kilkenny the following year. Finally, Antrim, Taaffe and Clanricarde were essentially royalists, although the first two did take the confederate oath, in 1643 and 1647 respectively.[39]

It is difficult to calculate with any certainty the number of soldiers who sat in the general assembly, although all the leading generals, Owen Roe O'Neill, Thomas Preston, Garret Barry, the earl of Castlehaven and Viscount Taaffe attended at one time or another.[40] A significant number of the aristocracy combined a military and political career, with Viscount Muskerry, the marquis of Antrim and the earl of Castlehaven providing the most notable examples, and the same may also have been true of the leading gentry. In any event, military matters (campaigns, supplies, discipline) rarely disappeared off the assembly's agenda.

Finally, the growing prosperity of many Irish towns provided the basis for a thriving merchant class, many of whom had become significant land owners in their own right. This group constituted less than 5% of MPs in the 1640-1 parliament, but played a much more prominent role in the confederate assem-

---

**38** Louth was appointed by the nuncio to the supreme council formed in September 1646 after the clerical faction seized power in Kilkenny. Order by the ecclesiastical congregation, 26 Sept. 1646 (Gilbert [ed.], *Irish confederation*, vi, pp 144-6). Richard Butler's promotion to the position of lieutenant-general of the Munster forces in 1647 triggered a crisis which saw Viscount Muskerry assume control of that army. Muskerry to Thomas Preston, 14 June 1647 (PRO SP Ire. 264/88 f.263). **39** Cokayne, *Complete peerage*, vol. 5 (1926) pp 299-300. Clanricarde records the reconciliation between Mayo and the confederate leadership "upon very poor and submissive terms on his lordship's part". Clanricarde to Ormond, 10 March 1645 (Lowe [ed.], *Clanricarde letter-book* pp 148-50). Antrim was nominated onto four supreme councils but was generally more interested in recovering his Ulster estates and supporting the royalist cause in Scotland. Taaffe proved an incompetent and duplicitous lieutenant-general of the Munster army, while Clanricarde eventually joined forces with the confederates in 1648 to oppose Owen Roe O'Neill. Unfortunately, Clanricarde's letter-book for the period 1647-50 is missing and it is unclear if the marquis actually took the confederate oath. **40** Assembly lists in Dublin City Library (Gilbert Collection) Mss 219, rolls 1-4; Walsh, *Irish remonstrance*, appendix 1, pp 31-2. Viscount Taaffe only took the confederate oath in the summer of 1647, but attended the final general assembly a year later. Rinuccini to Panzirolo, 14 Aug. 1647 (Aiazza [ed.], *Embassy* p. 300); Taaffe to Ormond, 11 Oct. 1648 (Bodl. Carte Mss 22 f.347).

blies.[41] Between 1642 and 1649 a majority of assembly meetings took place in the house of Kilkenny merchant, Robert Shee, while the leading families of Galway, Limerick, Cork, Waterford, Wexford and Kilkenny were all well represented.[42] Apart from their political activities, these men provided desperately needed loans and financial assistance to the confederate government and controlled the vital foreign trade markets.[43] Merchants, however, rarely appeared on any confederate councils or committees, all of which remained under the control of the traditional ruling classes.

The predominance of Anglo-Irish surnames in the general assemblies is hardly surprising given the large number of parliamentarians, lawyers and merchants at these meetings. In each of these groups the old English enjoyed a clear majority over the native Irish. Nonetheless, native Irish names regularly appear on the surviving lists. Based on surnames alone (admittedly a highly unsatisfactory method) the percentage of native Irish at the assemblies averaged about 22%. More importantly, increasing social, political and financial inter-action had blurred the existing ethnic boundaries in Ireland long before 1641. Little evidence exists of ethnic divisions in assembly politics during the 1640s, with native Irish and old English present in every faction. Social standing (calculated primarily on the basis of land ownership) and the issue of religion proved the most divisive factors, rather than ethnic considerations.[44]

In conclusion, the constituent elements in the general assembly reflected the diverse nature of confederate support among the catholic elite, and the total lack of representation from among the lower social orders. Assembly members dealt primarily with issues of land and religion, rather than poverty or inequality, and proved at times more concerned by the breakdown in social order which accompanied the uprising, than the activities of their enemies. Nonetheless, despite the conservative nature of the assembly, serious opposition emerged in later sessions to the policies pursued by the executive supreme council. Prior to 1646, the clergy proved particularly adept at exploiting this discontent, but after that date leading moderates, in particular Nicholas Plunkett (the assembly chairman), became increasingly influential.

**41** Cregan, D.F., "Confederate catholics" pp 505-06. **42** Among the names that appear are Browne, French, Lynch, Martin, Kirwan (Galway); Stackpole, Creagh, White, Fennell (Limerick); Tirry, Roche, Hore, Gould (Cork); Walsh, Wadding, Power, Sherlock, White (Waterford); Shee, Archer, Comerford (Kilkenny); Furlong, Hay, Hore (Wexford). **43** Patrick Archer of Kilkenny, for example, lent money to both confederates and royalists, and helped finance Antrim's mission to Scotland. Gilbert [ed.], *Irish confederation*, v, pp 1, 223-6. **44** Peace faction – Donough MacCarthy (Viscount Muskerry), Richard Bellings, Donough O'Callaghan, Gerald Fennell. Clerical faction – Piers Butler, Owen Roe O'Neill, Oliver Plunkett (Lord Louth), Dermot O'Brien. Moderates – Nicholas Plunkett, Randal MacDonnell (Marquis of Antrim), Patrick Darcy; Phelim O'Neill.

## Supreme councils, 1642–1649

For much of the 1640s the supreme council, functioning as the executive arm of government, was the dominant force in confederate politics. The council controlled all confederate civil and (until 1644) judicial affairs, while also acting as the final court of appeal in much the same way as the House of Lords did in England. In the absence of a council of war, the supreme council supervised the confederate military effort with varying degrees of success, and on the international front corresponded with the courts of Europe. Each general assembly elected a new council, whose authority expired whenever the next assembly met.[45] Despite the theoretical superiority of the confederate legislature, the continuous sessions of the supreme council enabled it to gain the upper hand, at least until late 1646.

Early councils consisted of 24 members, six from each province, including three resident or full-time members.[46] The meetings usually took place (as with the general assembly) in Robert Shee's house in Kilkenny.[47] In February 1646, the assembly reduced the number on the council to nine, to improve efficiency and speed up the decision making process. When the clerical faction seized power later that same year, they appointed a new council of 17, the first and only occasion the general assembly was not involved in the procedure.[48] Its powers remained the same with the important exception that "all orders affecting the business of the kingdom" had to be co-signed with the ecclesiastical congregation, and from September 1646 until March 1647, clerical representatives sat at the council board.[49] The dominance of the clergy proved short-lived, and in March 1647, with the moderates in the ascendancy, the assembly elected yet another council, reverting to the original format of 24 members.

The final election in December 1647 proved extremely controversial, with the co-opting of 36 supernumeraries, or alternates, onto the core group of twelve resident members (three from each province).[50] The clerical faction accused their opponents of changing the electoral format to gain control of the council. This

---

45 The structure and functions of the council were outlined in the confederate "model of government". Orders of the general assembly met at Kilkenny, 24 Oct. 1642 (BL Add Mss 4,781 ff 4-11). A judicature was established by the general assembly in August 1644. Order by the commissioners of the general assembly, 30 Aug. 1644 (Gilbert [ed.], *Irish confederation*, iii, pp 266-7). 46 A full list of council members from 1642 to 1649 is in appendix 2 (table 13). 47 Cregan, D.F., "Confederation of Kilkenny" (PhD thesis) pp 72-3. 48 Orders of the general assembly, Jan. 1646 (Bodl. Carte Mss 16 ff 470-80). The assembly reforms in early 1646 are discussed in chapter 3 pp 103-5. See also Order by the ecclesiastical congregation, 26 Sept. 1646 (Gilbert [ed.], *Irish confederation*, vi, pp 144-6). 49 Massari, "Irish campaign" p. 548; Order by the ecclesiastical congregation, 26 Sept. 1646 (Gilbert [ed.], *Irish confederation*, vi, pp 144-6). 50 Cregan mistakenly believed that the final general assembly in September 1648 elected a new supreme council. Cregan, D.F., "Confederate catholics" p. 512. In fact, the new faces who

*Table 4: Supreme council – numbers on the council*

| Year | Number on council |
| --- | --- |
| 1642 | 24 |
| 1643a | 24 |
| 1643b | 24 |
| 1644 | 24 |
| 1645 | 24 |
| 1646a | 9 |
| 1646b | 17 |
| 1647a | 24 |
| 1647b | 12 (+36) |

charge appears to be without foundation, as despite the addition of the supernumeraries, the balance of the original election was more or less retained, with the nuncio's supporters still in the minority.[51] In fact, the council eventually numbered 49 members, following the inclusion of Robert Devereux from Wexford as one of the three residents for Leinster, although not originally elected for that province. Officially, the extra member was recognition of the fact that Leinster had far more counties than any other province, and as a result contributed most to the central exchequer. Devereux's subsequent support for the Ormond peace treaty, however, suggests an alternative motive behind his nomination.[52]

The general assembly also appointed a president and secretary from among the residents. The wily veteran, Viscount Mountgarret, held the post of president on every council from 1642 until late 1646, chairing meetings and acting on occasions as effective head of state. During the same period, Richard Bellings, Mountgarret's son-in-law, functioned as secretary, overseeing all official correspondence. These appointments enabled Mountgarret and Bellings, both lead-

appeared at the council board from the summer of 1648 onwards consisted of those supernumeraries selected by the assembly in December 1647. See appendix 2. **51** Order of the general assembly, 12 Nov. 1647 (Gilbert [ed.], *Irish confederation*, vi, pp 208-23); Report on the affairs of Ireland, 1649 (Aiazza [ed.], *Embassy* pp 519-21). Of the original twelve elected, five were openly hostile towards the nuncio, the other seven being neutral or supporters of Rinuccini. After the addition of the supernumeraries, 25 were anti-nuncio, 23 neutral or supportive. This represented a significant though hardly overwhelming gain for the peace faction. **52** The other provinces agreed to an extra member from Leinster as long as no precedence was drawn from it. Order of the general assembly, 12 Nov. 1647 (Gilbert [ed.], *Irish confederation*, vi, pp 208-23).

ing figures in the peace faction, to significantly influence council policy until the rejection of the first Ormond treaty in August 1646.[53]

When the clerical party seized power the following month, Rinuccini assumed the position of president, breaking the monopoly of the peace faction for the first time. Six months later, in March 1647, the moderates at the general assembly secured the nomination of the marquis of Antrim to replace the nuncio, but no information survives regarding the position of secretary. Throughout the summer of 1647, Nicholas Plunkett and Nicholas French (assisted initially by Patrick Darcy) dominated the executive.[54] At the penultimate assembly in November of that year, both the positions of president and secretary appear to have been left vacant, probably in the forlorn hope of encouraging a more consensual approach to policy formation.[55] After the outbreak of civil war in May 1648, however, the peace faction stalwarts, Mountgarret and Bellings, resumed their earlier posts at the council table.

The first general assembly in October 1642 established the principle of provincial balance on the supreme council. Assembly members voted for candidates from provincial lists, each province providing six successful candidates.[56]

---

53 How exactly these men monopolised the two most important positions in the confederate association is unclear. Mountgarret functioned as the confederates' elder statesman, having sat in the Irish parliament as far back as 1613. An ideal figurehead in many ways, he was by no means the dominant figure in the confederate aristocracy, a position held by Viscount Gormanston, and after the latter's death in July 1643 by Viscount Muskerry. Bellings was unquestionably an able politician, and his marriage to one of Mountgarret's daughters did his career prospects no harm. Their strong advocacy of a peace settlement with the royalists also ensured they remained prominent, at least as long as the peace faction dominated affairs in Kilkenny.  54 One recent account describes Antrim as controlling confederate policy throughout 1647, while in fact the marquis was largely a peripheral figure in Kilkenny. Ohlmeyer, *Civil war and restoration* p. 192. He was active on the council for about two months after his election in March 1647, but more or less disappears from view then, although his name does appear on some council documents as late as July of that year. See PRO SP Ire. 265/19 f.107, 265/19 f.121, 265/19 f.138.  55 Order of the general assembly, 12 Nov. 1647 (Gilbert [ed.], *Irish confederation*, vi, pp 208-23).  56 According to Bellings, the assembly split into provincial groups, and "caused the names of all those in their province who, without any probability of success, might pretend to that employment to be written in a large sheet of paper, drawing a line from each of their names to the edge of the paper, then choosing some discreet persons to be overseers … every one of the members returned from that province gave his vote by stroking those set down in the paper to the number prescribed by the Assembly. This being done, and return made of those thus chosen by the Clerk of the House, he, in as many sheets of paper, writes the names given in by the four provinces, drawing likewise lines from each of them, whereon the prelates, and noblemen, and all other members of the Assembly, were to mark their strokes being first solemnly sworn upon the Holy Evangelists by those appointed to oversee the election, to make choice of the trustiest and ablest men to undergo that charge, to the number of half of those presented by each province, and those thus chosen having been taken of the oath of councillors were, after the recess of the Assembly accepted and obeyed as

While provincial balance may have made good political sense in the early days of the confederate association, to encourage support throughout the kingdom, it actually discriminated against the province of Leinster. In the Irish parliament (the model for the general assembly) Leinster returned 41% of the representatives, Ulster 26%, Munster 22% and Connacht 11%.[57] Based on these figures, a proportional distribution of council seats would have given Leinster 10 seats, Ulster 6, Munster 5 and Connacht only 3.

Over the following years, however, Leinster did in effect gain seats at the expense of Ulster, while the Munster and Connacht figures remained relatively stable. The non-resident Ulster members rarely travelled to Kilkenny, while prominent confederates such as Thomas Preston (Leinster general), Patrick Bryan (Leinster army committee), and Thomas Tyrrell (Leinster member of the committee of instructions) regularly attended council meetings.[58] The revised make-up of the council more accurately reflected the relative importance of each province within the association. The confederate power-base, centred on south Leinster and east Munster, provided the bulk of money and supplies, and many living there resented having to subsidise what they called "the burnt countries".[59]

Despite its relative poverty and geographic isolation, Connacht managed to retain six seats on the supreme council. This fact underlined the enormous influence of Galway politicians and clerics, who ensured that confederate government did not neglect the interests of this sparsely populated province.[60] Ulster, on the other hand, possessed few individuals of national standing politically, with provincial leaders concentrating for the most part on military affairs. Moreover, Ulster had been over-represented in the Irish parliament (a fact redressed in the general assembly), and contributed little to confederate coffers, as Scottish covenanters, royalists and parliamentarians controlled much of the province. For these reasons, as well as the practical difficulties in travelling to Kilkenny, there were rarely more than four Ulster representatives present at council meetings.[61]

the Supreme Magistrates of the Confederate Catholics". Bellings' History in Gilbert (ed.), *Irish confederation*, i, p. 112. This elaborate procedure is not mentioned elsewhere, and may well have been discontinued after the first assembly meeting. **57** The full list of constituencies in the Irish parliament is in Kearney, *Strafford in Ireland* pp 223-59. **58** The names of Preston and Bryan appear regularly on council documents from 1644 onwards. This may well have been due to reform proposals in 1644 which recommended that those involved in the affairs of the confederate forces sit on the supreme council "for the better management of military affairs". Propositions touching the present government offered by a committee to the general assembly, June 1644 (Marsh's Library, Mss z 3.1.3). **59** Ormond's uncle, James Butler, expressed his outrage at Leinster and Munster having to support financially confederate members from the depopulated areas of the country. Papers of James Butler, 12 Oct. 1648 (Bodl. Carte Mss 22 ff 352-4). According to Lenihan, the confederate territorial tax base was centred on Wexford, Kilkenny, Tipperary and Limerick. Lenihan, "Catholic confederacy" p. 188. **60** The desire to appease the earl of Clanricarde may also have helped Connacht's case. **61**

*Table 5: Supreme council: representative profile*[62]

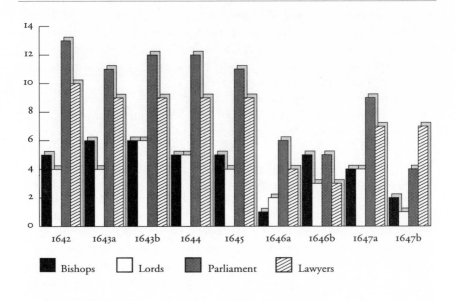

In terms of political leadership, a considerable degree of continuity existed between the confederate era and the early decades of the seventeenth century. The same parliamentarians and lawyers who had led the opposition to the policies of the Dublin administration dominated confederate councils throughout the 1640s.[63] Individuals such as Viscount Mountgarret, Patrick Darcy and Nicholas Plunkett were familiar figures on the Irish political scene long before the outbreak of the uprising. Constancy of personnel also proved a feature of confederate supreme councils, at least until 1646, with a core group of 24 members sitting on three or more councils.

The typical supreme council for the period 1642 to 1646 lined up as follows:

*Leinster: (6)* Viscount Mountgarret; Richard Bellings; Nicholas Plunkett; Archbishop Fleming (Dublin); Viscount Netterville; earl of Castlehaven
*Munster: (6)* George Comyn; Daniel O'Brien; Edmund Fitzmaurice; Gerald Fennell; Archbishop Walsh (Cashel); Viscount Muskerry[64]

Officially, however, the principle of provincial balance was retained in elections to the council. Any attempts to alter this would certainly have commented on by Rinuccini and others as happened during the controversial election in December 1647. **62** "Parliament' indicates the percentage of assembly members who sat in previous parliaments in Dublin. "Lawyers" indicates the percentage of assembly members who attended Inns of Court in London. **63** Veterans included people such as Daniel O'Brien and Viscount Mountgarret, both of whom had sat in the 1613 parliament. **64** Viscount Roche, active on early councils, was effectively

*Connacht: (6)* Patrick Darcy; Geoffrey Browne; Lucas Dillon; Archbishop O'Queely (Tuam); Roebuck Lynch; Bishop Bourke (Clonfert)[65]

*Ulster: (6)* Bishop MacMahon (Clogher); Turlough O'Neill; Archbishop O'Reilly (Armagh); Alexander MacDonnell; Thomas Fleming; Marquis of Antrim.[66]

These 24 individuals effectively dictated confederate policy until the rejection of the first Ormond peace treaty in August 1646. Although half of this number belonged to the peace faction, the list also included six bishops and some leading moderates.[67] Apart from the obvious advantage of numerical superiority, the predominance of the peace faction stemmed from the unity and energy of its adherents. They worked closely together, often meeting in private to discuss tactics, and tended to be among the most active members of council.[68] Along with Mountgarret and Bellings, Viscount Muskerry emerged as the most influential peace faction leader, ably assisted by the earl of Castlehaven, Gerald Fennell, Lucas Dillon and Geoffrey Browne.

Moreover, until 1645, a viable alternative to a speedy peace deal with the marquis of Ormond simply did not exist. The clerical faction lacked decisive leadership or a coherent strategy, and dissenting voices in the assembly focused almost exclusively on internal administrative and political reform. It was not until the arrival of Rinuccini in late 1645, that the clerics, driven by the nuncio's dynamic personality, developed an effective policy of opposition. As for the moderates, most of those active in the period 1642-6 supported the peace initiative. Plunkett and his allies only adopted an independent political strategy as a result of the confederate split in 1646.

The rejection of the peace treaty in August 1646 led to the overthrow of many of the "old guard" and the introduction of a significant number of new faces, as first the clerical faction and then the moderates gained control of the supreme council. In December 1647, however, with the re-emergence of the peace faction, a number of familiar faces returned to the council table. The general assembly re-elected 14 of the original 24 members from October 1642 onto the final supreme council. Of those missing, three (Viscount Gormanston, Archbishop O'Queely and Robert Lombard) were dead , the aged archbishop of Armagh had opted out of political life after 1646, James Cusack had become

---

superseded in 1644 by his great rival, Viscount Muskerry. **65** Clonfert, appointed to the judicature in 1644, was replaced on the council by Dermot O'Shaughnessy. **66** Although Antrim only definitely sat on two councils prior to 1646, he may well have been the missing Ulster member in 1645. See appendix 2. **67** Nicholas Plunkett, Patrick Darcy, Roebuck Lynch, the marquis of Antrim, Alexander MacDonnell (Antrim's brother) and Turlough O'Neill (Phelim's brother) were all considered moderates at one time or another. **68** Rinuccini, for example, complained of the peace faction meeting in secret to turn everything to their own ends. Rinuccini to Pamphili, 6 March 1647 (Aiazza [ed.], *Embassy* p. 258).

confederate attorney-general, while two others (Philip Mac Hugh O'Reilly and Coll MacBrien Mac Mahon) disappeared from the national stage after 1643.[69]

Between October 1642 and September 1646, only 35 different people sat on the six supreme councils elected during that period. In the remaining two years, until the dissolution of the confederate association, 61 individuals were appointed onto just three councils, including 37 first-time members. Prominent newcomers included the fervent clerical supporters, Oliver Plunkett (Lord Louth) and Piers Butler of Moneyhore, County Wexford, both from old English backgrounds. The moderates received crucial support from Bishop French of Ferns, Geoffrey Barron and Phelim O'Neill, underlining the clerical and ethnic mix among those who favoured a compromise settlement. Finally, apart from the return of the previous leadership, the peace faction was boosted by the election of new figures such as Lord Athenry and John Dillon.

Of all the provinces, Connacht's membership pattern on the supreme council proved remarkably cohesive. Throughout the 1640s (ignoring those whose only nomination was as an alternate in December 1647), 56 different individuals sat on the council.[70] Leinster and Munster provided 16 members each, with 14 coming from Ulster. Only 10 different individuals, however, represented Connacht on the supreme council between 1642 and 1649, and all except Lord Mayo hailed from the Galway area.[71] Leading figures in this group included Malachy O'Queely (the archbishop of Tuam, until his death in October 1645), his successor, John Bourke, Lucas Dillon, Patrick Darcy, Geoffrey Browne and Roebuck Lynch. Following the collapse of the first Ormond peace treaty, Dermot O'Shaughnessy, Richard Blake and Lord Athenry figured prominently. Apart from geographical and social connections, these men also shared close links with the most powerful catholic nobleman in Ireland, the marquis of Clanricarde, a fact which enabled them to exercise a disproportionate influence on confederate affairs.[72]

In the province of Ulster, the Stuart policy of plantation had resulted in the displacement of many of the traditional landowning class, who now sought to

---

**69** Viscount Gormanston died in July 1643, while Archbishop O'Queely was killed in October 1645. O'Reilly of Armagh was almost 70 years old, while Cusack was appointed attorney-general at the first general assembly, and appears to have concentrated exclusively on legal matters after 1642. Acts of the general assembly, 24 Oct. 1642 (Gilbert [ed.], *Irish confederation*, ii, pp 73-90). Cregan suspects that Robert Lombard died in 1643 as nothing more is heard of him after that date. Cregan, D.F., "Confederation of Kilkenny" (PhD thesis) p. 134. **70** Rinuccini is not included here as he did not represent any one province. **71** O'Queely was born in the diocese of Killaloe in Munster, but his archbishopric was based in Galway. Cregan, "Counter-reformation episcopate" p. 98. Mayo in fact only sat on the first council, and as a supernumerary on the last. For the rest of the period, the Galway influence was unchallenged. **72** The confederates made many appeals to the marquis to join their ranks, but, according to Rinuccini, he remained "arrogantly aloof". Rinuccini to Panzirolo, 14 Aug. 1647 (Aiazza [ed.], *Embassy* p. 300).

reverse the process and regain their property. They looked to Owen Roe O'Neill for military leadership, but in the political sphere few spoke on their behalf. Not only was Ulster under-represented on the council, but the councillors from the province belonged almost exclusively to those termed the "deserving Irish", natives who received estates in the plantation settlement. Needless to say, such people proved less than whole-hearted in their support for a new land deal, and by 1648 most openly opposed Owen Roe O'Neill.[73]

Members of this group included Turlough O'Neill, brother of Phelim, Viscount Iveagh, another important Ulster landowner, and the marquis of Antrim, although to what extent he ever supported confederate policies remains open to question. Antrim's primary loyalty was to his family and the Stuart monarchy, while the confederates, if they featured at all, came a very poor third.[74] During the marquis' long absences abroad, his brother, Alexander, protected the MacDonnell interests on the supreme council. Thomas Fleming, a Cavan resident, was related to Lord Slane, and remained politically close to the Pale gentry throughout the 1640s. Of the Ulster delegates, only Heber MacMahon, bishop of Clogher and close ally of Owen Roe O'Neill, effectively represented the dispossessed of the province.[75]

In the case of Leinster, the relative scarcity of Pale nobility on the council is striking. Traditionally one of the most influential groups in Irish politics, they played a crucial role in the initial stages of the uprising and the subsequent development of confederate governmental structures.[76] The early deaths of two of their most influential personalities, Viscount Gormanston and Lord Slane, effectively sidelined the Pale nobility for the rest of the decade. Their replacements on the council, Viscount Netterville and later Lord Louth, did not command the same level of support. Furthermore, the location of the confederate capital in Kilkenny, greatly enhanced the prestige of the Butler lords to the detriment of all other peers. Finally, the Pale emerged as a central theatre of war during the 1640s, forcing the nobility there into an active military, rather than political, role.

As for the clergy, the bishops averaged five members on each supreme council, with the archbishops obviously prominent.[77] The only additions to

[73] The split in the Ulster ranks in 1648 is discussed in chapter 6 p. 181. [74] Ohlmeyer, *Civil war and restoration* (1993) is an excellent study of Antrim's career, although it overstates the extent of the marquis' involvement with, and influence over, the confederates. [75] MacMahon was also the only man, along with Nicholas Plunkett, to have sat on all nine supreme councils. See appendix 2 (table 13). [76] Viscount Gormanston in particular was a central figure in the early days of the rebellion, and in the formation of the confederate association. Examination of Edward Dowdall, 13 March 1642 (TCD Mss 816 f.44); Orders of the supreme council, 18 June 1642 (PRO SP Ire. 260/67 ff 234-53) etc. [77] The four archbishops were all over fifty years of age at the outbreak of the rebellion- Dublin (51), Tuam (55), Armagh (60), Cashel (61). Although Tuam and Cashel remained active, this group were to some extent eclipsed by Clogher (41) and Clonfert (51). The former's close links with Owen Roe ONeill and Rinuccini

their council group came after the upheavals of September 1646, when the age-ing archbishops of Armagh and Dublin were effectively replaced by the younger, more active, bishops of Ferns and Limerick. The vast majority of prelates never sat on any council, even after the papal nuncio seized power, although most of them attended the general assemblies.[78] Many clerics had strong links with the landowning classes and shared their concerns for law and order and the sanctity of property.[79] With the exception of Thomas Dease of Meath, however, they adopted a more radical position on matters of religion, favouring a retention of church property seized from the protestants and full legal recognition of the Catholic Church. Indeed when united on these issues, the clergy formed a powerful faction which proved increasingly difficult to ignore from 1644 onwards.

In conclusion, on one level the supreme council was a remarkably homoge-neous body, controlled by a handful of individuals, mainly lawyers and former parliamentarians, who dictated confederate policy. Despite differences in priori-ties and policies, the members all belonged to the same class and shared com-mon concerns and goals. Without exception, however, confederate councillors lacked executive experience due to the Dublin government's policy of excluding catholics from office. According to James Butler, a kinsman of Ormond, the council meant well but could not govern "being not bred nor acquainted with state matters nor experienced in marshall affairs".[80] The general assembly proved equally critical of the council's failure to enforce law and order, from "whence issued a general contempt of government".[81] Clearly all their legal and parlia-mentary experience had not adequately prepared the confederate leadership for executive responsibilities. Nonetheless, despite these limitations, the council for the most part effectively carried out its duties in extremely difficult circum-stances.

---

assisted his rise to prominence, while the latter was nominated to head the new judicature in 1644. Order by the commissioners of the general assembly, 30 Aug. 1644 (Gilbert [ed.], *Irish confederation*, iii, pp 266). **78** Apart from those already named, only two other bishops were elected onto the supreme council, both as supernumerary members in late 1647. No evidence survives to show if Kirwan of Killala or Magennis of Down/Connor actually ever sat at the council board. **79** Cregan provides information on the extent of land-holdings by the Irish catholic bishops in Cregan, "Counter-reformation episcopate" p. 101. **80** As a result, Butler believed that confederate government was "so odious and to the whole nation so destructive, as of necessity it must be altered". James Butler to Ormond, 12 Oct. 1648 (Bodl. Carte Mss 22 f.350). **81** Order of the general assembly, 12 Nov. 1647 (Gilbert [ed.], *Irish confederation*, vi, pp 208-23); Orders of the general assembly, Jan. 1646 (Bodl. Carte Mss 16 ff 470-80). Clear paral-lels exist with the experiences of the parliamentary side in the English civil war, and of the Scottish covenanters. Zagorin argues that the English parliament in 1640 was "utterly without corporate experience as an executive body", and was forced to "assume the functions of gov-ernment which until then had been exercised by the king, the privy council and a host of royal officials". Young, *Scottish parliament* p. 327.

*Negotiating teams – committees and delegations, 1642-1649*

Between 1642 and 1649, the confederates authorised a handful of individuals to negotiate various agreements with the royalists. These negotiators enjoyed a considerable degree of autonomy from central control, a fact they often sought to exploit, at least prior to 1646.[82] The prejudices, concerns and ambitions of those involved in the talks, therefore, helped shape the final terms of the peace settlement. In many ways their contributions to events greatly exceeded that of Owen Roe O'Neill, Thomas Preston, the earl of Castlehaven and a host of better known confederate figures. With this in mind, the following section examines the make-up of the numerous delegations and committees established by the confederates.

The first official contact between the confederates and royalists occurred in March 1643 when a delegation from Kilkenny presented a remonstrance to the king's representatives at Trim, outlining their reasons for taking up arms. There had been a flood of catholic petitions, dating right back to the outbreak of the revolt, but the two sides had not met face-to-face except on the battlefield.[83] No official negotiations took place at Trim, as the royalists simply agreed to accept the remonstrance and pass it on to the king. Informal discussions, however, almost certainly took place between the two parties, who knew each other well.

The original confederate delegation, led by Viscount Gormanston, consisted of representatives from each of the four provinces – Robert Talbot from Leinster, Lucas Dillon of Connacht, the Munster lawyer, John Walsh, and Turlough O'Neill, an Ulster landowner. Barnaby Fitzpatrick, lord of Upper Ossory, was also selected, but neither he nor O'Neill actually travelled to Trim.[84] Gormanston, Dillon and O'Neill had already emerged as central figures in the confederate government, following their election in November 1642 onto the first supreme council. This council then appointed the delegation to present the confederate remonstrance. In future, all negotiating teams would be chosen directly by the general assembly.[85]

---

**82** Clanricarde shrewdly noted the peace faction's preference for negotiating through committees rather than large representative bodies, presumably because they were easier to control. Clanricarde to Ormond, 3 Oct. 1643 (Carte, *Ormond*, v, pp 472-4). **83** The confederate supreme council presented a petition to Ormond in July 1642 which he passed on to the king. Confederate petition, 31 July 1642 (Rawlinson MSS, B.507 f.43). Charles responded by authorising official contacts with Irish catholics early in 1643. Charles to Ormond, 12 Jan. 1643 (Carte, *Ormond*, v, pp 1-3). **84** Appointment of confederate representatives, 11 March 1643 (Gilbert [ed.], *Irish confederation*, ii, p. 224). Neither name appears on the remonstrance document. Remonstrance of grievances, 17 March 1643 (ibid. pp 226-42). The royalist delegation was led by Clanricarde, and included the earl of Roscommon, Viscount Moore and Maurice Eustace, all of whom also sat in the Irish parliament. **85** The council, however, rather than the assembly appointed the team to arrange a cease-fire with Lord Inchiquin in 1648. Articles of

### Table 6: Committee membership, 1642–1649

| | 1643a | 1643b | 1644a | 1644b | 1645 | 1646 | 1648 | | Province |
|---|---|---|---|---|---|---|---|---|---|
| Talbot R. | o | o | o | o | o | o | x | 7 | Leinster |
| Walsh J. | o | o | | | | | x | 3 | Munster |
| O'Neill T. | x | x | | | | | | 2 | Ulster |
| Dillon L. | x | x | | | | | | 2 | Connacht |
| *Upper Ossory* | o | | | | | | o | 2 | Munster |
| *Gormanstown* | x | | | | | | | 1 | Munster |
| Browne G. | | x | x | x | x | o | x | 6 | Connacht |
| *Muskerry* | | o | o | x | x | x | | 5 | Munster |
| Plunkett N. | | x | x | x | x | | | 4 | Leinster |
| Barnewall R. | | o | | | | | x | 2 | Leinster |
| Magennis E. | | x | | | | | | 1 | Ulster |
| O'Brien Der. | | | o | o | o | o | | 4 | Munster |
| MacDonnell A. | | | o | x | x | | | 3 | Ulster |
| Martin R. | | | o | o | | | | 2 | Connacht |
| *Mountgarret* | | | | x | x | x | | 3 | Leinster |
| Darcy P. | | | | x | x | x | | 3 | Connacht |
| Dillon J. | | | | o | o | o | | 3 | Leinster |
| *Dublin* | | | | x | | | | 1 | Leinster |
| *Antrim* | | | | o | | | | 1 | Ulster |
| Evverard R. | | | | o | | | | 1 | Munster |
| *Tuam* | | | | | | | x | 1 | Connacht |
| O'Neill P. | | | | | | | x | 1 | Ulster |
| O'Reilly M. | | | | | | | x | 1 | Ulster |
| *Taaffe* | | | | | | | o | 1 | Connacht |
| *Westmeaath* | | | | | | | o | 1 | Leinster |
| Burke T. | | | | | | | o | 1 | Connacht |
| O'Callaghan D | | | | | | | o | 1 | Munster |
| | 6 | 9 | 7 | 13 | 9 | 7 | 12 | | |

'x' indicates that the committee member also sat on the supreme council at that time, while 'o' means they did not.[86]

---

agreement, 20 May 1648 (Bodl. Carte Mss 22 ff.99). **86** Unlike the supreme councils and the general assemblies, the commissions for all the negotiating committees still survive, so a complete list of members can be presented. See BL Stowe Mss 82 f.116, Add Mss 25,277 f.62; Gilbert (ed.), *Irish confederation*, ii, pp 224-5; iii, pp 65, 269; v, pp 286-311; vi, p. 288. Table 6 lists the various individuals who took part in these talks, starting with the presentation of the

The other notable feature of this first confederate delegation, is that four of them, Gormanston, Upper Ossory, Dillon and Walsh, attended the 1640-1 parliament, while Robert Talbot had the distinction of being expelled from the 1634 parliament for an offence "which tended to the dishonour of (the lord deputy) and this house".[87] Only Turlough O'Neill had no parliamentary background, but he may be seen as a proxy for his more controversial brother, Phelim, member of parliament for Dungannon and one of the leaders of the initial uprising in October 1641. Apart from Gormanston and Talbot, the entire team had received legal training, and this policy of appointing negotiators with legal or parliamentary experience persisted throughout the 1640s.

Following the encounter at Trim, the second general assembly met in May 1643 to debate a possible truce with the royalists, and to select commissioners for the subsequent talks with the Dublin administration. Once again Viscount Gormanston led this delegation, and he appears to have resigned his seat on the supreme council to concentrate on the negotiations.[88] Alongside Gormanston, the team consisted of those who had delivered the remonstrance in Trim (minus Ossory), augmented by Viscount Muskerry of Munster, Ever Magennis representing Ulster and Geoffrey Browne, nephew of Patrick Darcy, and a leading figure in Galway political circles. Nicholas Plunkett and Richard Barnewall, both of Leinster, joined the group after Gormanston's death.[89]

The assembly retained a provincial balance on the new committee, and all the members, apart from Robert Talbot, John Walsh and Richard Barnewall, also sat on the existing supreme council. Furthermore, seven of the nine delegates were parliamentary veterans, while six had trained as lawyers. Once again the two Ulster representatives proved the exception, as neither Turlough O'Neill or Ever Magennis had ever attended parliament, while Magennis

remonstrance at Trim in March 1643, until the dissolution of the confederate association in January 1649. 1643a refers to the Trim meeting, 1643b to the delegation appointed to conclude a cessation with Ormond, which was eventually signed in September of that year. 1644a is the team which travelled to Oxford to negotiate directly with the king, while 1644b refers to the committee of treaty elected by the general assembly to continue those talks with Ormond. Although this committee stayed in existence until the publication of the peace in August 1646, I have included a list of the committee members who actually signed the Glamorgan treaty in August 1645 and the Ormond treaty the following year, to highlight a number of important absentees. The final list comprises the members of the second committee of treaty appointed by the assembly in October 1648, to conclude a second peace with Ormond. The names of the nobility and bishops are in italics. **87** Clarke, *Old English in Ireland*, pp 84-5. **88** The order of the supreme council on 20 June to treat for a cessation, was based on an order of the general assembly exactly one month earlier. Order of the supreme council, 20 June 1643 (BL Stowe Mss 82 f.116). It is of course possible that Gormanston was elected to the council in June 1643, and replaced after his death the following month. **89** *A collection of all the papers which passed upon the late treaty touching the cessation of arms in Ireland* ..., Dublin 1643 (RIA vol. 38, box 34, tract 1).

appears to have possessed no legal expertise, which clearly placed him at a distinct disadvantage. Negotiations took place throughout the summer of 1643 between the confederate delegation and the royalists, led by James Butler, earl of Ormond.

The arrival of Ormond onto the political scene assisted the confederates in some ways, but also caused complications. A number of the confederate delegates were either directly related to him, or enjoyed close business and professional links, a fact which may have facilitated the talks process.[90] Conversely, the blatant conflict of interest always threatened to undermine the integrity of the confederate team, and opponents of the first peace treaty later exploited this in their propaganda.[91] Initially, however, the negotiations continued smoothly and both sides agreed to a one year cessation of arms on 15 September 1643.[92]

The first serious peace talks began six months later in Oxford, the royalist capital, following the appointment of delegates by the general assembly in November 1643. Viscount Muskerry led the confederate team which included Talbot, Browne, Plunkett and another distinguished lawyer, Richard Martin of Galway. Both Plunkett and Browne were also elected to the supreme council at this time, a move which ensured that the confederate executive stayed fully informed of developments in Oxford. Dermot O'Brien of Munster, and Alexander MacDonnell (Antrim's brother), completed the group. MacDonnell, the sole delegate from Ulster, could hardly be said to have represented any provincial interests, other than those of the tiny group of catholic landowners. This fact is borne out by the total absence of any articles relating to the dispossessed of Ulster in the first peace treaty.[93]

After the failure of the Oxford conference the talks moved back to Ireland. Ormond continued to dominate the royalist negotiating team, assisted by the

---

90 Viscount Muskerry was married to Ormond's sister Eleanor. Cokayne, *Complete peerage*, vol. 3 (1913) pp 214-15. Patrick Darcy held lands from Ormond in Carlow, but in 1645 wrote to the lord lieutenant that he had received no rent from them "since the troubles". Patrick Darcy to Ormond, 25 Oct. 1645 (NLI Ormonde Mss 2313 f.31). 91 The author of the *Aphorismical discovery* was particularly colourful in his description of the close links between the royalists and certain confederates. For example, Bellings was "a toad in faction and a creature of Ormond", while Darcy was "Ormond's counsel and Clanricarde's minion". Gilbert (ed.), *Contemporary history*, i, p. 40. 92 Richard Bellings claimed that Richard Barnewall was not party to the agreement, but his signature appears with all the others on the document itself. Bellings' History in Gilbert (ed.), *Irish confederation*, i, p. 163; Articles of cessation, 15 Sept. 1643 (Gilbert [ed.], *Irish confederation*, ii, pp 365-76). 93 Appointment of commissioners to Oxford, 19 Dec. 1643 (Gilbert [ed.], *Irish confederation*, iii, p. 65). Muskerry did not sit on the supreme council prior to his trip to Oxford, perhaps reflecting a desire to distance himself from confederate government while in the presence of the king. Ohlmeyer describes Alexander as acting as a "watchdog" for his brother's interests. Ohlmeyer, *Civil war and restoration* p. 153 n. 9.

lord chancellor, Richard Bolton. On the confederate side, in July 1644 the general assembly elected a committee of treaty to travel to Dublin.[94] This committee received instructions from the aptly named committee of instruction, both of which answered, in theory at least, to the assembly. In practice the two committees became largely autonomous, while at the same time working closely with peace faction elements on the supreme council.[95] The composition of these bodies, therefore, proved crucial in determining the final shape of the Ormond peace treaty.

The establishment of powerful working parties in Kilkenny mirrored developments in England at this time, particularly on the parliamentarian side. In February 1644, the committee of both kingdoms, consisting of members of the English parliament with the addition of Scottish commissioners, replaced the committee of safety. Functioning essentially as the executive branch of government, it exercised wide-ranging powers independent of parliament, although (like the confederate supreme council) it could not decide on matters of war or peace. A bitter dispute erupted in Westminster as to whether the members of the committee should be bound by an oath of secrecy. The House of Lords vehemently opposed this move, arguing that such an oath impinged on the sovereignty of parliament, but only succeeded in delaying its introduction.[96] The issue of secrecy also surfaced in Ireland soon afterwards, with the confederate council and committees accused of misleading the assembly over the peace treaty.[97]

Although the general assembly nominated the committee of treaty, Ormond still influenced the final selection, albeit indirectly. As Rinuccini explained, the confederate leadership persuaded assembly members to choose people who were either connected, or on good terms, with the lord lieutenant to facilitate the talks process.[98] From the outset, therefore, a majority on the confederate negotiating teams sympathised with the royalist position and favoured an early peace, with a minimum of concessions. This was to have disastrous repercussions for confederate unity after the declaration of the treaty terms in August 1646.

**94** Commission for confederate delegates, 31 Aug. 1644 (Gilbert [ed.], *Irish confederation*, iii, p. 269). From September 1644 Bolton was engaged in complex negotiations with Patrick Darcy on constitutional issues. Peace debates, Sept. 1644, ibid. pp 280-1. **95** This autonomy was best illustrated when in 1645 the earl of Glamorgan insisted on excluding the general assembly from negotiations on religious concessions, and dealing instead directly with the committee of treaty. Lowe, "Negotiations between Charles I and confederates" p. 341. **96** Roberts, C., *The growth of responsible government in Stuart England* pp 145-6; Morrill, *Revolt of the provinces* pp 57-8. **97** Walter Enos claimed that the peace treaty published in August 1646 was not the same as "that which then (in the month of February and August) was in agitation and publicly read in the assembly". Enos "Survey" in Gilbert (ed.), *Irish confederation*, vi, p. 394. It is interesting that the establishment of committees in Kilkenny occurred shortly after the return of the confederate delegation from England in June 1644. **98** Report on the state of Ireland, 1 March 1646 (Aiazza [ed.], *Embassy* p. 133).

Ormond further exacerbated the problem by refusing to deal directly with the catholic bishops.[99] Quite apart from the lord lieutenant's intolerance of catholic clergy, it certainly would have been difficult for him politically (particularly following Inchiquin's desertion to the parliamentarian side in July 1644) to negotiate with representatives of the Catholic Church. Nonetheless, this stipulation effectively sidelined from the talks one of the most influential groups in confederate politics, and contributed greatly to clerical resentment. In order to mollify clerical opinion and save face, the general assembly appointed the aged archbishop of Dublin as one of the delegates, fully aware that ill-health would prevent him from travelling to Dublin.[100]

The committee of treaty consisted of the seven men who travelled to Oxford, augmented by six new members, including Viscount Mountgarret and the earl of Antrim. These noblemen appear to have been little more than figureheads, and indeed Antrim left for England shortly after the assembly dispersed in September 1644. Their names alone, however, gave considerable authority to any recommendations made by the committee. The assembly also appointed three leading legal figures, Richard Everard of Munster, John Dillon of Leinster and Patrick Darcy from Galway, to assist Nicholas Plunkett.[101] Finally, Mountgarret, Muskerry, Dublin, Plunkett, MacDonnell, Darcy and Browne were all members of the supreme council, underlining the continuing close links between elements on the confederate executive and the negotiating committee.

In a significant development, the assembly abandoned the principle of provincial balance, with Leinster (five members) gaining at the expense of Ulster (two members). Moreover the most active core of the committee – Muskerry, Plunkett, Darcy, Browne, Dillon, Talbot and O'Brien – did not include an Ulster representative.[102] Even at the conclusion of the process in 1646, not all the committee members signed the first Ormond treaty (seven signatures appear on

99 On 9 August 1644 Ormond wrote to Muskerry, anxious that no clergy be selected onto the confederate negotiating team. Gilbert (ed.), *Irish confederation*, iii, pp 251-2. Earlier that same year, the catholic earl of Clanricarde wrote to the confederates, that as a public minister "it will not be allowed me to receive and entertain any of the clergy". Clanricarde to Viscount Netterville, 23 April 1644 (Lowe [ed.], *Clanricarde letter-book* p. 76). 100 The fact that Dublin was (according to Rinuccini) "exceedingly corpulent" and travelled with difficulty, undoubtedly affected his contribution to the talks process. Rinuccini to Pamphili, 31 Dec. 1645 (Aiazza [ed.], *Embassy* pp 105-7). 101 Antrim left for England having failed to gain absolute control of confederate military forces. Ohlmeyer, *Civil war and restoration* pp 149-50. 102 In any event, Ulster's interests did not feature prominently in the objectives of its two provincial representatives (the earl of Antrim, or his brother, Alexander MacDonnell). The observation on the most active members of the committee is based not only on a knowledge of the negotiations, but also on the number of signatures on committee of treaty documents. See Bodl. Carte Mss 16 f.300, 304, 422, 566 etc.

the document). Walter Enos, in his survey of the peace settlement written in late 1646, further claimed that although the treaty contained the names of Viscount Mountgarret and Dermot O'Brien, neither had actually signed the document.[103] Therefore, only five of the thirteen original commissioners were directly involved in concluding an agreement with the royalists, hardly a representative sample of confederate opinion.

Unfortunately, little is known of the role played by the committee of instruction during the talks process, as references to its activities are sparse and uninformative. By 1648, the committee consisted of 50 or more general assembly members, but only Thomas Tyrrell (chairman between 1644-6) can be definitely identified.[104] It appears that the supreme council and committee of instruction effectively amalgamated after 1644, as official documents were frequently signed in the name of "the council and committee". Moreover, complaints emerged around this time of the council becoming too large and unwieldy.[105] The committee disbanded in June 1646 after sanctioning the terms of the Ormond treaty, and reformed two years later during the final assembly to supervise further negotiations with the royalists. Unless some new evidence comes to light, however, the operations (and personnel) of this committee will remain shrouded in mystery.[106]

After the collapse of the first Ormond treaty, formal negotiations between royalists and confederates ceased for almost two years, despite attempts by the general assembly to reopen channels of communications in early 1647.[107] In July

103 A copy of the Glamorgan treaty, concluded on behalf of eight confederate commissioners, including Mountgarret and O'Brien, appears in BL Add Mss 25,277 f.62. Enos made this assertion in the survey of the peace published at the end of 1646. Enos "Survey" in Gilbert (ed.), *Irish confederation*, vi, p. 371. The fact that Enos was anxious to denigrate his peace faction enemies, including Mountgarret, undoubtedly lends credibility to a claim which would have worked in the viscount's favour at that particular time.  104 Nicholas French referred briefly to the creation of the committee. Bindon (ed.), *Historical works*, vol. 2, p. 43. Ormond wrote of articles appearing "under the hand of Mr Thomas Tirrell who sat in the chair of a committee of instructions appointed by the said assembly". Ormond to Nicholas Plunkett, 25 Jan. 1647 (Lowe [ed.], *Clanricarde letter-book* pp 348-9). Richard Blake commented that the committee was comprised of over 50 members of the general assembly, without providing further details. Blake to Rinuccini, 19 Oct. 1648 (Gilbert [ed.], *Irish confederation*, vi, p. 296).  105 Rinuccini talked of those "whose office was to hear and examine the conditions of peace, and report on them to the public". He continued that these people eventually joined the supreme council as supernumeraries, increasing the size of the council to such an extent that it was almost impossible to pass any decisions. Report on the state of Ireland, 1 March 1646 (Aiazza [ed.], *Embassy* p. 133).  106 According to Bellings, in June 1646, the committee "having performed what they were convened for were dismissed". Bellings' History in Gilbert (ed.), *Irish confederation*, vi, p. 6. On 15 November 1648, the general assembly called a meeting of the committee of instructions to further the proceedings of the treaty. Order of the general assembly, 15 Nov. 1648 (Bodl. Carte Mss 22 f.625).  107 Negotiations conducted on an *ad hoc* basis by Hugh Rochford, Geoffrey Barron and

of that year Ormond finally left Ireland, handing Dublin over to the forces of the English parliament, and for the rest of the year military considerations proved paramount. Calamitous defeats in Leinster (Dungan's Hill) and Munster (Knocknanuss) forced the confederates to reconsider their strategy. In May 1648, the supreme council instructed three agents to negotiate a cease-fire with Lord Inchiquin, the protestant commander in Munster. John Walsh, a Munster lawyer and former MP who had negotiated the first truce with Ormond in September 1643, led the team. The signing of an agreement on 20 May precipitated a complete rupture in confederate ranks, resulting in a civil war.[108]

On 4 September 1648, the last general assembly met in Kilkenny and reactivated talks with Ormond who returned to Ireland at the end of the month. For practical purposes, assembly members appointed commissioners (as before) to conduct the negotiations, but on this occasion the committee of treaty had to report directly to the assembly, rather than the supreme council.[109] This final team, consisting of twelve men, represented in some ways a fresh start, as only Geoffrey Browne and Robert Talbot had been involved in previous treaty negotiations, although lawyers and former parliamentarians still predominated. Viscount Muskerry, perhaps in light of his previous experiences, declined an offer to be directly involved.[110] Other delegates included Viscount Taaffe for Connacht, and the earl of Westmeath for Leinster, both late converts to the confederate cause. Phelim O'Neill and Miles O'Reilly represented the "deserving Irish" of Ulster, anxious for a settlement with the king. As before, Ormond proved reluctant to deal directly with the catholic hierarchy, but unlike 1644, the assembly refused to compromise on the issue and selected the most senior and prominent prelate present (John Bourke, archbishop of Tuam).[111]

Despite a strong peace party presence, the negotiations quickly became bogged down on the familiar constitutional and religious themes. In an effort to break the deadlock, a number of leading confederates joined the talks, including Nicholas Plunkett (recently returned from Rome) and Patrick

Gerald Fennell, among others, continued for a number of months. Nothing was achieved, however, besides the temporary re-establishment of a truce. Peace negotiations, 1647 (Bodl Carte Mss 20 f.315, 372-4). **108** Articles of agreement, 20 May 1648 (Bodl. Carte Mss 22 f.99). The other two confederate agents were Richard Everard, a former member of the committee of treaty, and Patrick Gough, a supernumerary member of the supreme council, both from Munster. **109** Viscount Taaffe explained this new policy in a letter to the marquis of Ormond. The committee of treaty was not allowed to make any alterations in the confederate terms until they first returned to the general assembly with Ormond's answers. Taaffe to Ormond, 11 Oct. 1648 (Bodl. Carte Mss 22 f.347). **110** Idem. **111** Ormond to Inchiquin, 12 Oct. 1648 (Carte, *Ormond*, vi, pp 568-9). Viscount Taaffe convinced the lord lieutenant that a treaty had a much better chance of being accepted if a leading bishop was party to the settlement. Taaffe to Ormond, 11 Oct. 1648 (Bodl. Carte Mss 22 f.347).

Darcy.[112] Both sides finally reached an agreement in January 1649, after news of the king's trial undermined confederate determination to press for further concessions. The treaty was not signed by any delegation or committee, however, but by Richard Blake, chairman of the assembly, on behalf of the entire association.[113] Despite this admirable show of unity, the confederates remained divided and hostilities continued until the intervention of Cromwell. His arrival in Ireland signalled the end of the negotiating era, as military affairs moved centre-stage.

What conclusions can be drawn from the negotiating process and those involved in it? Despite the various military and political upheavals of the period, the personnel remained remarkably consistent. Until 1646, the peace faction dominated the confederate contribution to the talks process, primarily through controlling the various committees, as much as the supreme council. The predominance of lawyers, and those with previous parliamentary experience, ensured that the negotiations concentrated on legalistic and constitutional matters, largely to the exclusion of all others. The more mundane needs of many confederates remained largely ignored, a fact cleverly exploited by the opponents of peace in 1646.

Crucially, the Catholic bishops took no part in early negotiations, despite the clergy's pivotal role in underpinning confederate authority, and the importance of religious issues. Their absence resulted not only from Ormond's desire to exclude them, but also from the lack of decisive leadership among the bishops themselves (at least until 1645). Similarly, Ulster was poorly represented, a fact which reflected the deep suspicion felt by many confederates towards the inhabitants of that particular province.

When serious peace negotiations started again in September 1648, after a gap of two years, the situation had changed dramatically, not only in England, following the collapse of the royalist position in the second civil war, but also in Ireland. Despite the open opposition of the clerical faction to the government in Kilkenny, and the resurgence of the peace faction, the moderates still succeeded in setting the confederate agenda. The role of the general assembly proved crucial in this regard, retaining a tight control on the talks process, and ensuring that the bishops, plus a more representative group from Ulster, became fully involved.

The second Ormond treaty, therefore, incorporated a wider range of confederate demands, particularly on religious and plantation issues. This agreement

---

112 The assembly created a number of special committees to help the negotiating process. The assembly orders survive in Bodl. Carte Mss 23 f.48, 58 and Gilbert (ed.), *Irish confederation*, vi, pp 154-5. 113 *The marquesse of Ormond's proclamation concerning the peace concluded with the Irish rebels … with a speech delivered by Sir Richard Blake … also a speech delivered by the marquesse of Ormond …*, London 1649 (BL Thomason tracts E545 f.12).

*Table 7: Committees: provincial representation*[114]

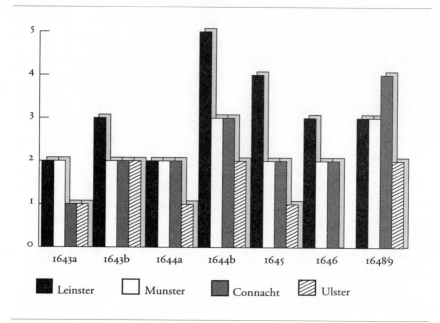

proved a more practical and popular basis (despite the continued opposition of Rinuccini, Owen Roe O'Neill and others) on which to dissolve the confederate association than its ill-fated predecessor. Further research is needed, however, particularly with regards to assembly membership, to enable us to fully understand the internal dynamics of the confederate association.[115]

---

114 The various committees are listed in table 6. 115 Using the existing assembly lists, it should be possible to identify each individual member, and start compiling their family, educational and political backgrounds.

# Confederate Ireland, 1642–1649

*ℰ১*

## A REAPPRAISAL

This union was our onlyest bulwark, and would prove (if not subverted)
formidable to our enemys at home and abroad: that commonwealth doth
prosper, whose citizens are of one accord.

Bishop French, *The unkind deserter of loyal men and true friends*, 1676[1]

The upheavals in Ireland during the 1640s were by no means a unique experience at a time of general crisis throughout the continent of Europe. Jeremiah
Whittaker declared in a sermon at Westminster on 23 January 1643 that "these
days are shaking and the shaking is universal: the Palatinate, Bohemia,
Germania, Catalonia, Portugal, Ireland, England".[2] The vast empire of the
Spanish Habsburgs suffered more than most, with the kingdom of Portugal
declaring independence in 1640, followed shortly afterwards by Catalonia's
switch of allegiance to France. A few years later in 1647, a revolt in Naples dealt
the Habsburgs, already threatened with financial bankruptcy, a further blow.[3]
The rulers of multiple kingdoms everywhere (including Charles Stuart) proved
particularly vulnerable to a variety of destabilising developments.

The causes of this general crisis remain a subject of intense debate among
historical scholars, with the argument focused primarily on the relationship
between society and the state. The growth of central government, as a result of
economic expansion and the demands of early modern warfare, created new
tensions. The existing ruling classes often came to view governmental policies as
dangerously innovative, even revolutionary, undermining their traditional role
in society.[4] During the early part of the seventeenth century the landed elite in

---

1 Reprinted in Bindon, S.H. (ed.), *The historical works of the right reverend Nicholas French
D.D.*, vol. 2, p. 151. 2 Ohlmeyer, Jane (ed.), *Ireland from independence to occupation, 1641-1660*
(Cambridge 1995) p. 1. 3 The main revolts during the 1640s are neatly chronicled in a single
volume in Merriman, R.B., *Six contemporaneous revolutions* (Oxford 1938). 4 According to
Hobsbawn, the crisis was economic in origin, starting during the 1620s recession and reaching
its peak between the 1640s and the 1670s, before a recovery in the latter part of the century
restored some degree of stability. Trevor-Roper describes it as a crisis in the relationship
between society and the state, caused primarily by the expansion of a parasitic bureaucracy.

Ireland shared these fears. They perceived the dynamic administration of Thomas Wentworth as threatening customary laws, as well as the existing social balance in Irish society. The lord deputy targeted catholics and protestants, settlers and natives, in his drive to maximise the return to royal coffers. As a result, he succeeded (remarkably) in alienating politicians and interest groups across the ethnic and religious divide, a fact which ultimately contributed to his downfall.[5]

The aggressive anti-catholic posturing of Scottish covenanters and the Westminster parliament exacerbated the feelings of insecurity among catholic land owners in Ireland. Already excluded from public office, they now faced the prospect of losing their valuable estates along with any remaining political influence. Below them, the small farmers and landless peasants (almost exclusively catholic) suffered increasing hardship as the economy slumped in the late 1630s. In normal circumstances the ordering of society in early modern Ireland, as elsewhere in Europe, tended to militate against cross-class solidarity.[6] By the early 1640s, however, the indebtedness of landholders, the discontent of the lower social orders and the common threat to their identity, helped Irish catholics overcome many of these social barriers and create a powerful alliance in the confederate association.

But is it possible to describe the confederates as nationalists, or were they merely disgruntled catholic subjects? Nineteenth century accounts, in portraying Irish history as a relentless march towards self-determination, oversimplified and thus discredited a complex phenomenon. Modern historians, rejecting this idealised version of events, have denied the possibility of any nationalist tendencies in Ireland prior to the United Irishmen in the 1790s.[7] Elliott, however, identifies

Such growth could only be tolerated in a society expanding in wealth and numbers, which was clearly not the case in the Spanish empire (or indeed the Stuart kingdoms). According to Trevor-Roper, governments, not their opponents, constituted the revolutionary element in society. This thesis is developed by Parker and Steensgaard, both of whom claim that the innovative policies of government, especially in the fields of finance and religion, caused the general crisis. Elliott argues that the increased scale of warfare created problems of a new magnitude, forcing governments to exercise greater control over the state. The methods employed in this task, however, failed to provide sufficient resources to ensure obedience to their will, leading to conflict. For writings on the "general crisis" see in particular two collections of essays, Aston, T. (ed.), *Crisis in Europe 1560-1660* (London 1965), and Parker, G. and Smith, L.M. (eds), *The general crisis of the seventeenth century* (London 1978). **5** Clarke, A., "Ireland and the general crisis", *Past and present*, no. 48 (Aug. 1970) pp 79-99; Wentworth's tenure in Ireland is described in detail in Kearney, H., *Strafford in Ireland* (1989). **6** Clarke describes how the gentry in Ireland was comprised of social equals of different religious and national origins. Clarke, "Ireland and the general crisis" pp 89-90. According to Gillespie the Irish economy was in poor shape by late 1641, due to political problems and a succession of poor harvests. Gillespie, "Irish economy", *Independence to occupation* p. 162. **7** According to Foster, for example, the confederates "were very far from nationalist revolutionaries, even if increased parliamentary

a new phenomenon in the early modern Europe, which he describes as corporate or national constitutionalism. This emerged essentially as the preserve of the dominant social group in the state, acting as defenders of a community whose rights and liberties were enshrined in a written constitution or a body of law. Not surprisingly lawyers played a leading role in all of this, helping to formulate the concept that each nation had a distinct historical or constitutional identity.[8]

Elliott also refers to the increasing usage of the term "patria" from the sixteenth century onwards, but cautions that supposed allegiances to national communities sometimes turn out to be nothing of the kind.[9] Morgan argues that in Ireland the ideology of "patria" first emerged in the mid-sixteenth century and became closely linked with the counter-reformation movement. This confessional nationalism, originating in the catholic colonial community, was adopted by Hugh O'Neill in the 1590s, but traditional Pale hostility towards the Ulster Irish prevented the creation of a broad nationalist movement.[10] The ideology did not die with O'Neill's defeat however, but prospered among exiled clergy and soldiers on the continent.

In Ireland itself the political elite (both catholic and protestant) aggressively defended the constitutional privileges of the Irish kingdom from the impositions of Westminster. During the 1640-1 parliament Patrick Darcy argued that Ireland was a separate and distinct kingdom, though subject to the crown of England. This doctrine received broad support across the political and religious divide, although the outbreak of the rebellion in October 1641 split Irish politics along sectarian lines once again. Nonetheless, the protestant community (as well as confederate catholics) continued to support the idea of Irish parliamentary independence throughout the 1640s and beyond.[11]

The national constitutionalism of the elite, combined with the widespread resentment of the religious policies of the state, produced a common patriotism among Irish catholics, particularly after the outbreak of the Ulster rising.[12] Richard Bellings described how those attending the historic meeting on the Hill

independence was an important part of the package". Foster, Roy, *Modern Ireland 1600-1972* (London 1988) p. 96. **8** Elliott, "Revolution and continuity", *General crisis* pp 110-33. Lawyers were also to play a crucial role in the development of the confederate association. See chapter 7 p. 213. **9** Elliott gives as one example the rebels of Ghent in 1578, who spoke of their "patrie", and referred to themselves as "patriotes". Elliott, "Revolution and continuity", *General crisis*, Parker and Smith (eds), pp 121-2. **10** Morgan, Hiram, "Faith and fatherland in sixteenth-century Ireland", *History Ireland*, vol. 3, no. 2 (summer 1995) pp 13-20. **11** Darcy, Patrick, *An argument delivered* ... (1643); See Clarke, "Colonial constitutional attitudes" pp 357-75. **12** The threat from Westminster and Scotland is referred to in all early petitions of the rebels. For example, the remonstrance of the catholics of Ireland on 28 December 1641 (Gilbert [ed.], *Contemporary history*, i, pp 360-1). In their demands presented to the king in Oxford on 28 March 1644, the confederates declared that "the parliament of Ireland is a free parliament of itself, independent of and not subordinate to the parliament of England; and that the subjects of Ireland are immediately subject to your Majesty as in right of your crown".

of Crofty in December 1641, greeted with wild applause Rory O'More's statement that the inhabitants of Ulster and the Pale belonged to "the same religion
and the same nation".[13] The catholic hierarchy eagerly embraced the concept of a
catholic Irish identity, declaring that any war fought to defend the catholic religion and the liberties of the kingdom was both "lawful and just".[14] The confessional nationalim of the clergy, however, owed more to developments on the
continent than in Ireland itself.

Lay confederates, although they initially formed a catholic association for
mutual protection, for the most part espoused an inclusive form of national
identity. They insisted that the king make no distinction between his Irish subjects on the basis of ethnicity or Christian denomination, treating all equally
before the law. The confederate motto, "Hiberni unanimes pro Deo Rege et
Patria", which means literally "Irishmen of one mind for God, King and
Country", perfectly epitomised this ideal.[15] The confederates national vision
incorporated the entire kingdom of Ireland, and all the people living there. This
fact often brought the confederate civil government into conflict with elements
of the catholic hierarchy, especially the papal nuncio, Rinuccini, who strongly
disapproved of the doctrine of inclusiveness.[16]

Place of birth, rather than blood, now provided the essential criterion for
membership of the Irish nation.[17] As a confederate delegation explained to the
marquis of Ormond during negotiations in 1644, "for he that is born in Ireland,
though his parents and all his ancestors were aliens, nay if his parents are Indians
or Turks, if converted to Christianity, is an Irishman as fully as if his ancestors
were born here for thousands of years and by the laws of England, as capable of
the liberties of a subject".[18] This remarkable statement, promoting an inclusive

Gilbert (ed.), *Irish confederation*, iii, pp 128-33. **13** The close social links between the leaders of
the Ulster rising and the Pale gentry undoubtedly reinforced this sense of common identity.
Bellings' History in Gilbert (ed.), *Irish confederation*, i, p. 37. **14** This declaration was made at
a meeting of the ecclesiastical congregation in May 1642. Acts of the ecclesiastical congregation, 10-13 May 1642 (BL Stowe Mss 82 ff 271-4). **15** This motto appeared on various official
confederate documents and flags. Moran (ed.), *Spicilegium Ossoriense*, vol. 2, pp 17-18. Father
Ignatius Fennessy, the Franciscan librarian in Killiney, clarifies the exact meaning of the motto
in a letter to *History Ireland*, vol. 2, no. 3 (Autumn 1994) p. 9. **16** In November 1647, for
example, he bitterly criticised an edict of the supreme council, signed by the bishop of Ferns
amongst others, offering an opportunity to heretics to join the confederate ranks. Rinuccini to
Panzirolo, 3 Nov. 1647 (Aiazza [ed.], *Embassy* p. 327). **17** John Morrill, in a recent essay, writes
how in "Ireland and in the Western Highlands, the sense of Gaelic and of sept or clan identity
retreated as a sense of inhabitant-of-Ireland and inhabitant-of-Scotland identity strengthened". Morrill, John, "Historical introduction and overview: The un-English civil war", *Celtic
dimensions*, (ed.) John Young, p. 13. It is interesting to note that the recent amendment to article 2 of the 1937 Irish constitution seeks to redefine Irishness according to non-territorial crite-
ria. **18** Confederate explanation of propositions, 28 Sept. 1644 (Gilbert [ed.], *Irish confederation*, iii, pp 298-305). While on one level asserting a separate national identity, the confederates
nonetheless favoured the continued observance of English common law, except of course

vision of Irishness, predates by almost 150 years Wolfe Tone's own efforts at uniting catholic, protestant and dissenter.[19]

While recognising their constitutional links with the crown of England, leading confederates at the same time perceived themselves first and foremost as
Irishmen. Owen Roe O'Neill, for example, reminded his troops that "they were
no mercenary soldiers but natives of the kingdom", while Thomas Preston, in an
early appeal to Clanricarde to join the confederate association, wrote "remember
you are an Irishman". Even among the lower social orders evidence exists of the
emergence of a common national identity. The French traveller, Francois le
Gouz, wrote in 1644 that invariably the people he met on his journey through
the kingdom described themselves as *Éireannach*.[20]

Despite the confederates' attempts at forging a common Irish identity, local
and provincial sentiment continued to exercise an important influence (as they
still do today). Nonetheless, the shared experience of creating, and maintaining,
an alternative government during the 1640s, helped break down many traditional barriers among the catholic population at least. The alliance proved fragile at
times, however, as the leadership in Kilkenny played a delicate balancing act,
attempting to control social unrest while negotiating a settlement with the state
which would in essence preserve the existing order. As Elliott argues, a group
(like the confederate leadership) that thinks in terms of restoration of traditional
rights is likely to balk at innovation.[21] This fact limited the scope of confederate
actions, but their attempts to return to the "old ways" often led to startling new
departures, so that the rebellion on occasion assumed the characteristics of a revolution.

Whether events in Ireland in the 1640s constituted a rebellion or a revolution
is a important and complex question. The confederates strongly objected to the
term "rebels", insisting they only fought to defend the royal prerogative, reli-

where it discriminated against catholics. Orders of the general assembly, 24 Oct. 1642 (BL Add
Mss 4781 ff 4-11). **19** The confederates, although suspicious of radical strains in protestantism,
were not adverse to an alliance with the established church. A declaration in 1644 states clearly "that each man known to be a moderate conformable protestant, may as well as the Roman
Catholic respectively, and enjoy their freedom of their own religion, and peaceably and quiet-
ly enjoy their own estates, so far forth as they or any of them shall join with us". *A declaration
of the lords and gentry and others of the provinces of Leinster and Munster in the realm of Ireland
of their intentions towards the English and Scottish protestants inhabiting in the kingdom* London
1644 (R.I.A. vol. 41, box 37, tract 1). **20** Lenihan, "Catholic confederacy" p. 13; Journal of
Colonel Henry McTully O'Neill, *Desiderata curiosa Hibernica* [Lodge, John (ed.)], vol. 2 p.
497; Preston to Clanricarde, 18 Jan. 1643 (Carte, *Ormond*, v, pp 384-5). **21** The correspondence of the catholic gentry immediately after the outbreak of the rebellion illustrates how
concerned they were at the breakdown in social order. Muskerry to the earl of Barrymore, 17
March 1642 (BL Add Mss 25,277 f.58); Clanricarde to Charles Coote, 17 March 1642 (Bourke,
*Clanricarde memoirs* p. 95); Elliott, "Revolution and continuity", *General crisis*, Parker and
Smith (eds), p. 129.

gious freedom and the constitution of the kingdom.[22] Almost all rebels in the early modern period, however, claimed to be loyal subjects, fighting in defence of traditional privileges. Heinz Lubasz provides an excellent and succinct definition of the difference between a rebellion and a revolution. He identifies a rebellion as opposition directed at particular laws, practices or individuals, which aims at specific and limited change (for example the replacement of the personnel of government) rather than the transformation of the system of domination. A revolution occurs when the demand for the particular is replaced by demands for more general and fundamental change.[23]

The problem in Ireland is that a number of different and sometimes competing processes occurred almost simultaneously. The initial uprising on 22 October 1641 was in essence a pre-emptive strike by catholic Ulster landowners, to counter the perceived threat from the English parliament and Scottish covenanters. In the process, they hoped to create a strong bargaining position for themselves in subsequent negotiations with the king. The failure to capture Dublin, the administrative centre of the kingdom, created a political vacuum in rebel held areas, as increasing numbers of people took advantage of the collapse of authority to settle old scores and overturn the plantation policies of successive administrations. This development threatened to destroy the existing social order, so that many catholic landowners felt obliged to join the rebels or be swept away by them. What Charles Tilly has termed a revolutionary situation began to emerge, with the existing polity fragmenting into two or more blocs.[24]

The early months of the uprising were characterised by confusion and chaos, as the disturbances began to spread throughout the country. Catholic leaders, terrified of the consequences of a truly populist uprising, but at the same time repulsed by the violent counter measures of the state, desperately sought to regain the political initiative. They gradually succeeded during the course of 1642, actively supported by the catholic clergy, whose collaboration in imposing an oath of association proved crucial to that success.[25]

---

**22** The first official contacts between the confederates and the royal commissioners were almost cancelled because of the latter's use of the term "rebels" to describe the Irish catholics in arms. The supreme council wrote to the commissioners on 9 Feb. 1643, refusing to meet, "until that foul imputation of rebellion, most undeservedly laid to our charge be taken away". They only relented when informed that the king himself had used the term in the original commission. Gilbert (ed.), *Irish confederation*, ii, pp 157-9, 163-4. **23** In addition, a revolution, to be more than a sequence of violent events, most result in effective change for a sustained period, even if the old power system eventually reasserts itself. Lubasz, Heinz, *Revolutions in modern European history* (New York 1966) pp 1-7. **24** Tilly, Charles, *European revolutions 1492-1992* (Oxford 1993) p. 10. **25** This "two risings" theory was first espoused by the catholic elite to distance themselves from the bloody consequences of the initial revolt. Writers like Nicholas Plunkett explained how the rising "was only the act of a few persons of broken and desperate fortunes", followed by "a rude multitude". Presentation by Nicholas Plunkett, Sept. 1661 (BL Add Mss 4,781 ff 155-61). Although this interpretation is largely accurate, recent

Between 1642 and 1649 the confederates controlled vast tracts of the kingdom including many of the principal cities. They adopted radical measures to retain (and legitimise) control over the waging of war. These measures included providing essential governmental and judicial services at both central and local levels. The confederates established a national parliament (the general assembly) which provided a forum for political debate, implemented various policy measures (including taxation), and initiated contacts with foreign courts.[26] An elaborate administrative system, with councils at national, provincial and county level, further underpinned the representative nature of their government. Against the backdrop of a major conflict, confederate achievements in this area proved truly remarkable.

The fact that the confederates never claimed sovereignty, and were ultimately prepared to accept Charles as head of state, does not negate the radical nature of their actions.[27] The outbreak of civil war in England enabled the regime in Kilkenny to seek an alliance with the king against their common enemy, the English parliament. From early 1643 onwards, with a brief interlude in late 1646, confederates of all political persuasions sought an accommodation with the state; therefore they can hardly be termed revolutionaries.[28]

The internal dynamics of the confederate association during this period of self-rule warrants particular examination. The traditional classification of the confederates into two hostile groups, old English versus native Irish, has led many historians to pay insufficient attention to the question of how the political process within the association actually operated. As a result, the emergence of a highly influential group of moderates, led by Nicholas Plunkett, which sought to chart a political course between the extremes of the clerical party and peace party, has not hitherto been recognised.

In an attempt to properly survey the political landscape of the 1640s it is necessary to start with the basic question of identity: who were the confederate

research shows that many of the leaders at local level came from the gentry class, and not from the lower social orders. Lenihan, "Catholic confederacy" p. 80. Nonetheless, the widespread perception at the time was that the rising had got out of control, hence the efforts by the Catholic Church and others to re-establish some form of order throughout 1642. **26** The parliament in 1613-15 was the first to include representatives of all 32 counties, but as with those of 1634-5 and 1640-1, the protestants had an artificially created majority. The figures are given in Clarke, *Old English in Ireland* p. 255. The confederate general assemblies at least reflected the numerical domination of catholics in the kingdom of Ireland, if not the social structure. **27** Confederate sensitivity on the issue of sovereignty was reciprocated at the English court. On 30 May 1645, for example, the Venetian ambassador in France reported that Queen Henrietta Maria opposed the idea of the papal nuncio (Rinuccini) residing in Ireland, as such a move "amounts in a way to declaring them sovereign". Gio. Battista Nani to the doge and senate, 30 May 1645 (*Calendar of state papers, Venetian*, vol. 26, p. 192). **28** Even at the height of its success, during the offensive against Dublin in late 1646, the clerical faction was still prepared to contemplate a further deal with the royalists. See chapter 4 p. 121f.

catholics? Previous accounts have answered this question in predominantly ethnic or religious terms. Internal confederate tensions have been ascribed to antipathy between the old English and native Irish, primarily over the terms of a religious and political settlement with the king.[29] There is unquestionably an element of truth in such claims, enough at any rate to give them some credibility. It is too simplistic, however, to ascribe confederate tensions to these factors alone.

Among the confederate landowning elite, intermarriage and shared interests had broken down traditional racial barriers to the extent that the native Irish Donough MacCarthy, Viscount Muskerry, was accepted without question as the head of the so-called old English party. The confederates made strenuous efforts to ensure ethnic harmony within their ranks, and problems more usually arose along class lines. Numerous accounts survive of the excesses of the "rude multitude" or "landless sort" by both native Irish and old English leaders.[30] The objections expressed towards the lower classes were based on the practical threat they posed to the existing social order, rather than on ethnic considerations.

Confederate criticisms of the Ulster forces of Owen Roe O'Neill support this hypothesis. The widespread hostility displayed towards them arose primarily because of their destructive behaviour during campaigns. They were vilified by people as diverse as Clanricarde and the papal nuncio, Rinuccini, as well as by more moderate figures like Nicholas Plunkett. The creaghts accompanying O'Neill also suffered physical attacks by bands of peasants in Connacht.[31] Ulster landowners, however, and indeed the native Irish of other provinces, do not appear to have been targeted in a similar manner.

While it is evident that the confederate association did not function as a wholly homogeneous entity, a remarkable degree of unanimity emerged on constitutional issues. A return to the old Gaelic political order held no appeal for conservative catholic landowners of either ethnic background. Their loyalty to

**29** Corish, "Ormond, Rinuccini, and the confederates, 1645-9", *NHI*, iii, pp 317-35; Jane Ohlmeyer talks of the confederate ranks being "irremediably split" between the old English and the old Irish. Ohlmeyer, *Civil war and restoration* p. 182.    **30** Henry McTully O'Neill, an officer in Owen Roe O'Neill's army, blamed many of the early atrocities of the rebellion on "some of the loosest of the Irish rabble". Journal of Henry McTully O'Neill, *Desiderata curiosa Hibernica*, vol. 2, p. 485. The earl of Clanricarde used similar language in November 1641, condemning the rebels as "loose people". Clanricarde to the earl of Essex, 15 Nov. 1641 (Bourke, *Clanricarde memoirs* p. 14). Bellings, colourful as ever, described attempts by the confederates to contain "the rascal multitude". Bellings' History in Gilbert (ed.), *Irish confederation*, i, pp 14-5.    **31** In February 1644, Clanricarde reported to Taaffe the destruction caused in Sligo by "those rude, barbarous people", while Rinuccini also denounced them as "barbarous". Clanricarde to Taaffe, 23 Feb. 1644 (Lowe [ed.], *Clanricarde letter-book* p. 46); Report on the proceedings of Owen O'Neill, May 1647 (Aiazza [ed.], *Embassy* pp 281-4). During the early part of 1647 the excesses committed by the Ulster troops near Kilkenny shocked the moderate leadership. Plunkett informed Thomas Preston of their departure, "after much evil committed". Plunkett to Preston, 27 April 1647 (PRO SP Ire. 263/124 f.209).

the crown of England and its appendage, the kingdom of Ireland, did not waver during all the upheavals of the 1640s.[32] The challenge facing the leadership in Kilkenny was how to ensure that any future peace treaty would be adhered to by Charles I.

Confederate politics divided primarily, as in England and Scotland, over the issue of settlement terms with the king. However, the concept of political parties controlled by a leader with a specific ideology or agenda was completely alien to the seventeenth century. In the confederate general assembly, as at Westminster, "parties" consisted of loose groups of individuals, dominated by one or two personalities, sharing a common goal. The vast majority of members remained uncommitted, ready to be swayed by the arguments of the day and generally more concerned with local rather than national issues.[33] The problem is to correctly identify the various groupings in Kilkenny during the 1640s.

In fact, three main power blocs existed in confederate politics, rather than two as is traditionally argued. These were the peace faction, the clerical faction, and a small but influential group of non-aligned moderates.[34] The peace faction favoured a limited settlement that would guarantee religious toleration, allowing catholics to worship in private without hindrance. The primary concern of its leaders was to preserve their estates and to gain access to public office. On the question of safeguards, they wanted royal concessions to be ratified in the Irish parliament, but on certain issues they accepted the good faith of both the king and his Irish deputy, James Butler, the marquis of Ormond.

The leaders of the peace faction had extensive parliamentary and legal experience, and provided an element of continuity in Irish political life. They dominated proceedings in Kilkenny until the signing of the first Ormond treaty in August 1646. Principal among them were Viscounts Mountgarret and Muskerry, Richard Bellings, Gerald Fennell and Geoffrey Browne. Their close links with the marquis of Ormond influenced many contemporaries (and ultimately historians) to christen the peace faction "Ormondists".[35] This term is misleading how-

---

**32** In 1661 Nicholas Plunkett stressed the point, in a petition to Charles II, that at no time did Kilkenny enter into a treaty abroad that would have diminished royal rights in Ireland. Presentation by Nicholas Plunkett, Sept. 1661 (BL Add Mss 4,781 ff 155-61). Although this statement is technically correct, the confederates *were* willing to offer the protectorship of the kingdom to Innocent X in return for massive financial and military aid. See instructions given by the supreme council to the agents travelling to Rome in January 1648 (BL Stowe Mss 82 ff 155-6). **33** This was true also at Westminster. Hexter, *Reign of King Pym* pp 63-7. See also Morrill, *Revolt of the provinces* p. 93. **34** Cregan believed confederate politics did not consist of rival parties differentiated by racial origin or any one factor. Instead there existed a series of interlocking and complicated relationships, with individual confederates divided on a whole series of issues, including provincial and personal rivalries. Cregan, "Confederate catholics" pp 506-9. Such an interpretation, however, precludes the possibility of collective political objectives within the association as can readily be substantiated by an examination of the surviving documentation. **35** The papal nuncio, Rinuccini, and other opponents of the peace faction,

ever, as securing an acceptable peace, rather than satisfying the political ambitions of the lord lieutenant, was the primary motivation for this group. Another
description, "old English", is equally flawed, as apart from Muskerry a number
of native Irish (including Donough O'Callaghan and Daniel O'Brien) featured
prominently in this faction.

On the opposite political wing the clerical faction emerged as an increasingly
vocal element in confederate politics after 1644. This group favoured a more radical religious settlement, arguing (not illogically) that only a full restoration of
the Roman Catholic Church, along with an independent Irish parliament, could
guarantee security for catholics.[36] After the collapse of the first Ormond peace in
August 1646, the clericalists (under the dynamic leadership of the papal nuncio,
Rinuccini) briefly seized power and adopted an aggressive military strategy to
gain control of the entire kingdom. Rinuccini, at least at first, could rely on the
support of the majority of the bishops, but eventually became more closely associated with Owen Roe O'Neill and the Ulster Irish.

This alliance between Rinuccini and O'Neill did not restrict support for the
clerical faction to one particular ethnic group. True, the majority of the nuncio's
adherents came from native Irish backgrounds, but they also included Oliver
Plunkett, Lord Louth, Piers Butler of Moneyhore and many others of old
English extraction. The more radical politics of the clerical faction found particular favour among the dispossessed catholics (particularly the Ulster exiles), who
hoped thereby to regain their estates. The powerful influence of the priests at
local level also ensured a groundswell of popular support.

Between both extremes stood a group of moderates, led by Nicholas
Plunkett, a leading Pale politician. Plunkett had attempted to steer a middle
course from the early days of the uprising, and only committed himself to the
confederate association at the meeting of the general assembly in October 1642.
Plunkett's popularity can be gauged from the fact that, despite this initial reluctance, assembly members still elected him to the powerful position of chairman.
He retained the post in every subsequent assembly, except for the last, summoned during his absence in Rome.

Plunkett also sat on all nine supreme councils between 1642 and 1649, while
as a member of the crucial committee of treaty he helped negotiate both the
Glamorgan and Ormond treaties. In August 1646, sent by the council to moder-

used the terms "Ormondist" or "Ormond's faction" in a derogatory sense, as a means of iden-
tifying the group of individuals who favoured a speedy settlement with the marquis of
Ormond. *Aphorismical discovery* in Gilbert (ed.), *Contemporary history*, i, p. 40;
Considerations upon the future assembly, 30 Dec. 1646 (Aiazza [ed.], *Embassy* p. 238);
O'Ferrall and O'Connell (eds), *Commentarius*, i, p. 425. Considering the dominance of the
Butler family in Irish politics, such links were somewhat inevitable. **36** The clerical congrega-
tion specifically listed their demands to the general assembly on 10 January 1647 (Bodl. Carte
Mss 20 ff 100-1).

ate clerical opposition to peace, he switched sides in a move which greatly facilitated Rinuccini's seizure of power. For the next twelve months however, Plunkett
and his moderate allies effectively dictated confederate strategy, and set the agenda for the final peace negotiations with the marquis of Ormond in late 1648. No
other confederate can match Plunkett's record of active involvement and political influence, a remarkable demonstration in the art of survival.

Despite his high political profile and controversial switch of allegiance in
1646, Plunkett appears to have alienated few people, even among those confederate colleagues who opposed him politically. Although Rinuccini blamed him
retrospectively for the collapse of clerical supremacy, the nuncio's final report
expressed more disappointment than bitterness. Before 1646 at least, Ormond
had no objections to dealing with Plunkett, despite the latter's reputation for
extreme catholic devotion.[37] This enduring ability to appeal to all sides enabled
Plunkett to exploit the widespread dissatisfaction with the excesses of the more
extreme factions, and to move the confederate association towards the political
middle ground.

The identity and influence of other leading moderates is more difficult to
establish, as they usually exercised that influence by supporting either the peace
or clerical factions. Plunkett's political allies rarely united as a coherent body,
and were apt to change their allegiances according to the circumstances at a
given time. This group included such diverse figures as Roebuck Lynch from
Galway, Randal MacDonnell, earl of Antrim, and Phelim O'Neill of Ulster,
along with an assortment of the more moderate bishops, principal among them
the influential John Bourke, archbishop of Tuam.

Plunkett, however, would not have achieved much without the consistent
support of Patrick Darcy and Bishop French. Plunkett and Darcy enjoyed a
common legal and parliamentary background, and joined forces during the early
days of the uprising. Darcy's power base lay in the town of Galway, which exercised a hugely disproportionate influence on confederate politics. Bishop French
only emerged onto the political scene in 1645 as a spokesman for the clerical faction, but he provided an invaluable link between the moderates and the more
conciliatory clerics. Politically, the triumvirate of Plunkett, Darcy and French
proved more than a match for their confederate opponents.

Plunkett and his associates not only sought an acceptable compromise agreement with the king in the interests of confederate unity, but also advocated radical reforms of the political system in Kilkenny. Their rise to prominence coincided with, and was enhanced by, that of the general assembly. According to the
1642 "model of government", the confederate legislature appeared at the apex of

37 Report on the affairs of Ireland, 1649 (Aiazza [ed.], *Embassy* pp 509-11). Ormond wrote to
Muskerry in 1646 that Plunkett was the ideal choice to conduct negotiations for the confederates. Ormond to Muskerry, 22 April 1646 (Bodl. Carte Mss 17 f.208).

the new political structure with ultimate responsibility for peace or war.[38] In reality, however, the supreme council, meeting in continuous session, assumed a dominant role.[39] Moreover, within the council itself, the peace party wielded considerable influence, increasingly to the exclusion of all others. The creation of a committee to conduct negotiations with Ormond further concentrated power in a few hands. Plunkett and his associates considered these developments harmful and divisive; their reforms proposed to remedy the situation by restoring control to the general assembly.

The reform measures adopted by the general assembly between June 1644 and November 1647 went a long way towards making the various councils and officials more accountable for their actions.[40] By advocating the notion of the primacy of the legislature over the executive branch of government, Nicholas Plunkett promoted the middle path of consensus politics. In that respect the summer of 1646 appears to have been something of a watershed. Prior to that Plunkett's loyalties may have been divided, serving both as chairman of the assembly and as a leading peace negotiator on the committee of treaty. After the rejection of the Ormond peace however, in August of that year, he became an undeviating advocate of unity and compromise, a popular policy with the majority of confederates.

Unfortunately for the confederates, the royalist commander, the marquis of Ormond did not reciprocate the flexibility and moderation shown by the new moderate leadership in Kilkenny. The marquis has excited little critical comment among modern historians, apparently happy to accept the image created by his eighteenth century biographer, Thomas Carte, of an honourable man, operating in extremely difficult circumstances.[41] Contemporary critics, however, described in detail Ormond's destructive role during the 1640s, and an examination of the peace process illustrates clearly that the lord lieutenant has a case to answer.[42]

Instead of promoting peace, Ormond encouraged confederate divisions by refusing to make any concessions on religious issues.[43] Despite clear evidence of internal tensions in Kilkenny by early 1646, he continued to insist on a treaty which was totally unacceptable to the catholic clergy, thus provoking a major

38 Orders of the general assembly met at Kilkenny, 24 Oct. 1642 (BL Add Mss 4,781 ff 4-11). 39 This fact was acknowledged by Richard Bellings in his memoirs. Bellings' History in Gilbert (ed.), *Irish confederation*, iii, p. 3. 40 For various reform documents see (1644) Marsh's Library Mss z 3.1.3; (1646) Bodl. Carte Mss 16 ff 470-80; (1647) Gilbert (ed.), *Irish confederation*, vi, pp 208-23. 41 Carte, Thomas, *History of the life of James the first duke of Ormond*, 6 vols (Oxford 1851). Beckett's hagiography is a good example of the favourable treatment the duke has received of late. Beckett, J.C., *The cavalier duke: A life of James Butler first duke of Ormond, 1610-1688* (Belfast 1990). 42 Bishop French, for example, bitterly criticised Ormond as the man that "let fall the venomous apple of discord in the middle of that united body". Bindon (ed.), *Historical works*, vol. 2, p. 151. 43 Clanricarde's letters from the 1645 general assembly describe the confederate frustration at delays in the treaty, and the role of the clergy in fomenting dissatisfaction. See Lowe (ed.), *Clanricarde letter-book* pp 155-76.

crisis in August 1646. His misdirected strategy substantially contributed to the failure to provide the king with any military assistance from Ireland. Ormond compounded this failing by surrendering Dublin to the English parliament in July 1647. This action, prompted by a variety of complex reasons, proved catastrophic for royalist interests in the kingdom, and delayed for almost a further two years a peace settlement in Ireland.

Hexter is credited with identifying the emergence of a middle party at Westminster in the early 1640s, led by John Pym.[44] Nicholas Plunkett played a similarly pivotal role in confederate Ireland, emerging in the process as one of the most influential Irish catholic politicians of the seventeenth century. His espousal of consensus politics, as well as his advocacy of the primacy of the legislature (and the need for an accountable executive), illustrate a level of political sophistication not hitherto associated with the confederate period. After years in exile during the Cromwellian era, Plunkett returned to prominence during the restoration period as a spokesman for Irish catholic landowners. Charles II had some sympathy for their plight, but vested interests, none more powerful than the marquis of Ormond himself, restricted the extent of the catholic recovery.[45]

The ensuing political process essentially degenerated into a sordid scramble for land, with Ormond's old confederate allies in the peace faction emerging as the main catholic beneficiaries.[46] Given the limited and disappointing nature of the settlement, it is hardly surprising that widespread grievances persisted. Catholic landowners slowly expanded their holdings during the reign of Charles II, while the succession of his catholic brother, James, further raised their hopes. James II fled from England in 1688 and arrived in Ireland the following year as a first step to regaining his throne. The parliament held in Dublin in 1689 under his authority was the last to admit catholics until the Mansion House meeting in January 1919.

The Jacobite parliament resurrected much of the old confederate programme, calling for the suspension of Poynings' law, significant religious concessions and a reversal of the acts of settlement.[47] Despite his desperate need for

---

**44** Hexter, *Reign of King Pym* (1941).  **45** Documents of 1660s relating to the settlement of Ireland (RIA Mss H.V.I ). BL Add Mss 4,781 is another copy of the same documents.  **46** Richard Bellings, Geoffrey Browne, Lucas Dillon, Geoffrey Fennell were well looked after by Ormond. The full list of those who recovered their estates is contained in the appendix to the 19th report of the deputy keeper of the public records in Ireland pp 41-87. Plunkett was also declared innocent, and recovered some land though not his principal residence near Trim. **47** Simms, J.G., *Jacobite Ireland, 1685-91* (London 1969) and *The Jacobite parliament of 1689*, Irish history series, no. 6 (Dundalk 1974). See also his two chapters in *NHI*, iii, pp 420-453 and pp 478-508. Simms is the only historian to have examined the Jacobite parliament in any detail. It appears that only one confederate, Alexander MacDonnell, sat in the 1689 parliament. He attended numerous general assemblies, and was a member of the last six supreme councils. He succeeded his brother, Randal, as marquis of Antrim in 1683, and sat in the

Irish catholic support, James II proved every bit as reluctant as his father to grant significant concessions. In any event, the crushing defeat at Aughrim in July 1691 destroyed any prospect of a catholic recovery, while the subsequent Williamite land settlement and the implementation of a more repressive set of penal laws heralded a new age of protestant colonial domination. Nicholas Plunkett, who died in 1680, did not live to see the final political extinction of the cause he served so well.

House of Lords in 1689. Cregan, D.F., "Confederation of Kilkenny" (PhD thesis) p. 336, n. 1.

# General assembly attendance

の

The general assembly of the confederate catholics of Ireland met on nine occasions between August 1642 and January 1649. Elections to the assembly were based on the 1542 franchise act, excluding protestants voters, using existing parliamentary boundaries.[1] The Irish parliament had grown considerably during the early part of the seventeenth century with the creation of new peers and the addition of new boroughs, mainly in Ulster. Between 1613 and 1634, membership of the House of Lords trebled to 123 lords spiritual and temporal, with protestants constituting the vast majority. A total of 256 MPs was returned to the Commons in 1634, a 10 per cent increase on 1613 – 106 members from Leinster, 56 from Munster, 28 from Connacht and 66 from Ulster. Thomas Wentworth subsequently disenfranchised seven "catholic" boroughs, but the parliament effectively overturned this decision in 1640-1.[2]

The confederates' desire to model their government along parliamentary lines suggests that attendance figures at the confederate assemblies probably approximated those of the 1634 parliament, although this is impossible to verify in the absence of full electoral returns. Large areas of Ulster and parts of Connacht remained outside confederate control throughout the 1640s, and were probably under-represented as a result, while the major towns appear to have returned more than their share of members. Moreover, the proceedings of the assembly tended to be a bit chaotic, with numerous accusations of non-elected individuals sitting in on meetings.[3]

1 The question of the franchise is examined in chapter 7 p. 207f. 2 Two books examine parliamentary membership prior to 1641. Kearney, H., *Strafford in Ireland* pp 223-63 and Clarke, A., *Old English in Ireland* pp 255-61. See also McGrath, Bríd, "A biographical dictionary of the membership of the House of Commons 1640-1641". 3 General assembly representation is discussed in some detail in chapter 7, pp 205-17. Complaints about irregularities arose at almost every session. Galway for example returned at least 14 representatives to the first assembly in 1647 compared to 8 members of parliament in 1640-1. BL Add Mss 4,781 ff 12-34. Bellings criticised what he saw as an unusually large attendance at the same meeting, while admitting that little could be done to rectify the situation. Bellings' History in Gilbert (ed.), *Irish confederation*, vii, p. 1. See map 2 for an outline of the parliamentary constituencies.

The imprecise estimate of representation in the confederate assemblies is due mainly to the destruction of confederate records in 1711, when official attendance lists for the general assemblies perished (if they had ever existed). Until now, historians believed that only two lists of any sort had survived. Thomas Bourke, official printer to the confederates, printed the first of these for the assembly of July 1644. Bourke's original pamphlet no longer exists, but Peter Walsh reproduced a copy in his *History and vindication of the loyal formulary or Irish remonstrance* in 1674, as did J.T. Gilbert in the *History of the Irish confederation* two centuries later. As Walsh was copying from a printed source the information is presumably relatively accurate.[4] Gilbert also published the second attendance list in *History of the Irish confederation*, a shorter version of which first surfaced over a hundred years earlier in the supplement to a historical compilation (by yet another Thomas Bourke) entitled *Hibernia Dominicana*.[5] The origins and dating of this second list will be discussed at a later stage.

The 1644 document is reasonably straightforward, although a number of the names appear twice. Making allowances for this, a total of 13 bishops, 18 lords and 166 knights, citizens and burgesses attended the assembly in July of that year.[6] This seems a credible figure, although somewhat on the low side for the knights and burgesses. The assembly met primarily to select a committee of treaty to negotiate a peace settlement with the royalists. Many delegates may simply not have bothered to travel to perform such a relatively straightforward task. Furthermore, the confederate forces were in the process of launching a major offensive in Ulster, which would have engaged the energies of many members.[7]

The possibility exists, however, that the list is not complete. For example, a series of letters between the supreme council and Ormond in early 1645 reveal that James Sall attended the 1644 assembly and yet he is not recorded in the document – a simple printing error perhaps, or his name may have been purposely removed following his defection to the royalist side.[8] Another problem, apart from Sall's omission, concerns Bourke's inclusion of the names of lords "now absent, by reason of impediments", like the earl of Castlehaven who led the expedition into Ulster that summer.[9] Nonetheless, these anomalies aside, it is possible to accept the 1644 list as both authentic and accurate.

The second printed list is more detailed, giving the names and places of origin of all those people who subscribed to the revised confederate oath of associa-

4 Walsh, *Irish remonstrance*, appendix 1, pp 31-2; Gilbert (ed.), *Irish confederation*, iii, pp 212-16. 5 Gilbert (ed.), *Irish confederation*, ii, pp 212-19; Bourke, Thomas (ed.), *Hibernia Dominicana*, supplementum, pp 882-5. 6 Walsh, *Irish remonstrance*, appendix 1, pp 31-2. 7 This fact is confirmed by the low percentage of Ulster members at the assembly. See chapter 7 (table 2). 8 Supreme council to Ormond, 21 Jan. 1645 (Bodl. Carte Mss 13 f.476); Advice tendered by James Sall, 20 June 1644 (BL Stowe Mss 82 f.136); Cokayne, *Complete peerage*, vol. 6 (1926) p. 23. 9 Walsh, *Irish remonstrance*, appendix 1, p. 31,

tion (including the four religious articles). It relates, therefore, to the crucial assembly held early in 1647 (the date given in *Hibernia Dominicana*), and not 1643 as Gilbert suggested.[10] This list consists of 11 bishops, 16 lords and 292 commoners – very credible figures once again. Problems exist, however, with some of the names, principally those of Viscount Gormanston who died in July 1643, and Viscount Taaffe who did not take the confederate oath until the summer of 1647.[11] An examination of the manuscript in Dublin City Library (the one used by Gilbert), clearly establishes that Gormanston's inclusion was simply a transcribing error.[12] In the case of Taaffe, his name may well have been added to the existing list once he joined the confederate association.

The 1647 assembly list printed by Gilbert is part of a contemporary manuscript, consisting of four rolls, each one preceded by an oath of association. Near identical copies of the rolls survive in the British Library, Bodleian Library, and Royal Irish Academy, as well as the Dublin City Library.[13] The Cromwellian regime systematically assembled this information to incriminate leading Irish catholics, and the following statement appears at the end of each manuscript- "a true copy of an alphabet of the subscriptions made by the Irish to the oath of association, remaining in the chief remembrancers office".[14] Roll 1 (the one used by Gilbert) clearly belongs to the 1647 assembly because of the oath that precedes it. Roll 4, much shorter and probably incomplete, is impossible to connect with any particular meeting or assembly.

Rolls 2 and 3, however, appear to be full lists similar to roll 1, except that they contain the original oath of association, prior to the 1647 amendments. They are in fact assembly attendance sheets, although Gilbert failed to recognise them as such. This new identification increases the number of surviving lists from two to four. Each one includes the names of the leading confederates, lords spiritual and temporal, knights and burgesses from the four provinces. Assembly meetings constituted the only place where such a large and diverse group of confederates came together, at which time they would renew their oath of association. The difficult part involves connecting each roll with a particular assembly. By examining the names, it may prove possible to overcome this problem, although (as with the lists in Walsh and Gilbert) there are difficulties associated with this approach.

The evidence from roll 3, the more straightforward of the two, suggests that it

---

**10** Gilbert (ed.), *Irish confederation*, ii, pp 212-9; Bourke, Thomas (ed.), *Hibernia Dominicana*, supplementum, pp 882-5. All the names in the latter version, the shorter of the two, also appear in Gilbert's copy. **11** Taaffe took the oath of association on assuming command of the confederate Munster army, shortly after Ormond fled the country at the end of July 1647. Rinuccini to Panzirolo, 14 Aug. 1647 (Aiazza [ed.], *Embassy* p. 300). **12** Dublin City Library, Gilbert Collection Mss 219. **13** Bodl. Carte Mss 70 ff 64-85; BL Add Mss 4,781 ff 12-34, Mss 35,850 ff 12-34; RIA Mss H.VI.I ff 15-48; Dublin City Library, Gilbert Collection Mss 219. **14** *Public records in Ireland*, 20th report of the deputy keeper (Dublin 1888), appendix 4, pp 25-7.

is a list of those who attended the general assembly during the summer of 1645, at a time of intensive negotiations between the confederates, Ormond and Glamorgan. Whereas between 1642 and 1644 the general assembly usually sat for four weeks, this particular session in 1645 lasted over three and a half months, with a one month adjournment in July.[15] This might well explain the exceptionally large numbers (12 bishops, 13 lords and 417 knights, citizens and burgesses) in attendance. Furthermore, the controversy over the various peace treaties would also have ensured a large turnout, not all of them elected representatives.

The inclusion of the earl of Westmeath and Viscount Mayo supports this dating, as the former only joined the confederate association in 1645, while the latter was finally reconciled with Kilkenny in March of that year after a long conflict.[16] As Richard O'Connell is styled bishop of Ardfert, and Heber MacMahon bishop of Clogher (the consecration of both men took place in June 1643), their inclusion is consistent with a 1645 dating.[17] Furthermore, the meeting could not have been any later than the summer of 1645 because the name of Malachy O'Queely, archbishop of Tuam (killed in October) appears on the list, along with Piers Crosby who returned to Ireland from France in 1643, and died in a confederate prison in 1646.[18]

Against all that, Nicholas French is described as bishop of Ferns, although his consecration did not take place until December 1645. Nonetheless, he had been nominated to the post the previous January. The inclusion of Richard Bellings (abroad on a mission throughout 1645), and the absence of leading members of the committee of treaty (Viscount Muskerry, Alexander MacDonnell, Lucas Dillon, Geoffrey Browne, John Dillon and Dermot O'Brien) creates further difficulties. Bellings' may simply have added his name to the list on resuming the post of secretary to the council late in 1645 . Although the committee of treaty met in Kilkenny during the summer, the intense negotiations with Ormond and Glamorgan would have restricted their attendance at the assembly. Overall, the balance of evidence, from those included (rather than those absent), supports a 1645 dating.

Roll 2 (allowing for those who appear twice) consists of 8 bishops, 13 lords and 318 knights, citizens and burgesses. An examination of the names narrows the date range considerably, particularly those of William Tirry, bishop of Cork and Cloyne who died in March 1646 and Viscount Castlehaven who deserted to the royalists in August of that year.[19] This suggests that the roll belongs to one of the earlier assemblies, a fact confirmed by the presence of Malachy O'Queely, archbishop of Tuam. Two former members of parliament Adam Cusack and

15 See chapter 7 (table 1). 16 King's Inns, Prendergast papers, iv, ff 426-30; Clanricarde to Ormond, 10 March 1645 (Lowe [ed.], *Clanricarde letter-book* pp 148-50). 17 Cregan, "Counter-reformation episcopate" p. 87. 18 Thanks to Bríd McGrath for information on members of the 1634 parliament. 19 Cregan, "Counter-reformation episcopate" p. 87; Tuchet, *Castlehaven's review* pp 125-33.

Theobald Purcell, both of whom died in 1644, are also on the list, which pushes the date back further again.[20]

Richard O'Connell, described as bishop-elect of Ardfert, was nominated to this post in September 1641 and consecrated on 10 June 1643. This fact alone appears to limit the number of possible assemblies to just two, October 1642 or May 1643, although these meetings may well have been two different sessions of the same assembly.[21] Supporting the 1642/3 hypothesis is the naming of Heber MacMahon as bishop of Down and Connor, as his transfer to Clogher took place in late May 1643.[22] The inclusion of Gormanston yet again (on the Bodleian and British Library rolls, but not the Dublin City Library version) also suggests a pre-July 1643 date.

Evidence from the depositions in TCD favours May 1643 over November 1643, or indeed October 1642. William Stafford of Wexford, who admits to being at the Waterford assembly in November 1643 (and is named on roll 2) also identifies two colleagues, Thomas Rosceter and William Hore, who accompanied him, neither of whom are included on the list. Another deposition names the entire Connacht delegation to the first assembly, half of whom do not appear on any of the surviving lists.[23] The absence of a number of bishops (particularly the archbishop of Armagh) further diminishes the possibility that this is a list from October 1642.

Against that, Owen Roe O'Neill arrived in Waterford city for the assembly meeting, while the previous May the general remained in Ulster, allowing Phelim O'Neill to visit Kilkenny.[24] Owen Roe O'Neill, not Phelim, is listed on roll 2 which swings the balance of probalities towards a November 1643 dating. Furthermore, there are an unusually high number of delegates from Waterford city listed, while the mayor of Waterford, Francis Briver, is the only civilian given a title. The problem with this is that Briver's term of office expired in September 1642, prior to the first official assembly meeting, and he may well have been removed before that for his refusal to admit confederate forces into the city.[25] The confusion of evidence suggests therefore that roll 2 is probably an assembly list for the period 1642-3, but until more evidence comes to light it is impossible to be any more precise.

**20** McGrath, "Biographical dictionary" p. 122; Kearney, *Strafford in Ireland*, p. 242. **21** On 13 November 1642 the first general assembly declared "the twentieth day of May next to be the first day of the sitting of this Assembly after the adjournment of the present meeting". Gilbert (ed.), *Irish confederation*, ii, p. 86. It is unclear from the surviving documentation if elections were held prior to this meeting on 20 May 1643. See also Cregan, "Confederation of Kilkenny" (PhD thesis) pp 65-8. **22** Cregan, "Counter-reformation episcopate" p. 87. **23** TCD Mss 819 f.226 (William Stafford, Jan. 1653), f.266 (William Stafford, Dec. 1653), Mss 831 f.170 (Walter Bourke, 12 Dec. 1642). **24** TCD Mss 1071 (Cín Lae Ó Mealláin) f.32; Journal of Henry McTully O'Neill, *Desiderata curiosa Hibernica*, [Lodge, John (ed.)], vol. 2, p. 497. **25** Smith, C., *The ancient and present state of the county and city of Waterford* (Dublin 1746) pp 159-66; *HMC*, 10th report, appendix 5 (London 1885) pp 279-80; Power, P. , *History of Waterford city and county* (Dublin 1990) pp 77-8.

*Table 8: General assembly members with parliamentary experience*

(The number of assembly lists they appear on is indicated after each name.)

**LORDS** Antrim (2); Brittas*(1); Cahir*(1); Castlehaven*(3); Costello-Gallen (1); Dunboyne (1); Fermoy (3); Fingal (4); Gormanston (1); Ikerrin (3); Louth (4); Mayo (3); Mountgarret (4); Muskerry (4); Netterville (4); Slane (1); Taaffe (1); Trimlseton (3); Westmeath (1) – **Total** 19

(* Both Brittas and Castlehaven had a right to sit in parliament from 1634, Cahir from 1640, but it is unclear if any of them did so.)

**COMMONS** Archer, Henry (2); Ash, Richard (2); Barnewall, Richard (3); Barron, Geoffrey (3); Bellew, John (4); Bellings, Richard (4); Blackney, George (3); Blake, John (2); Blake, Richard (1); Blake, Valentine (1); Bourke, Theobald (3); Bourke, Thomas (2); Browne, Geoffrey (3); Browne, William (1); Butler, Piers (4); Butler, Richard (2); Butler, Thomas (3); Byrne, Bryan (4); Byrne, James (3); Cheevers, Marcus (2); Clinton, Peter (2); Coghlan, John (1); Coghlan, Terence (2), Comerford, Edward (4); Creagh, Pierce (3); Crosby, Piers (2); Cruise, Walter (4); Cullen, John (1); Cusack, Adam (1); Cusack, James (4); Darcy, Patrick (4); Dempsey, Barnaby (3); Dillon, Henry*(2); Dillon, James (2); Dillon, Lucas (2); Dowdall, Laurence (3); Esmond, Thomas (3); Fitzgerald, John (1); Fitzgerald, Lucas (2); Fitzgerald, Maurice(4); French, Patrick (2); Grace, Robert (3); Haly, John*(4); Haly, Richard (2); Hartpole, Robert (4); Hennessy, Thomas (3); Holliwood, Christopher (1); Hope, Alexander(2); Hore, John (3); Lynch, Nicholas*(2); Lynch, Robert (4); MacMahon, Coll. (1); Martin, Richard (2); Nugent, John (3); Nugent, Thomas*(2); O'Brien, Dan. (3); O'Brien, Der. (3); O'Brien, Don. (3); O'Connor, Teig (4); O'Neill, Phelim (3); O'Reilly, Philip (2); Plunkett, Nicholas (4); Power, John (4); Purcell, Thomas (1); Rochford, Hugh (3); Roche, Redmond (1); Rothe, Peter (1); Shee, Robert (4); Sherlock, Christopher (1); Stanley, John (3); Strange, Richard (3); Sutton, Nicholas (2); Talbot, Robert (4); Walsh, John (4); Warren, John*(1); White, Dominick (3); White, Henry*(1); White, Nicholas (1) – **Total** 78

(*These names appear but it is not clear if they refer to the MPs in question.)

A number of former MPs were active in confederate ranks, but their names do not appear on any of the surviving lists: Browne, Dominick; Cappock, Thomas; Christabel, James; Davills, Thomas; Kavanagh, Morgan; Maguire, Roger; Nettervill, Lucas; Walsh, Walter.[26]

---

**26** Roger Maguire was almost certainly present at the assembly in October 1642, while Walter Walsh attended the 1648 assembly. Acts of the general assembly, 24 Oct. 1642 (Gilbert [ed.], *Irish confederation*, ii, pp 73-90); The names of the lords and others now assembled in the assembly at the city of Kilkenny, 10 Oct. 1648 (Bodl. Carte Mss 22 f.339). Bríd McGrath's thesis contains a store of information on the catholic members of parliament in 1640-1. McGrath, B., "Biographical dictionary" (PhD 1988).

*Table 9: General assembly members with legal training*[27]

---

(The number of assembly lists they appear on is indicated after each name.)

Allen, John (3); Archer Thomas (1); Archer, Walter (1); Aylward Peter (1); Baggot, John (4); Barnewall, George (2); Barnewall, John (1); Barnewall, Richard (3); Barnewall, Robert (1); Barron, Geoffrey (3); Bellings, Richard (4); Berford, Richard (4); Bermingham, Richard (3); Bermingham, William (3); Blake, John (2); Blake, Richard (1); Blake, Valentine (1); Bodkin, Dominick (3); Bourke, Edmund (1); Bourke, John (3); Bourke, Thomas (2); Browne, Geoffrey (3); Browne, James (1); Browne, William (1); Bryan, Patrick (4); Butler, Edmund (4); Butler, Edward (2); Butler, James (3); Butler, Piers (4); Butler, Richard (2); Butler, Thomas (3); Cheevers, John (2); Cheevers, Marcus (2); Clinton, Peter (2); Comyn, George (4); Cowley, James (2); Cusack, Adam (1); Cusack, James (4); Darcy, Patrick (4); Devereux, Robert (3); Dillon, James (2); Dillon, John (2); Dillon, Lucas (2); Dongan, Thomas (2); Dormer, Michael (1); Everard, Joesph (1); Fanning, Geoffrey (2); Fennell, Gerald (4); Finglas, John (2); Fitzgerald, Christopher (2); Fitzgerald, Gerald (4); Fitzgerald, Lucas (2); Fitzgerald, Richard (2); Fitzgerald, Thomas (4); FitzPatrick, Barnaby, Lord of Upper Ossory (4); Grace, John (1); Haly, John (4); Haly, Nicholas (3); Haly, Richard (2); Hore, John (3); Hore, Matthew (4); Hore, William (2); Hussey, Edward (1); Kirwan, Patrick (1); Lynch, Nicholas (2); Lynch, Roebuck (4); MacCarthy, Callaghan (1); MacCarthy, Florence (3); MacDaniel, James (1); Magrath, Turlough (1); Martin, Anthony (2); Martin, Richard (2); Netterville, Patrick (4); Nugent, Peter (1); Nugent, Robert (2); O'Brien, Turlough (1); O'Callaghan, Callaghan (3); O'Flynn, Fiachra (2); O'Meara, Thomas (1); O'Neill, Phelim (2); O'Neill, Turlough (4); O'Reilly, Philip (2); O'Rourke, Hugh (1); Plunkett, Nicholas (4); Power, Edmund (3); Power, Richard (1); Purcell, Garrett (1); Purcell, Theobald (1); Purcell, Thomas (1); Roche, John (1); Rochford, Hugh (3); Rothe, Peter (2); Ryan, Thomas (3); Shee, Edward (1); Shee, Marcus (1); Shee, Richard (2); Shee, William (1); Sherlock, John (1); Stackpole, Bartholomew (2); Strange, Richard (3); Tyrrell, Thomas (3); Wadding, Paul (1); Wadding, Richard (4); Walsh, John (4); Walsh, Patrick (2); Walsh, Robert (1); White, Arthur (1); White, Dominick (2); White, Henry (1); White, James (1); White, John (1), White, Thomas (1) – **Total** 112.

**27** This list is comprised of those confederates who attended an English inns of court during the reigns of James I and Charles I. A few may have completed their education prior to 1603, but not enough to alter the overall figures in any significant manner. Those who may have been trained on the continent are not included. At the outbreak of the Irish rebellion in October 1641 most Irish catholics were expelled from the English inns of court so some of the above did not complete their studies. D.F. Cregan, "Irish recusant lawyers in politics in the Reign of James I", *Irish jurist*, vol. 5 (1970) pp 306-20; Joseph Foster, *Register of admissions to Gray's Inns 1521-1889* (London 1889); *The records of the honourable society of Lincoln's Inn* (London 1896); *Register of admissions to the honourable society of the Middle Temple* vol. 1 (London 1949); *Students admitted to the Inner Temple 1547-1660* (London 1877).

## Table 10: Regular general assembly members[28]

*Members whose names appear on all four lists*

BISHOPS Cashel; Clogher; Clonfert; Killaloe – **Total** 4

LORDS Clanmalier; Fingal; Louth; Mountgarret; Netterville; Upper Ossory – **Total** 6

COMMONS Baggot, John; Bagnall, Walter; Bellings, Richard; Bellew, John; Berford, Richard; Birne, Brian; Bryan, Patrick; Butler, Edmond; Butler, Piers; Carroll, John; Cheevers Arthur; Comerford, Edward; Comyn, George; Cruise, Walter; Cusack, James; Darcy, Patrick; Dongan, Edward; Doyne, Terence; Duff, James; Duff, Paul; Fennell, Gerald; Ferrall, Francis; Fitzgerald, Edmond; Fitzgerald, Gerald; Fitzgerald, Maurice; Fitzgerald, Thomas; Fleming, Thomas; Haly, John; Hartpole, Robert; Higgins, Daniel; Hore, Matthew; Lacy, John; Lynch, Robuck; MacDonnell, James; Netterville, Patrick; Netterville, Robert; O'Connor, Teig; O'Neil, Turlough; Plunkett; Ambrose; Plunkett, Nicholas; Power, David; Power, John; Preston Thomas; Shee, Robert; Slingsby, Henry; Talbot, Robert; Wadding, Richard; Wadding, Thomas; Wall, Edward; Walsh, John; Warren, Alexander; Wogan, Nicholas – **Total** 52

*Members whose names appear on three lists*

BISHOPS Ardfert; Armagh; Leighlin; Tuam; Waterford – **Total** 5

LORDS Castlehaven; Fermoy; Ikerrin; Iveagh; Muskerry; Trimleston – **Total** 6

COMMONS Allen, John; Barnewall, Richard; Barron, Geoffrey; Bath, James; Bellings, Barnaby; Bermingham, William; Birne, James; Blackney, George; Bodkin, Dominick; Bourke, John; Brown, Geoffrey; Butler, James; Butler, Theobald; Butler, Thomas; Colclough, Anthony; Creagh, Pierce; Darcy, Thomas; Dempsey, Barnaby; Dowd, Edward; Dowdall, Lawrence; Doyle, James; Esmond, Thomas; Everard, Richard; Fallon, Stephen; Fitzgerald, Piers; Fitzpatrick, Florence; French, Christopher; Gough, Patrick; Gould, John; Grace, Robert; Green, George; Haly, Nicholas; Henes, Thomas; Hollywood, Nicholas; Hore, John; Hore, Philip; Kealy, Edmund; Kearney, Philip; Lacy, Walter; MacCarthy, Dermott; MacCarthy, Donough; MacCarthy, Florence; MacCarthy, Teig; MacGeoghegan, Conly; O'Boyle, Turlough; O'Brien, Conor; O'Brien, Daniel; O'Brien, Dermott; O'Callaghan, Callaghan; O'Callaghan, Donough; O'Connor, Don; O'Rody, Thaddeus; O'Sullivan, Daniel; Power, Edmond; Prendergast, James; Preston, James; Preston, Robert; Rochford, Hugh; Ryan, Thomas; St.Leger, George; Stafford, William; Stanley, John; Strange, Richard; Tyrrell, Thomas; Warren, Edmond; Warren, William; Wolferston, Francis; Young, William – **Total** 68

---

**28** Among the regular lay members of the general assembly, almost one in three had parliamentary experience, while a similar percentage had received some degree of legal training.

*Table 11: General assembly electorate, 1642-1649*[29]

**ANTRIM:** Patrick O'Neile

**CORK:** Thomas Browne; Carroll Connolly; Robert Coppinger; Walter Coppinger; Patrick Gallwey; Walter Gallwey; William Gordon; James Gough; David Gould; James Gould; Phillip Gould; David Hally; – Harding; Phillip Martell; Thomas Martell; Patrick Meade; James Morrough; Nicholas Pounch; Edmund Roche; George Roche; James Roche; John Roche; Morris Roche; Walter Ronayne; – Skeddy; Edward Supple; David Terry; Dominick Terry; George Terry; Robert Terry; William Walter

**DOWN:** Ever McGennis

**DUBLIN:** John Finglass; Philip Hoare; Richard Murphy

**GALWAY:** Richard Martin

**KILDARE:** Christopher Archbold; William Archbold; Thomas Ashe; John Lattin; Robert Moore; James Walsh

**KILKENNY:** James Bryan; Helias Shee

**LAOIS:** John Fitzgerald

**LOUTH:** Peter Bath; James Clinton

**MEATH:** Christopher Barnewall; Patrick Barnewall; Patrick Betagh; William Fitzgerald; Edward Geoghan; Adam Missett; Melchoir Moore; Nicholas Plunkett; Patrick Welden

**ROSCOMMON:** John Kelly

**TIPPERARY:** Gerald Fennell; Robert Fleming; Patrick Netterville

**WATERFORD:** James Walsh; James Fitzgerald; Teige O'Bryan

**WESTMEATH:** James Nugent; Richard Tyrrell

**WEXFORD:** Nicholas Heyr; William Hoare; Thomas White

**Total:** 69 voters (15 counties)

**29** This list is simply a small sample of the confederate electorate. The Clarendon State Papers contain the only surviving copy of a confederate electoral return. It is for the city of Cork in December 1646 and includes a list of voters. Bodl. Clarendon MSS 29 f.8. The other names are contained in evidence presented to the court of claims in 1663. Geraldine Talon (ed.), *Act of settlement* (forthcoming).

*Table 12: Continuity of membership*

---

*1634 Parliament:*              115 catholics in the commons
*1640 Parliament:*              101 catholics in the commons

A total of 183 catholic members were returned to the House of Commons in 1634 and 1640 (33 of the 115 catholic members in 1634 were returned again in 1640), 82 of which, or 45%, subsequently sat in confederate assemblies.[30]

*1642/3 General assembly:*      318 commoners
                                146 (46%) do not appear on any other list

*1644 General assembly:*        166 commoners
                                17 (10%) do not appear on any other list
                                82 (50%) attended previous assembly (1642/3).[31]

*1645 General assembly:*        396 commoners
                                152 (39%) do not appear on any other list
                                195 (49%) attended previous assemblies.[32]

*1647 (Jan.)General assembly:*  292 commoners
                                91 (31%) do not appear on any other list
                                201 (69%) attended previous assemblies

**30** This figure includes Muskerry and Dunboyne who sat in the House of Commons before moving to the Lords. **31** 1644 is the first assembly for 67 people (40%), who also appear on later lists (1645 & 1647). **32** For 49 people in 1645 (12%), the only other list they appear on is the following one in 1647.

# Membership of the supreme council

᎒᎒

For much of the 1640s the supreme council, functioning as the executive arm of government, dominated confederate politics. And yet, despite the council's pivotal role from 1642 onwards, acknowledged by all historians, no definitive membership list exists. Without knowing who was present at meetings, it is difficult (if not impossible) to interpret the council's actions. Dónal Cregan did some excellent research in this area but it is by no means complete and there are problems with some of his conclusions.[1] Nonetheless, Cregan's list is an obvious starting point for anybody determined enough to undertake this task.

The immediate problem is a familiar one for anybody involved in research on confederate Ireland, namely that the bulk of the records no longer survive. As a result, most of the information concerning supreme council elections has been lost. In only three cases do the sources provide a full list of elected members – the first council elected in October 1642; the council appointed by the war party after the rejection of the Ormond peace in September 1646; and the final council, nominated in acrimonious circumstances in December 1647.[2] For all the others, the researcher must rely on signatures appended to supreme council documents.[3] This method is surprisingly comprehensive, but nonetheless must be approached with some caution. Contemporary complaints exist of non-elected members sitting in on council meetings, particularly during the period 1644-6, when the committee of instruction probably amalgamated with the supreme council, making the identification of council members all the more difficult.[4]

---

1 Cregan, D.F., "The confederate catholics of Ireland: The personnel of the confederation, 1642-9", *IHS*, vol. 29, no. 116 (Nov. 95) pp 490-512. 2 Gilbert (ed.), *Irish confederation*, ii, pp 73-90 (Oct. 1642); vi, pp 144-6 (Sept. 1646); vi, pp 208-23 (Dec. 1647). 3 The most valuable sources for these documents are the Carte manuscripts in the Bodleian Library, Oxford, and the state papers relating to Ireland in the Public Records Office, London. Gilbert's printed collections and the *Commentarius* also provide much information. 4 Rinuccini identified the growth of the supreme council as a major impediment to decisive government. Report on the state of Ireland, 1 March 1646 (Aiazza [ed.], *Embassy* p. 133). Furthermore, most of those

Finally, there is the question of provincial representation. The first assembly, in October 1642, elected six members from each province, and the confederates retained the principle of equality throughout the 1640s.[5] The Ulster delegates, however, far from the confederate heartland in south Leinster and east Munster, had a poor attendance record. Their places on the council board may well have been taken on an informal basis by the extra Leinster and Munster delegates whose names appear on the documents.[6]

The accompanying table outlines the membership of each supreme council from 1642 until 1649, and differs most noticeably from Cregan's model insofar as he identified ten councils, whereas there were in fact only nine.[7] The problem arises with the second general assembly of 1647. According to normal procedures, the assembly selected a new council of 12 resident members to replace the existing body, but the elections proved contentious and civil war threatened to engulf the confederate association. Eventually, a compromise was reached with the addition to the council of 36 supernumeraries (or alternates) to fill the gaps in the case of absentees.[8] When the confederates did split into warring factions over the truce with lord Inchiquin, in May 1648, a number of these supernumeraries began to sit at the council board.[9] This development led Cregan to the mistaken conclusion that a new supreme council had been elected. The final general assembly, from September 1648 until January 1649, dissolved the confederate association and did not appoint a new council.

Elections to the first five councils, between 1642-6, were relatively non-contentious. Each council had 24 members, most of whom have been correctly identified by Cregan. In fact, additional research indicates only five changes from Cregan's list before 1645. The first concerns the council elected in June 1643, where Cregan lists an extra Munster delegate at the expense of Ulster. Viscount Muskerry of Munster however, only headed the committee negotiating a truce with Ormond, although he may have sat in on a number of council meetings in an unofficial capacity. The name of the missing Ulster member unfortunately does not survive.

For the council elected in November 1643, Cregan omits one of the Munster representatives, Viscount Roche (although his signature appears on a council document in June 1644), and the archbishop of Armagh, who along with the other metropolitans sat on every council until 1646.[10] On the other hand,

involved in the treaty negotiations were also members of the supreme council, making it easy to confuse the council with the committee of treaty. **5** Acts of the general assembly, 24 Oct. 1642 (Gilbert [ed.], *Irish confederation*, ii, pp 73-90). **6** This issue is discussed in chapter 7 p. 220f of above. **7** Table 13 provides a full list of supreme council members from 1642-9. **8** Orders of the general assembly, 12 Nov. 1647 (Gilbert [ed.], *Irish confederation*, vi, pp 208-23); Rinuccini to Panzirolo, 24 Dec. 1647 (Aiazza [ed.], *Embassy* pp 343-6). **9** See council documents in Bodl. Carte Mss 22 f.99, 115-20 etc. **10** Supreme council to Urban VIII, 14 June 1644 in Bourke, Thomas (ed.) *Hibernia Dominicana*, supplementum, p. 877. For reasons

Cregan mistakenly includes Ever Magennis of Ulster, whose name disappears from council lists after 1643 until December 1647.[11] Thomas Preston is also named by Cregan, but as the 6 Leinster representatives are already accounted for, he probably sat in on council meetings in his capacity as general of the Leinster army, the most important in the confederate association.

The mistaken titles on certain documents has added to the confusion. The signatures of Richard Barnewall, Robert Talbot and John Walsh appear on what Gilbert identifies as supreme council documents, during the third general assembly in November 1643. In fact, these letters have nothing to do with the council, but deal instead with matters arising from the truce agreed with the royalists in September of that year. The three people mentioned above were part of the confederate delegation which negotiated the settlement with Ormond, and not members of the supreme council.[12]

The next divergence from Cregan concerns the council elected in August 1644. Nicholas Plunkett, chairman of the general assembly, is absent from Cregan's list, although named as a member of every other council. It is extremely unlikely that Plunkett, one of the most popular and active Leinster representatives, would not have been nominated to the council in 1644. After August 1644, he became increasingly involved in the peace negotiations with the royalists, spending a lot of his time in Dublin. This might explain the absence of his signature from council documents during much of this period. In early 1645, however, Plunkett wrote to the confederate agent Matthew O'Hartegan in Paris on behalf of the supreme council, and his name appears on other council documents that year.[13]

Although John Walsh's name appears on Cregan's list, his council membership in the period 1644-5 must be considered doubtful. Walsh was elected as judge of the new judicature established by the general assembly in August 1644. The bishop of Clonfert resigned his seat on the council after his appointment to the judicature, but would hardly have done so had Walsh remained at council board. None of the other judges (Richard Berford, John Dillon and Richard Martin) were members of the supreme council, reflecting a desire of the confederates to separate the judicial and executive functions of government.[14] Removing Preston's name (for the reasons outlined above), and including the marquis of Antrim for Ulster completes the list.[15]

---

which are not immediately apparent, the archbishop of Cashel was not elected onto the first supreme council in November 1642. Acts of the general assembly, 24 Oct. 1642 (Gilbert [ed.], *Irish confederation*, ii, pp 73-90). **11** O'Ferrall and O'Connell (eds), *Commentarius*, iii, pp 170-1. **12** Truce documents, Nov. 1643 (Gilbert [ed.], *Irish confederation*, iii, pp 41-3, 50). **13** Appointment of Michael Walsh by the supreme council, 9 Aug. 1645 (PRO SP Ire.260/145 f.401); Plunkett to O'Hartegan, 9 Jan. 1645 (Gilbert [ed.], *Irish confederation*, iv, pp 119-21). **14** Order by the commissioners of the general assembly, 30 Aug. 1644 (Gilbert [ed.], *Irish confederation*, iii, pp 266-7). **15** The 1644 general assembly also elected Antrim onto the com-

*Table 13: Supreme council membership 1642–1649*

|  | 1642 | 1643a | 1643b | 1644 | 1645 | 1646a | 1646b | 1647a | 1647b |  | province |
|---|---|---|---|---|---|---|---|---|---|---|---|
| *Clogher* | x | x | x | x | x | x | x | x | x | 9 | Ulster |
| Plunkett N. | x | x | x | x | x | x | x | x | o | 9 | Leinster |
| Darcy P. | x | x | x | x | x | x |  | x | o | 8 | Connacht |
| Bellings R. | x | x | x | x | x | x |  |  | x | 7 | Leinster |
| Dillon L. | x | x | x | x | x | x |  |  | x | 7 | Connacht |
| *Mountgarret* | x | x | x | x | x | x |  |  | o | 7 | Leinster |
| O'Neill T. | x | x | x | x | x |  |  | x |  | 6 | Ulster |
| Fennell G. | x | x | x | x | x |  |  |  | x | 6 | Munster |
| Browne G. | x | x | x | x | x |  |  |  | o | 6 | Connacht |
| Comyn G. | x | x | x | x | x |  |  |  | o | 6 | Munster |
| *Dublin* | x | x | x | x | x |  |  |  | o | 6 | Leinster |
| O'Brien Dan. | x | x | x | x | x |  |  |  | o | 6 | Munster |
| *Clonfert* | x | x | x |  |  | x |  | x | o | 6 | Connacht |
| *Tuam* | x | x | x | x | x |  |  |  |  | 5 | Connacht |
| *Armagh* | x | x | x | x | x |  |  |  |  | 5 | Ulster |
| Fitzmaurice E. | x | x | x | x |  |  |  |  | o | 5 | Munster |
| *Roche* | x | x | x |  |  |  |  | x |  | 4 | Munster |
| Magennis E. | x | x |  |  |  |  |  |  | o | 3 | Ulster |
| *Mayo* | x |  |  |  |  |  |  |  | o | 2 | Connacht |
| *Gormanston* | x |  |  |  |  |  |  |  |  | 1 | Leinster |
| Lombard R. | x |  |  |  |  |  |  |  |  | 1 | Munster |
| MacMahon Coll. | x |  |  |  |  |  |  |  |  | 1 | Ulster |
| Cusack J. | x |  |  |  |  |  |  |  |  | 1 | Leinster |
| O'Reilly P. | x |  |  |  |  |  |  |  |  | 1 | Ulster |
| Lynch R. |  | x | x | x | x |  | x | x | x | 7 | Connacht |
| *Cashel* |  | x | x | x | x |  | x |  | o | 6 | Munster |
| *Netterville* |  | x | x | x | x |  |  |  |  | 4 | Leinster |
| *Castlehaven* |  | x | x | x | x |  |  |  |  | 4 | Leinster |
| Fleming T. |  | x | x | x | x |  |  |  |  | 4 | Ulster |
| *Antrim* |  | x | x |  |  |  |  | x | o | 4 | Ulster |
| *Iveagh* |  | x |  |  |  |  |  |  | o | 2 | Ulster |
| MacDonnell A. |  |  |  | x | x | x | x | x | o | 6 | Ulster |
| *Muskerry* |  |  |  | x | x | x |  | x | o | 5 | Munster |
| O'Shaghnessy D. |  |  |  | x | x | x |  | x | o | 5 | Connacht |
| O'Callaghan D |  |  |  |  | x | x |  |  |  | 2 | Munster |
| *Ferns* |  |  |  |  |  |  | x | x | o | 3 | Leinster |
| Butler P. |  |  |  |  |  |  | x | x |  | 2 | Leinster |
| O'Sullivan Br. D. |  |  |  |  |  |  | x | x |  | 2 | Munster |
| *Louth* |  |  |  |  |  |  | x | x |  | 2 | Leinster |

*Table 13: Supreme council membership 1642–1649*

| | 1642 | 1643a | 1643b | 1644 | 1645 | 1646a | 1646b | 1647a | 1647b | | province |
|---|---|---|---|---|---|---|---|---|---|---|---|
| O'Neill O.R. | | | | | | | x | x | | 2 | Ulster |
| O'Neill P. | | | | | | | x | | o | 2 | Ulster |
| Preston T. | | | | | | | x | | | 1 | Leinster |
| *Glamorgan* | | | | | | | x | | | 1 | Munster |
| Rinuccini G.B. | | | | | | | x | | | 1 | |
| O'Boyle T. | | | | | | | | x | x | 2 | Ulster |
| *Limerick* | | | | | | | | x | x | 2 | Munster |
| *Athenry* | | | | | | | | x | x | 2 | Connacht |
| Blake R. | | | | | | | | x | o | 2 | Connacht |
| Geogh P. | | | | | | | | x | o | 2 | Munster |
| Everard R. | | | | | | | | x | o | 2 | Munster |
| O'Brien Der. | | | | | | | | x | | 1 | Munster |
| Rochford H. | | | | | | | | x | | 1 | Leinster |
| Dillon J. | | | | | | | | x | | 1 | Leinster |
| Barron G. | | | | | | | | | x | 1 | Munster |
| Bryan P. | | | | | | | | | x | 1 | Leinster |
| O'Neill H. og | | | | | | | | | x | 1 | Ulster |
| Devereux R. | | | | | | | | | x | 1 | Leinster |
| Barnwall R. | | | | | | | | | o | 1 | Leinster |
| Talbot R. | | | | | | | | | o | 1 | Leinster |
| *Costello-Dillon* | | | | | | | | | o | 1 | Leinster |
| Nugent T. | | | | | | | | | o | 1 | Leinster |
| Dongan J. | | | | | | | | | o | 1 | Leinster |
| Bagnal W. | | | | | | | | | o | 1 | Leinster |
| *Killala* | | | | | | | | | o | 1 | Connacht |
| Blake V. | | | | | | | | | o | 1 | Connacht |
| Burke J. | | | | | | | | | o | 1 | Connacht |
| *Dunboyne* | | | | | | | | | o | 1 | Munster |
| Walsh J. | | | | | | | | | o | 1 | Munster |
| Cahan J. | | | | | | | | | o | 1 | Ulster |
| *Down/Connor* | | | | | | | | | o | 1 | Ulster |
| O'Reilly M. | | | | | | | | | o | 1 | Ulster |
| Maguire R. | | | | | | | | | o | 1 | Ulster |
| | 24 | 24* | 24 | 24 | 24* | 9 | 17 | 24 | 49 | | |

* 1643a and 1645 – one Ulster member missing from each list

1647b – "x" represents a resident member, "o" a supernumerary or alternate

The establishment of the committees of treaty and instruction by the assembly in August 1644, further complicates matters. Created to undertake treaty negotiations with the marquis of Ormond, these two committees worked closely with the supreme council to the extent that the three groups practically amalgamated. A number of prominent individuals sat as members of at least two of the bodies, signing documents on behalf of the "council and committee".[16] As a result of this confusion, Cregan can only provide 21 names for the council elected in 1645, two of which (Robert Talbot and Patrick Bryan) are almost certainly wrong. Although both were leading members of the committee of treaty, it is not possible to confirm their membership of the supreme council until the election in December 1647. Preston, yet again, is mistakenly included, leaving only 18 correct names.

Two of the missing members are Malachy O'Queely, archbishop of Tuam, and Hugh O'Reilly, archbishop of Armagh. O'Queely, one of the most prominent and powerful figures in confederate politics, sat on every supreme council until his death in October 1645, while O'Reilly represented Ulster until 1646.[17] Similarly, Daniel O'Brien of Munster and Thomas Fleming of Ulster were regular members until the general assembly reduced the size of the supreme council in February 1646. That leaves two places unaccounted for, with the regular pattern of provincial representation suggesting one more person from both Ulster and Connacht. The most obvious candidate for Connacht is Dermot O'Shaughnessy who had replaced the bishop of Clonfert on the council the previous year. Considering the remarkable stability in Connacht representation, it is not unreasonable to assume that he retained his seat in 1645, especially as he sat on every subsequent council until 1649 (bar the truncated version in 1646). As in June 1643, the final name from Ulster remains elusive, with a number of possible contenders, including the marquis of Antrim and Viscount Iveagh.

Concerns about the size and effectiveness of the supreme council, as well as the influence of non-elected individuals, led the general assembly to streamline its membership. As a result, assembly members elected only nine people onto the council in February 1646, two from each province, with Richard Bellings as secretary.[18] Cregan provides nine names, but the inclusion of Geoffrey Browne of Galway is a mistake, despite his presence on every previous supreme council. The two Connacht representatives in 1646 were the celebrated lawyer Patrick Darcy and Sir Lucas Dillon. The ninth member of this truncated council was in fact Viscount Muskerry, representing Munster along with Donough O'Callaghan. Muskerry proved extremely active in the military, administrative

mittee of treaty. Ohlmeyer, *Civil war and restoration* p. 149. **16** See PRO SP Ire 260/154 f.423, 261/5 f.6, 261/12 f.76 etc. **17** Rinuccini describes Tuam's death as a great loss to the council. Rinuccini to Pamphili, 20 Nov. 1645 (Aiazza [ed.], *Embassy* p. 88). **18** Orders of the general assembly, Jan. 1646 (Bodl. Carte Mss 16 ff 470-80).

and diplomatic spheres throughout 1646, and his name appears on almost all official confederate documents of the period.[19]

Later that same year, the clerical party, led by Rinuccini, assumed control of confederate affairs and appointed a new supreme council of 17 members, all correctly listed by Cregan. A number of council documents from late 1646 also contain signatures of people not in this original group, the most common being that of the Cistercian priest, Father Patrick Plunkett, brother of Nicholas and later bishop of Ardagh. Along with Terence O'Brien (later bishop of Emly), the Jesuit Robert Nugent and others, Plunkett represented the ecclesiastical congregation, which governed in association with the supreme council. These clerics were not, however, strictly members of the council.[20]

In early 1647, the general assembly rejected the first Ormond peace treaty, but exonerated its authors from any blame. A group of moderates, centred around Nicholas Plunkett and Bishop French, made strenuous efforts to promote confederate unity, a fact reflected in the composition of the new supreme council. This body consisted of members from the peace and clerical factions (as well as leading moderates), with the four provinces equally represented. Cregan names 21 of the 24, to which can be added Turlough O'Boyle and Owen Roe O'Neill, both of Ulster, and Donal O'Sullivan Beare representing Munster.[21] According to Inchiquin, Richard Bellings of Leinster sat on the council during 1647, but this is highly unlikely. As a leading supporter of the first peace treaty, his election in March 1647 would surely have been remarked upon (as was that of Muskerry) by various hostile commentators such as Rinuccini.[22]

Finally, as already mentioned, only one supreme council sat between December 1647 and January 1649. The full list of members, resident and supernumeraries, totalling 49 people, 12 from each province, plus Robert Devereux of Wexford as one of the three Leinster residents, is published by Gilbert, and also in the *Commentarius*.[23] The accompanying table provides almost a full list of

**19** See Bodl. Carte Mss 17 f.160; PRO SP Ire. 261/23 f.100, 261/27 f.105 etc. **20** See PRO SP Ire. 262/14 f.148, 262/31 ff 193-4, 262/56 f.223, 262/66 f.243 etc. **21** Bodl. Carte Mss 21 f.571 provides of the names of 21 council members, though not the same 21 names supplied by Cregan. The document, however, records the election of a Teig O'Connor Roe to represent Connacht. This name does not appear on any council document during the year, and as six Connacht members are otherwise accounted for O'Connor's inclusion must simply be a mistake, or else somebody else took his place during the course of the year. The following correspondence – supreme council to Andrew Lynch, 9 April 1647 (NA Miscellaneous Doc., Old Series 64-91, no. 83); supreme council to Henry Talbot, 28 March 1647 (Bodl. Carte Mss 20 f.558); supreme council to Taaffe, 27 Sept. 1647 (Bodl. Tanner Mss 58/2 f.529) – completes the list. **22** Inchiquin to Lenthall, 18 Nov. 1647, *Tanner letters*, McNeill (ed.), pp 274-8; Rinuccini to Pamphili, 24 March 1647 (Aiazza [ed.], *Embassy* p. 264); Report on the affairs of Ireland, 1649 (ibid., pp 509-11). **23** O'Ferrall and O'Connell (eds), *Commentarius*, iii, pp 170-1; Orders of the general assembly, 12 Nov. 1647 (Gilbert [ed.], *Irish confederation*, vi, pp 208-23). The last Ulster name in the *Commentarius* is given as "Emerus MacMahony", whereas the original

supreme council membership from 1642 to 1649, but still can not be described as definitive. Apart from the two Ulster names missing (May 1643 and 1645), the gaps in documentary evidence, the problems concerning the period 1644-6 when a multiplicity of councils and committees abounded, and the odd inexplicable inclusion, would undermine any such claims. Nonetheless, the additional information gathered here provides a further valuable insight into the dynamics of confederate government.

document in the Carte collection, reprinted by Gilbert, correctly identifies this person as Ever Magennis.

# Memoirs of Nicholas Plunkett &
# Nicholas French

ເຈ

In the decades following the Cromwellian conquest, a number of confederates found solace in writing their memoirs. These authors frequently sought to apportion blame for disastrous defeats and ruinous exile, or else hoped to ingratiate themselves with the new regime in Ireland. The account entitled *Aphorismical discovery* belongs in the first category, Richard Bellings' narrative in the second. Two manuscripts in the National Library of Ireland, entitled "An account of the war and rebellion in Ireland since 1641" and "A light to the blind", have been ascribed to a Nicholas Plunkett.[1] Unfortunately, internal evidence suggests both documents were written at the beginning of the eighteenth century, decades after the death of the renowned lawyer and confederate of that name in 1680.

A Nicholas Plunkett of Dunsoghly, writing some time after the final Jacobite defeat in 1691, is the known author of the "Account", although the latest book on the 1641 uprising ascribes the manuscript to the confederate Plunkett.[2] A detailed article by Patrick Kelly in *Irish historical studies* clearly refutes this suggestion. There are a number of references in the "Account" to events in the early eighteenth century, although Kelly concedes that the narrative of the 1640s may well be older or "based on material committed to writing a long time before". It is possible, therefore, that Nicholas Plunkett of Dunsoghly had access to material belonging to his confederate namesake, which he used in compiling his own history.[3]

Unfortunately, even if this were the case, it would be of little use in attempting to discover the political philosophy of the confederate Plunkett. The opinions of the eighteenth century author, blatantly pro-Ormond and bitterly anticlerical, pervade the narrative. Rinuccini is described as "the fatal and pestilent

---

**1** NLI Mss 345 (An account), 476-7 (Light to the blind). **2** Perceval-Maxwell, *Irish rebellion* p. 79. **3** Kelly, Patrick, " 'A light to the blind', the voice of the dispossessed elite in the generations after the defeat at Limerick" *IHS*, vol. 24, no. 96 (Nov. 1985) pp 431-62. It is possible that Nicholas Plunkett may have been a grandson, or some other relation, of the confederate Plunkett who was also from Dunsoghly.

nuncio", while Bishop French, Plunkett's great ally during the 1640s, is dismissed as "that upstart mean creature". Even the confederate Plunkett does not escape criticism, being proclaimed as "one of the great lawyers of the last age", but "who in his bigotry was a while of the nuncio's party".[4] These clearly were not the opinions of the leading political moderate of the 1640s.

The authorship of the second document, "A light to the blind", is as yet undetermined. Written shortly after the "Account", it is markedly different in tone, calling for Irish catholics of all backgrounds to unite, and help restore the Stuart monarchy with the support of the French. Although Plunkett, a powerful advocate of confederate unity, would have sympathised with these sentiments, he did not write this tract. Again the document appeared long after his death, and the most likely author (according to Kelly) was Colonel Nicholas Plunkett, brother of the third earl of Fingal.[5]

It may seem pedantic and unnecessary to clarify these points, but given Plunkett's central role in the events of the 1640s, and the evident confusion still existing on the subject, it is vital to ascertain if either of these works can be ascribed to him. The answer is an emphatic no, and the confederate Plunkett's memoirs (if they ever existed) probably have not survived. Apparently, all that remained for historians were a few official letters, written in his capacity as chairman of the general assembly, or as a member of the supreme council.[6] On reading through a number of documents in the British Library, however, another source recently came to light.

Between 1660 and 1662, Irish catholics entered into negotiations with the recently restored Stuart monarchy. They were seeking a royal commitment to honour the terms of the second peace treaty signed with the marquis of Ormond, Charles I's lord lieutenant at the time. With Charles' son back on the throne, and Ormond reappointed as lord lieutenant, Irish catholics hoped to recover at least some of their estates. Their delegation was headed by none other than Nicholas Plunkett, who presented a variety of documents at court, outlining the case for restoration, while at the same time repudiating the charges of disloyalty brought by the protestants of Ireland.[7]

Plunkett's submissions dealt at some length with the causes and course of the uprising, and although he constructed his arguments with a very specific audience in mind (mainly English protestant royalists), the documents nonetheless shed an important light on his attitude to events in the 1640s.[8] Charles II eventually banished Plunkett from court early in 1662, following the discovery of instructions from the supreme council and catholic hierarchy in

---

4 NLI Mss 345 ff 24-5, 57, 63, 559. 5 NLI Mss 476-7 ff 50-270; Kelly, "A light to the blind" p. 443. 6 See for example, PRO SP Ire. 263/31 f.48, 263/110 f.184, 263/124 f.209; Bodl. Carte Mss 20 f.133, 207 etc. 7 Papers relating to Ireland, 1642-1648 (BL Add Mss 4781) contains documents and papers presented at the court of Charles II in 1660-2. 8 References are made to his submissions throughout the main text.

January 1648, authorising Plunkett to offer the protectorship of the kingdom to Innocent X.[9]

Many of his ideas are echoed in the writings of his great ally (and companion on that mission to Rome in 1648) Nicholas French, bishop of Ferns. French emerged as a prolific author during his twenty five years in exile, producing *A narrative of the earl of Clarendon's settlement and sale of Ireland* in 1668, *The bleeding iphigenia* in 1674 and finally *The unkind deserter of loyal men and true friends*, published in 1676, two years before his death. Some of these works appear to contradict one another, but claims that Peter Talbot in fact wrote *Sale and settlement of Ireland* were strenuously denied by the eighteenth century antiquarian Walter Harris. Samuel Bindon, who published a collected volume of the bishop's writings in 1846, agreed with Harris, and in the absence of any definite evidence to the contrary, French is still the accredited author of all three books.[10]

Unlike Nicholas Plunkett, Bishop French, exiled in Louvain, felt no need to pander to the sensibilities of English royalists. Deeply disillusioned by developments in Ireland after the restoration of the Stuarts, he retrospectively blamed the duke of Ormond for the collapse of the catholic interest. French's bitterness distorts much of his writings, but the memoirs are still a valuable source of information on moderate confederate opinion.

**9** Supreme council instructions to agents travelling to Rome, Jan. 1648 (BL Stowe Mss 82 ff155-6); Papers relating to Ireland, 1642-8 (BL Add Mss 4781 f.146). **10** Bindon, S.H.(ed.), *The historical works of the right reverend Nicholas French D.D.*, 2 vols (Dublin 1846). Once again, references are made to his works throughout the main text.

# Bibliography

രു

MANUSCRIPT SOURCES, IRELAND

DUBLIN

*Dublin City Library, Pearse street:* Gilbert collection:
Mss 101 A collection of some of the murders and massacres committed of the
Irish in Ireland since the 23 October 1641
Mss 176 Ireland – fragment of a journal 1641-1647
Mss 205 Ireland – privy council papers, 1640-1707
Mss 214 Plunkett mss – A treatise or account of the war and rebellion in Ireland
since the year 1641
Mss 219 Collection of the proceedings of the commissioners, 1660
Mss 254 Memoirs of George Leyburn

*Franciscan Archives, Killiney*
Vol. D IV 1-1272, Miscellaneous documents, 5 Nov. 1641-29 Dec. 1642

*Jesuit Provincial Archives, Leeson street*
Original manuscripts B, 1576-1698
27 April 1648 Declaration against cessation with Inchiquin
4 May 1648 Delegation of authority to nuncio and four bishops
27 May 1648 Declaration of censure
20 Jan. 1648/9 Roman catholic prelates to Mr Verdier
29 Jan. 1648/9 Supreme council at Kilkenny to Mr Verdier
Dispersal of Irish bishops around Europe (*c.*1653)

*King's Inns*
Prendergast papers vols 1-14

*Marsh's Library*
Mss z 3.1.1 Order of the lord chancellor to grant forth an attachment against
such persons as have infringed the privileges of this House … 17 June 1647

Mss z 3.1.3 Propositions touching the present government offered by a committee to the general assembly, June 1644

*National Archives:*

Mss 3171-85 Paulet papers from papers relating to Garrylough estate in the
Fitzpatrick papers

Miscellaneous old series no. 83: Copy of the petition of Andrew Lynch to the
supreme council of confederate catholics of Ireland and order thereon 9 April
1647

Transcript of Carte papers, vols 2-24 (24 Oct. 1641- 29 May 1649)

*National Library*

Mss 345 Plunkett Mss: Account of the war and rebellion in Ireland since 1641

Mss 476-7 A light to the blind

Mss 2307-15 Ormond papers: 15 July 1640-26 April 1649

Mss 8517 Esmond papers

Mss 9051 Articles of peace, January 1648-9

Mss 19080 Abstract of the decrees of the court of claims

D.3951-4384 Calendar of Ormond deeds, 1640s

Ms G.O. 16 pp 107-8 Oath of association (including preamble)

Private Collections (Reports)

    Dopping-Hepenstall, vol. 14 report 407 p. 2888

    Sarsfield, vol. 11 report 309 p. 2385

    Gormanston vol. 4 report 103 pp 1032-3

    De Freyne vol. 18 report 505 p. 3656

*Royal Irish Academy*

H.V. I: Documents relating to the settlement of Ireland 1660-1670s

H.VI. I: Collection of documents relating to the settlement of Ireland 1660

*Trinity College*

Mss 615 Journal of the Irish House of Lords, March 1639/40-May 1646

Mss 809-41 Depositions 1640s-1650s

Mss 846 Aphorismical discovery of treasonable faction

Mss 1071 Cín Lae Ó Mealláin

Mss 1178 Petition of parliament to lord justices and council, 23 June 1642

Mss 1181 Account of moneys due to the duke of Ormond 1641-1660

Mss 1184 Ordonnances de l'assemblée générale ..., 24 Oct. 1642

Mss 6404 Ware manuscripts, diaries and notes


GALWAY

*University College Galway*

Book A – Galway corporation records

## MANUSCRIPT SOURCES, ENGLAND

### LONDON

*British Library*
Additional Mss:
  4,763 Milles collection
  4,781 Papers relating to the settlement of Ireland 1660-62
  4,819 Pococke collection
  18,980-1 Rupert correspondence
  20,100 Brief narrative, 1 Nov. 1641-15 June 1642
  24,863 Miscellaneous papers 1640-60
  25,277 Political and miscellaneous papers
  28,937 Miscellaneous papers 1583-1679
  31,885 Miscellaneous entry book of Thomas Arthur 1619-1666
  35,850-1 Hardwicke papers
  38,856 Hodgkin papers
  39,672 Autographs from Morrison collection
  46,920-31 Correspondence from Sir Philip Perceval
Egerton Mss:
  917 Miscellaneous papers
  1048 Collection of parliamentary documents 1624-59
  2541-2 Miscellaneous historical papers of Sir Edward Nicholas 1598-1660
Harley Mss: 6988 Royal letters and warrants 1625-55
Lansdowne Mss: 692 Transcripts of miscellaneous papers
Sloane Mss: 1008 letters and papers of Dr. E. Borlase relating to 1641
Stowe Mss: 82 miscellaneous papers

*Public Records Office*
SP/63 State papers, Ireland: 260-6, 274-5, 303
SP/94 State papers, Spain: 42
PRO 31/8/198 Transcript of the Digby manuscripts

### OXFORD

*Bodleian Library*
Carte Mss: 1-25, 44, 63-68, 70, 118, 168, 176, 273
Clarendon Mss: 20-36, 91, 98
Rawlinson Mss: B.507
Tanner Mss: 57-60

PAMPHLETS (WITH LOCATION)

*Articles of agreement made, concluded and agreed on at Dublin the eighteenth day of
   June 1647 ...*, Dublin 1647 (BL Thomason Tracts E394 f.14)
*Articles of peace, 17 January 1648 ...*,Cork 1648/9 (RIA vol. 58, box 56, tract 1)
*The bloody diurnall from Ireland being the papers and propositions, orders an oath
   and several bloody acts and the proceedings of the confederate catholics assembled
   at Kilkenny ...*, London 1647 (BL Thomason Tracts E386 f.16)
*A bloody fight at Balrud-Derry in Ireland ...*, London 1647 (BL Thomason Tracts
   E401 f.18)
*Bloody fight at Blackwater in Ireland ...*, London 1646 (RIA vol. 48, box 44, tract
   6)
*A collection of all the papers which passed upon the late treaty touching the cessation
   of arms in Ireland ...*, Dublin 1643 (RIA vol. 38, box 34, tract 1)
*The copy of a letter sent from the lord chief justices ...*, London 1641 (BL Thomason
   Tracts E173 f.32)
*The copy of a letter written from the lord viscount Gormanston unto Sir Phelim
   O'Neal ...*, London 1642 (BL Thomason Tracts E155 f.22)
*Declaration of the Lords and Commons assembled in parliament...*, London 1643
   (RIA vol. 38, box 34, tract 4)
*A Declaration of the lords and gentry and others of the provinces of Leinster and
Munster in the realm of Ireland of their intentions towards the English and Scottish
Protestants inhabiting in the Kingdom ...*, London 1644 (RIA vol. 41, box 37, tract
   1)
*A declaration by the lords justices and council ...*, Dublin 1641 (BL Thomason
   Tracts 669 f.3)
*A declaration made by the rebels in Ireland against the English and Scottish protes-
   tant inhabitants within this kingdom ...*, London 1644 (BL Thomason Tracts
   E17 f.14)
*A declaration of the resolutions of his majesty's forces published by the marquess of
   Clanricard against the parliament of England ...*, London 1648 (BL Thomason
   Tracts E456 f.10)
*The demands of the rebels in Ireland unto the state and council of Dublin, 3 Feb.
   1641 ...*, London 1641 (NLI Thorpe I, no. 310)
*The earl of Glamorgan's negotiations and colourable commitment in Ireland demon-
   strated or the Irish plot ...*, London 1645/6 (BL Thomason Tracts E328 f.9)
*An exact and full relation of the great victory obtained against the rebels at
Dungan's Hill in Ireland 8 Aug. 1647 ...*, London 1647 (NLI Thorpe IV no. 447)
*Two great battles fought in the kingdom of Ireland ...*, London 1646/7 (BL
   Thomason Tracts E375 f.4)
*The grounds and motives inducing his majesty to agree to a cessation of arms for one
   whole year with the Roman Catholics of Ireland ...*, Oxford 1643 (RIA vol. 38,
   box 34, tract 7)

*The Irish cabinet or his majesties secret papers..taken in the carriages of the Archbishop of Tuam ...*, London 1645/6 (RIA vol. 45, box 41, tract 4)

*The Irish Monthly Mercury,* number 1 ..., Cork 1649 (NLI Lough Fea XII no. 277)

*The Irish papers containing the lord Digby's letter and the lord Inchiquin's answer ...*, London 1646 (BL Thomason Tracts E355 f.26)

*The king's letter to the marquesse of Ormond, etc ...*, London 1646 (RIA vol. 48, box 44, tract 8)

*The king's majesties manifesto to the kingdom of Ireland, undertaken and published by the marquess of Clanricarde ..., 1647* (RIA vol. 55, box 50, tract 5)

*The last articles of peace, 30 July 1646 ..., 1646* (RIA vol. 48, box 44, tract 3)

*A letter from the right honourable lord Inchiquin and other commanders in Munster to his majesty ...*, London 1644 (BL Thomason Tracts E8 f.37)

*The lord marquess of Argyle's speech to a grand committee of both Houses of Parliament, 25 June 1646 ... also his majesty's letter to the marquess of Ormond* London 1646 (BL Thomason Tracts E341 f.25)

*A manifestation directed to the honourable Houses of Parliament in England sent from the lord Inchiquin etc. ...*, London 1644 (BL Thomason Tracts E6 f.10)

*The marquesse of Ormond's proclamation concerning the peace concluded with the Irish rebels....with a speech delivered by Sir Richard Blake ... also a speech delivered by the marquesse of Ormond ...*, London 1649 (BL Thomason Tracts E545 f.12)

*His majesty's answer to a message sent unto him by the House of Commons at York, 19 March 1641 ... also two remarkable letters from Ireland ...*, London 1642 (BL Thomason Tracts E140 f.25)

*A mighty victory in Ireland obtained by the lord Inchiquin near Englishman's Hill ...*, London 1647 (BL Thomason Tracts E417 f.14)

*More victories lately obtained in Ireland ...*, London 1647 (BL Thomason Tracts E409 f.2)

*News from Dublin in Ireland ...*, London 1647 (BL Thomason Tracts E416 f.22)

*A perfect narrative of the battle of Knocknones, within the county of Cork ..., 1647* (NLI Thorpe IV no. 451)

*The propositions sent by the Irish Parliament held at Kilkenny to the commissioners at Dublin ...*, London 1647 (RIA vol. 53, box 50, tract 10)

*Oath of the confederate catholics ...*, London 1644 (BL Thomason Tracts E17)

*Orders established in the popish general assembly held (under the specious pretence of supreme authority, and being his majesty's good subjects) at the city of Kilkenny ...*, London 1643 (BL Thomason Tracts E60 f.19)

*Papers presented to the parliament against the lord Inchiquin ...*, London 1648 (BL Thomason Tracts E435 f.33)

*The pope's brief or bull of dispensation ...*, London 1642 (BL Thomason Tracts E113 f.4)

*Queries concerning the lawfulness of the present cessation, by David, Bishop of Ossory ...*, Kilkenny 1648 (RIA vol. 58, box 56, tract 6)

*The rebels letter to the pope, 20 Jan. 1642 ...*, London 1642 (BL Thomason Tracts E131 f.23)

*A remonstrance of the beginnings and proceedings of the rebellion ... including the acts of the Kilkenny Congregation 10-12 May 1642 ...*, London 1642 (BL Thomason Tracts E110 f.9)

*A remonstrance from the lords and commons assembled in parliament at Dublin ...*, Dublin 1646 (RIA vol. 48, box 44, tract 16)

*Three letters intercepted by Sir Tho. Fairfax in Cornwall ...*, London 1646 (BL Thomason Tracts E329 f.12)

*A treacherous plot of a confederacy in Ireland ...*, London 1641 (BL Thomason Tracts E179 f.15)

*A true copy of the laws and rules of government, agreed upon and established by the nobles of several counties of Ireland ...*, London 1641/2 (BL Thomason Tracts E138 f.5)

*The true demands of the rebels in Ireland ...*, London 1642 (BL Thomason Tracts E135 f.4)

*True intelligence from Ireland ...*, London 1642 (BL Thomason Tracts E153 f.13)

*A true relation of every remarkable circumstance in the relieving of Tredagh, by Capt. Thomas Steutevile ...*, London 1642 (BL Thomason Tracts E135 f.26)

*A true relation of a great victory obtained by the forces under the command of the lord Inchiquin in Munster in Ireland ...*, London 1647 (BL Thomason Tracts E418 f.6)

*Two letters of the lord Digby to the lord Taaffe, the rebels general in Munster, taken in the said general's cabinet in the late battle between him and the lord Inchiquin ...*, London 1647 (BL Thomason Tracts E419 f.8)

*Two letters sent from the lord Inchiquin unto the speaker of the honourable House of Commons ...*, London 1647 (BL Thomason Tracts E389 f.1)

*Two ordinances of the Lords and Commons assembled in Parliament: one commanding that no officer or soldier either by sea or land shall give any quarter to any Irishman or any papist born in Ireland ...*, London 1644 (BL Thomason Tracts E14 f.7)

*The victorious proceedings of the protestant army in Ireland ...*, London 1647 (BL Thomason Tracts E413 f.5)

## PRINTED SOURCES

*Acts and ordinances of the Interregnum, 1642-1660* 3 vols (London 1906)

Aiazza, G. *The embassy in Ireland of Monsignor G.B. Rinuccini, archbishop of Fermo in the years 1645-49* translated by Annie Hutton (Dublin 1873)

*Analecta Hibernica* (Reports)

— no. 15 (1944) O'Grady papers; Longfield papers

— no. 20 (1958) Colclough papers; Nugent papers

— no. 25 (1967) Kavanagh papers; Gormanston papers

Bindon, S.H. (ed.). *The historical works of the right reverend Nicholas French D.D.* 2 vols (Dublin 1846)

Borlase, Edmund. *The history of the execrable Irish rebellion traced from many preceding acts to the grand eruption the 23 October 1641, and thence pursued to the act of settlement, 1662* (Dublin 1680)

Bourke, Thomas. *Hibernia dominicana* 2 vols (Kilkenny 1762- Supp. 1772)

Bourke, Ulick. *Clanricarde memoirs* (London 1757)

*Calendar of state papers, domestic series, 1645-47* (London 1891)

*Calendar of state papers relating to Ireland, 1633-47* (London 1901)

*Calendar of state papers, Venetian,* vols 25-8 (London 1924-7)

Clarendon, Edward Hyde, earl of. *The history of the rebellion and civil wars in England* 6 vols (London 1888)

Clarke, Aidan (ed.). "A discourse between two councillors of state, the one of England and the other of Ireland." *Analecta Hibernia,* no. 26 (1970) pp 159-75

Croker, T.C. *The tour of the French traveller Monsieur de Boullaye le Gouz in Ireland AD 1644* (London 1837)

Darcy, Patrick. *An argument delivered by Patrick Darcy esquire by the express order of the commons in the parliament of Ireland, 9 June 1641* (Waterford 1643; reprinted 1764)

Fitzpatrick, Thomas. *Waterford during the civil war* (Waterford 1912)

Foster, Joseph (ed.). *The register of admissions to Gray's Inn 1521-1889* (London 1889)

French, N. *The bleeding iphigenia* (Louvain 1674)

—. *A narrative of the earl of Clarendon's settlement and sale of Ireland* (Louvain 1668)

—. *The unkind deserter of loyal men and true friends* (Louvain 1676)

Gardiner, S.R. *The constitutional documents of the puritan revolution, 1625-1660* (Oxford 1962)

Gilbert, J.T. *A contemporary history of affairs in Ireland from 1641-1652,* 3 vols (Dublin 1879)

—. *History of the Irish confederation and the war in Ireland,* 7 vols (Dublin 1882-1891)

Historical Manuscripts Commission. *2nd Report* (London 1874), *4th Report* (1874), *8th Report* (1881) appendices

—. *Calendar of the manuscripts of the marquess of Ormond* 8 vols, new series (London 1902-20)

—. *Manuscripts of the duke of Portland* vol. 1, 13th Report, appendix part 1 (London 1891)

—. *Manuscripts of the marquess of Ormond* vol. 1, 14th Report, appendix part 7 (London 1895)

—. *Manuscripts of the viscount de L'Isle,* vol. 6, *Sidney papers, 1626-98,* 77th Report (London 1966)

—. *Manuscripts of Ormond, earl of Fingal, Jesuits, corporations of Galway and Waterford etc.,* 10th Report, appendix part 5 (London 1885)

—. *Report on the manuscripts of the earl of Egmont*, vol. 1, Parts 1/2 (London 1905)

—. *Report on the manuscripts of the marquess of Ormond*, vol. 2 (London 1899)

Hogan, James (ed.). *Letters & papers relating to the Irish rebellion between 1642-46* IMC, no. 16 (Dublin 1936)

Jennings, Brendan (ed.). *Wild geese in Spanish Flanders, 1582-1700*, IMC (Dublin 1964)

*Journal of the House of Commons of the kingdom of Ireland*, vol. 1, 1613-1666 (Dublin 1796)

Leyburn, George. "Memoirs of George Leyburn, 1722" *Clarendon historical society's reprints*, series 2 (1884-6) pp 273-354

[Lodge, John (ed.)]. *Desiderata curiosa hibernica* 2 vols (London 1772)

Lowe, John (ed.). *Clanricarde letter-book 1643-1647* (Dublin 1983)

Massari, Dionysius. "My Irish campaign", *Catholic bulletin*, vols 6-10 (1916-20)

McNeill, Charles (ed.). *The Tanner letters*, IMC, no. 30 (Dublin 1943)

Moran, P. F. (ed.). *Spicilegium Ossoriense, being a collection of original letters and papers illustrative of the history of the Irish church from the reformation to the year 1800* 3 vols (Dublin 1874-84)

More O'Ferrall, E.G. (ed.). "The dispossessed landowners of Ireland, 1664" *The Irish genealogist*, vol. 4 (1971/2) no. 4 pp 275-302, no. 5 pp 429-49

Nalson, John (ed.). *An impartial collection of the great affairs of state* 2 vols (London 1682-3)

O'Ferrall, Richard and O'Connell, Robert. *Commentarius Rinuccinianus, de sedis apostolicae legatione ad foederatis Hiberniae catholicos per annos 1645-9*, ed. Stanislaus Kavanagh, IMC, 6 vols (Dublin 1932-49)

"Oireachtas library list of outlaws, 1641-1647", presented by R.C. Simington and John MacLellan, *Analecta Hibernica*, no. 22 (1966) pp 318-67

*Public records in Ireland* 19th Report, appendix 5 (Dublin 1887)- Abstract of the decrees of the court of claims (1663)

— 20th Report, appendix 4 (Dublin 1888)- Kilkenny confederate records

*The records of the honourable society of Lincoln's Inn*, vol. 1 (London 1896)

*Register of admissions to the honourable society of the Middle Temple*, vol. 1 (London 1949)

*Register of the privy council of Scotland 1638-43* (Edinburgh 1906)

Rushworth, J. *Historical collections of private passages of state, weighty matters of law, remarkable proceedings in five parliaments* 7 vols (London 1680-1701)

Smith, W. J. (ed.). *Herbert correspondence*, IMC, no. 66 (Dublin 1963)

*Statutes at large passed in the parliament held in Ireland*, vol. 2, 1634-1662 (Dublin 1786)

*Students admitted to the Inner Temple 1547-1660* (London 1877)

Talon, Geraldine (ed.). *Act of settlement 1662: Court of claims* (IMC, forthcoming)

Temple, John. *The Irish rebellion or an history* (London 1646)

Tuchet, James. *The earl of Castlehaven's review or his memoirs* (London 1684)

"Unpublished letters and papers of Owen Roe O'Neill" presented by Jerrold Casway, *Analecta Hibernica*, no. 29, (1980) pp 220-48

Walsh, Peter. *The history and vindication of the loyal formulary or Irish remonstrance* (1674)

Ware, James. *The whole works of Sir James Ware concerning Ireland*, vol. 2 (Dublin 1745)


SECONDARY WORKS


Armstrong, Robert. "Protestant Ireland and the English parliament, 1641-1647" (PhD thesis, TCD 1995)

Arnold, L.J. "The Irish court of claims of 1663", *IHS*, 24, no. 96 (Nov. 1985) pp 417-30

Ashton, Robert. *The English civil war: Conservatism and revolution 1603-1649* (London 1978)

Aston, Trevor (ed.). *Crisis in Europe, 1560-1660* (London 1965)

Aylmer, G.E. *Rebellion or revolution ?* (Oxford 1986)

Bagwell, Richard. *Ireland under the Stuarts* 3 vols (London 1909-16)

Beckett, J. C. *The cavalier duke: A life of James Butler first duke of Ormond, 1610-1688* (Belfast 1990)

—. "The confederation of Kilkenny reviewed", *Historical studies*, vol. 2 (London 1959) pp 29-41

Bottigheimer, Karl. "Civil war in Ireland: The reality in Munster", *Emory university quarterly*, vol. 22 (Spring 1966) pp 46-56

Bradshaw, Brendan. "Geoffrey Keating: Apologist of Irish Ireland", *Representing Ireland: Literature and the origins of conflict, 1534-1660*, eds B. Bradshaw, A. Hadfield, W. Maley (Cambridge 1993) pp 166-190

—. "Native reaction to the westward enterprise: A case study in gaelic ideology", *The westward enterprise: English activities in Ireland, the Atlantic and America, 1480-1650*, eds K. Andrews, N. Canny, P. Hair (Liverpool 1978) pp 58-75

—. *The Irish constitutional revolution of the sixteenth century* (Cambridge 1979)

Brady, Ciaran. "The decline of the Irish kingdom", *Conquest and coalescence: The shaping of the state in early modern Europe*, ed. M. Greengrass (London 1991) pp 94-115

Brown, Keith. *Kingdom or province? Scotland and the regal union 1603-1715* (London 1992)

Burke, W.P. *History of Clonmel* (Waterford 1907)

Caball, Marc. "The gaelic mind and the collapse of the gaelic world: An appraisal", *Cambridge medieval celtic studies*, no. 25 (Summer 1993) pp 87-96

—. "Providence and exile in early seventeenth-century Ireland", *IHS*, vol. 29, no. 114 (Nov. 1994) pp 174-88

Canny, Nicholas. "In defence of the constitution? The nature of Irish revolt in the seventeenth century", *Culture et pratiques politiques en France et en Irlande 16th-18th Siècle*, eds Louis Cullen et Louis Bergeron (Paris 1990) pp 23-40

—. "The formation of the Irish mind: Religion, politics and gaelic Irish literature 1580-1750", *Past and present*, no. 95 (May 1982) pp 91-116

Carte, Thomas. *History of the life of James the first duke of Ormond* 6 vols (Oxford 1851))

Casway, Jerrold. "Owen Roe O'Neill's return to Ireland in 1642: The diplomatic background", *Studia Hibernica*, no. 9 (1969) pp 48-64

—. *Owen Roe O'Neill and the struggle for catholic Ireland* (Philadelphia 1984)

Clarke, Aidan. "Alternative allegiance in early modern Ireland" *Journal of historical sociology*, vol. 5, no. 3 (Sept. 1992) pp 253-66

—. "Colonial constitutional attitudes in Ireland 1640-1660" *P.R.I.A.* vol. 90, section c, no. 11 (1990) pp 357-75

—. "The 1641 depositions", *Treasures in the library TCD*, ed. P. Fox (Dublin 1986) pp 111-22

—. "The genesis of the Ulster rising of 1641", *Plantation to partition*, ed. Peter Roebuck (Belfast 1981) pp 29-45

—. *The graces 1625-41*, Irish history series no. 8 (Dundalk 1968)

—. "The history of Poynings' law, 1615-1641", *IHS*, vol. 18, no. 70 (Sept. 1972) pp 207-22

—. *The old English in Ireland 1625-1642* (London 1966)

—. "Ireland and the general crisis", *Past and present*, No. 48 (Aug. 1970) pp 79-99

Cokayne, G.E. *The complete peerage* 12 vols revised edition (London 1910-59)

Coonan, T.L. *The Irish catholic confederacy and the puritan revolution* (Dublin 1954)

Corish, P. J. "Bishop Nicholas French and the second Ormond peace 1648-9", *IHS*, vol. 6, no. 22 (Sept. 1948) pp 83-100

—. "The crisis in Ireland in 1648: The nuncio and the supreme council: Conclusions", *Irish theological quarterly*, vol. 22 (Jan. 1955) pp 231-57

—. *The origins of catholic nationalism*, vol. 3, *A history of Irish catholicism* ed. P. J. Corish (Dublin 1968)

—. "Rinuccini's censure of May 22 1648", *Irish theological quarterly*, vol. 18 (Oct. 1951) pp 322-37

—. "Two contemporary historians of the confederation of Kilkenny: John Lynch and Richard O'Ferrall", *IHS*, vol. 8, no. 31 (Mar. 1953) pp 217-36

Cregan, D.F. "The confederate catholics of Ireland: the personnel of the confederation, 1642-9", *IHS*, vol. 29, no. 116 (Nov. 1995) pp 490-512

—. "The confederation of Kilkenny: Its organisation, personnel and history" (PhD thesis, UCD 1947)

—. "The confederation of Kilkenny" *The Irish parliamentary tradition*, ed. Brian Farrell (Dublin 1973) pp 102-15

—. "Daniel O'Neill, a royalist agent in Ireland 1644-50", *IHS*, vol. 2 (1940-1) pp 398-414

—. "Irish catholic admission to the English inns of court 1558-1625", *Irish jurist*, vol. 5 (summer 1970) pp 95-114

—. "An Irish cavalier: Daniel O'Neill in the civil wars 1642-51", *Studia Hibernica*, no. 5 (1965) pp 104-33

—. "Irish recusant lawyers in politics in the reign of James I" *Irish jurist*, vol. 5 (winter 1970) pp 306-20

—. "The social and cultural background of a counter-reformation episcopate, 1618-60", *Studies in Irish history presented to R. Dudley Edwards*, eds Art Cosgrove and Donal MacCartney (Dublin 1979) pp 85-117

—. "Some members of the confederation of Kilkenny" *Measgra i gcuimhne Mh'ch'l U' Chléirigh*, ed. S. O'Brien (Dublin 1944) pp 34-44

Curry, J. *An historical and critical review of the civil wars in Ireland* (Dublin 1775)

Cunningham, Bernadette. "Native culture and political change in Ireland 1580-1640", *Natives and newcomers: Essays on the making of Irish colonial society 1534-1641*, eds C. Brady and R. Gillespie (Dublin 1986) pp 148-70

Dunne, Tom. "The gaelic response to conquest and colonisation: The evidence of the poetry", *Studia Hibernica*, no. 20 (1980) pp 7-30

Edwards, R.D. and Moody, T.W. "The history of Poynings' law: Part 1, 1494-1615", *IHS*, vol. 2, no. 8 (Sept. 1941) pp 415-24

Elliott, John. *National and comparative history* (Oxford 1991)

Farrell, Brian (ed.). *The Irish parliamentary tradition* (Dublin 1973)

Foster, Roy. *Modern Ireland 1600-1972* (London 1988)

Gardiner, S.R. *History of the civil war* 4 vols (New York 1965)

Gardner, W. *The life of James first duke of Ormond, 1610-1688* 2 vols (London 1912)

Giblin, A. "Geoffrey Baron, 1607-51", *The commemoration of the siege of Limerick* (Limerick 1951) pp 51-7

Gillespie, Raymond. "Harvest crises in early seventeenth-century Ireland" *Irish economic and social history*, vol. 11 (1984) pp 5-18

—. "Mayo and the rising of 1641", *Cathair na mart*, vol. 5 (1985) pp 38-44

Hardiman, James. *The history of the town and county of Galway* (Galway 1820)

Hazlett, Hugh. "A history of the military forces operating in Ireland 1641-1649" 2 vols (PhD thesis, Queens University Belfast 1938)

Hexter, J.H. *The reign of King Pym* (Cambridge 1941)

Hollick, Clive. "Owen Roe O'Neill's Ulster army of the confederacy, May-August 1646", *Irish sword*, vol. 18 (1991) pp 220-6

Hutton, Ronald. *The Royalist war effort 1642-1646* (London 1982)

Hynes, Michael. *The mission of Rinuccini, nuncio extraordinary to Ireland 1645-1649* (Louvain 1932)

Jackson, Donald. *Intermarriage in Ireland 1550-1650* (Montreal 1970)

Kearney, H.F. "Ecclesiastical politics and the counter reformation in Ireland 1618-48", *Journal of ecclesiastical history*, vol. II, no. 2 (Oct. 1960) pp 202-12

—. *Strafford in Ireland 1633-41: A study in absolutism* (Cambridge 1989)

Keeler, M.F. *The long parliament, 1640-1641: A biographical study of its members* (Philadelphia 1954)

Kelly, Patrick. "'A light to the blind', the voice of the dispossessed elite in the generations after the defeat at Limerick", *IHS*, vol. 24, no. 96 (Nov. 1985) pp 431-62

Kerrigan, Paul. *Castles and fortifications in Ireland 1485-1945* (Cork 1995)

Leerssen, J.T. *Mere Irish and f'or-ghael* (Amsterdam/Philadelphia 1986)

Lenihan, Pádraig. "The catholic confederacy 1642-49: An Irish state at war" 2 vols (PhD thesis, UCG 1995)

—. "The Leinster army and the battle of Dungan's Hill, 1647", *Irish sword*, vol. 18 (1991) pp 139-53

Lindley, K.J. "The impact of the 1641 rebellion upon England and Wales 1641-5", *IHS*, vol. 18, no. 70 (Sept. 1972) pp 143-76

Little, Patrick. "'Blood and friendship': The earl of Essex's efforts to protect the earl of Clanricarde's interests, 1641-6", *E.H.R.*, vol. 112, no. 448 (Sept. 1997) pp 927-41

Lowe, John. "The Glamorgan mission to Ireland 1645-6", *Studia Hibernica*, no. 4 (1964) pp 155-96

—. "The negotiations between Charles I and the confederation of Kilkenny 1642-9" (PhD thesis, University of London 1960)

Lubasz, Heinz. *Revolutions in modern European history* (New York 1966)

Lydon, James. "'Ireland corporate of itself': The parliament of 1460", *History Ireland*, vol. 3, no. 2 (summer 1995) pp 9-12

Lynch, John. *The life and death of the most reverend Francis Kirwan, bishop of Killala*, translated by C.P. Meehan (Dublin 1884)

MacCuarta, Brian (ed.). *Ulster 1641: Aspects of the rising* (Belfast 1993)

Malcolm, J.L. "All the King's men: the impact of the crown's Irish soldiers on the English civil war", *IHS*, vol. 21, no. 83 (March 1979) pp 239-64

McGrath, Br'd. "A biographical dictionary of the membership of the House of Commons 1640-1641" (PhD thesis, TCD 1998)

Meehan, C.P. *The confederation of Kilkenny* (Dublin 1882)

Merriman, R.B. *Six contemporaneous revolutions* (Oxford 1938)

Moody T.W., Martin F.X. and Byrne F.J. (eds). *A new history of Ireland*, vol. 3, *Early modern Ireland 1534-1691* (Oxford 1991)

Morgan, Hiram. "Faith and fatherland in sixteenth-century Ireland", *History Ireland*, vol. 3, no. 2 (summer 1995) pp 13-20

Morrill, John. "The British problem c.1534-1707", *The British problem c.1534-1707: State formation in the Atlantic archipelago*, eds B. Bradshaw and J. Morrill (London 1996) pp 1-38

—. *The nature of the English revolution* (London 1993)

—. (ed.). *Reactions to the English civil war 1642-1649* (London 1982)

—. *The revolt of the provinces: Conservatives and radicals in the English civil war 1630-1650* (London 1976)

Ó hAnnracháin, Tadhg. "'Far from terra firma': The mission of Gian Battista Rinuccini to Ireland 1645-1649" 2 vols (PhD thesis, European University Institute 1995)

Ó Buachalla, Breandán. "James our true king: The ideology of Irish royalism in the seventeenth century", *Political thought in Ireland since the seventeenth century*, eds D. George Boyce, R. Eccleshall, V. Geoghan (London 1993) pp 7-35

—. "Poetry and politics in early modern Ireland", *Eighteenth-century Ireland, iris an dá chultúir*, vol. 7 (1992) pp 149-175

O'Dowd, Mary. "Women and war in Ireland in the 1640s", *Women in early modern Ireland*, eds Margaret MacCurtin and Mary O'Dowd (Edinburgh 1991) pp 91-111

Ohlmeyer, Jane. "The 'Antrim plot' of 1641- a myth?", *Historical journal* vol. 35, no. 4 (1992) pp 905-19

—. *Civil war and restoration in the three Stuart kingdoms: The career of Randal MacDonnell, marquis of Antrim, 1609-1683* (Cambridge 1993)

—. (ed.). *Ireland from independence to occupation 1641-1660* (Cambridge 1995)

—. "The wars of religion, 1603-1660", *A military history of Ireland*, eds T. Bartlett and K. Jeffrey (Cambridge 1996) pp 160-87

O'Malley, William. "Patrick Darcy, lawyer and politician, 1598-1668" (MA thesis, UCG 1973)

Ó Siochrú, Micheál. "The confederation of Kilkenny", *History Ireland*, vol. 2, no. 2 (summer 1994) pp 51-56

O'Sullivan, M.D. *Old Galway* (Cambridge 1942)

Parker, G and Smith, L.M. (eds). *The general crisis of the seventeenth century* (London 1978)

Pearl, Valerie. "Oliver St. John and the 'middle group' in the long parliament: Aug. 1643-May 1644", *English historical review*, vol. 81 (1966) pp 490-519

Perceval-Maxwell, M. "Ireland and Scotland 1638-1648", *The Scottish national covenant in its British context*, ed. John Morrill (Edinburgh 1991) pp 193-211

—. *The outbreak of the Irish rebellion of 1641* (Dublin 1994)

Perry, Nicholas. "The infantry of the confederate Leinster army, 1642-1647", *Irish Sword*, vol. 15 (1983) pp 233-41

Power, P. C. *History of Waterford city and county* (Dublin 1990)

Quinn, D.B. "The early interpretation of Poynings' law, 1494-1534", *IHS*, vol. 2, no. 7 (March 1941) pp 241-54

Richardson, H.G. and Sayles G.O. *The Irish parliament in the middle ages* (Philadelphia 1960)

Roberts, Clayton. *The growth of responsible government in Stuart England* (Cambridge 1966)

Russell, Conrad. *The fall of the British monarchies 1637-1642* (Oxford 1991)

Sessions, W.K. *The first printers in Waterford, Cork and Kilkenny pre-1700* (York 1990)

Simms, J.G. *Jacobite Ireland, 1685-91* (London 1969)

—. *The Jacobite Parliament of 1689*, Irish History Series no. 6 (Dundalk 1974)

Simms, Katharine. "Bardic poetry as a historical source" *The writers as witness: Literature as historical evidence*, ed. Tom Dunne, *Historical studies 16* (1987) pp 58-75

Smith, Charles. *The ancient and present state of the county and city of Waterford* (Dublin 1746)

Smith, David L. *Constitutional royalism and the search for a settlement, 1640-49* (Cambridge 1994)

Stephen, Leslie and Lee, Sidney. *Dictionary of national biography*, vols 1-22 (Oxford 1917)

Stevenson, David. *Alasdair MacColla and the Highland problem in the seventeenth century* (Edinburgh 1980)

—. *Scottish covenanters and Irish confederates: Scottish-Irish relations in the mid-seventeenth century* (Belfast 1981)

Stradling. R.A. *The Spanish monarchy and Irish mercenaries: The wild geese in Spain 1618-1668* (Dublin 1994)

Taylor, J.F. *Owen Roe O'Neill* (Dublin 1896)

Tilly, Charles. *European revolutions 1492-1992* (Oxford 1993)

Underdown, David. *Pride's purge* (London 1985)

Warner, Fred. *The history of the rebellion and civil war in Ireland* (London 1767)

Young, J.R. (ed.). *Celtic dimensions of the British civil wars* (Edinburgh 1997)

—. *The Scottish parliament 1639-1661: A political and constitutional analysis* (Edinburgh 1996)

# Index

❧

adventurers act, 29, 60, 63, 71, 72, 79
Antrim, earl/marquis of, *see* MacDonnell, Randal
Athenry, Lord, *see* Bermingham, Francis
Audley, Colonel Mervin, 76
Aylmer, Garrett, 36

Bagenal, Colonel Walter, 115, 132, 133, 203
Bandonbridge, battle of (1642), 31, 143
Barnewall, Nicholas, Viscount Kingsland, 215
Barnewall, Patrick, 28
Barnewall, Richard, 64, 203, 229, 263
Barron, Geoffrey: 40, 42; speech to assembly, 133; negotiations with Ormond, 138,149; as moderate, 165, 181, 224; talks with Rinuccini, 175
Barry, Colonel John, 64, 68, 95, 136, 137, 171
Barry, Garrett, 50, 216
Barry, Robert, 91
Bath, James, 37
Bellings, Richard: account of period, 12; and Ulster insurgents, 25; as secretary of supreme council, 49, 65, 103, 219-20, 266; support for peace, 65-7, 194, 245; and 6th general assembly, 101; letter to ecclesiastical congregation, 111; imprisoned by clerical faction, 116; released, 126; account of 7th general assembly, 127-35 *passim*; plotting with Digby, 153; and Rinuccini, 164, 169; support for Inchiquin truce, 181; commandeers Jesuit printing press,

183; and Loughrea assembly, 203; influences council policy, 219-20;
Benburb, battle of (1646), 31, 107, 118
Berford, Richard, 36, 37, 86, 263
Bermingham, Francis, Lord Athenry, 140, 164, 181, 215, 224
Bindon, Samuel, 271
Blake, Richard: 224; as moderate, 141, 161; mission to Spain, 162; chairman of general assembly, 191, 196, 235; speech at signing of peace, 201; chairman of Loughrea assembly, 203; parliamentary experience, 212;
Bolton, Richard, 77-9, 231
Borlase, Edmund, 156
Bourke, Hugh, 38, 80
Bourke, John, lieutenant-general of Connacht, 51
Bourke, John, bishop of Clonfert/ archbishop of Tuam: 124, 223, 224, 234; confederate lord chancellor, 85, 263; opposition to Rinuccini, 173; 178; at final general assembly, 187; as "secondary assessor", 197; as moderate, 247
Bourke, Miles, Viscount Mayo, 37, 216, 254
Bourke, Oliver, 34-5
Bourke, Theobald, Lord Brittas, 216
Bourke, Thomas, Viscount Clanmorris, 37, 215
Bourke, Ulick, earl/marquis of Clanricarde: 13, 28, 67, 115, 140, 213; background, 29; attitude to uprising,